GROUCHO

GROUCHO
by
HECTOR ARCE

G. P. PUTNAM'S SONS
NEW YORK

SBN: 399-12046-7

Library of Congress Cataloging in Publication Data

Arce, Hector.
  Groucho.

  Bibliography
  Includes index
  1. Marx, Groucho, 1890-1977. 2. Comedians—United
States—Biography. I. Title.
PN2287.M53A7   1978   790.2'092'4   [B]   78-16019

PRINTED IN THE UNITED STATES OF AMERICA

To the memory
of my father,
Bert T. Arce

Introduction

Now, toward the end of 1976, it was time to move on. The two book collaborations which had brought me to Groucho Marx's door were successfully completed. Though I'd be turning my professional attention away from a man I'd come to know and love, my emotional ties would always remain strong ones.

One day, during the course of a telephone conversation with my literary agent in New York, the said lady, Julia Coopersmith, observed, "You've grown very attached to Groucho, haven't you?"

Of course I had. I'd never been a Groucho Marx fan per se, and I'd come to know him very late in his life. My own father had died the month before I met this very human and humane living legend. With no great protestations of filial devotion, which would have been awkward for me to voice and for him to hear, I'd come to look on this endearing old man as my surrogate father.

Julie Coopersmith must have filed this information away, for a couple of weeks later she suggested I should write the authorized biography of Groucho Marx.

I immediately resisted the idea. Though my attachment to

Groucho was a deep one, working in his household had been marked by pandemonium and hysteria. He seemed to flourish in such an atmosphere, but every time I'd return to that famous Beverly Hills house on Hillcrest Road I'd felt like an out-patient returning to the asylum. I yearned for quiet and reflection on my next book.

"You have to do it," Julie insisted. "You're the only writer who's had total access to him. You've probably spent more time alone with him than anyone outside his household." This, I conceded, was true.

Despite my great reservations, I allowed myself to be convinced. Julie said she would contact Erin Fleming, Groucho's personal manager, to see if the idea was a viable one. It was.

A verbal agreement was worked out, in which I would have total literary control, and Groucho wrote a letter authorizing me to write his comprehensive biography which was attached to the book contract. (After his death, the authorization was to be continued by the executors of the Marx Estate, the trust department of the Bank of America in Beverly Hills.)

Then I began to search out the telling details which would flesh out the story. I'd already absorbed many of them from Groucho directly during our previous collaborations.

Groucho's son Arthur, in a previous book, had already opened a Pandora's box of revelations: the alcoholism and emotional illnesses of virtually every woman whose life was touched by his father and the unflattering look at Groucho as a deeply flawed human. My plan was to temper Arthur's indictment with a more dispassionate look at Groucho. Another book had contained some rather shabby confessions which resulted in Groucho's filing of a multi-million-dollar lawsuit. Groucho justifiably took great pride in the style and good taste intrinsic to all his work, qualities the second book lacked, and I wanted to return them to my work.

Too soon, however, his frail health worsened. Unpleasant headlines followed. The events surrounding his final illness left me depressed and demoralized. I told Groucho's old friend Norman Krasna I couldn't continue with my book. Being drawn into the contretemps between Groucho's children and his manager-companion, I felt, had jeopardized the objectivity vital to the work.

"You have to finish it, dear boy," Norman said. He went on to explain that my close vantage point was an unparalleled one. "In fact," he went on, "I have a title for you: *Warts and All.*"

His encouragement echoed that of Groucho. Months before his final illness, I'd come back from a research trip to New York laden with revelations about Groucho's personal life, even more intimate than he in his unflinching candor had already supplied. Hesitantly I outlined what these new insights were, the truths of which he confirmed. Then I asked him how deeply I should delve into these facts.

Groucho answered without hesitation, "Tell it all."

He may have felt that in me he would get a fairer shake. Maybe, in agreeing to share his innermost turmoils, he was making one final contribution to the world. He would show the phobias, the frustrations, and the complexes that go into the making of a great comedian. After a lifetime of the insecurity that plagues all great funny men, he at last felt comfortable enough with his own person to know, as I also now realize, that nothing I reveal about him can diminish the legend and the man.

HECTOR ARCE
Beverly Hills, California
May, 1978

PROLOGUE

A bare-chested Julius Henry Marx, in the summer of his eighty-fifth year, basked in the early afternoon sun, one of his round-the-clock nurses applying suntan lotion and flirtatious affection in equal measure. Lying on a chaise longue on the terrace behind his bedroom-study, the world today was beating a path through his sliding glass doors . . . physicians, attorneys, accountants, literary collaborators, fan mail answerers . . . the procession seemed endless.

It was fitting that after years of touring the hinterlands, he should let the world come to him. That night, more guests, from star-struck celebrities to hangers-on, would arrive to pay homage to the legendary Groucho. And if he footed the bills for the unceasing round of parties in his newly decorated home, the company was always enthusiastic and receptive to the songs he sang at the after-dinner musicales. What price glory? No one knew better than he.

Presently, Erin Fleming—who in other ways embodied the whole world to him—arrived, accompanied by Groucho's publicist, Tom Wilhite. A press release had been written about his newest literary collaboration, a book on his old quiz show. His approval was but a formality. It had already been left up to Erin, the ultimate hyphenate: girlfriend-mother-actress-adviser-manager. Today another set of hyphens—court jester-siren—would be tacked on to the string. Soon another—daughter—might be added, for talk had it that Groucho planned to adopt his longtime companion.

Erin started talking, but because he was speaking himself, he hadn't heard. "I beg your pardon?" he asked her.

"You beg her bottom?" I interjected, for that's what I thought he'd said.

"She's got a cute bottom," the old man noted.

"How would you know?" she asked coquettishly.

"I felt it this morning," he replied. "Feels great."

"That's incest!" she exclaimed in mock outrage.

"So that's what happens in the hills of Trousdale?" I asked.

"Give me incest all the time," the old man said. He started to laugh.

"Don't say things like that," Erin said, now turned serious. "That will give me a bad reputation."

"You *have* a bad reputation," Groucho corrected.

"You gave it to me and—"

"That's all I gave you," Groucho interrupted, "but that isn't what I wanted to give you."

"That's not my fault," Erin said quietly.

"Not mine either," Groucho replied.

After some discussion, blame was shifted to the composer-pianist Erin was hoping to marry.

Before her arrival, Groucho had been reminiscing about the early days of vaudeville. Then he turned to Erin. "You wouldn't know. You're only a minor."

"Thank you for calling me a minor. Actually I'm the oldest virgin here."

Groucho's laugh turned into a wheeze. After he caught his breath, talk shifted to the print of one of the quiz shows Wilhite wanted to see.

"I don't know where it is," Erin said. "I used to have that show in the house until it was rented out permanently."

"What kind of house was it, Miss Fleming?" Groucho asked. "Was it the kind of house that I thought it was?"

"Most likely," she replied, "it was your house created by your ex-wife, who's now in the house business."

"Was it a whorehouse?" he persisted.

"I have no idea," Erin said. "I wouldn't know what that is, being a virgin."

Groucho's wheezing laughter came up again. He had difficulty catching his breath.

"Why are you wheezing?" she asked. "I *am* a virgin."

"Temporarily," Groucho said.

"Temporarily," she agreed.

"As of June fifth," Groucho said. "I think someday . . . she will get her wish."

"What's my wish?" Erin asked.

"Marriage," Groucho said. "It's my wish for you."

"Why would you wish that on me?"

"It's the greatest gift I could give you."

The statement was eloquent in its simplicity. A not unpleasant silence ensued. It was broken when the nurse advised Groucho it was time to turn over on his back. As he did so, he noticed Wilhite for the first time. "Hi, Tom. Have you been here all this time?"

"I've been here," Wilhite replied.

"Do you have some evil purpose?" Groucho asked.

"He's going to make you famous," I explained.

If that was the case, Wilhite could stay with the rest of us to bask in Groucho's sunshine. There might also be enough room on the outer edges of the immense spotlight that would follow him for the rest of his days, should any of us want to join Groucho there. Beneath its warm and mellow glow, faults and imperfections were filtered out. Obvious from that perspective were the forces that shaped him, masked were those which he had shaped, sometimes inadequately. His life had been marked by public triumph and private despair. Yet, Julius Henry Marx, in the summer of his eighty-fifth year, was at peace with the world and reasonably at peace with himself.

CHAPTER ONE

Like every other magician, Yasha was held in small esteem by the community. He wore no beard and went to synagogue only on Rosh Hashonah and Yom Kippur, that is, if he happened to be in Lublin at the time. Esther, on the other hand, wore the customary kerchief and kept a Kosher kitchen; she observed the Sabbath and all the laws. Yasha spent his Sabbath talking and smoking cigarettes among musicians. To the earnest moralists who attempted to get him to mend his ways, he would always answer: "When were you in heaven, and what did God look like?"

Isaac Bashevis Singer, The Magician of Lublin

The Marx Brothers never let facts get in the way of a good story. While sharing reminiscences, each would embroider a layer, the five of them working the final product into a rich tapestry under which the homespun base was hardly visible.

Groucho, true to his public image, wielded the needle to a greater degree than his brothers. Since he also insisted on having the last word, his version was accepted as gospel, or whatever its equivalent is to essentially irreligious men.

Conversely, given durable material which had stood the test of time, he could undo its amusing or enthralling threads so that it was barely held together by his distinctive brand of illogical logic.

The emigration from Germany of his maternal grandfather, Louis Schoenberg, is a case in point.

A few years ago, Maxine Marx, Chico's daughter, wrote Groucho a letter, in which she asked him why his grandfather had uprooted his wife and family to bring them to the New World.

"In addition to being one of Hanover's greatest magicians," he facetiously replied, "Opie worked on umbrellas. He came because he heard there was a big need for umbrella makers in this country."

Groucho, as was his wont, evaded the question. The Schoenbergs knew that Americans weren't in need of umbrellas to protect them from the molten metal cascading from the heavens; nor did they believe that the metal would spontaneously form fabled sidewalks of gold as it hit the ground.

The reasons for leaving their native land were largely the same ones that, from 1860 to 1890, brought the greatest influx of German immigrants in the history of the United States. Nearly five million— Prussians, Saxons, Bohemians—chose to escape from the uncertainty of political, religious, and—especially—economic considerations, as their homelands were being violently forged into a unified German state.

After the financial panic of 1873, massive unemployment swept the continent. The mass European exodus quickened, and other nationalities followed.

The life the newcomers left behind them wasn't as easy as *Duck Soup*. When, in 1886, the Statue of Liberty was unveiled on Bedloe's Island in New York harbor, the immigrants could well relate to the poem inscribed thereon. It was written by the American poet Emma Lazarus, herself of Portuguese-Jewish ancestry. The New Colossus was America, and the message she offered to foreign countries, particularly those in northern and western Europe from which eighty-five percent of the country's new inhabitants had thus far emigrated, reeked of left-handed condescension: "Give me your tired, your poor, your huddled masses

16

yearning to breathe free; The wretched refuse of your teeming shore; Send these the homeless, tempest-tossed to me."

The sentiments didn't offer immigrants any substantial alternative to their previous indentured positions. But still they came.

With open arms, the "wretched refuse" were welcomed by native Americans, with the unspoken caveat that they stay at arm's length and mingle only among themselves. These immigrants would become the manpower the United States so urgently needed as the nation evolved from a rural society into an industrial state. Menial jobs awaited all the hale and hearty.

Some might aspire to greater and more distinguished heights. America was the land of the possible, if not necessarily the probable, and hope was packed along with the minimal amount of luggage permitted them in steerage.

The passage by ship from Bremen to New York was thirty dollars. Because this route offered the cheapest fare to America, most Germans settled in New York. The Dublin to Boston route was cheapest for the Irish, and for the same practical reason most of them settled in New England.

Many of the German immigrants already had relatives in America who arranged passage for them through American Jewish peddlers. Interest and carrying charges increased the debt to forty dollars, to be paid back over a specified period of time. Thus were the newcomers introduced to the most American of institutions: the installment plan.

If in later years the Marx Brothers came to be labeled the quintessential anti-Establishmentarians, they may have been prepared for this role by the family's dubious heritage, spanning three generations, of being somehow beyond the pale.

Conjecture in this case has more validity than the sketchy details any of the Marxes or the Schoenbergs were able to supply about their forebears. Perhaps their assumption was that they had no background to speak of.

Circumstantial evidence must be relied on for information about Louis (Lafe) Schoenberg, the founding father of what was to

17

become a matriarchal dynasty. He was born about 1830 in Holland, the son of the Abraham Schoenbergs. Since theirs was a German surname and Lafe spoke German like a native, perhaps his own father was a traveling man, as his son was later to be. None of his grandchildren, who preferred to call him Opie, the colloquial German word for grandfather, knew why he was called Lafe. Somewhere in his past there might have been a Scandinavian in the woodpile.

Louis or Lafe or Opie grew to be a handsome man, well over six feet tall, who possessed incredible strength. According to family folklore, he once happened upon a horse-drawn cart mired in the mud. He unhitched the horses and lifted the wagon out of the puddle. He retained this strength in his old age, his grandsons looking on with awe as he once pushed a grand piano across a room.

He was also given to displays of legerdemain. Like Singer's magician, Yasha Mazur, he was a maze of personalities, "religious and heretical, good and evil, false and sincere. He could love many women at once . . . He lusted after women, yet hated them like a drunkard hates alcohol."

The indiscriminate lust of his youth, which he delighted in describing to his pubescent grandsons as their own passionate juices started flowing, may have caused the scandal which drove Lafe out of his hometown. Throughout Europe, Jews led a highly restricted life. Most were tremendously religious and steeped in the tradition of family and responsibility. There was simply no room for godless priapism. Nor were there polite nineteenth century euphemisms for men who had turned their backs on centuries-old beliefs. They were outcasts, doomed to vagrant lives.

Lafe went on the road, performing feats of strength and creating third-rate magic out of his threadbare bag of tricks. In his off-hours, the dashing figure bedded down impressionable females.

In later years, he would talk about the time he arrived in a Dutch town. A crowd had gathered to watch his magic act. He offered to sever a man's head and put it back on again, but he cautioned the audience not to make a noise, lest the trick be ruined. Lafe, assuming no one would have the courage to volunteer, had underestimated the hard-headed Dutch. A man in the audience got up and said, "Here I am."

No one had called his bluff before. Lafe couldn't perform the trick, he confessed to the audience, which rewarded him for his honesty by throwing stones at him as he hot-footed it out of town. Not long after, probably through necessity, he added the repairing of household goods to his working repertory.

Sometime in the early 1850s, he met his future wife Fanny at the fairgrounds in Dornum, Germany, a desolate, lowland town of eight hundred inhabitants off the sandy North Sea shore, a few miles east of the Dutch border. The town was a stopping-off place between Essen and Wilhelmshaven. Plattdeutsch was spoken in the area, an idiom as close to Dutch as it was to German.

Fanny was a small, dumpy woman, a devout Jew, already in her early twenties, living in a society where most girls were married off by their middle teens. Her only solace, outside her religion, was the harp she expertly strummed, a half-size model instead of the conventional one because it was more suited to her short frame.

Her marital prospects must have seemed as bleak as the surrounding landscape. No doubt, like the dozens of girls who had preceded her, Lafe assisted her in her fall from grace.

"She must have come from a family of means," Maxine Marx theorizes, "because the harp isn't the kind of instrument you went and picked up for a few German marks.

"Opie was a very handsome strapping fellow, and why he was attracted to her, God knows. There were only two ways she could have married him. One was to run off with him, but this would have been totally out of character for her. The other was to get pregnant by him. If she was pregnant, her family would have had to let her marry him. I think they did and they gave her the harp and a little money and that was it."

This assumes that Fanny and Lafe fell genuinely in love and, despite her family's objections, insisted on marrying. Lafe had probably moved on when other girls had been caught up in similar embarrassments. Had the ceremony been performed with her father's shotgun held to his head, Fanny's family would have done more to help the young married couple than they evidently did.

19

As for Lafe, he didn't give any indication later that he'd been trapped into an unwanted marriage. Marriage to Fanny represented a partial return to respectability. If he'd been the unprincipled whoremaster and low-life type Singer's fictional magician penitently described himself as, he would have deserted his wife at the earliest opportunity.

But they were to stay together for nearly fifty years. Lafe fathered Fanny's eleven children and remained reasonably faithful to one woman for the only time in his life. He would even go through the charade, for his wife's sake, of resuming contact with a God he'd never believed in.

The Schoenbergs made Dornum their home base as they traveled throughout Hanover eking out an existence. In the face of constant adversity, the laughter generated by Lafe became their saving grace. Like many religious, straitlaced women, Fanny's sense of humor was largely untapped, and it needed a rapscallion like her husband to bring it out and to lighten life's load. Their grandfather's cockeyed view may have been the most precious legacy he passed on to the Marx Brothers.

"When he was feeling chipper," Harpo wrote in *Harpo Speaks!*, "Grandpa used to perform magic for me. He conjured pennies out of his beard, and out of my nose and ears, and made me practice the trick of palming coins. Then he would stoke up his pipe and tell me about the days when he and Grossmutter Fanny toured the German spas and music halls. Grandpa performed as a ventriloquist and a magician ... while Grandma played the harp for dancing after he did his act."

As the children were born, they were added to the troupe. Fanny would be responsible for the bulk of their education. Personal ambition, however, she couldn't teach them, and judging from family folklore, few of the Schoenberg children learned it by themselves.

Minna, the third youngest, was born in 1864. The girl developed an extraordinary love for the family's world of ragtag entertainment, though she manifested no discernible talent. Her older sister Hannah was regarded as the gifted one, possessing a clear soprano voice. But she was hampered by a placid nature; if she were to have a future in this world—it was unthinkably expensive for her to train for an operatic career—she would have to be pushed. And why push an innocent girl into a field of vagabond rogues and their loose female companions?

Young Adolf, born in 1868, was the second youngest and seemed possessed of both talent and determination. The need for recognition and applause was nurtured by the mediocre theatricals in which his family specialized. He too had a pleasant singing voice, even though on its own it offered scant promise of putting any pumpernickel on the family table.

Lafe and Fanny had endured nearly a quarter of a century of unrelenting hardship before they decided the family should emigrate. It took them several more years to raise the steerage fare for themselves and their eight surviving children. The girls hired out as domestics and the boys performed handyman jobs beside their father until they finally scraped up enough money in 1880 for ten passages to America.

Simon Marrix was born in 1861, in the French province of Alsace. When he died seventy-two years later, none of his five sons knew the names of his parents, nor could they confirm that they were related to the dozens of people in New York who shared their father's adopted name.

Like his future father-in-law, Simon rarely talked about his background, erasing it from his mind like his French nationality, rubbed out by the Germans after they annexed Alsace, the spoils of the Franco-Prussian War, in 1871.

True, he spoke a German dialect in addition to his native French, as most Alsatians did, but he was emotionally, romantically French.

During his impressionable teens, one international crisis after another brought France and Germany to the brink of another war. When Simon was fourteen, an article appeared in the *Berlin Post*, headlined "Is War in Sight?" It touched off a panic in France.

Three years later, the burgeoning socialist movement was driven underground in Alsace and further repressive measures were taken by occupying Germans.

Simon, apolitical throughout his life, knew he could never bear arms against France. And he didn't want to live among the German

21

Huns. He began making plans to emigrate to America before he could be conscripted into the German army.

Several of his cousins were already in the United States. One of them sponsored his immigration, and Simon arrived in New York in 1881. He was twenty, a handsome, dapper bantam rooster. Despite the oppression of his Alsatian upbringing, he was a natural boulevardier.

Shortly after his arrival, his cousin—who had adopted the name of Marx—suggested Simon do the same. With the preponderance of German immigrants on the lower East Side, where the two shared a room, adopting the German name would help him in business.

The German-English name of Marx had several variations, Marxen and Marxsen among them. The name had two meanings: the son of Mark or Marcus and dweller at a mark or boundary stone.

If it was any consolation to Simon, Marx was also a French name. Marks—the original spelling—described people who came from the French frontier district of Marck, near Calais, across the Strait of Dover from England.

Simon reluctantly agreed to adopt the name. One of his uncles had married in the United States, and his thirteen Marx children were well entrenched in the American way. One of them—Max—was a theatrical tailor who would one day number George M. Cohan, Sam Harris, and Douglas Fairbanks, Sr., among his closest friends. Another—Samuel—would soon be one of the leading political lights at Tammany Hall. Simon polished off his German pronunciation and prepared to meet the world as custom tailor. The French are nothing if not practical.

The Schoenbergs arrived in New York just in time to be included in the federal census of 1880. Louis, age fifty, and his wife Fanny, forty-nine, claimed to be housing three children at their flat on the lower East Side, located at 376 East Tenth Street. They were Minnie, age fifteen; Adolf, twelve; and Henry, seven. (Apparently, Minna no sooner arrived in the United States than she Americanized her name in honor of Minnie Maddern, a leading child actress of the day, whom the Schoenberg girl idolized.) There is no record in this census of the five older children. Some of them may have already married. It seems more likely that they were hidden away when the man from the government came to ask his intimidating questions.

It was a common practice for Jews on the lower East Side to rent a big, expensive apartment and sublet sections of it. A Jewish tailor might rent a two-room flat, keeping one room for himself, his wife and two children; the second might be sublet to another tailor, wife, and child, who would in turn hang a blanket down the middle of the room and rent half of it to a third family. Some census takers, as a result, came more often than every ten years. Police would sweep down on the tenements and arrest those responsible for these impossibly crowded conditions, the landlord and the prime tenant.

Adding to the crowded conditions was the fact that the lower East Side served as a cut-rate food basket for the rest of New York. People came by public conveyance from other parts of the city in daily droves. Grocery stores there were fairly uniform in their offerings: a coal bin outside, along with barrels of herring packed in aromatic brine and pickles in various stages of processing. Carts wended their ways down the narrow streets offering large, flat, circular loaves of corn bread. Forequarters of beef selling at seven to ten cents a pound were carried by kosher butchers. A three-pound chicken could be bought for fifty cents.

The Schoenbergs were part of the second wave of Germans to emigrate to America. Many of them settled in the Yorkville section, where the future Marx family would live. By the mid-nineteenth century, Yorkville had a highly Teutonic flavor, and by the 1890s the neighborhood had the reputation among other burghers as being a place where solid, rotund people spoke in gutturals and dispensed sauerkraut and lager beer.

The first wave of Germans, arriving between 1837 and 1860, were the formal-speaking Old Guard which writer Stephen Birmingham would later categorize as *Our Crowd*: names like Lehman, Goldman, Straus, Lazarus, and Seligman. Most were luxuriously ensconced in Fifth Avenue mansions between Sixtieth Street and Eightieth Street.

There was a man among them who denied his Jewish heritage.

August Schönberg, born in the Rhineland Palatinate in 1816, had come to the United States by way of Frankfurt, Naples, and Havana in 1837 in his capacity as agent for the Rothschilds, the leading Jewish banking house in Europe. He settled in New York, turned gentile, changed the "Beautiful Mountain" meaning of his German name to its French equivalent, Belmont, and married the daughter of Commodore Matthew Perry. For the next fifty years the Belmonts would dominate New York society. If August Belmont was a distant relative, there was no way Lafe could approach him. They were separated by caste and religion.

Economics, however, separated them most of all. While Belmont was building a magnificent residence on Fifth Avenue near Washington Square, Lafe was peddling and repairing umbrellas door-to-door.

"Since neither my grandfather nor my grandmother spoke any English," Groucho wrote in *Groucho and Me*, "they were unable to get any theatrical dates in America. For some curious reason there seemed to be practically no demand for a German ventriloquist and a woman harpist who yodeled in a foreign language."

Lafe plied his trade for less than a year, grossing a grand total of $12.50. Shortly after celebrating his fifty-first birthday, he opted for an early retirement. Omie, as Fanny was to be called by her grandchildren, apparently had no objection. Perhaps the two deemed their life's work a success, the gauge being the family's arrival in America; with this modest accomplishment, they could now rest. Lafe, sensing that retirement at fifty-one might strike many as premature, tacked twelve years on his age, and embarked on a new life of good works, which primarily entailed assisting Omie in maintaining a God-fearing Orthodox household.

His children, who'd been helping to support him for years, took care of his simple needs for the next thirty-eight years. Lafe could survive on cold potatoes and pumpernickel. His daily pleasures were equally homely: ten long black cigars, rolled from the leavings of a tobacco factory, and a pint of whiskey, concocted from the residue of a nearby distillery. When he died in 1919, his children supplied him with the ultimate face-saving gesture. They insisted he was 101 years old, when in fact he was eighty-nine.

The girls took up the economic slack of the household by working at a straw hat factory in the neighborhood, putting in ten hours a day, six days a week. Still later they did piecework at home. Within ten years the New York garment industry would be almost wholly populated by such Jewish seamstresses, working out of their tenements and small lofts.

Adolf, as soon as he was of age, got a job as a pants-presser at a garment factory. What the other sons did none of the present-day Marxes seems to recall.

Inevitably, the paths of Simon and Minnie would cross. The lower East Side was a small area geographically, crammed though it was by the burgeoning German colony.

They met on a Saturday night, at a dancing school on lower Second Avenue conducted by a Mr. Englehart.

Simon was a marvelous dancer, needing no lessons, but the school had a constantly changing array of young girls to meet and conquer. He was as lecherous as his future father-in-law had been in his own youth. Girls in the neighborhood warned Minnie of his inconstancy. With his Gallic posturings, he was already an exotic in her eyes. Their admonitions only served to double his attractiveness.

Minnie was blonde and curvaceous, with flirtatious blue eyes and a ready, musical laugh. She was unlike any girl Simon had ever known, a candy-box package of cuddly manipulation. She was also shrewder and tougher than the man on which she set her sights.

She was nineteen and Simon was twenty-three when Lafe and Fanny bowed to the inevitable and allowed them to marry in 1884. Simon was making a comfortable living from his one-time-only customers, who mistook him for the three other more competent Marxes in Manhattan who were also tailors. If Minnie sensed that his prospects over the long haul weren't the brightest, she ignored it. The belief that love will find a way is strongest at the beginning of relationships.

Simon moved his new wife to the upper East Side, their first flat being located at 354 East Eighty-second Street. Minnie considered herself more German than Jewish and found little in common with the Russian Orthodox Jews who'd started to settle on the lower East Side. The bride brought Opie and Omie along as her dowry. Soon various other Schoenbergs would be joining them.

Three thousand miles away from his homeland and three years after his escape from German subjugation, Simon Marx (né Marrix) let down his guard and was irrevocably subjugated by the German horde.

CHAPTER TWO

"When we were little," the Mock Turtle said, "we went to school in the sea. The master was an Old Turtle. We used to call him Tortoise . . . because he taught us."
                    Lewis Carroll, Alice's Adventures in Wonderland

Only in the distinctive speech pattern of late nineteenth-century New York could "Tortoise" for "taught us" be truly considered a pun. The city's nationalistic elements staked their segregated claims on various parts of Manhattan Island, preserving their Old Country traditions, becoming a melting pot only in the forging of an inflection and pronunciation which would later be called a New York accent.

New Yorkese had a strongly German base, but other minorities of the period also contributed to this comic, dissonant babel. It was an accent to be used in everyday speech by all the Marx Brothers, but associated by the public with the most vocal of them. Groucho's delivery was faster, due no doubt to his exceedingly agile mind and the desire to get a word in edgewise in a cacophonous, constantly expanding household.

27

"My theory is that everything Groucho said was funny," Dick Cavett states, "because he said it in his voice."

Once, in a darkened Beverly Hills theater, I reveled in Groucho's loud and sarcastic remarks about the feature. Sibilant shushes assailed us. A male six rows or so in front of us called out, "Who do you think you are—Groucho Marx?" Groucho merely snickered.

In the midst of the climactic emotional scene a misty-eyed Richard Harris, having lost Vanessa Redgrave to Franco Nero, sang poignantly, "Once there was a fleeting whisp of glory called Camelot ..." At that juncture Groucho loudly said to me, "I think it would be a good ideahr if we went to the terlet."

Several people groaned at the breaking of this fragile mood. One of them might even have said, "Good riddance."

The film ended while we performed our ablutions and we had to weave our way through the mingling crowd to return to our seats. Fans, recognizing Groucho, followed us. They now found all his devastating cracks retroactively funny. Some asked for his autograph.

"No," he answered in a mock-hurt voice. "You told me to shut up."

First generation German-Americans retained the stocky physiques of their European-born fathers for good reason. *Ess, ess, mein kind* became the byword of mothers throughout the city. A roly-poly body, they felt, could best fight off the most common, ravaging diseases of the area and the time: pneumonia and tuberculosis.

For those who were also Hebrew, their mothers' cries—"Eat! Eat!"—held a special urgency. So many of their infants had been carried away by the disease that tuberculosis had come to be called Jewish asthma.

Simon and Minnie lost their first son, Manfred, who'd been born a year after their marriage, to the illness.

The death of their infant left Minnie with a storehouse of unexpressed love, which was to be squandered on Leonard—later to be known as Chico—who was born on August 21, 1887.

Leonard was indisputably his mother's child, having inherited her fair hair and blue eyes, and her flirtatious, manipulative personality. If, however, children are as innately perceptive as some would have it, Chico must have sensed that much of the love with which his mother engulfed him was a simple case of transference. He was receiving, in addition to his own, a residue of love for his dead brother. This early realization would leave him emotionally crippled. Greedy for even more love, he would continue his childhood pattern of testing those near to him to see how much he could get away with throughout his life.

Adolf was born fifteen months later on November 23, 1888. The angelic blond child with the green eyes was a favorite of his father, whose charm and warmth he had inherited. Adolf apparently didn't notice or resent his mother's preference for his older brother. Seemingly, he was satisfied with whatever crumbs were thrown his way.

By 1890, eighty percent of the population of New York was of foreign parentage. The Irish, having come first, during the famine of 1846 to 1850, dominated not only Boston. One-third of New York's population of 1,500,000 was now Irish-American, and fully twenty-five percent was Irish-born. Within the next ten years, the German-born would attain such percentages, and prolific families like the Marxes would be largely responsible.

Such demography, however, did not interest Minnie. For her, the momentous event that kicked off the 1890's was her brother's decision to quit the garment factory, change his name to Al Shean, and become an entertainer.

He, along with Sam Curtis, Arthur Williams, and Ed Mack, assumed the stage name the Manhattan Comedy Four. They came to be one of the most popular four-man acts of the period, as well as one of the most durable. Their bookings ran for ten solid years.

The quartet developed a distinctive combination of sophisticated music and robust comedy. They could toss off some maudlin oldtime songs, like "After the Ball," but their greatest hit was their harmonic interpretation of Dave Nation's "It Isn't What You Used To Be, It's What You Are Today."

The ascent to stardom begun by her brother in 1890 was

29

probably more exciting to Minnie than the birth of her son Julius on October 2 of the same year.

By 1898, the City of New York had developed more stringent reporting requirements, coincidental with the creation of a greater New York City incorporating all the boroughs. Previously, eighty-five percent of all births and deaths went unrecorded. No city records exist which verify the births of Chico, Harpo, and Gummo, either at the Eighty-second Street address, or at the modest Yorkville brownstone at 239 East 114th Street, where the Marxes later moved. They might have been born in flats on East 122nd and East 135th streets, also in Yorkville, where the family briefly lodged before vacating both premises in the middle of the night, several steps ahead of the landlords. It was cheaper to pay a ten-dollar moving fee than to cough up a twenty-five dollar monthly rent.

Originally, Yorkville was an area of meadows, deep valleys, and rocky cliffs. It was a game hunter's dream, abounding in rabbits, woodcock, and English snipe.

Later, frame shacks were hurriedly thrown up, standing defiantly against the wind, sleet, and snow of over fifty bitterly cold winters. They housed the most wretched element of the city.

In the 1870s, modest businesses began springing up along such thoroughfares as Lexington and Third avenues. More substantial buildings—modest brownstone homes and apartments—were constructed on the side streets between Eighty-fifth and 125th streets.

The area of Yorkville abutting on Central Park was among the last to be developed. Most Fifth Avenue mansions were concentrated between Eighty-sixth and Ninety-second streets, and housed such distinguished citizens as Andrew Carnegie, Arthur M. Huntington, Robert C. Lewis, and Henry Phipps. Not until 1898 would construction begin further uptown.

Both Groucho and Gummo were born at the 114th Street address, in the middle of Yorkville. A housing development covering several blocks would later be erected in the area, swallowing up the building as well as several surrounding streets. It stands to this day on the edge of Spanish Harlem.

Groucho's was the only birth of the four surviving older brothers to be recorded, which suggests there were complications during the delivery. Midwives supervised the vast majority of births at the time, and physicians were called only in an emergency. The attending physician would then report the delivery to the appropriate agency.

The infant was named after Aunt Hannah's husband, Julius Schickler. Like many Jews before him, he found peddling the quickest way to get started in America. The wagonload of fruits and vegetables he carted from door to door early in the week was based on Thursday nights and Friday mornings at the big peddlers' market on Hester Street. He identified himself as a grocer in the New York City directory of 1888, where he was listed as living at the then respectable, middle class address of 999 Tenth Avenue, along with Hannah and her daughter Polly. Schickler hadn't fathered Polly and her brother Lou. No surviving members of the family recall the name of Hannah's first husband or if she'd previously been married at all.

Groucho, in writing about the situation, opted for respectability even if it was gained at his Cousin Polly's expense. "An aunt of mine had a daughter by her current husband," he wrote in *Groucho and Me.* "When he got a look at the kid, he blew to Canada and was never seen again." He didn't explain why Polly's brother was a Schoenberg who later changed his name to Shean along with Uncle Al.

According to Groucho, Schickler—nicknamed The General—"was five-feet-one in his socks, holes and all. He had a brown spade beard, thick glasses, and a head topped off with a bald spot about the size of a buckwheat cake. My mother somehow got the notion that Uncle Julius was wealthy, and she told my father, who never did quite understand my mother, that it would be a brilliant piece of strategic flattery were they to make Uncle Julius my godfather."

At the moment of his birth, "Uncle Julius was in the back room of a cigar store on Third Avenue, dealing them off the bottom. When word reached him that he had been made my godfather, he dropped everything, including two aces he had up his sleeve for an emergency, and quickly rushed over to our flat."

Groucho would later take further comedic license by saying The General felt so responsible for his namesake that, two weeks after his birth, Uncle Julius moved in with the Marxes and remained with them until Groucho married. Like many of Groucho's stories, it was more fiction than fact, and perhaps says something about his desparate need to prove that someone cared. For Julius Henry (the middle name came from the youngest of the Schoenberg uncles) was a child not even a mother of Minnie's temperament and prejudices could love.

Her first two sons, with their fair coloring and regular features, were Aryan in appearance. As they grew older and their light-colored hair began to darken, Minnie wasn't above putting peroxide in their bath water in an effort to keep them forever blond. Peroxide could do little to alter the appearance of her third son. He had coarse, kinky black hair and olive skin, and he wouldn't be believable as a blond. Some recessive genes in Simon and Minnie had combined to create this Semitic child with an already prominent nose. Hopefully, his face would grow into it.

In addition, there was a cast in Julius's left eye, which his parents didn't bother to consult a doctor about. Whatever the problem, which seemed to cure itself over the years, the young boy would look at you with one eye and seem to be staring over your shoulder with the other.

"I had one beautiful eye," Groucho once remarked to me. "The other one was not so pretty." Thinking I'd find out the medical term for his affliction, I asked him, "What did you call it?" He snapped back, "I called it Sam."

Understandably, when Uncle Al came calling with his new wife, Aunt Johanna, and she remarked on his beautiful brown eyes, Groucho was thrilled ... even though his eyes were grey. He remembered it as the first kind word he'd ever received from a woman, his mother included. Aunt Jo had complimented him on the feature he felt most self-conscious about.

But young Julius had other insecurities. Leonard was his mother's favorite; Adolf was adored by his father. The Marx parents seemed to have run out of laps for their youngest to crawl on.

When Milton (Gummo) was born on October 23, 1892, Leonard and Adolf also noticed a cooling of their parents' ardor. Milton was a listless, sickly child who'd later be diagnosed as having a rheumatic heart. Both Simon and Minnie were forced to divide attention between their favorites and the newest Marx from then on.

For Julius, there was no breaking through the emotional barrier. Certainly, Simon loved all his sons—he called each of them "Darling"—but Minnie's indifference was to adversely affect Groucho and shape his attitude toward women for the rest of his life.

Julius would walk around the apartment, his eagerness for a hug or a pat on the head transparent. Minnie laughed at his obviousness. She called him, quite accurately, *Der Eifersüchtige* ... The Jealous One. The label, coming so early in his life, stuck in his subconscious.

I once had the temerity to suggest to Groucho that he apparently wasn't Minnie's favorite.

"That's not true," he exploded. "My mother treated us all equally ... with contempt!"

Toward the end of his life, still possessed of enormous pride, he found it unseemly to open up eighty-year-old wounds.

"I was a model boy," he insisted. "I never did any harm. I loved my mother and father. I was honest and sincere. I never told a lie, unless I had to ... which was Always ... from the song of the same title."

Julius compensated for this indifference by falling in love with his pillow. "I used to rub it, and it would put me to sleep. I wouldn't go anyplace without it. Once, mother sent me to the Catskills. I don't know where she got the money. I came home the next day. I forgot my pillow. I'd go to bed with it every night. My brothers kept looking at me in an odd way. I didn't understand why. Everybody strokes his pillow ... even Lincoln."

In 1895 the Marxes moved to 179 East Ninety-third Street, also in Yorkville, where the family would live for the next fifteen years. It was the apartment all the brothers would consider their ancestral home.

The four-story brownstone building was located between Lexington and Third avenues, and rent on their three-bedroom flat was twenty-seven dollars a month.

Simon and Minnie shared one bedroom; Opie and Omie, the second; the four boys shared the third, crammed like sardines in one double bed. With only the coal stove in the parlor, the doors of all the bedrooms were kept open during the bitterly cold winters in the naive hope that some of its warmth would waft their way.

Soon after they had moved, Aunt Hannah was stricken by a debilitating, usually fatal illness. Cousin Polly, a teen-ager, came to live with the family after the Schickler house was given up. Hannah turned to Christian Science and was miraculously cured. She joined the growing menage, along with Uncle Julius. Inexplicably, his burgeoning career as a grocer had been marked down like so much day-old bread. Cots were set up all over the apartment to accommodate them and other Schoenbergs who tended to use the apartment as an emergency flophouse.

"We didn't bathe often," Groucho recalled. "We never saw a shower. We had one bathroom. All we had was a tin tub. We used to stand in line to take a leak." Groucho early noticed that, in addition to having a more outgoing personality as well as his mother's love, nature had favored Chico, in a more basic regard.

"We were so poor that when somebody knocked on the door we all hid," Groucho recalled. If the mild-mannered rent collector, Mr. Hummel, persisted in pounding, Gummo was sent to the door, usually in his night clothes. "I'm sick," he would truthfully say, "and my mother isn't home." Well, batting .500 isn't bad. The landlord's agent would go away to return another day.

The apartment drew relatives and friends from all of New York, some to play penny ante poker with Minnie in the kitchen and others to repair to the dining room for pinochle with Simon and Mr. Hempelmeyer from next door.

Simon had a little room off the kitchen where he conducted his business. He was an abysmal craftsman, but an inspired chef. A huge vat which was used for boiling clothes on Monday was more usually filled with epic amounts of beans or potatoes or chowder.

Minnie was a sloppy housewife and an inept cook. She'd gladly leave her husband in charge of the kitchen, and there were always a few women relatives around to do the housework. The family's Orthodox practices were entirely due to Omie's efforts. If she wanted to have two separate sets of dishes and utensils, she'd have to care for them.

Groucho and Shelley Winters once appeared together on Dick

Cavett's show. Shelley, who was playing Minnie in the Broadway production of *Minnie's Boys*, asked, "Groucho, tell me really—truly—how did Minnie, your mother, handle all these boys, who were obviously a handful?"

"Completely ignored us," Groucho replied. "She put us out in the street and let us play, that's all. When we got hungry we went in the house." For a helping, not of mom's apple pie, but pop's kügel or strudel.

Often, the young Marxes seemed to get more attention from neighbors than from their own parents. Felix Marx, a cousin of Simon's who made his living as a barber, was a neighbor for a brief time. He would often give the boys pennies for candy, and his wife kept a clean rag at the ready to wipe their running noses.

Across the street, at 172 East Ninety-third Street, Adam and Elisabeth Wagner lived with their three daughters and one son. One of the daughters—Marie—was a topflight tennis player and the object of a very young Harpo's intense adoration. Mrs. Wagner, an accomplished baker, often supplied the boys with cookies and fruit tarts from her kitchen. She didn't socialize with Minnie, however, disapproving of "that woman with the pile of dyed hair who lets her boys run wild."

The boys—Gummo included—were developing strong, wiry bodies, but without a spare ounce of flesh on them. Simon thought they should have a reservoir of fat to fight off any incipient diseases. He developed a game at breakfast every morning.

He would set out three sweet rolls and the three sons who finished their starchy breakfasts first could partake of the lagniappe. This was a gambit Chico relished, since the odds favored him. He'd developed into a fast eater, and a trencherman to boot. Groucho approached breakfast more methodically. He would usually finish a strong second, with Gummo behind him. Invariably, the dawdling Harpo was left with his empty hand stretched out.

One morning, however, Groucho and Gummo won and placed, and it was a tossup as to whether Chico would beat Harpo to the finish line. Harpo was a fraction of a second faster, but as he reached out, Chico brought forth a meat cleaver, crashing it down on the table, splitting the top in two. Harpo withdrew his hand just in time.

A few weeks later, a distant in-law by the name of Samuel Wolfenstein, who ran a men's wear emporium on Waverly Place, agreed to advance Minnie enough money to take herself and two of her children to Dornum. Minnie was ecstatic. Besides Chico, who would she take? Groucho made a deal with Harpo, giving him his sweet roll that morning.

Groucho would later say that both Harpo and Gummo agreed to accept express wagons in lieu of the trip, but it's doubtful that Gummo at three would possess enough reason to understand the terms of the agreement. Harpo, however, understood that a sweet roll in the hand is better than no hand at all.

The Wolfensteins, with their two daughters, and Minnie and the two boys traveled by cattle boat. All Groucho remembered of the trip was the visit to the cemetery in Germany where his great-grandparents had been buried.

Both Leonard and Adolf were now of school age, and they would embark on their studies under the "Rah, rah, royal purple" banner of P.S. 86 at Ninety-sixth Street and Lexington Avenue, with varying degrees of success.

Chico's extraordinary head for figures—the perfumed, curvaceous ones were still beyond his capabilities—boded well for him. His teachers assured him that, if he applied himself, he could find comfort and security in the groves of Academe. His brain was a mental adding machine which Harpo couldn't keep up with, even if he were spotted two hours and the fingers and toes of the entire household.

Family legend has it that Harpo was so dim he was kept in the first grade for five years. The number is somewhat inflated.

Children such as Adolf were known as slow learners in those days. His school difficulties might well have been solved by a remedial reading course, had there been such a subject in the school curriculum at the time.

The lack of mental agility would turn him red with frustration, particularly after his younger brothers began developing greater skills than he possessed.

Harpo later rationalized that his teacher, Miss Flatto, had fallen hopelessly in love with him. Unable to bear the thought of parting, so his version went, she kept him in the first grade for another year. Only until she herself was promoted to teaching the second grade was he allowed to move along with her.

He was into his second year in the second grade when his formal schooling ended forever. (Contrary to popular folklore, he hadn't yet begun to shave.) Two Irish toughs, bigger than Harpo even though he might have been a couple of years older, would throw him out the first-story classroom window whenever Miss Flatto left the room. He would trudge up the school steps and return to the classroom a step behind his teacher, who demanded to know what he was doing out of the classroom. Harpo's code of honor was too well developed to tell. He did decide after a while that defenestration might lead to decapitation. The next time he was flung out the window, he picked himself up, dusted himself off, and went home. His education had ended at the age of eight.

Harpo's next few years would be spent exploring the neighborhood. There was an ice cream parlor on Third Avenue operated by Mr. Jergens, who would own the first automobile in the neighborhood. A block away, on Lexington, was the neighborhood tabacconist, Mr. Gehrke. Everybody called him Gookie. He would work behind the store window, rolling cigars, his tongue hanging out and his eyes crossed. He was as oblivious to the faces he was making as he was to the people who would come from blocks away to see him make them. Harpo committed the expression to memory. It would serve as inspiration years later when he joined his brothers in their as yet unplanned vaudeville act.

The Old Homestead Beer Garden was a popular neighborhood saloon. Behind the main building was an open-air stage where continuous shows were put on in summer by jugglers, comedy teams, trick musicians, yodelers, and magicians.

One illusionist who lived in the neighborhood, being Hungarian-born and already a huge star, wouldn't gravitate to a German beer hall. He was Ehrich Weiss, a rabbi's son, who lived next door to the Wagners and across the street from the Marxes during the 1890s. Inspired by a famous French magician of the mid-Victorian period, Robert Houdin, he changed his name to Harry Houdini. He'd pulled a disappearing act in real life, for none of the Marxes ever remembered seeing him on the street. By 1904, after a triumphant European tour, he was firmly entrenched in his custom-designed digs on West 114th Street.

Aunt Hannah had discovered that Groucho possessed a sweet and clear boy soprano voice. As a result of her encouragement and the promptings of his older brothers, he raised his voice in song at the Old Homestead. At age five, Julius Marx had made his public debut.

Simon, who had recently changed his name to Sam, was a teetotaler. He seemed content to spend all his time at the home he as a tailor occasionally worked out of. During the day, his cutting table and sewing bench would be brought out of the room off the kitchen and set up in the dining room, and swatches and bolts of material would be strewn throughout all three chambers. Then, as dinner hour approached, everything would be put away as he began to prepare dinner.

Minnie, in the meantime, was running a less affluent version of a Fifth Avenue salon, meeting with friends to trade chitchat or to play poker, to which she'd become addicted.

"Our father was a good man in bed," Groucho told me, "but the town schlemiel. I don't mean to say he wasn't a nice man, because he was. But he was ignorant. Our mother was the boss. After all, who was stronger: Napoleon or Josephine?"

Sam would later be called Frenchy by his sons, who in their distinctive, twisted brand of logic, had noticed that he'd turned his back on everything French, the language included. The family conversed in both German and English, often in the same sentence. The only concession Sam made to his heritage was to stand and hold his hand over his heart whenever "La Marseillaise" was played.

Although well-groomed, Frenchy didn't frequent the barber shop, as the average man did, to swap stories and read the *Police Gazette*. There was no cubbyhole along the wall in any of the neighborhood barber shops with his name on it. The straight-edged razor with the ivory handle, the leather strop for honing, and the china shaving mug were all kept at home in the one bathroom.

Marx père wasn't a regular guy like Uncle Al, who would come calling with the latest snappy stories, indulging each nephew with a silver coin as he left.

Al was doing much better financially than his brother-in-law. Frenchy would always be a mediocre tailor, his spotty wages augmented by what his permanent guests—the Schoenbergs and the Schicklers—were able to bring in.

Groucho didn't choose to recall the many days Frenchy went out with a supply of yard goods, which he would sell door to door, bringing home the foodstuffs which he would later transform into the evening meal. Because the family had no icebox, food for the day's meals had to be bought every day.

Nor did he mention how loving their father was with his sons. Frenchy was a demonstrative man, given to displays of spontaneous affection, whereas Minnie's were usually more perfunctory. His sons responded in kind, indulging this sentimental man at the same time they were making him the butt of their jokes. Every story they told about him revealed him as being not too bright, an attitude toward their father they must have inherited from Minnie.

Julius's assessment was even harsher than his mother's. Frenchy didn't notice. He went on calling Julius "Darling" as he did all his boys.

What Julius perceived was the way Minnie was able to dominate the household and their lives. Creditors could be put off, children could do her bidding. The sound of her laughter was the energizer, and her family would join in despite its often mocking tone. Derision was as much a part of Minnie as the more physical, sensuous desire to have her bare feet rubbed, an act of obeisance her sons eagerly performed, and a practice each in turn would expect from his own children.

If the laughter was too painful for those with thin skins, they'd have to develop thicker ones. Julius was the most vulnerable. He wasn't a tough guy like Leonard. He didn't have Adolf's incurable belief that under the six-foot pile of manure there must be a pony. Julius couldn't hide behind Milton's invalidism. His arsenal, stockpiled at an early age, was the word, flitting and darting, mercilessly strafing the target, wounding as he'd been wounded. His sardonic tone was the outcry of the idealist who lives within every disillusioned cynic.

"My mother was a wonderful woman," Groucho would say. "She made us what we are. We owe it all to her."

Thus spoke Groucho, the misogynist, about himself and his

brothers: Chico, the unregenerate Don Juan and compulsive gambler; Gummo, the life-long hypochondriac; Zeppo, whom Groucho would later describe as having ice water running through his veins. Only Harpo seemed to have emerged unscathed. Or did he?

Two events in 1896 set the family and Groucho off in new directions. Omie's health failed and she took to her bed.

"We were having a pillow fight in our room," Groucho recalled, "when Frenchy came in and told us to stop. Omie had died."

"Barukh Dayan Emet," said acquaintances when they heard the news. Blessed be the true judge. No flowers were permitted, according to Orthodox ritual, as Omie, at the age of sixty-six, was laid to rest.

Her death, after a period of mourning, liberated the family. Orthodox practices were simply too rigorous to observe in such a casual household and were eventually dropped. Opie, in tribute to his dead wife, took over the modicum of religious training the boys would receive. He supervised their Bar Mitzvahs. After that, the Marx clan, while not turning their backs on religion completely, concentrated on more secular matters.

Back in Europe, according to a tale of the time, the Archbishop of Budapest had been born a Jew and converted to Catholicism. His assistant was also a converted Jew. Experiencing the smells of a kosher restaurant, the Archbishop turned to his associate and said, "To think that's the religion we left."

The Marxes didn't have the tradition of kosher cuisine retained by other non-practicing Jews, having never been exposed to it. Groucho wouldn't eat his first bagel until he was eighty-one, according to his son Arthur in *Son of Groucho.*

He was as ambivalent about his religion as one of the characters in a story he liked to tell. "There were two Jews in Israel," Groucho said. "They were both pissing. One looked over at the other. He asked, 'Are you a Jew?' The guy said yeah. 'Do you live in Israel?' Yeah. The man asked, 'Why aren't you circumcised?' To which the other one replied, 'I'm not sure I'm going to stay.'"

His second wave of liberation was marked by the beginning of Groucho's academic career. Jewish custom required that a youngster's mother or teacher drop a bit of honey on the first book he read. The child licked the honey to forever associate sweetness with learning. In Groucho's case, the whole jar must have been spilled. His choice of reading was initially indiscriminate, but his nose wouldn't be too far away from a book for the rest of his life.

Hope was offered in the Horatio Alger stories devoured by Groucho. Be he bootblack, plumber, or newsboy, Alger's hero earned his just reward, surmounting impossible obstacles and achieving the pinnacle of success.

Uncle Al was the only male role model of his acquaintance that Groucho early wanted to emulate. He instilled a desire in the child to go on the stage.

Groucho's reading introduced him to many others.

The greatest, as he was to millions of other boys, was Frank Merriwell, the hero of one of the dime store novels, *Tip Top Weekly*, which Chico brought home every week. He was created by George Patten, who was as prolific as the character he created was mythic, turning out 20,000 words a week which reached 124 million readers.

Physically, Merriwell was a splendid specimen: "His handsome proportions, his graceful, muscular figure, his fine, kingly head and that look of clean manliness ... stamped him as a fellow of lofty thoughts and ambitions."

Merriwell's priorities were also admirable. He loved his mother, his alma mater, and his country; he abhorred poor sportsmanship, drinking, and bullies.

His real-life embodiment might have been another of Groucho's boyhood idols, Richard Harding Davis. Novelist, journalist, man-about-town, and the top war correspondent of his era, Davis personified masculinity and derring-do. His personality was an attractive, rakish mixture of vanity and self-mockery.

Groucho's mirror-image, however, was closer to that of Teddy Roosevelt, who achieved fame as the roughest of the Rough Riders in the Spanish-American War of 1898. Within three years he would become president. Dumpy-looking, with thick spectacles and a mouth filled with teeth which protruded from his walrus mustache, Roosevelt would have cut a comical figure if his heroism hadn't already become part of American folklore. He was also the living embodiment of the country's energetic mood. This was the Cocksure Era: optimism, confidence, and innocence all wrapped up into one idealistic package. Teddy Roosevelt's passion for reading created a special empathy in Groucho. The new president was reputed to read two or three books every day, and would eventually write twenty-four of them himself.

When he wasn't at home reading or at any of the vaudeville houses catching Uncle Al's act, Groucho would be out with his brothers on the street, experimenting with life.

Cousin Polly had married a tailor named Sam Muller, who had a shop on Lexington Avenue not far from the Gookie cigar store. In exchange for letting them put a poster in his store window, the managers of the Star Melodrama Theatre on 102nd Street gave Muller two free tickets a week. Often, when he couldn't use the tickets, he would give them to the boys. Previously exposed to vaudeville turns, they now saw stage plays for the first time. Soon after, Groucho appeared on the stage of that theater, singing a solo in the olio.

Despite the great ambivalence about his upbringing, Groucho would often turn defensive when I'd reflect that his parents didn't do right by him and his brothers.

"I wasn't robbed of my childhood," he protested. "None of the boys were. We had the typical New York childhood of the time. We played stoop ball."

Each boy, a team unto himself, would try to hit a five-cent rubber ball with a broom handle. If he made contact, he would then run from fire hydrant to fire hydrant. Because Groucho's eyesight wasn't the best, he was less adept than Chico and Harpo. Because of his weak heart, Gummo was forced to sit on the stoop and watch.

The boys also got into their fair share of trouble. The four of them had already made a shambles of Cousin Polly's wedding reception when they'd jumped on a strange contrivance in the men's room—a urinal—which broke away from the wall and unleashed a torrent of water. The bridegroom had to pay for the damage before the reception could continue.

They also jumped on trolleys without paying, dodging the ticket taker as long as they could before leaping off, only to hop onto the next trolley to again do the same thing.

There was the rest of the city to experience, and it wasn't limited solely to Manhattan. The outlying counties that had been consolidated into the boroughs of Greater New York had brought the city's population to nearly 3,500,000 by 1900. The expansion actually began in 1883 with the opening of the Brooklyn Bridge.

During the summer, the boys would often go—usually with Minnie, who loved the water—to Rockaway Beach, or to Coney Island's Steeplechase Park, with its spectacular nighttime fireworks displays.

When they couldn't hitch a ride, they walked. Sometimes they'd amble down the wide, tree-lined main avenues of picturesque Manhattan, where the rough granite blocks of the streets were being paved over with asphalt, to take in the parade of open victorias and horseless chuggers.

Other times they'd walk by the tracks of the New York & Harlem Railroad, which was a "roofless tunnel" between Forty-second and Ninety-sixth streets. Pigs and goats were raised along these dirt banks, and there was still an Irish shanty or two to be seen as they ambled from Yorkville toward the theater district.

It was, all in all, a clean city. A city commissioner, George E. Waring, had organized a crew of 2,000 uniformed men and 750 horses and carts. The men were dressed in white uniforms—they were known as the White Wings—symbols that the city could be made clean and kept clean.

A new class of pleasure riders could be seen on the Third Avenue cable cars, noisy family parties traveling from one end of the line to the other. On other routes, people would go for joy rides on lit-up trolley cars, amateur bands in the front seats playing for them.

Many in the ghettoes developed more adventurous palates and began sampling cuisine not native to their own lands. All New York seemed to develop a taste for spaghetti and hot dogs. Lobster places sprang up all over the city.

In Central Park, the Old Money nobs and nouveaux riches took up bicycle riding with equal enthusiasm. The boys would develop squatters' rights on the choice park benches, charging spooning couples ten cents to vacate them.

Back in their own neighborhood, they'd hop on the back of the ice wagon to steal a free ride. Some youngsters wearing skates would hold on to the back of the wagons as they were wheeled down the street, but the skateless Marx boys had to forego this activity.

Among the first mansions to be built in Yorkville, much of which was still a series of shanty towns with many open spaces, was that of Jacob Ruppert, the owner of the nearby brewery. Located at Fifth Avenue and Ninety-third Street, opposite the Central Park reservoir, it was a major structure beside which small farms still operated well into the twentieth century. It was also the first bastion of respectability that the Marx Brothers would storm. If that building were a woman, she would be Margaret Dumont.

Within its iron-spiked fence stood the house and an orchard. Two watchdogs performed double duty, on the alert for neighborhood boys with designs on the peaches and apples ripening on the rows of trees along Ninety-third Street. The poaching of the fruit, with its accompanying plots and subterfuges, took on the character of a summer and fall military campaign for the Marxes. They would return home with eye-opening stories of being threatened with a shotgun by old man Ruppert or nearly having their limbs torn apart by the dogs, omitting the fact that they'd been tearing apart some limbs themselves in their quest for the forbidden fruit.

Some forbidden fruit was still beyond them. Sex was nonexistent as a subject at school or as a topic of dinner conversation at home. "We lived near Central Park," Groucho recalled, "and we heard of fellows taking girls in the bushes. But I didn't know what they were doing."

Young Julius well knew that a boy and a girl didn't sleep together unless they were married, having had an immediate example of such a taboo in his own home.

One day, Frenchy was found with a Schoenberg cousin in the bed he normally shared with Minnie. Such a gambit in a round-the-clock open house is a tribute to his daring, if not his intelligence. The wailings Minnie raised ended with the banishment of the young girl from the house. Pleadings by others that Simon was the instigator had no effect on Minnie. How could the girl be so stupid? And did they expect her to kick her own husband, the father of her sons, out of the house? The matter was closed, and nothing more would be said of it. The message gathered by the boys was an obvious one: it was all right to play around; if any problems ensued, the female was always to blame.

In an era when *la belle poitrine* was displayed—women had no compunction about openly breast-feeding their babies—the chance sighting of a shapely ankle beneath a hobble skirt was cause for ecstatic transports. As to what delight was located where female limbs met the body, it was described by a ditty the boys picked up in the neighborhood:

> I took my girl to the engine house,
> The engine went by steam;
> A red hot coal flew up her hole;
> And burned her magazine.
> Her magazine was hairy,
> As hairy as could be;
> Two black eyes and a bloody nose,
> And her ass was painted green.

"That's the way kids talked," Groucho explained. "It's as good as Shakespeare."

Groucho recalled a childhood venture to Hammerstein's Theatre on Times Square. A boy and girl act was on the bill. The girl sat on a bench while the fellow tried to flirt with her.

"So he came up to her and said, 'You're a very attractive broad,'" Groucho recalled. "Then he added, 'It's a nice day, isn't it?'" She said, 'It *was*.' They were cancelled after the first performance because he used the word 'broad.' Everybody was talking about it."

As for the ultimate four-letter word, Groucho once heard a joke on the street and didn't know why it was funny. He had to ask Chico what the word meant.

Jewish peddlers would ply their wares, calling out their inventory as they slowly made their way down each street. Anyone interested in buying would lean his head out the window and yell down the number of his apartment so that the order could be delivered.

A peach seller made his way down the street one day. A woman in an apartment building shouted down to him, "I want a dozen."

The man nodded and waved.

"4 Q," the woman yelled.

"Fuck you too!" the man angrily replied.

And then there was Leonard. There was always Leonard or Lenny or Leo or Chico. Whatever they called him, he was the bane of his parents' existence, the apple of his mother's eye, and the object of more jealous sibling rivalry than all the other brothers combined.

It's difficult imagining anyone being as precocious as Chico was in one respect. He became a compulsive gambler at the age of nine, the same year Omie died.

He had, of course, seen his parents playing poker and pinochle for small stakes. Had Omie lived she might have told him as well as his parents that the Talmud, which sets forth Hebrew law and tradition, equates gambling with thievery. Also, in ancient Israel a gambler wasn't considered a fit witness in a Jewish court of law.

Chico would have surely disagreed, answering, "Do you want to bet?"

Psychological studies have concluded that compulsive gamblers are compulsive liars as children. Chico's bald-faced untruths, however, were often caused by the fact that he was already a compulsive gambler, a reversal of this particular cause and effect theory.

He would hock the suits his father tailored, and once even went so far as to pawn the shears Frenchy relied on to make a living. Never in his later career did he offer an acting performance to match those in which he presented explanations for his failure to bring home his weekly salary from the various post-grammar school jobs he held.

Chico quickly learned that a new pair of pants would get him $2.50 from the pawnbroker. Frenchy, in self-defense, began making suits with two pairs of pants, one for the customer and one for Chico to hock. "That, I believe, was the origin of the two-pants suit in America," Groucho cracked.

Minnie thought Leonard's passion for gambling might be blunted if he learned to play the piano. If he became proficient enough, he might even be able to accompany Julius when he sang.

The piano was bought for five dollars down and one dollar a week. It was a scarred, secondhand upright that had to be hoisted with a crane through a window. A Viennese piano teacher, a lady with an imposing mustache, was hired to teach Chico for twenty-five cents a week. Unfortunately, she could only teach the right hand, and she faked with the left. Chico, in imitation, became quite an adept one-handed piano player.

By 1899 there were one million pianos in the United States for a population of 75 million people, and the number of pianos was increasing five times as fast as the number of people.

True to prevailing fashion, Minnie set the upright in the middle of the room. More fashionable households had taken to draping the backs of the pianos in plush velvet or silk damask. The Marxes didn't have the money for such fripperies. The only thing draping the back of their piano was Julius. Looking over Chico's shoulder as the latter practiced, he picked up rudimentary skills. When Groucho played the piano, he would always use his left hand and let the right one limp along, playing the instrument in Chico's mirror image.

The piano was fine as a hobby, but Chico had greater enticements on the street. At the age of eleven, he began staying out all night.

He'd fallen in with a tough street gang. As a result, he had to learn to use his fists, or broken bottles if the odds didn't favor him.

As the boys grew bigger, another double bed was bought for their room. The floor was now carpeted with wall-to-wall mattresses. Chico and Harpo shared one bed, and Groucho and Gummo the other.

Frenchy would wait up for the wayward Leonard, usually falling asleep in the easy chair in the parlor. When he'd awaken in the middle of the night, he'd occasionally see that the beds were fully occupied. Earlier, when Chico had come in, he'd get into Harpo's side of the bed, nudging his brother over so that he was now sleeping where Chico usually slept.

Their father was a poor disciplinarian. Spanking his children caused him to cry longer than the miscreant. He'd force himself to punish the boy, taking a whisk broom and shouting, "No-goodnik, stay out late," as he got in some rather feeble licks. He couldn't

47

bear to spank any of his boys with his full might. Then Frenchy would depart the room, leaving a dazed and confused Harpo wondering what nightmare he'd just awakened from.

Chico was twelve when he ran away from home for the first time. His parents were hollow-eyed with worry. They found him and brought him back, but he was to make off often over the next few years.

Harpo in the meantime had obtained his first full-time employment after five years of assorted jobs, having been hired as a bellhop at the Hotel Seville, a tony theatrical haven down on East Twenty-eighth Street. His salary was twelve dollars a month, which he dutifully brought home, though he was allowed to keep the fifty cents extra he received weekly for walking the dog belonging to Cissie Loftus, a famous English music hall and vaudeville star.

All of America seemed to be progressing as it entered the twentieth century. More immediately, Uncle Al was also on to bigger things. He disbanded the Manhattan Comedy Four in order to team up with Charles L. Warren in a ragtag skit called "Quo Vadis Upside Down." The act was to last for ten years.

At home, Frenchy and Minnie were commiserating with each other. They were at a loss as to what to do about Leonard.

Julius had always been the dutiful son. His odd jobs hadn't begun to pay as well as Adolf's, but he too could be trusted to bring home all his earnings, such as the weekly dollar he received for singing in the boys' choir at the Episcopal Church on Madison Avenue.

His oldest brother was charming and irresponsible and outspoken, and a delinquent to boot. He was getting the bulk of parental attention, and goodness had nothing to do with it, as Mae West would later maintain.

Julius was going on ten when he decided to assert himself, although he was to do so in a comparatively timid way.

The Saint Patrick's Day parade of 1900 was exceptionally glorious, as Julius watched it from in front of the Ruppert mansion.

Riding in the parade, sitting in a luxurious barouche, was Tom Sharkey. The heavyweight fighter had fought the champion, Jim Jeffries, the previous November. He was the loser in a hotly disputed twenty-five-round decision, being bettered in a lackluster match by an opponent reputed to be the strongest man ever to hold the title. As the carriage arrived at the corner, Julius turned into the Groucho the world would come to know. He yelled, "Hey, Sharkey, what did Jeffries do to ya?"

Many boxing fans believed Jeffries hadn't done anything to Sharkey, and that the challenger was robbed of the decision. Groucho was jabbing at Sharkey's most sensitive point.

The fighter leaned halfway out the carriage and yelled, "Come over here, ya little bastard, and I'll kill ya!"

Groucho didn't move, smiling as the parade resumed, as he marveled at his own daring.

That summer, Frenchy and Minnie found they were expecting another child. Julius was caught in an emotional tailspin. He'd been getting a disproportionately smaller share of care and affection than his three brothers, and now it would be further diluted with the arrival of a fourth.

Perhaps as compensation for the seeming emotional deprivation, he committed a petty crime at Bloomingdale's.

"I wanted to be a writer and I had nothing to write with," he told Dick Cavett. "I had a lead pencil, but I wanted a printing press. Now they had them for sale for $1.98. They were toy-size and had letters in it, you know, you'd pick out the letters 'H' and 'G,' whatever letters you wanted. I stuck it under my coat. A floor-walker came along and he saw a peculiar bulge and he says, 'What have you got under there?' And I said nothing and he reached in and pulled out this printing press, and he got a cop, who arrested me. Old man Bloomingdale came along around this time and said, 'What are you doing there? What's the policeman for?' The floorwalker said, 'Well, the kid stole a printing press.' The old man said, 'Let him go, all the kids steal in this neighborhood.' They let me go, but they didn't let me keep the printing press."

The boy was ordered never to set foot in the store again, a warning he obeyed for over seventy years. Thus ended his life of crime.

The baby was born on February 25, 1901, and named Herbert by his thirty-seven-year-old mother. He wasn't dark-haired and fair-skinned like their previous boy, Milton. At last, Minnie had a *real* blond.

49

CHAPTER THREE

"Did you hear? They shot McKinley!"
"You don't say! Of McKinley and who?"
Apocryphal dialogue of the period

Weber and Fields . . . Smith and Dale . . . Wheeler and Woolsey
. . . Clark and McCullough.

They came in pairs, these comedy teams that were the mainstay
of the two-a-day, one of them the shark and the slicker, the other a
rube besting the first at his own game through sheer naiveté.

Vaudeville had seeped into every corner of the North American
continent and there just weren't enough quality acts to keep up
with the demand. Pallid imitations sprang up, long on nerve and
short on talent. They were hissed; they were pelted with fruit and
vegetables; yet they were virtually indestructible.

Vaudevillians' lives revolved around their shows. Constant travel
made it difficult for them to keep up with current events. The age
of the topical comedian was yet to come. Thus, some performer
surely asked, when hearing of the assassination of the President,

"Of McKinley and who?" If McKinley were half of a comedy act, he might be fully deserving of that final, fatal criticism. For there were enough dreary performers around who warranted being driven off the stage.

No one was more critical of the vaudevillian than his fellow performer. Class distinctions were closely observed. The headliner on the bill ignored the lesser acts, and the lesser acts turned up their noses at the acrobats and animal acts, and not only because of their gamy smell. These were the dumb acts which closed the show, the objects of the audience's much divided attention. Once they came on, many spectators, eager to beat the rush, would begin to leave their seats.

At the beginning of its sixty years of existence, vaudeville was more democratic. From 1870 to 1890, afterpieces—in which all the performers on the bill appeared—were prevalent. But as it developed, vaudeville began to showcase the artist and the star, who didn't care to have his name linked with lesser members of the cast. The dumb act, and later the Biograph short subject, came to replace the afterpiece as the show-closer.

Vaudeville—its name comes from the French "vau-de-Vire," the valley of the Vire in Normandy famous for its light and convivial songs—had its root in the ethnic variety shows of the mid-nineteenth century. At that time, Irish acts predominated, blackface was a close second, and Dutch or German dialects were third.

They were racial comics, but extraordinarily faithful to the reality of their types. This was the essential difference between vaudeville and burlesque, from which it had broken off.

The root of burlesque is the Italian word *burla*, which means a jest or a mockery, and the low comedy and nudity that evolved out of it clearly showed how different it was from vaudeville. Burlesque turned its back on respectability; vaudeville yearned for and almost achieved it.

Vaudeville was the entertainment of the bourgeoisie, which was too conventional to wallow in burlesque and lacked the culture to discern the offerings of the legitimate, classical theater.

It may have begun in February, 1881, when Tony Pastor opened the Fourteenth Street Theatre with *Pie-Rats of Pen-Yan*, a satire of

Gilbert and Sullivan's *Pirates of Penzance*. The offering didn't go over well.

Pastor tried again the following October when he presented a "novel entertainment" designed to attract respectable women patrons and their escorts. Eight contrasting acts were put forth, headed by Ella Wesner, who sang English music hall numbers and interpolated them with a fetching monologue.

Benjamin F. Keith took the idea and expanded it into modern circuit vaudeville in 1885, offering shows to which children could take their parents.

Not until February, 1890, however, did the vogue of "ladies" attending vaudeville shows begin; evidently a distinction between "respectable women" and "ladies" existed at the time. They braved the curtained boxes on the balcony of Koster and Bial's Theater on Twenty-third Street. The object of their curiosity was Carmencita, the Spanish dancer who'd been immortalized on canvas by Sargent and Chase. She became the talk of the town.

Before long, the social status of legitimate actresses was also upgraded, as they began to socialize over teacups in Fifth Avenue mansions.

Vaudeville wasn't a subject read about in books of the time, other than the yearly compendium of two-acts, sketches, monologues, and parodies known as *Madison's Budget*, a best seller at a dollar, which every small-time performer cribbed from. The major influence on young Julius was his Uncle Al, whose career was thriving. In addition to making the princely sum of two hundred dollars a week, he was regarded as an eminence in the neighborhood whenever he came calling. The boy told his mother that if he didn't become a doctor he might follow in Uncle Al's footsteps.

At the end of his seventh year in school, in the summer of 1903, Minnie informed Groucho she'd gotten a job for him at Hepner's, a wig factory on West Forty-fourth Street, in the theatrical district. His salary would be three dollars a week.

"I should work all summer?" Groucho asked. His catholic tastes had led him far afield from the required reading at school, and there were many books outside his structured curriculum that he wanted to crack open before his final year in grade school.

"It's a full-time job," Minnie told him. "All year round."

Thus, without a whimper, Groucho's academic career came to an end. "I went into show business because I didn't want to finish school," he later said without much conviction. "I wanted to become an entertainer."

Withdrawing her third eldest from school wasn't seen as an act of cruelty by Minnie, depriving as it did the one son with the greatest potential as a scholar. The profession of medicine was forever closed to him. Nor was there any subconscious effort to keep Chico, the only one of her sons thus far to finish grade school, academically superior.

The family needed the extra money. Harpo was working and bringing his salary home. Leonard more often brought home excuses from his job instead of contributing his fair share. Had he brought his earnings home instead of gambling them away, perhaps Groucho might have finished grade school and gone on to a higher education. The accusation went unspoken.

In later years Groucho would take considerable pride in having written seven books without the benefit of a high school education. Yet there were grammar schools then and grammar schools now. The curriculum, with its emphasis on reading and the classics, might well have qualified a grammar school graduate of that day to enter a liberal arts college today. Not until 1918 would New York drop achievement levels, and add subjects with vocational and recreational orientations.

According to the 1903 New York City Teachers' Syllabus, English was to account for 320 minutes of the weekly 1,500-minute, five-day school week. It was divided into English appreciation, reading, composition, spelling, and memorizing. The last concentrated heavily on the works of Shakespeare, Tennyson, and Byron.

Seventh grade mathematics consisted of algebra, geometry, accounting, the metric system, and conversion to and from foreign money.

The first six grades were taught 120 minutes weekly of American history, with the emphasis on New York's role in national events. History in the seventh and eighth grades delved into English history from 55 B.C. until 1901 and the accession of Edward VII to the throne.

Seventh graders had one hour of music a week, learning songs in unison, two- and three-part harmony and writing "diatonic intervals from hearing."

In 1909, a national study filed with the United States Commissioner of Education revealed that on a national level eighty to ninety percent of the students did not continue from primary school, or the first six grades, to grammar school, grades seven and eight. Julius's education exceeded the norm. In not allowing him to renew his academic career for another thirty-eight weeks, Minnie thought she was performing a service. He'd be around the world of entertainment, and who knew where that would lead?

Groucho's duties at Hepner's involved the lugging of five-gallon tin cans to a general store on Tenth Avenue, where they would be filled with kerosene. Then he would haul them back to Hepner's, where he used the kerosene to wash the greasepaint out of the wigs. He was as close to the world he aspired to as the manure-shoveler at the circus. A boy of his sensibilities could see the work offered no future other than a case of permanently stooped shoulders.

One incident in particular made him aware the job hadn't even prepared him with a rudimentary knowledge of the field. His boss sent him out one day to purchase a copy of the *Dramatic Mirror*. Its editor was Harrison Grey Fiske, the husband of Minnie Maddern Fiske, one of the great ladies of the theater, and the former child actress Groucho's mother adored. At the newsstand, Groucho said, "I want a copy of the *Theatrical Looking Glass*."

"What?" the newsman asked.

"Theatrical Looking Glass," the boy repeated. Any Lewis Carroll fan would have made the same mistake.

After much laughter, the newsman gave the boy a copy of the *Mirror*. Groucho returned to the factory, feeling somewhat sheepish, but newly determined to move on. He wanted to be nearer the center of the arena, and to know what to call it when his opportunity came.

He decided to look for an opening as a singer.

In later years, Minnie would develop a public persona, a combination of P.T. Barnum and Florence Nightingale, and would receive credit for launching the Marx Brothers as well as Al Shean.

It was an assessment Groucho violently disagreed with. He insisted he got his first jobs on his own.

In addition to his daily rounds at the booking offices, he'd taken to reading the want ads. One summer day in 1905, he came upon a notice in the classified section of the *New York Morning World:*

Boy Singer wanted for Touring Vaudeville Act. Apply Leroy, 816 3rd Ave., between 2 and 4. $4 a week job.

"When I saw the ad," Groucho wrote in *The Groucho Phile,* "I ran all the way from our house on 93rd Street to 33rd Street . . . Then I ran up five flights of stairs and knocked on the door. A man answered. He was in a kimono and wearing lipstick. This was the profession I wanted to get into?"

Groucho won the job with his rendition of "Love Me and the World Is Mine." An East Side tough named Johnny Morris was hired as the buck, or tap, dancer to round out the Leroy Trio.

Leroy opined that this would be a distinguished vaudeville tour. The act was slated to open at the Ramona Amusement Parlor in Grand Rapids and then go on to play the New Novelty Theatre in Denver. No mention was made of any stops between.

"When I said goodbye, my mother cried a little," Groucho wrote in *Groucho and Me,* "but the rest of the family seemed able to contain themselves without too much effort. As a parting gesture, just as I was leaving, the dog bit me."

The troupe traveled by day coach to Grand Rapids. The show opened with four blacks dressed as Orientals, calling themselves the Wangdoodle Four. The Leroy Trio would be the second of the five acts.

What Groucho would most remember about the tour was the mistreatment he received from Leroy and Morris. He'd saved his money, keeping it in a grouch bag, a chamois sack with a leather drawstring which most actors of the time carried. Leroy somehow convinced Julius that they should travel south, perhaps to Colorado Springs, in search of bookings. They arrived at Cripple Creek, 125 miles south of Denver and about fifty miles west of Colorado Springs, apparently off course, where he was left stranded. Leroy and Morris had absconded with his eight dollars.

56

Groucho's concept of homosexuals was the prevalent one. Of course, Leroy bore some resemblance to a woman, and a couple of the Wangdoodle Four had jokingly threatened to use him as one. With Leroy there could be no doubt about sexual orientation. But Morris was tough and male and didn't fit the stereotype. Julius was learning something new every day, as necessity required if he was to survive.

He was hired to drive a grocery wagon ten miles between Cripple Creek and Victor through a mountain range. At one point, the narrow road looked down on a gorge of four thousand feet, making for a terrifying ride.

"I didn't know anything about horses except that they ate sugar," Groucho recalled. "The only horses I had seen up to that time were either on carousels or the broken down ones that pulled wagons on the streets in New York. Nevertheless, I introduced myself to the team and told them who was boss. I was scared. If I went faster it would be over sooner, I thought. However, one of the horses went on a sit-down strike in the middle of the road. He probably saved my life. The horse wouldn't budge until a new driver came along. I was fired, of course."

Minnie wired him the money to come home.

As for Leroy and Morris, the paths of offbeat love may have run as roughly as more conventional ones. A Gene Leroy opened as a single at the Crystal Theater in Denver a month later.

Back in New York after his misadventure, Groucho found conditions much the same as when he had left.

Herbert would soon be five, and was as spoiled as ever. Leonard was still a headache, even in absentia. He had totally disappeared. Adolf was looking for a job. Opie, claiming to be eighty-six instead of his actual seventy-four, and increasingly daffy, was looking forward to a winter of ice skating in Central Park.

Rather wondersome in its presumption had been the act Uncle Henry and Milton had put together during Julius's absence. Henry, a sweet, deaf man, had an overpowering ambition to follow his brother Al into show business. He induced his nephew Milton to join him in a mock ventriloquist act, in which Milton would put a papier-mâché head over his own and move mechanically as if Henry were pulling the strings. Even if their material had been

57

topnotch, they would have had trouble. Henry was deaf and Milton stammered. As Milton labored to get out a line, Henry was on to his next one, the punch line coming before the setup of the joke. The act failed within two weeks.

Julius spent the next three months at occasional jobs, usually singing illustrated songs in a beer garden. His one credit had stimulated Minnie to take more of an interest in him. She was now acting as his unofficial agent.

Mother and son met Lily Seville, an English performer, at a theatrical agency one day.

"She was the most beautiful woman I'd ever seen," Groucho said of the twenty-three-year-old girl he'd soon be trodding the boards with in a singing version of *The Lady and the Tiger.*

She'd been booked for seven weeks on the Interstate vaudeville circuit in Texas and Arkansas, and hired Julius for fifteen dollars a week. They would be billed as "Lady Seville and Master Marx."

"She was a lousy singer," Groucho recalled, "but who cared?" He developed a huge crush, as they toured from Hot Springs to Dallas to Houston to San Antonio to Waco.

His first notice in *Variety,* excluding the listing of his name on the bill in other cities on the tour, appeared on February 2, 1906. It was written by an out-of-town correspondent covering the doings at the Majestic Theatre in Fort Worth:

> Week 22, Miles McCarthy & Co., in a "Race Tout's Dream," made a hit, Martha Florrine's lions, tigers and jaguars, were well trained and the act daring, every one being glad when it was over. The Musical Goodmans made a pronounced hit of an only fair act by hard, rapid work. . . . Lily Seville and Julius Marx, singers, were fair.

This wasn't a particularly auspicious write-up of the launching of one of the most venerable show business careers. Julius didn't mind, as long as Lily Seville was around.

Her presence soon proved scarce, however. One look at the trainer who handled Martha Florrine's lions, tigers, and jaguars, and Lily thought there was no one she'd rather be manhandled by. That he was Martha Florrine's husband caused no constraint.

The tour ended in Waco, and after the final performance, Lily kissed Master Marx on the cheek, handed him his ticket to New York, and ran away with the animal trainer.

She'd seen Julius putting his money in his grouch bag. When he opened it on the train he discovered that what he thought was sixty-five dollars in folding money was actually old folded newspaper. At age fifteen, he now had two theatrical credits. Unfortunately, Julius hadn't much to show in the way of money, his earnings having gone to the wholesale financing of elopements.

His next job kept him closer to home.

On April 21, 1906, Gus Edwards advertised his new production of "Postal Telegraph Boys" with Miss Gracie Emmons and "eight boys carefully selected from the Postal Telegraph Co."

Julius was one of the boys. He'd been recruited off the street by director William Lykens and was selected after an open casting call.

Gus Edwards composed over five hundred popular songs, among them "School Days," "In My Merry Oldsmobile," and "Sunbonnet Sue." He'd mounted his first "School Boys and Girls" production the previous year, in 1905. It would be the model for dozens of school acts throughout the next few years.

The number of young talents who started with Edwards and went on to fame was monumental. Among them were George Jessel, Eddie Cantor, George Price, Walter Winchell, Mitzi Mayfair, Ray Bolger, Hildegarde, Mae Murray, Helen Menken, Jack Pearl, Sally Rand, Ricardo Cortez, Mervyn LeRoy, Eleanor Powell, Herman Timberg, and Vivian and Rosetta Duncan.

The performers in the second production, aside from Miss Emmons, weren't billed. Groucho recalled that Bert Wheeler was in the same act, but he didn't remember any others. Jessel and Winchell, for example, worked for Edwards two years later.

Julius was going on sixteen but he looked closer to twelve. He was picked to perform a solo in the show. Later, when the sheet music of "Farewell Killarney" was published, young Julius's picture was on the cover.

The act gave benefit performances at upper Broadway restaurants for a week, raising money for victims of the San Francisco earthquake, before opening at the Alhambra Theatre on April 27.

"After playing around for a short time," the *Variety* review read in part, "this latest act of Gus Edwards is at the Alhambra for its first week in New York. . . . Five selections, all published by Mr. Edwards' company, are sung, but two only are melodious. The girl, Miss Emmons, has a weak voice, and does not add to the sketch, while of the boys, there is only one with a good voice, he having a solo."

Julius, the boy soloist, was disappointed that he hadn't been further identified.

After closing at the Alhambra, the troupe participated in a monster benefit to raise money for the Relief Fund of the San Francisco Sufferers mounted by the Combined Theatre Managers of New York.

The performance started at 11 A.M. on May 4 and ended at midnight. Among those participating on the stage of the Metropolitan Opera House were Paderewski, Enrico Caruso, Fritz Kreisler, and John McCormack.

Julius sang his solo about two in the afternoon. The song he selected, "Somebody's Sweetheart I Want To Be," composed of course by Edwards, had been introduced the previous year by Lillian Russell when she appeared at Proctor's Twenty-third Street Theatre in a concert of songs composed by Edwards.

A total of $33,000 was raised for earthquake victims during the thirteen-hour program.

Julius had just started touring with the Edwards troupe to Albany and New Bedford when an item appeared in the June 9 edition of *Variety:*

Lily Seville, the English singing comedienne, sails to-day for home. Miss Seville returns in September to fulfill twenty weeks now booked over the Keith Circuit.

The lady was getting a lot of mileage out of those sixty-five dollars.

No sooner did Julius's tour with Edwards end than he was hired to go on the road in a melodrama. *The Man of Her Choice* was the usual recital of virtue triumphant, and Julius would be cast as a wise-cracking office boy. His salary would be ten dollars a week, as opposed to the fifteen Lily Seville had paid him, but he was fully determined to hold on to the money this time.

The production toured to Washington, Baltimore, and Wilmington for three weeks. When he retired at night, Groucho would move a bureau to block the door of the hotel room in which he was staying.

On September 8, 1906, the *New York Dramatic Mirror* gave the play a positive review, and singled out "Julius Marx, who made quite a hit in a 'kid' part as Jimmy Armstrong, the office boy. Some incidental vocal solos by Elizabeth A. Chester, Mabel Mordant, and Julius Marx were well received."

Groucho, in recalling his performance, took greatest pride at his line at the first act curtain. "Stop!" he cried at the villain, a revolver in his hand. "Move one step and I'll blow you to smithereens."

"You know," he said, "I still don't know what 'smithereens' means."

The production proceeded throughout the Northeast for the next four months.

On October 22, 1906, augmenting the symbolism of his Bar Mitzvah three years previously, young Julius truly became a man.

Most of the girls he'd liked had been put safely on a pedestal. Throughout his childhood he'd developed crushes on the most unattainable of girls. His most daring experience up to that time came at the age of fourteen. "It was the first time I kissed a girl and she stuck her tongue in my mouth," he recalled. "I couldn't sleep for a week. It was almost like getting laid." But not quite.

The Man of Her Choice had opened that fall night at the Français Theatre in Montreal. Leaving the stage entrance after the performance, Groucho was accosted by a prostitute.

"She took me down in the cellar. There was an iron grating and we crawled there and we got to the cellar."

"What did she look like?" I asked.

"Great legs," Groucho replied.

When the troupe arrived in Ottawa, the next stop on the tour, Julius noticed some suspicious symptoms. He went to a doctor.

"She gave me the clap. The first time I got laid and I got the clap. You know, once you have it, you never get over it. The vestiges of that always remain in some part of your body."

61

He would approach all the future women in his life feeling tainted, unworthy, somehow unclean. Many years later, Groucho got considerable mileage from a line he spoke when resigning from the Friars Club: "I don't care to belong to any social organization that would accept me as a member." Similarly, he had grave doubts about any woman who'd accept him as a husband or a lover.

The deep-seated rage toward his mother, which he refused to admit even to himself, extended into a distrust of all women. Any act of love or kindness was suspect. They all wanted something.

His total conditioning in this attitude was caused by Minnie's treatment of him in the past and, as it would prove to be, in the immediate future.

He was still with the company, touring in Canada and the Midwest, when a series of prominent ads appeared in *Variety:*

A Very Big Hit
Master Julius Marx
With "The Man of Her Choice" Co.

Minnie sent him clippings of the ad, which she had placed in four consecutive weekly issues.

His mother had performed a spontaneously generous gesture toward him. Julius was genuinely moved. She must be proud of him after all.

As for Minnie, two of her sons had already started in show business. She had an idea.

CHAPTER FOUR

NIGHT-IN-GALE, any of various small European thrushes with a russet back and buff to white underparts; it is characterized by the varied, melodious singing of the male, especially at night during the breeding season.

Webster's New World Dictionary

Edward Claudius Wayburn had co-directed the original Gus Edwards production of "School Boys and Girls." In later years, he would be credited with those inspired touches that made stars out of the merely talented. It was he, backstage folklore has it, who induced Eddie Cantor to get out of blackface and become a white-faced song and dance man; he convinced Will Rogers to talk more and twirl his lariat less; he coached a pantomime juggler named W.C. Fields in reading lines on stage. He was also the chief "girl picker" for Ziegfeld.

Ned Wayburn, in other words, was no theatrical tyro.

Minnie had met him when Julius was a member of the Edwards troupe. She renewed the acquaintance, and in an impassioned plea, the likes of which defense attorneys delivered to save murderers from the gallows, convinced Wayburn to sponsor a singing trio. It would center on her talented son Julius, and would include Milton and a girl singer of Wayburn's choosing. She would turn out to be a girl named Mabel O'Donnell.

The Gerry Society had been formed at the turn of the century for the express purpose of keeping children under sixteen off the New York stage. Where there's a will there's a loophole, and what ensued was a rash of performances from orchestra pits and balcony boxes, rendered by beardless youths and breastless girls.

The Wayburn act had a major advantage. Though the principals appeared to be on the verge of adolescence, Julius and Mabel were almost seventeen and sixteen respectively and Milton, though only fifteen, was taller and looked older than the other two. And, if need be, his papers could be doctored.

The group began rehearsing six weeks before the scheduled late September, 1907, opening at Pastor's. They were untested, but on the strength of the Wayburn name, they'd be starting their careers in vaudeville's big time. Fortunately, Milton didn't stammer when he sang and wasn't the inspiration, as Groucho was later to claim, for the composing of "K-K-K-Katy."

The Marx Brothers would later talk about the tribulations of working in small-time vaudeville, reminiscing about the four shows a day on weekdays and the five shows on weekends; the exhausting overnight hops from one town to another whenever they played a split week; the necessity of wearing knee pants and long stockings and talking in falsetto in order to qualify for half fares on the train.

Despite the fact they received last billing, they started at the top, and stayed there for a couple of years. Obviously, they weren't the dismal talents they claimed to be.

Minnie suggested they be named the Nightingales, after the way in which they sang. The dictionary definition seems more apt, for these singing males became ever more melodious during the breeding season, which lasted 365 nights a year.

One aspect of their act presaged their descent to the small time. Wayburn would be their mentor, but damned if he'd finance their start. As a result, the act was designed to perform "in one," after the curtain had dropped for scene changes for more elaborate acts.

Minnie solved the problem of costumes by purchasing white duck suits, which were on sale at Bloomingdale's, for less than ten dollars. She bought straw hats, also on sale, to go with the suits. Mabel wore a party dress. Tacky.

The act opened on September 3 at the Garrick in Wilmington. Wayburn suggested a few changes and assured them they'd do well when they opened September 16 at Pastor's.

Thus prepared, Ned Wayburn's Nightingales presented their thirteen-minute offering to a receptive New York audience.

Variety reviewed the presentation in the September 21 issue:

> Two clean cut, good-looking boys and a little mite of a girl with a voice that seems ten sizes too large for her make up a most pleasing singing trio.
>
> The voices blend well and are handled with judgment usually lacking in children.... The act was a solid hit at Pastor's, and will please anywhere through the usefulness and the good singing of the trio.

Variety, of course, tended to favor the performer. The September 28 review in the waspish *Dramatic Mirror*, while not as effusive, was also positive:

> A small act billed as Ned Wayburn's Nightingales was offered last week at Pastor's. The performers are two boys and a girl, who are evidently pupils of Mr. Wayburn, as they are allowed to use his name. They do a rather neat little turn of songs and dances, and pleased those who like to encourage precocious children.

The Nightingales proceeded on tour. Minnie was delighted to hear of their good reception. She and Frenchy went to Philadelphia for the October 21 opening at Keith's.

Variety's "Philadelphia Chatter" column by George M. Young took note of their appearance:

> "The Nightingales" proved surprisingly good for youngsters, singing each of their numbers well and being rewarded

with liberal applause. A "plant" used in the box does not help the act any.

Both the Marx parents had contagious laughs, but Frenchy's was more booming. Minnie suggested it might not be a bad idea if Frenchy were to make vocal his enjoyment of the show. His laugh was to become familiar and obvious to theater managers, as it already was to the *Variety* correspondent in Philadelphia.

The two Marx brothers, Julius and Milton, traveled up and down the Eastern seaboard with Mabel O'Donnell, doing quite well.

Each member of the act was making twenty-five dollars a week, and sending the bulk of it home. Wayburn, presumably, got a percentage, although it was soon to end.

The establishment of the new order was announced in an ad in *Variety*, which appeared on November 30, 1907:

THE THREE NIGHTINGALES
Big Hit Everywhere
Minnie Marx, Manager

At last, Minnie had found her calling. Or so she thought. The Wayburn name was dropped from the act, amicably one assumes, since Wayburn would in the future work again with all the brothers.

Minnie decided that a quick costume change should be inserted midway through the expanded show, which now had a few choreographed dances. The three would open their act in their original costumes, then take turns going offstage to change into the second outfit.

They were no longer the nervous performers of only three months before when they re-opened the week before Christmas at Pastor's in New York.

The *Variety* review by Dash told the story:

The "Three Nightingales" form the only one of the juvenile acts that shows any change since last seen, and they only in dressing. The boys are wearing frock coats and high hats, while the girl is sporting a new dainty pink costume. . . . The three children have splendid voices that blend beautifully. The act is ... a big hit. The white costumes worn at the opening should be sent to the cleaner.

Now that Minnie was fully in charge, she thought an essential change was necessary. Mabel O'Donnell would have to go. Despite her powerful voice, Mabel tended to sing off-key. More importantly, a girl in the act entailed additional tour expenses. Unlike the boys, she couldn't double up in hotel rooms.

Julius wasn't sorry to see Mabel go. For several weeks now, her feelings for him had been apparent. His latent masochism required that he love more than be loved, and he didn't know how to cope with this turnabout. It was a position in which he would rarely find himself in the future.

A singer named Lou Levy was hired to replace Mabel.

"He was from Brooklyn," Groucho recalled, "and had a wonderful voice. Minnie was lucky to get him. By this time our voices were changing, and we'd tried to put a little comedy in the act because of it."

Minnie began making more elaborate plans for the act. Lou would need a white duck suit, as well as a frock coat. Julius should have another costume for the "butcher boy" number. But more important than outfits were bookings.

An ad appearing in the May 23 issue of *Variety* facilitated her work somewhat. Henderson's Coney Island was advertising for new acts, and interviews were being conducted at the United Booking Office in the St. James Building. Minnie concluded a deal with Jule Delmar of UBO for The Nightingales to appear at Henderson's Coney Island the week of June 1.

"When we reported for our opening date," Groucho recalled, "Mother found the manager had advertised for a quartet. He was going to produce a quartet or nothing."

Adolf was working in a nickelodeon on Thirty-fourth Street. Under Leonard's tutelage, he'd developed a piano-playing repertoire of two numbers: "Waltz Me Around Again, Willie," played two octaves high and fast for comedies; "Love Me and the World Is Mine," with a tremolo in the bass for dramatic scenes and a trill in the right hand for love scenes. He would play either song during

67

chase scenes at double-tempo so that they couldn't be recognized.

"One afternoon, in the middle of the movie," he wrote in *Harpo Speaks!*, "my mother marched down the aisle of the theatre to the piano. She ordered me to leave at once and come with her."

While en route to Brooklyn, she told him what was expected of him. Adolf protested that he'd never sung in public before. "He never should have sung in private either," Groucho told me. "In those days, anyone who really couldn't sing was a bass. All he did was 'boom-boom.' He became our bass."

Thus, Harpo's career began. He appeared wearing Groucho's white ducks. One sight of the audience and he wet his pants. If he was a nervous wreck as well as a terrible singer, Rush, the *Variety* reviewer, didn't notice:

THE NIGHTINGALES
Singing Quartet
20 mins., One
Henderson's

Under this title are brought together a quartet of youngsters who, for individual merit as singers, attain a high degree of excellence. They are nice looking, fresh boys and there is a certain agreeable youthfulness about their singing that places it apart from the conventional music of male quartets.... The boys, however, are wasting a good deal of valuable time in the exploitation of ineffectual comedy and dialogue. The talk is far from funny and makes the turn seem to lag. The greater part of it could be dropped altogether, and the precious moments thus saved devoted to more singing. The singing scored with unwavering certainty, but the talk dropped heavily and made a serious handicap to what might have been an unqualified success. The drag was particularly noticeable at the opening. As a straight singing number "The Nightingales" can be made into a sure winner with very slight eliminations. It has elements of good entertainment.

With hindsight we can laugh at Rush's rush to judgment and deride his lack of perception. Couldn't he discern that this was a comedy team in embryo, needing only nurturing and polishing before it emerged full blown on the world's consciousness? No.

Neither could Minnie. *Variety* was her Bible and Talmud and Koran. The audience's spotty laughter had seemed to support Rush's assessment. The Four Nightingales simply weren't that funny. Minnie told the boys to play it straight from then on.

Adolf was to remain in the act. "Minnie figured if she could get twenty-five dollars for one son," Groucho said, "and she could get fifty dollars for two, then she could get seventy-five dollars for three."

The Four Nightingales had been performing on the United vaudeville circuit in the Northeast for six months when, inexplicably, their bookings dropped off. Neither Minnie's entreaties nor Frenchy's lavish home-cooked meals could entice the bookers to hire the boys.

As the boys grew older—Adolf was now twenty, Julius eighteen, and Milton sixteen—their boyish charm took on that hard edge that comes with life's experiences. They had lost their credibility as innocents on the stage.

They had long since lost their sexual innocence, but Minnie was surprisingly tolerant of her children's promiscuity. Maxine Marx, the oldest and most analytical of her grandchildren, said, "She always encouraged her sons to chase after fast women. She believed that as long as they were satisfied with all the loose women available to them, they would have no reason to get married. And as long as she could keep them from getting trapped into marriage, she could continue to exercise control over them."

Minnie in pursuit of bookings and the brothers in pursuit of fast women both found fulfillment in the South from Florida to Texas.

Groucho recalled some of their misadventures during the late spring and early summer months of 1909 in an article, "Up from Pantages," which he wrote for the *New York Times* in 1928.

Looking back over twenty years, I can remember playing a movie and vaudeville house in the business section of Jacksonville, Florida. It was a long, dark narrow hall, filled with folding yellow chairs, the kind that are used by undertakers to make the mourners more uncomfortable, and by politicians for their pre-election rallies. It wasn't really a theatre, but a gents' furnishings store that had been converted into a theatre simply by removing the counters, shelves, and some of the rubbish, and by installing an electric piano.

There was no stage. There was, however, a long, narrow platform about as wide as the scaffolding used by painters and stone masons, and it was on this precarious ledge that most of the performance was given. If the act involved dancing, acrobatics or anything strenuous there was a brief intermission to enable the performer to jump to the floor for that part of the act.

The dressing room was large and roomy and had perfect ventilation. It was, in fact, a trifle too roomy, as it comprised the whole backyard and was shared alike by a grocer, a butcher and a blacksmith. It was not much for privacy but great for congeniality and comradeship. One had for companions a crate of chickens, three pigs that were about to be slaughtered, some horses waiting to be shod, two girls who later became known as the Dolly Sisters and a covey of the largest rats that ever gnawed at an actor's shoe.

The program consisted of four turns. At least that was the manager's contention, but actually there were only two acts. The manager built up the bill by advertising the mechanical piano as an act, and also a reel of the most flickering films that ever ruined an audience's eyes.

The first performance began at noon and then every hour on the hour until midnight, or longer, if the business warranted it. The manager was a Greek who had been in the theatrical business only a few months—just long enough to master such a childish profession—and he had therefore set himself up as critic, censor, master of ceremonies, stage manager, ticket chopper and, frequently, bouncer.

We had named ourselves the Nightingales, a title that certainly bore no relation to our singing, but it promised much and in those days, bookings were made on promises. The opening performance Monday found us Marxes singing lustily to what we imagined was a spellbound and enraptured throng. We had just arrived at the point in the chorus where we hit the big harmony chord, this chord that was supposed

70

to put the song over with a bang, when we heard a terrific noise which might have come from a wild bull, but which turned out to be the manager running down the aisle, waving arms, head and hands, and shouting, "Stop it! Stop it, I say! It's rotten. Hey, you fellers, you call that singing? That's terrible! The worst I ever heard. My dog can do better than that. Now you go back and do it over again and do it right or you don't get a nickel of my money, not a nickel."

Embarrassed and red-faced, we slunk to the side of the stage, too dazed to utter a word of defence. We were certainly the saddest-looking nightingales that ever chirped a song. While we cowered in the corner, the Florida Belasco announced to an audience which was entirely too sympathetic to suit us that these hams—pointing to us—could sing rotten in Tampa, could sing rotten in Miami and, if they so desired, could sing rotten in St. Petersburg, but when they sang in Jacksonville, the biggest and best town in the State, they would have to sing on key or they didn't get any money. Ordering us back to the stage, he jumped off the ledge and ran up the aisle to hearty applause and vocal encouragement from the local music lovers. Apparently there was no more than the usual amount of discords on our second attempt, as there were no interruptions, except the customary jeers and catcalls which always accompanied our musical efforts.

In Orange, Texas, we lived at a wormy-looking boarding house run by a landlady who looked like a cross between one of the Whoops Sisters and a coach dog. Her rates were five dollars a week—a little high, she conceded, but she set a grand table, easily the best in Texas.

If it was all the same to us, she would prefer her money in advance. We held out for four and a half apiece, and after much general haggling we compromised on four seventy-five, this to include laundry.

For our first meal, which she announced as lunch, we had chili con carne, bread and coffee. This was not an unusual lunch for Texas and we thought nothing of it. The chili was good—everybody makes good chili down there—but the coffee was terrible. It may have been good to the last drop, but I never got that far; the first drop was awful. That evening for dinner we had chili and a depressing-looking vegetable which we finally agreed to call okra, and for all I know may still be known by that name. The following morning for breakfast we had bacon and chili, and for lunch we each had a big bowl of steaming chili.

What the baby of song and story is to its mother, what the saxophone is to a jazz band, what Gilbert was to Sullivan—those were all nothing to what chili was to this landlady. It was her piece de resistance, her monument to Mexico with a low bow to all of Central America. By Thursday, despite the fact that we still had a healthy equity in the $4.75 we had paid in advance, we had retreated to the general store in the village and there rounded out the week on canned goods, dried fruits, brick cheese and Coca-Cola.

Later on that season we played an open-air theatre in Gulfport, Miss. It was just a short way as the wind blows from the swamps of Louisiana, and was set in a clearing in the woods. It had the appearance of an early frontier fort and we later discovered it was just about as safe. The wind had been blowing steadily from the marshes all day and by show time that night the air was black with blood-hungry mosquitoes which, if they had been labeled like asparagus, would have been known as the giant variety extra size. The dressing room had sides and a floor, but a thrifty management, knowing the actor's love for the great outdoors, had decided that a roof would be superfluous, and had therefore taken that lumber and with it built a few extra benches for the customers. This was fine for the manager and the customers but hard on the performers. The make-up lamp on the shelf acted like a village church bell calling the faithful to the meeting house, and these faithful fell on us, hook, line and stinger. Like thousands of miniature monoplanes they swooped down while we, armed with towels, socks, rolled up newspapers and fans, tried vainly to repel them. It was like trying to stop a cyclone.

Stung beyond endurance, our screams of anguish finally brought the manager on the run, and we told him, between slaps, fans and curses, that, wedded as we were to our art, we would have to abandon it for the time being unless something drastic was done in the way of relief. The manager promised us that he would return in a few moments with a remedy that he had used for years, a remedy that had never failed. Then, leaving us, he rushed out to mollify an audience that was threatening to tear down what theatre there was, unless the promised and advertised entertainment was forthcoming.

In a few moments he was back with a half dozen smudge pots filled with pitch and pipe, and which when lit quickly drove out the man-eating insects. We got dressed and went out on the stage, puffed and swollen, but still the Nightingales and still singing off-key.

While singing our opening number, we smelled smoke, and were happy because of it, figuring the more smoke, the less mosquitoes. But by the time we came to our third song we noticed a certain warmth in the rear that we realized could not be entirely due to the Southern climate, and when we came to our last song, we saw the audience rushing out of a theatre that was entirely in flames. We rushed after them, happy that we had lost the mosquitoes. But we also had lost our wardrobe and our trunks, and we later discovered we had lost the manager with what salary was coming to us.

Groucho would recall another occasion when the audience vacated an open-air theater for a different reason. It happened in Nacogdoches, Texas. A runaway mule proved more entertaining to the townspeople, who left The Four Nightingales standing on the makeshift stage in mid-performance.

The performers waited for the audience to return. Once most of them were back in their seats, Julius said, "Nacogdoches is full of roaches." The audience laughed at the rhyme and from that point on The Nightingales gave expression to all the high spirits they'd been publicly repressing. Yes, they could be funny, they informed Minnie upon their return to New York, and from now on they would be. Minnie paid them scant notice. A more pressing matter was at hand.

The writing was on the cracked plaster wall of the apartment on

Ninety-third Street. The Nightingales had outworn their welcome in the East. Minnie broached the idea of working out of Chicago, more central to the vaudeville circuits servicing the Midwest and South.

The Marxes—Frenchy, Minnie, Adolf, Julius, Milton, Herbert, and Opie—settled at 4649 Calumet Avenue, in the Fuller Park section of Chicago. But it soon became obvious that the house couldn't accommodate all the Schoenbergs who'd made known their intentions of coming out to join them.

By juggling books, signing promissory notes, and borrowing from her brother Al, Minnie was able to put down one thousand dollars of the $21,000 asking price on a three-story brownstone house at 4512 Grand Boulevard. Minnie also made a smaller acquisition in the form of a pool table, quite possibly sensing the imminent return of her prodigal son.

The World's Fair of 1893 had signaled the start of Chicago's development as a major city. Carl Sandburg in 1916 would describe the city as "stormy, husky, brawling," and these qualities were evident even in Chicago's cultural institutions.

The year the Marxes moved there, one-fifth of all motion pictures in the world were being made in Chicago. Essanay Studios on the North Side was the nucleus of the film colony, and would soon introduce to the screen such stars as Wallace Beery, Gloria Swanson, Lewis Stone, Colleen Moore, and Tom Mix. Carl Laemmle had just opened the Chicago Theatre, and he would later found Universal Pictures in California. Hungarian-born Adolph Zukor, who'd been in the fur business in Chicago, was now thriving in New York making the short subjects for a company that would be the forerunner of Paramount Pictures.

Opie made the easiest adjustment. Each morning, in what was to become a ritual, he would call down from the top of the stairway, *"Meine Kinder, ich habe Hunger."* After a simple breakfast of cold potatoes and pumpernickel, he would settle on the porch and count the passing cars.

Julius was more restless. He soon gravitated to Washington Street which numbered among its shops the Covici-McGee bookstore. Within its walls in the next few years, he would meet Ben Hecht, Maxwell Bodenheim, Ashton Stevens, Sandburg, Sherwood Anderson, Edgar Lee Masters, Clarence Darrow, and Theodore Dreiser.

Twenty-year-old Julius, exposed to writers en masse, discovered he was able to verbalize and share concepts and philosophies with them that he couldn't with the denizens of the dressing rooms. He had found his intellectual home.

"I think writers are the most important part of show business," Groucho once told me. He'd already stressed that writers were the most important people in the larger world too.

"Is that why writers are your closest friends?" I asked.

"Partly," he replied. "My whole life is my friends. Friendship is more important than marriage. You know, most important friendships are between men. Women are more concerned about what dress they're wearing and how their hair is styled."

"What does it take to be a good friend?" I asked.

"Tolerance . . . the ability to overlook things people may say."

This was one of the rare instances during our association when Groucho didn't attempt to conceal his sentiments behind a facade of humor. He truly believed what he said and the subject was too profound to joke about. Yet within this belief lay the crucial distinction which was to color his relationships with women. They were frivolous objects designed to appease physical hungers at home or to wear on your arm in public.

Actually, Groucho hadn't had much of a chance to develop his own thinking about women. His attitudes had been shaped by the casual morality of his grandfather, his father, and his Uncle Al.

Shean came visiting soon after the Marxes moved to Chicago. Away from his wife, Johanna, he was every bit the swordsman with the ladies that his father and brother-in-law had been. Never one to hide his light under a bushel—performers aren't paid to be modest—he nevertheless had managed his affairs with more discretion. Now that his nephews were of age, he would talk more openly about his chance encounters.

Ironically, the most important meeting during his visit to Chicago turned out to be with a male. Ed Gallagher was also an entertainer, and the two men decided to team up. Though their first ventures

75

were in musical comedy, they were to become the most famous team in vaudeville.

What prompted Minnie to suggest the move to Chicago was its importance as a vaudeville center. Three major circuits—the Orpheum, Sullivan and Considine, and Pantages—all booked their talent in Chicago. The lesser Gus Sun circuit also booked most of its attractions there.

A good act could work in Chicago for a solid year without having to tour. But as far as the Windy City was concerned, the Marx tribe would have to prove itself all over again.

Minnie decided to put together a singing-dancing troupe to be called the Six Mascots. Two girl singers were hired, along with basso Freddie Hutchins, to join Adolf, Julius, and Milton. The girls dropped out soon after, and through necessity, Minnie and Aunt Hannah joined the act, women in their fifties pretending to be schoolgirls. The act, fortunately, was booked in Chicago area theaters for four consecutive months. It didn't travel well, however. None of its members wanted to be too far away from home when it inevitably folded.

The Six Mascots ended in a ludicrous way. During the course of one performance, Minnie and Aunt Hannah sat on the same chair simultaneously. The chair collapsed. Sometimes audience laughter isn't appreciated, even by a fledgling comedy team.

Leonard, during his semi-estrangement from the family, had worked as a wrestler, prizefighter, pool hustler, whorehouse pianist. In 1907, at age twenty, he became a song-plugger with Shapiro, Bernstein & Co. in Pittsburgh. Within a year he was the manager of the operation. (Julius, while touring with the *Man of Her Choice* company, had also plugged songs. "I was paid five dollars a week whenever I was in Philadelphia, at the Jerome H. Remick Company. I stood in a box and sang songs to Jeanette Dupree.")

Leonard often accompanied his assistant, Arthur Gordon, who was a much better singer than his boss. The two decided to form an act.

In the meantime, the three other brothers in show business, having seen the success of the musical tabloid, particularly if it

76

were a school act in the Gus Edwards stripe, mounted "Fun in Hi Skule."

Minnie usually toured with the boys, leaving Frenchy at home to supervise Herbert's education and look after Opie, who was showing signs of forgetfulness. He was relegated to the sole show business responsibility of booking hotel and boarding house accommodations for the act, Frenchy long having shown a lack of understanding about the world of entertainment. His sons later told of asking him to catch the act in a huge Chicago theater, to see if their routines were audible enough. He went backstage after the performance and said he'd heard every word.

"That's great, Pop," Chico said. "Where were you standing?"

"Standing?" Frenchy asked. "Who was standing? I was sitting in the front row."

Minnie returned home so that Frenchy could go on the road as a salesman. Back in Chicago, her mind stayed on the road with the act. Julius had adeptly taught himself to play the guitar and Leonard could play the piano. It was time for Adolf to learn to play an instrument too. She shipped him a used harp.

When Leonard and his partner returned to Chicago, Minnie took over. First, she decided the singer of the duo should have an Italian name. Gordon became Gordoni. Then she suggested they should be represented by Minnie Palmer, the eminent lady producer. Her real surname was Marx.

Minnie had shrewdly changed her name, borrowing some of the majesty of the Palmer House, "the palace of the world," which had been a Chicago institution since 1873. There was also a real Minnie Palmer, a petite, blonde vaudeville performer who'd developed an Eastern following. Borrowing her name gave added prestige, since it was vaguely familiar to people Minnie would be dealing with. She proved to be formidable in appearance, more so than the real article, if not necessarily as effective. Minnie would arrive for meetings heavily corseted and wearing a blonde wig. If she and Frenchy were invited on to a friend's home for dinner, Minnie would take off the corset as soon as they were safely amid the civilians, wrapping it in newspapers with the strings hanging out.

She booked Marx and Gordoni at the Willard Theatre in Chicago for the week ending July 22, 1911. Leonard's reunion with his younger brothers, after a separation of nearly five years, would have to wait. They'd be on the road for over a year, while Leonard worked with three different men, first Gordoni, then his cousin Lou Shean, and finally George Lee.

The boys were in Seattle, preparing for their opening August 7 at the Pantages Theatre. The school act had a very vocal Adolf spouting many multi-syllable words, in his role of a red-wigged Patsy Brannigan, a stock character of the period, to the German professor played by Julius.

Adolf wore a funny hat that looked like an inverted bucket. "Take dot ding off," the professor would instruct him. Adolf would tip the hat forward from the rear, and flop it back on his head when the teacher turned away. The act concluded with a doggerel song designed to have the audiences yelling for more.

It was "Peasie Weasie," a song with ten comic verses, one of which was:

A humpback went to see a football game,
The game was called on account of the rain.
The humpback asked the halfback for his quarter back,
And the fullback kicked the hump off the humpback's back.

The performers would leave the stage for a moment, then Julius would stick out his head from the side of the curtain. "More?" Audiences knew that these comedy songs had many choruses and they would applaud until they'd heard them all.

The troupe also used to sing parodies of well-known airs. Julius had an affinity for shirts, judging from a couple of the lyrics. "There was I waiting at the church" became "There was I waiting in my shirt." The *Habañera* from *Carmen* had new English lyrics: "I want my shirt, I want my shirt, I won't be happy without my shirt . . ."

No less a personage than W. C. Fields, then performing a comedy juggling act, could attest to the extraordinary reception the school act received. "They sang, danced, played the harp and kidded in zany style, were vaudeville headliners," he wrote in *W.C. Fields by Himself.* "Never saw so much nepotism or such hilarious laughter in one act in my life. The only act I could never follow. In Columbus I told the manager I broke my wrist and quit."

Each of the brothers was making thirty-five dollars a week, with the rest of the cast of twenty splitting up the balance of the nine hundred-dollar weekly gross. Minnie, apparently on a winning streak, was mounting a vaudeville revue throughout the East with the assistance of her brother Henry as she also prepared to open a musical tabloid to tour in the West. The troupe of eighteen opened in late October of 1912 in "Golden Gate Girls," an act written by Al Shean.

Minnie met the boys in Waukegan, where they were performing the school act. In the orchestra pit was a young violinist, Ben K. Benny. Because the stage name Benny Kubelsky had adopted was similar to Ben Bernie's, he would soon be changing it to Jack Benny.

The curtain went up for the evening's performance with Julius sitting at the desk and Adolf entering the schoolroom wearing his hat, most notable for two spikes sticking in front. Impaled on one was an orange; on the other was an apple. As Adolf approached the desk he noticed that Julius was staring into the orchestra pit with a stunned look on his face. Adolf turned around to discover Leonard sitting at the piano, silently running his hands over the keyboard. Adolf snatched the fruit off his hat and threw it at his wayward brother. Leonard threw it at Julius, who in turn threw it at Milton. The stage by this time was splattered with apple sauce and orange juice. The curtain was rung down before the end of the performance. Leonard had, in his own fashion, come home to stay.

Leonard returned to the family act with an Italian accent which he'd perfected on the road, and patterned after his favorite barber. He also demonstrated a shrewder business head than his mother, and was openly critical of several of her practices. It was inappropriate, he argued, to use the Marx house in Chicago as a booking office for the act, with Frenchy cooking his way into the bookers' hearts. Nor should their father bribe bookers with a nice piece of woolen goods. The kickback was a way of life for less than sterling talents, but the act was better than that. Minnie was too quick to take the first offer.

She had placed an ad in the September 30, 1911, issue of *Variety:*

Three Marx Brothers and Co.
Presenting that classy school act different from all others
Now completing a successful tour of the PANTAGES CIRCUIT
Although offered an immediate return over the time,
unfortunately Eastern bookings made it impossible to accept.
                    Direction, Miss Minnie Palmer

"Don't you see anything wrong with that ad?" he asked Minnie. She didn't.

"Well, if the act is so successful and has all these Eastern bookings, and couldn't accept a return on the Pantages, why are you advertising for more bookings?"

Minnie had no reply. Her favorite son was back with the family, and if he wanted to assert himself in this way, she would tolerate the impertinence.

Leonard also had more personal suggestions to offer his brothers. "Chico was a character," Groucho said. "By the time any show opened he'd fucked half the chorus. Women were crazy about him. He'd walk up to a girl and say, 'Do you fuck?' And many times they said yes."

Chico's daughter Maxine concedes her father had a great self image. "He knew he was irresistible. But the thing about Chico and men like him is they only pick on women they're sure of. They have an instinct. They know the women who are going to respond to them."

"He had that look of shy innocence," his first wife, Betty, recalled. "With women he was very sweet. That's why he could go from one to another . . . and then he wouldn't know them the next week."

In the casual backstage morality of the time, Adolf, Julius, and Milton would have had to be two-headed grotesqueries not to experience active sex lives. Their activities accelerated after Leonard rejoined them. He had them popping in and out of hotel rooms as if they were actors in a French farce.

"These men were such libertines, and totally amoral," Maxine

80

said. "All of them would do and say anything. But if a woman said a four-letter word, they'd get *so* upset."

Leonard would pass on these girls to his younger brothers as if they were clothes he'd outgrown. One of the girls in the act, after dallying with all four, announced she was pregnant.

"Who was responsible?" I asked Groucho.

"*We* were," he replied. They shared the blame along with the abortionist's bill. Their behavior was in sharp contrast to that of one of the characters in a story Groucho often told: "O'Flaherty and Ryan had an office together. They were both fucking the same secretary. She got pregnant. Ryan said to O'Flaherty, 'Go to the hospital. See how she is and what the bill is.' O'Flaherty came back to the office and said, 'She had twins. Mine died.'"

Julius was as sexually active in the hotels he was now stopping at as in the dressing rooms. "The whole first part of my life was spent sleeping with colored girls," he told a *Playboy* interviewer. "In those days, all hotels had black chambermaids. You'd give her a couple of bucks and take her in your room and lay her."

The brothers would also frequent hook shops. "We were a big hit there. We were entertainment. Harpo and Chico played the piano and I sang. The girls used to come to watch us at the theater, and if they liked us, they'd send a note backstage inviting us over after the show."

Love was an alien word in young Julius's vocabulary. He hadn't had an emotional alliance up to now. Those women he'd hungered for were beyond his reach, as if he'd picked them knowing they were unattainable. His sexual experiences were fast and furtive and selfish. Julius wasn't sure a true lady would enjoy sex, a concept favored by the great majority of American men of the time.

"Sex is the world's greatest invention," Groucho once told me, smirking slightly at the analogy. To me, it was a revealing choice of words. If sex were a machine, then it was all right to be handled in Groucho's mechanical fashion, and the more often, the better. Yet, despite this highly charged activity—or because of it—there were dark undercurrents Julius could neither ignore nor explain. There had to be more to life than this. "There were a lot of times I wanted to jump out the window," Groucho said. "I didn't like staying in hotel rooms on upper floors because I was afraid I'd get this sudden urge to jump out the window." He continued pushing bureaus against doors, a futile exercise against the demons that bore down on him, not from the outside, but from within.

It was a hard and unrelenting life, physically punishing and devoid of security. Performers who weren't well established never knew if their new acts would be accepted. The gossip traveled along the circuit much faster than the subjects of such talk. Acts coming into a new town could be closed before they opened, and no recourse was available to them.

The brothers tried a new musical tabloid in the late winter of 1913, "Duke of Bull Durham." It played in Great Lakes cities for six weeks, then folded. Much time and money had been lost. The brothers returned to performing the better accepted "Mr. Green's Reception." Even so, it took Minnie an additional six weeks to get new bookings.

Glamor had nothing to do with their hellish, exhausting nomadic existence.

Consider, for example, how complicated it was for an act to close one night in Terre Haute, Indiana, and open the following day in Evansville, only one hundred miles away. By direct trains, with stops at every hamlet along the way, the trip should have taken three hours at most. Instead, eight hours would often elapse before the performers reached their destination. After finishing their last show in Terre Haute, they would board the midnight train south. After riding for an hour, it would be necessary to get off at a small town along the route and wait four hours before a second train would pick them up for the remaining two-hour trip to Evansville. At the deserted station midway—who but a fool would be there in the middle of the night?—performers' trunks were dumped off, and the troupers would have to transport them on a truck to the baggage car of the next train, and assist the baggageman in loading their gear. There was no other way to be sure the wardrobes and props wouldn't be left behind.

According to show business legend, monologist Art Fisher coined the nicknames by which the Marx Brothers would forever be known during a poker game backstage in Galesburg, Illinois. A popular comic strip of the time was "Sherlocko the Monk," and vaudeville as a result was infected with Henpeckos, Tightwados, and Nervos. As Fisher was dealing, he said, "This one's for you, Harpo," to Arthur, whom he knew to play the harp. (Adolf had anticipated the anti-German sentiment of the coming world war and changed his name to Arthur a couple of years previously.)

"This one's for you, Gummo," Fisher continued. Milton always wore gumshoes, or rubbers, to help ward off colds. (At the age of seventeen, it was discovered he'd never had a rheumatic heart. The ailment was then diagnosed as a slight heart murmur which didn't require extreme physical restrictions. Gummo, however, continued coddling himself for the rest of his days, as his son Robert put it, taking pills for diseases that hadn't yet been invented.)

Leonard became Chicko. "Chickens" were girls, and if that poker game had taken place five years later when "chickens" were being called "flappers," Chico would have been known as Flappo. (The K was dropped because of a typesetter's error. Chico liked the look of it and kept the new spelling.)

Groucho was the serious one, Fisher felt, and apparently not a model of good cheer. His everyday attitude was a somber one, and no wonder that he was invariably thought to be the oldest of all the brothers.

I once asked Groucho about his name. "I hate it," he said. "It's terrible. It sounds like I'm the kind of guy who goes around whipping little children."

If differences with other acts caused friction, imagine how difficult it must have been for partners in the same act, working together year after year. Sometimes they'd accuse each other of walking through performances or stepping on laugh lines. The brothers were curiously free of such dissension. True, every six months or so, Chico and Harpo would lock themselves up in a room with Groucho and threaten to quit the act if he didn't stop his displays of temperament and petulance. But they were developing a camaraderie they'd scarcely had as children. Their money was going into the same pot—collected by Minnie, who in turn doled out allowances—and common sense dictated that they adopt an all for one and one for all approach to their craft.

This wasn't the case of Gallagher and Shean. In true "Sunshine Boys" fashion, they stopped speaking—later they wouldn't remember why—and went their separate ways.

The split was to bolster the brothers' career. Uncle Al agreed to write an act for them, to be called "Home Again," which evolved from "Mr. Green's Reception." The opening scene on the docks had Groucho saying, "Next time I cross the ocean, I'll take the train."

After finishing the sketch Uncle Al presented it to his nephews. A dismayed Harpo found he had only three lines. "He wasn't the greatest talker," Groucho said. "Al did him a favor. He told Harpo he shouldn't even have those three lines, and he should do everything in pantomime. That's how it all started."

Unfortunately, Uncle Al hadn't done the same for Gummo. He was to play Groucho's son, a cane-carrying dandy who wore white gloves. Gummo had grown into a strapping, good-looking man who easily attracted girls—until he opened his mouth. His stammer was incurable, and it seemed to become more pronounced any time he stepped on a stage. "Whenever he was nervous, he would stammer," his son Bob said. "He was most nervous on the stage because he hated performing. Out of self-defense, this uneducated man had developed a fantastic vocabulary. He'd read the dictionary like it had a plot. He knew not less than a dozen synonyms for every word that might make him stammer."

The act had a trial run at the Hippodrome in Chicago, before opening September 28, 1914, at the Majestic Theatre in Dallas. From there it would work its way east.

Through years of performing and experimentation, the brothers had developed gestures, attitudes, inflections, and postures which made people laugh. They'd come to know what evoked the laughter, though they'd never understand why.

Reed of *Variety,* in his out of town review of September 26, gave notice that "Home Again" was a winner:

> This merry little musical short gives the Four Marx Brothers opportunity to do some very effective work in their several lines. They all have talent, and they shine in this piece which allows them to display their own brand of rollicking humor in

which they excel. ... The story concerns Henry Schneider (Julius Marx) who is returning with his family and friends from a voyage across the ocean. ... Milton Marx is seen as Harold Schneider whose chief work is to look handsome, which he does without question. Leonard Marx is seen as an Italian character, and his specialty at the piano, in which he does comic things with his hands and fingers, is one of the best features. He gets a laugh about every minute, is at ease and graceful, and makes good all the time. Arthur Marx is billed as a "nondescript." He is made up as a "boob" and his makeup is not pleasant. He gets a good many laughs but a change should be made in his character. He plays the harp well, and does some comedy with the strings that is in a class by itself. ...

When the trade paper erred in its assessment, it did so in the performer's favor, sometimes describing him as being better than he actually was. But *Variety's* coverage was traditionally positive and constructive, and the brothers, like hundreds of acts before them, took heed of the comments.

The act was playing at the Majestic in San Antonio when the *Variety* of the previous week reached them. Minnie had done it again:

If this act doesn't increase the average weekly receipts for the season so far, at least the amount of its salary while in your house, you don't have to pay it any salary. Four Marx Brothers and Co. (17 people) in *Home Again*, 38 minutes of laughs. Includes References.

Leonard shot off a letter to his mother: "Since when has any theater manager been honest with actors? Do you want us to work for nothing?"

"We're too good for that," Leonard told his brothers of such practices.

After five months on tour, the "Home Again" company was set to open at the Palace Theatre in New York on February 22, 1915. Martin Beck, who controlled the eighteen Orpheum theaters

85

throughout the West, had opened the Palace on March 24, 1913, planning it as the first link of an Eastern chain which would challenge the pre-eminent Keith circuit.

Beck had invested over one million dollars in the theater. Stickily romantic paintings of the period hung in the lobby along the great marble stairs leading to the auditorium. The 1,800 seats were upholstered in flowered cretonne. Despite the somewhat garish decor, Beck had succeeded in immediately establishing the biggest of the big-time theaters at Broadway and Forty-seventh Street. It supplanted Hammerstein's at Broadway and Forty-second as the zenith of vaudeville.

The Palace could become a springboard to fame. At the very least it offered performers the assurance of more human treatment on the lesser circuits after a successful Palace run. Success wasn't automatic. Performers were severely tested by an often unruly audience, the most critical in vaudeville. The admission price was steep—fifty cents for an average matinee or one dollar for evening performances. Thus the pressure audiences placed on the entertainers was so nerve-racking that some faint hearts refused to accept Palace bookings. Neither the Four Cohans nor Al Jolson ever played the Palace. Some acts, if not ready, would ask for postponements until they felt they were in top form.

The Four Marx Brothers in "Home Again" shared equal billing on the second spot with the Edward Abeles Co., which was staging a comedy playlet, *The Memorandum Box*. The headliner was Madame Emma Calvé, built up by the management as "the most important musical booking in the history of the Palace," and the world's foremost prima donna.

After rollicking with two comedy troupes at the opening Monday matinee, the assemblage wasn't of a mood to appreciate Madame Calvé, no matter how indelible her art. There were no *Night at the Opera* shenanigans by the Marxes interfering with the diva. The brothers knew this would be suicidal. The Madame incurred the gallery's displeasure on her own. She didn't return for the evening's performance.

As for "Home Again," Sime's *Variety* review of February 27 set the seal on the audience's verdict:

With the disappointment and additions, the Palace program didn't commence to look like a Palace bill until the second part, when the Four Marx Brothers in "Home Again" started it on the move, with May Irwin carrying it along. . . . The act proved its value by holding up this spot for 39 minutes in the biggest vaudeville theatre in America. The company, talk, music, comedy, and setting made themselves liked, along with the individual members of the Marx family, especially Arthur Marx, in his silly boy character, who attracted much notice to himself and ways of making fun. . . .

CHAPTER FIVE

Don't say "slob" or "son of a gun" or "hully gee" on this stage unless you want to be cancelled peremptorily. Do not address any one in the audience in any manner. If you have not the ability to entertain Mr. Keith's audiences without risk of offending them, do the best you can. Lack of talent will be less open to censure than would be an insult to a patron. If you are in doubt as to the character of your act, consult the local manager before you go on the stage, for if you are guilty of uttering anything sacrilegious or even suggestive you will be immediately closed and will never again be allowed in a theater where Mr. Keith is in authority.

Sign posted backstage at four hundred Keith's Theaters

The Marx Brothers had arrived. Their credentials as journeymen vaudevillians were finally established with the successful engagement at the Palace. They could now continue with the same arduous grind as before, with no letup in sight. The only visible change in their standing was a slight rise in the performers' pecking order. Theater managers, when giving them instructions, often added at the end of a sentence, "Please." They were now headliners in smaller theaters, usually those with split-week bookings, and were being more prominently billed behind the top acts at the most important theaters in the country. The family couldn't as yet be considered affluent, but it was comfortable. With the troupe grossing $1,500, each of the brothers was making nearly $150 a week.

"We were just young men trying to make a living," Groucho said. Their life had fallen into a routine, as he put it, of "two-a-day, smoke cigars, play cards, pick up girls."

They weren't aware of the marked changes throughout the world of entertainment that were in the offing. Of most immediate importance was the subtle way vaudeville was degenerating into a more respectable form of burlesque. William Morris, then the head vaudeville booker along with the Keith-Orpheum circuit, predicted the oncoming doom of vaudeville, noting that it was beginning to trade on notoriety instead of talent.

The freak act was one manifestation of the decline of vaudeville. Willie Hammerstein was responsible for its introduction, having raised the bail for two girls, Lillian Graham and Ethel Conrad, accused of shooting W. E. D. Stokes, of the Social Register, in the leg. Trading on the purple headlines, he billed the women at the Victoria as "The Shooting Stars."

E. F. Albee, head of the Keith circuit, had returned from a Western tour to discover that Mrs. Florence Carman, who'd been acquitted in a sensational murder case, was appearing at the Prospect Theatre in Brooklyn. The United Booking Office soon issued an Order:

To representatives of acts: We understand that some of you have been offering persons as vaudeville acts who have recently gained notoriety through criminal court trials. Such acts have nothing to commend them but their notoriety, and in order that you may know of our disposition regarding acts of this character, we hereby notify you that we do not desire them, would not play them under any circumstances, and consider it an insult for you to offer them to our company.

90

Please, therefore, do not even suggest acts of this character to this office in the future.

The legitimate theater during the 1914-1915 season was in the midst of a depression, and the thirty-six Broadway houses were having great trouble filling their 54,000 seats. They were competing with a dozen vaudeville houses, fifty vaude-film houses and a great number of straight picture theaters. Business on Broadway wouldn't pick up until the fall, as the impact of European orders for war goods was felt in America.

On March 3, 1915, the Liberty Theatre in New York booked a motion picture created by D. W. Griffith called *The Birth of a Nation.* All the nickelodeons that had been springing up in store-front buildings over the last ten years and all the shorts that ended the vaudeville programs during the same time may be regarded as precursors to the new dramatic art form.

An English entertainer the brothers had met in Canada in 1913 had committed his future to the medium, and on the strength of one picture, *Tillie's Punctured Romance,* was already a major star. His name was Charlie Chaplin.

"We were in Winnipeg one day," Groucho said. "We had a three-hour wait before taking the train to California. I passed a theater which was on the Sullivan-Considine circuit and heard a tremendous roar of laughter. I paid my ten cents and walked in. A little man was on the stage. He was doing a pantomime act, the greatest I'd ever seen. I went backstage and introduced myself to the guy. Chaplin wasn't any too clean. He'd worn the same shirt for six weeks because he was only getting twenty-five dollars a week." (Groucho was extremely fastidious. Such careless grooming would be the telling detail he would notice. He once spotted William Faversham in a hotel lobby. The English actor was the matinee idol of the day, the leading star of the Charles Frohman Company for six years. "I lost all respect for him when I saw him."

If the brothers weren't aware of the changes in vaudeville that would be affecting their future, Fred Allen, at least in retrospect, was. In *Much Ado About Me,* he described what was happening:

91

The motion picture companies were erecting theaters in every city. Millions of dollars were being spent to advertise motion pictures and the stars were being developed in the new medium. Hollywood was soon to consign big-time vaudeville to the horse and buggy era. Big-time vaudeville theaters in most cities were antiquated buildings run by local managers who never tinkered with tradition.

The Marxes were at a critical juncture in their career, as were all vaudevillians. Fortuitously, Chico asserted himself. Endowed as he was with native shrewdness, he had already anticipated the need to mount new acts. He also sensed that the act required new leadership. He persuaded Minnie to settle down at home in Chicago, emphasizing the necessity of her full-time presence there to supervise and discipline her youngest son, who was turning into a miniature Chico.

Left unspoken was his low opinion of her managerial competence. Vaudeville was getting more competitive, and though the brothers were doing well, bookings didn't come as readily as before. Minnie's sheer love of the entertainment world no longer qualified her to operate in this cannibalistic field. Chico took over. His negotiations came to be conducted as if he were involved in a huge poker game; fortunately, the bluffs he used in business dealings met with better results than those he employed at the card table. He also became his brothers' morale booster. Gummo was a lost cause, but there was still hope for Harpo and Groucho. "Chico kept telling us we were good," Groucho said. "Harpo and I were always scared. We didn't think we could make it."

With his wife again at home, Frenchy went on the road selling cardboard boxes to grocery stores. Minnie often set up his itinerary so that it coincided with that of their sons. Gummo, who was seriously contemplating leaving the act, would work with his father during the morning. He proved so effective that he began to think a job in sales would be a viable alternative to the dreaded stage.

In later years, the brothers got great comic mileage out of Frenchy's seeming disorientation while on the road. He would call his wife from another town and ask, "Minnie, where am I?" He had been astute enough in the past to negotiate favorable boarding house rates, as well as to book complicated connections on the train routes the brothers traveled. He had grown strangely stupid in a very short time.

"Frenchy was not a bright man," Chico's first wife, Betty, said. "But he was a simple, nice man. When he asked, 'Where am I?' he meant, 'Where am I going next?' The boys didn't explain that. It wouldn't have been as funny. The other way, it's funny . . . stupid but funny. I had a bad habit of correcting them. I didn't know any better. I'd say, 'It wasn't like that.' You don't do that to a comedian."

Not all of Groucho's stories denigrated his father. Once, the act returned to Chicago for an engagement at the Majestic in December of 1915. The booking could mean their return to the big time and the Marxes were understandably nervous about this homecoming. Because Frenchy's prop laugh had long since become familiar to Chicago theater managers, he would on occasion hire a claque to roar approval, paying for their tickets plus a dime for their trouble. Minnie instructed him to round up fifty boosters for the opening.

The fifty boosters Frenchy brought laughed and applauded wildly. In Groucho's opinion, their enthusiasm, simulated though it was, helped keep the act on in the big time.

Although Groucho had led his brothers into show business, Chico and Harpo were getting the lion's share of the critical notices. Groucho was hampered by the fact that he sang in one key and the German accent he had appropriated from Omie and Minnie was dangerously close to becoming passé. The German-Dutch comic, a mainstay of vaudeville since the 1880s, ridiculed an older generation of immigrants. There weren't enough of these dialects left in everyday American life to warrant all that mimicry on the stage. The accent in itself was no longer funny.

The brothers were in their next-to-final day of a one-week run at Shea's Toronto, when, on May 7, 1915, a German submarine sank the *Lusitania* off the Irish coast, with the loss of 1,198 lives, 139 of them American. A wave of anti-German feeling swept North America.

Groucho had used his German dialect at the afternoon show, but changed it to a Yiddish one that evening. It was the first step toward dropping the German dialect altogether. (Chico kept his Italian accent since it lent itself more easily to comic misinterpretation and outrageous puns.) Groucho discovered that audiences laughed longer than usual. The Marx Brothers' distinctive brand of lunatic comedy was about to be born, and cataclysm was acting as its midwife.

The dark clouds of war had been moving inexorably across the Atlantic Ocean, threatening to unleash a storm over the United States as they already had over Europe. Minnie was torn by the First World War, not knowing where her allegiances should lay. She couldn't envision her sons fighting against the Fatherland. The Conscription Act had just been proposed in 1916, and would be passed the following year. Minnie saw a solution. Under the act, the President was authorized to exempt from the draft persons engaged in vital industries, including agriculture. She instructed the brothers to purchase a twenty-seven-acre tract of farmland on U. S. 66 at Route 45 in what is now La Grange, Illinois, twenty miles outside of Chicago.

With the purchase of the farm, half of the family moved to La Grange, including the gentleman farmers who would be doing their bit for the upcoming war effort.

"The first morning on the farm," Groucho said, "we got up at five. The following morning, we dawdled in bed until six. By the end of the week we were getting up at noon, which was just enough time for us to get dressed to catch the 1:07 to Wrigley Field, where the Chicago Cubs played."

Their intentions were nevertheless honorable, and they played the role of farmers as well as they could. One day, fifteen-year-old Herbie was sitting by a haystack, a piece of straw in his mouth, when Chico walked by. "Howdy, Zeke," he said. "Howdy, Zeb," Chico replied. Zeb became Zeppo when he joined the brothers in the act.

Their only income from the farm was the quarters they received for shagging balls from the adjoining golf course. After hearing that a butter-and-egg man was coming to the farm on a buying trip, the family took quick measures. The eggs laid by their own chickens

94

had been eaten by rats, so they went to a nearby grocery store and bought several dozen which they placed in baskets. The buyer looked at the chickens, and then at the eggs. "It's amazing," he said. "This is the first time I've ever seen Rhode Island Reds lay white eggs."

"Oh?" asked Zeppo.

"Yes. They're usually brown."

The brothers, after the summer layoff, returned to the vaudeville tour in September. By now, each of the brothers had established his priorities. Groucho's were reading and girls; Chico's were gambling and girls; Gummo's were pill-taking and girls. Harpo's were girls too, and most importantly, his harp. He would later transport audiences with his sublime renditions on the instrument. At the outset, he had trouble transporting the harp itself. It took up the room of a fifth brother, but through sleet and storm no brother was ever so lovingly looked after. He had taught himself to play, tuning the instrument incorrectly and placing it on the wrong shoulder. Nevertheless, with nobody's help, he had become an artist. His brothers, who had little regard for his brainpower up to now, began to look on him as a wizard. After an episode in a Midwestern town, they thought he might also be a warlock.

The brothers were playing the end of a split week in Burlington, Iowa, in December of 1916. The theater, which seated five hundred, was damp and dimly lit.

Since Groucho was the only brother who could be routed out of bed before noon, it was his responsibility to rehearse the orchestra. He walked into the theater, the picture of a successful entertainer, a diamond stickpin in his tie, cane in hand, smoking a cigar.

He was confronted by the manager, Jack Root. "Don't you see the sign?" Root snarled. "It says NO SMOKING. That'll cost you five dollars."

Root, a native Austrian, had been the first light heavyweight boxing champion. Groucho drew from his extremely limited reservoir of physical courage. The sign was hanging high on a side wall, barely visible. "Why don't you hang the sign in a closet?" Groucho asked. "Then you can be sure no one will see it."

"A wise guy, huh?" Root said. "That'll cost you another five."

Groucho, muttering under his breath, threw the cigar away and started rehearsing the music. He told the brothers what had happened when he returned to the hotel.

Shortly before the two-thirty matinee curtain, Chico called for Root. The brothers were in makeup and costumes when the theater manager arrived.

"Unless you cancel that ten dollar fine, we're not going on," Chico said.

"The hell you say," Root countered.

The brothers then started taking off their makeup. Harpo stepped in. "I'll tell you what," he told Root. "We'll take ten dollars and you take ten, and let's throw the whole twenty in the Salvation Army pot on the corner."

Root refused. Stomping noises from the restless audience, however, made him change his mind. Root agreed to the condition.

The act played without further incident for the rest of the run. When it closed on Saturday night, the performers had forty minutes to get dressed, pack, load scenery on trucks, and get to the train depot.

In the midst of the activity, two of Root's assistants came in bearing four big canvas bags. They were loaded with coins. This was a standard practice among chiseling theater managers. They would pay off acts in dimes, nickels, and quarters just before train time, when there was little chance to verify totals. Once aboard the train, the actors invariably found they'd been short-changed.

The brothers scooped up the bags. Harpo called back at Root as they left, "You son of a bitch! I hope your lousy theater burns down!"

Before dawn of the following day, the theater did exactly that. "That's why Harpo doesn't talk," Groucho would later say. "It's too big a risk."

One day, Chico dropped a bombshell. A sultry brunette one. Her name was Betty Karp. She was twenty years old, and without fanfare she had become Mrs. Chico Marx.

Betty was of Russian-Jewish background, and her upbringing had

96

been one of great privation and near starvation. Though born in the United States, her mother had taken her back to Russia to live as a child. In bouncing back and forth, she had developed a physical resilience and a conservative manner which belied her erotic hothouse appearance.

She and Chico had met through one of Betty's childhood friends, who had worked for Chico as a song-plugger in Pittsburgh. "When he came to New York with the act, my girlfriend wanted me to meet him," Betty said. "Of course, I knew all about him. He used to three-sheet, which meant he stood in front of the large posters with his picture on them, in front of the theater. I guess it was a good way to pick up girls. When we were introduced, he told me he wanted to take me home. He seemed a little dangerous to me. An actor . . . who wanted an actor? They're here today and gone tomorrow. I pushed my girlfriend onto him, and he took *her* home. The next day he called and asked me for a date. I accepted. Then I thought it over. He was leaving the next day. Why should I have to wrestle him or something? So I stood him up."

The relationship would have been aborted then if Betty hadn't had an actress friend who persisted in dropping names of all her acquaintances. Betty bore it for as long as she could before timorously offering, "I know an actor too."

"Who?" the girl asked.

"One of the Marx Brothers," Betty replied.

"Why, they're playing in Brooklyn!" the girl said.

"I didn't know anything about Brooklyn," Betty recalled. "I lived in Manhattan. But my friend convinced me to go with her. It took her so long to make up that by the time we got there, the last act was already on. It was lucky they were the Marx Brothers. We went backstage after the show, and told the stage manager we were looking for Leo."

As the brothers came offstage and saw the two girls, they all claimed to be Leo.

"I didn't recognize any of them with their makeup on," Betty said. "I said no to each of them, even Chico. But then he said, 'You're the girl who stood me up.' He made another date with me to come to the theater and then go out for dinner. I accepted again. This time, he completely forgot about it, and I waited around for him like a big jerk. That was our romance. When we finally got together, I never let go. He was a charmer, and I was never sorry, really."

The couple was so naive about the how's and why's of weddings that they neglected to invite their families. They were married at a friend's house by a rabbi. Groucho was incensed, and didn't invite Chico and Betty to his own wedding three years later.

Chico moved his wife to Chicago. "It was an army," Betty said. "Poor me, I was practically an only child. I had a brother who had never lived with us. I came into this enormous house with so many people. I was treading on everybody's toes, saying all the wrong things.

"The boys all lived at home when they came off the road. Chico and I had a room, the boys were two to a room . . . Al Shean and his wife also lived there . . . a nephew of Minnie's from Germany was there . . . the man they called The General, and Aunt Hannah. There was also Opie. He was an amazing old man, and he was still figure skating on the ice. He was getting senile, though."

Betty didn't hesitate, when asked, to offer her uncommonly frank opinions, and this quality in her was often offputting. Yet, her compliments were equally honest, uncolored and never fawning. Groucho's recently cultivated mustache was a case in point.

"I've always hated mustaches," she recalled. "It was less trouble for Groucho to grow his own instead of gluing on a false one for the act. 'Groucho,' I told him, 'I don't know why you want to hide your beautiful mouth with a mustache.' He did have a beautiful mouth. It was beautifully shaped, almost feminine. After I told him how I felt, he shaved off the mustache."

Before long, Betty was part of the family. "They were very funny. You could hear them two blocks away. The house was full of music and laughter. Food was always available, and the soup pot they were served from was as big as a table."

Groucho looked kindly on her, and Betty had also found an ally in her mother-in-law. "I got along wonderfully with Minnie," she recalled. "She had a cute way about her and a terrific sense of humor. She was quite a person. She never put herself out for anyone, but she never interfered. If anything, she tended to side with me."

Once, Betty had asked Minnie why she always favored her daughter-in-law over her son. "My son loves me, and nothing can change that," Minnie replied. "But I have to make you love me too."

"Minnie knew what I had in Chico, and she was glad I had it. Some of the worry was taken off her shoulders."

In reconstructing the earliest days of their marriage, Betty discovered Chico had been unfaithful on their honeymoon, and continued to womanize at every opportunity.

"I was young and dumb," Betty said. "Nothing mattered, as long as I had Chico. My mother-in-law felt sorry for me. A girl would call Chico on the phone and she would say, 'Don't you call here again. He's a married man.' It had never dawned on me. Whenever a girl called and I answered the phone, I'd say, 'He'll be here in another hour.' In those days I wasn't suspicious. It took me a long time, and then I was *very* jealous and *very* suspicious.

"Groucho felt sorry for me, too, because Chico was always away, either chasing girls or gambling. He had a little automobile, a Beatle, and he polished it constantly. Groucho loved cars, and he went from the cheapest to a Cadillac. It took him forever to get a Cadillac, but he paid cash for his. Chico bought a Cadillac right away, but on time. One day Groucho said, 'Come on, I'll take you for a ride.' I got into the car with him, and he went and bought some cheese. It smelled simply awful. I had a super-sensitive nose, smells still kill me, and I said, 'It stinks.' I'd insulted Groucho, because he was super-sensitive about *everything*. For the rest of the summer he did *not* take me for another ride."

In April of 1917, the United States went to war. Theater business quickly dropped off. Before the end of the year a 10:45 P.M. curfew would be put into effect on Broadway as a means of conserving fuel. Vaudeville houses tried to keep their heads above water by featuring war song contests. It was too early for the brothers to determine how the war would affect their bookings, because the summer season was upcoming and they traditionally took the summers off. Vaudeville closed down because of the lack of air conditioning in the great majority of the country's theaters.

The brothers were called up for their physicals. Apparently,

99

President Wilson had made an exception of the Marx Brothers. They weren't entitled to exemptions as farmers.

The four, as legend has it, turned up at a Chicago recruiting station to enlist in the Illinois Infantry. One was rejected for poor eyesight. A second had flat feet. A third reportedly had a physical disability incurred by an operation. The fourth was deferred "for general reasons."

"That's nothing," Groucho allegedly said to the recruiting sergeant. "You should see the fifth Marx brother. Two heads!"

Actually, men from the ages of twenty-one to thirty were being drafted. Chico, thirty and married, was legitimately exempt. Groucho's poor eyesight disqualified him. Harpo had suffered from albuminuria since he had been a child and because of it wasn't able to tolerate alcohol until he reached middle age. Only Gummo, with his heart murmur, was found acceptable. He left the act forever.

"Over There" for Gummo would prove to be the North Side of Chicago. He remained stateside during the war and his primary function seemed to be the procurement of chorus girls for his senior officers. He would also supply them with wheels, borrowing Harpo's car or allowing them the use of a secondhand Allis Chalmers, which he and Groucho had bought for three hundred dollars.

Groucho was left with no transportation to call his own.

"Gummo and I were in love with two beautiful Jewish girls on the North Side," Groucho said. "Every time we wanted to use the car, Zeppo would take out the ignition, and we had to take the El. The car had no brakes, and it had a hole in the top. We were playing the Majestic Theatre at the time. Once, when we left the show, it was raining. It was the kind of car that you had to press the brakes on Thirty-ninth to stop at Forty-fifth. We took the girls home. When we got Gummo's girl home, her father was standing at the door. He looked at Gummo and said, 'If I ever see you again, I'll kill you.' That's as close as Gummo got to getting a Purple Heart."

Groucho remedied the situation by purchasing a secondhand Scripps Booth."If you leaned against the front door it would open. I once took a girl out and leaned against her. She flew out of the door and skidded into a drug store on the corner."

The brothers embarked on the 1917-1918 tour in late August. Betty Marx was now a part of the act. One day, dancing off the stage, Harpo purposely tripped Betty, and she fell to the floor in a graceless sprawl. The audience roared. Only her feelings were injured. She let Harpo know. "What are you complaining about?" he asked. "You got a laugh, didn't you?" Always anything for a laugh.

Groucho, as a nouveau man of the world, had recently taken up golf. He was playing with a friend one day at Lincoln Park in San Francisco. It was a case of beginner's luck when on that January day, he shot a hole-in-one.

"The next day my picture was in the local newspaper," Groucho recalled. "It was stuck between the pictures of Walter Hagen and Bobby Jones. The headline read, MARX JOINS THE IMMORTALS.

"That afternoon I went out again on the golf course. There was a bunch of photographers following us around. I got to the same hole, but this time I took a twelve. The photographers folded up their equipment and walked away.

"The following day there was another story in the paper. This time there was a blank hole where my picture had been before. The pictures of Hagen and Jones remained. Above the story was another headline: MARX LEAVES THE IMMORTALS."

I once asked Groucho what the basic elements in the telling of a good story were. "You know," he replied, "I never claimed to be a joke teller. In fact, I've fucked up a lot of jokes. But I think to tell a good story you have to go over it like you do a comedy script. You cut away all the dead wood so that nothing but the basics remains." In Groucho's case, it might sometimes mean cutting away the truth, as he did in this case. Neither Hagen nor Jones had achieved golfing immortality at the time Groucho shot his hole-in-one. Although Hagen was conceded to be the top professional in the country at the time, he won his first National Open in 1914, and wouldn't win his second and final Open until 1919, the following year. From 1916 to 1922, Jones played in eleven major tournaments without winning one. He would win his first National

Open in 1923, winning thirteen additional championships by 1930.

The January 31, 1918, issue of the *San Francisco Examiner* reported the story in a different way, under a headline stating MARX HOLES OUT IN ONE 7TH GREEN AT LINCOLN PARK:

> This is not a press agent story, although it may bear some of the earmarks of the same.
>
> Julius Marx, who plays with his three brothers and a lot of damsels on the Orpheum time for income and golf on various links for amusement, made golfing history yesterday morning by holing out in one on the seventh green at Lincoln Park. His feat was attested by a fellow thespian, Frank Crumin, and the two were just about to hie themselves to a notary to make affidavits when another witness, who happened to be a newspaper man, appeared on the scene and took what he had seen and the word of the two thespians and let it go at that.
>
> Crumin, who is a bit of a golfer himself, says that Marx was all besmeared with fortune, but Marx knows that he played the shot and played it right and that the ball went just where he wanted it to. The seventh at Lincoln Park is a 153-yard, par 3 hole, a nice mashie shot, but a difficult single shot hole.
>
> Incidentally, Marx quit his game right then and there. He didn't want to spoil his record.

The February 15, 1918 issue of *Variety* also told of the incident:

> JULIUS MARX (4 Marx Bros.) is a golfer. His latest exploit, made recently over the Lincoln Park link, San Francisco, when he holed out in one, on the seventh, besides making him a record holder, places him in a division with "Jerry" Travers, Francis Ouimet and other Class A men. The hole is 153 yards, par 3. Responsible witnesses saw the play and are prepared to make affidavit it was accomplished. Marx at the time was playing a match, but refused to continue, fearing to besmirch his brilliant record.

Travers and Ouimet were conceded to be the greatest golfers of the day, though their names didn't come down in sports history with as much luster as those of Hagen and Jones. What the relating of the story reveals about Groucho is that his reminiscences had come to be miniature Greek tragedies. He built himself to a prominence he didn't possess at the time, only to be done in by a tragic flaw of his own making.

Meanwhile, Minnie had decided to return to show business, and entered the fray as the guiding spirit behind the brothers' attempt to forsake vaudeville. She hired Jo Swerling to write a romantic farce, to be called *The Street Cinderella*. Uncle Al would direct, and the music was to be written by Gus Kahn and Egbert Van Alstyne.

The national flu epidemic, which ultimately caused nearly 500,000 deaths, spread all over America early in September of 1918. Virtually all theaters were shut down. Wartime prohibition went into effect the same month. But the imperturbable Marx Brothers started rehearsals. Musical comedies and revues dominated the Broadway stage during the war years, and more than a hundred headline vaudeville acts had graduated to the legitimate theater. The Marxes were determined to become the second wave to sweep over Broadway.

The show opened on September 28 in Grand Rapids, with a chorus of twelve singing:

> *We are the girls from the nursery rhyme*
> *We're here to make you happy.*
> *We'll sing in tune and dance in time*
> *And hope you won't get nappy.*

A second wave of Spanish influenza had struck the country. The audience was required to sit one seat apart and alternate rows were kept empty. Many held handkerchieves over their noses. The Marxes knew this wasn't a silent criticism of their offering, but even they couldn't recover from this semi-quarantine, funereal reception.

The show moved on to Benton Harbor, Michigan, where on October 3, five days after its opening, *The Street Cinderella* was swept into a storm drain.

The only reward that Groucho reaped from the experience was a friendship with veteran actor Edward Metcalfe, who introduced him to the brilliant patter of "some English operettas." From that point on Groucho became the world's most rabid fan of Gilbert and Sullivan.

The Marxes licked their wounds at the farm in La Grange—the house on Grand Boulevard was now closed up—before returning to a "Home Again" variation, "'N' Everything," which opened in November in Gary, Indiana.

They continued with the show for the next twenty-seven months, until February, 1921, firmly re-establishing themselves as vaude-villians. They were so successful that they were soon booked exclusively on the big-time Eastern circuits.

The family was still living in Chicago in the summer of 1919. One day, Chico told Betty, "I've got to go to New York, and I'm late."

"Why are you late?" she asked.

"All the Eastern booking was done weeks ago," he replied.

"If you have to book in New York, what are you doing in Chicago?" Betty said. "Why don't you all move to New York?"

Betty had reasons of her own for wanting to move back to New York. She was feeling increasingly insecure about her marriage, and wanted to be closer to whatever of her immediate family remained.

Chico went to his brothers. "Why don't we all move to New York? Why are we wasting the whole summer here?"

Whiling away the weeks playing cards and sunning at the beaches hadn't seemed like a bad idea until Chico impressed on them the importance of being nearer to the action. They had already received a clue it was time to move on when they played Keith's Philadelphia that July and the theater's newly installed air conditioning received equal billing with the act.

Yearning for the big time, which meant Broadway, the Marxes returned to New York. They took up separate residences. Their lives as somewhat independent adults had begun.

The legitimate theater began looking even more attractive after a month-long Actors' Equity strike proved successful. As a result, performers' bargaining positions were strengthened. The strike, which had closed down all Broadway theaters, had cost the owners $250,000 a week in lost revenues. Management felt actors, who were losing $100,000 weekly, could be starved into submission.

Many of the great stars of the theater had sided with management. George M. Cohan, who was a producer as well, was among them. His partner, Sam Harris, who was to become a close friend of the Marxes, took the actors' side during the strike. Groucho, although not directly affected, never forgave Cohan for his treachery. Once, when George Jessel was at his house for dinner and extolling the greatness of Cohan, Groucho exploded. "He was a no good son of a bitch! He kicked Ethel Levey in the stomach when she was seven months gone!" (Ethel Levey was Cohan's first wife and Groucho never amplified on the source of this information.) Nothing Jessel said about Cohan could make Groucho change his mind.

The turning point in the strike occurred when the biggest star of all, Ethel Barrymore, sided with the actors. The settlement set precedents for the care and feeding of actors which remain to this day.

In November of 1919, Chico convinced producer Charles Dillingham to sign the brothers to a three-year contract. It would go into effect the following season with the brothers starring in their first Broadway show.

In the meantime, Groucho was ready to make a long-term commitment of his own. He was approaching thirty when he began seriously thinking about marriage. He was ripe for wedlock. He had been having an affair with a girl in the act, and she became pregnant. The girl loved Groucho, though she thought he would never marry her because there had been other men in her life. Groucho never believed in the double standard, and he probably would have married her if she had informed him of the situation. She chose to get an abortion instead. The relationship was permanently damaged, and the affair wasn't revived.

Zeppo had met a shy, pretty blonde, Ruth Johnson, in Cleveland, and had dated her several times. Subsequently he recruited her for the act.

"I think Ruth discovered that perhaps Zeppo didn't count for much in the act," Chico's first wife, Betty, said. "She was using her head. She may have liked Zeppo better at first, but she discovered Zeppo wasn't making as much money as Groucho. When Groucho went for her, I didn't see that Zeppo was broken-hearted."

Harpo one day suggested that the modestly talented Ruth be replaced. "The girl stays," Groucho snapped. "I'm going to marry her."

The ceremony took place February 4 in Chicago. The celebration was somewhat muted, Opie having passed away shortly before the wedding.

Out in Hollywood, Charlie Chaplin was making over one million dollars a year. Thirty-five million Americans were going to the movies weekly, and he was the prime drawing card. He had invited the brothers to dinner when they appeared in Southern California. "He was so rich," Groucho said, "that he had a butler behind each chair, and the dinner was served on solid gold plates."

As for the brothers, their mother Minnie was still doling out their allowances. Groucho talked to Chico. "It's not right. We're two married men, and we still depend on our mother to tell us how much we can have." Shortly thereafter, Minnie was informed she would no longer be handling the finances for the act. At the age of thirty, Groucho attempted to declare his independence from the indifferent Minnie. Groucho became the authority figure, largely deciding for his brothers how much they should dole out to their parents. Opting for financial security—there was clearly little choice, since Minnie hadn't offered him an emotional alternative—Groucho embarked on a lifetime of tightfistedness which would shame a Jack Benny.

After their appearance in Los Angeles, the act headed north to San Francisco, where it appeared in mid-March of 1920 at the Orpheum. The *San Francisco Chronicle* review by Marjorie Driscoll singled out Harpo:

> ... quite correctly billed as a red-headed nondescript. He works entirely in pantomime and he does everything from harp solos, both serious and comic, to comedy falls that would make a slapstick picture-producer pale with envy. He is quite the funniest comedian that has stirred the mirth of Orpheum audiences for many a moon.
>
> Julius Marx is a clever eccentric dancer, comedian, and general utility man. Herbert Marx is a dapper society dancer,

106

and Leonard Marx is a piano-teasing character comedian with gifted fingers. . . ."

When the brothers returned to New York in the early fall, victims of exhaustion and malaise, they again voiced misgivings about the path their career was taking. They met with Jo Swerling, Al Posen, and Max Lippman, to discuss what potential they might have in motion pictures. They decided to test themselves by making one. Each man chipped in one thousand dollars to make *Humorisk*, a silent movie spoofing silent movies. It was written by Swerling, one of the Marx sketch writers, who had been best man at Groucho's wedding. Posen agreed to act as business manager. (He wasn't sophisticated enough in the field to know he could legitimately claim the title of producer.) Lippman's contribution, other than money, no one could later recall. Looking on as kibitzers were Oscar Mirantz and Nathan Sachs. "Mike" Mirantz was married to Betty Marx's first cousin, Florence, and "Nuck" Sachs' friendship with the brothers went back to their days on Ninety-third Street. An attorney, he was credited by Groucho with helping the act maintain a high taste level.

The supporting cast was made up of a husband and wife team named Ralston, a line of chorus girls from a Shubert unit working in New York, and several fringe performers from the Marx Brothers act. One reputedly was Mildred Davis, who later would marry Harold Lloyd.

The movie was shot at Fort Lee, New Jersey, and at a converted warehouse doubling as a studio at Fortieth Street and Tenth Avenue in New York.

The one-reeler commenced with Harpo sliding down a coal chute (he was the love interest) and ended with Groucho trudging off in ball and chain, getting his just deserts as the villain of the piece. In between was a singular hodgepodge lacking rhyme or reason—mostly reason. The film had no structure. At no time during its shooting had there been a screening of the daily rushes.

One scene took place in a cabaret. Al Posen invited his mother to come see the crazy new business he was involved in. She arrived at the height of one of the daily crises and discreetly seated herself at a table away from the commotion. Later it was discovered the table occupied by Mrs. Posen was an integral part of the action. She was persuaded to come back for the next three days to sit in the same place until the scene was completed.

No one save the cameraman had ever been involved in a motion picture. The cinema was an infant medium at the time, and the final creation by this group was equally embryonic.

The budding studio conglomerate wanted to see the final product. "None of us was very hopeful about the proceedings," Groucho wrote in the *Saturday Evening Post* in 1931, "but we said without really believing our words that you can't tell until an audience sees it. We'll get the thing previewed in some theater around New York, and then we'll know if we have a picture or not. But we knew what we had, and so did the managers who viewed *Humor Risk.* Not one of them wanted the picture shown in his theater. We even offered to pay a small rental but the managers seemed to be too considerate of their audiences."

Ben Ginsberg, Swerling's assistant, revealed that he had an uncle who owned a movie theater in the Bronx, and he thought his uncle would agree to screen the picture before an audience.

The theater was featuring a program of screen mysteries the day the Marxes and their associates descended. Suddenly the audience was beset by the biggest mystery of all. One feature ended and *Humorisk* began. It was flashed on the screen without title or credits, the producers having forgotten to make them. It could have been *Humorisk, Humor Risk* (as Groucho spelled it) or *Flight of the Bumble Bee,* as far as the audience was concerned.

The picture, to put it mildly, was not well received. The hisses, snickers and incipient violence drove home the sad fact that they had a bomb on their hands. The print was burned. Posen tossed the negative in his closet.

The brothers returned to vaudeville which, in an effort to compete with the ever-burgeoning legitimate theater, was now mounting four shows a day. The Marxes had set a record among big-time acts by having played sixty consecutive weeks in first-class New York theaters, a fact which offered some consolation.

The brothers knew that with 12,000 vaudeville acts idle, they had to widen their range. It was gratifying to them that Gallagher and Shean were the brightest lights of vaudeville, and that their imitators were so numerous the Keith office issued an order limiting bills to one Gallagher and Shean imitation. But their success had no direct relevance to them.

They teamed up with Herman Timberg, a comedy monologist who had appeared on the same bill with the Marx Brothers when they toured in "Home Again." Timberg had started in show business with the original Gus Edwards "School Boys and Girls" act. He was known to dance and play the violin—at the same time.

The brothers, whose "Peasie Weasie" finish was a crowd pleaser, couldn't match Timberg's ploy for milking audience applause. Taking his first bow, he would look into the wings as if someone were calling him, then walk offstage to see what that imaginary person wanted. The audience applause would bring him back, and then he would repeat the procedure all over again. He would take his final bow, with the audience going wild, believing it had won out over the person beckoning from the wings.

Benny Leonard, the lightweight boxing champion, was sweet on Timberg's sister Hattie. He was also a stagestruck admirer of the Marx Brothers. Leonard financed the act called "On the Mezzanine." The Marx Brothers would star, with Timberg's sister cast in a feature role. Not wishing to be accused of nepotism, Timberg renamed his sister Hattie Darling. She also managed the act, protecting her boyfriend's investment.

The brothers held a special affection for athletes, and no one was more of a celebrity in their eyes than Leonard, the first great Jewish lightweight, considered by many the greatest champion of all time in that weight class.

Groucho recalled crossing the Brooklyn Bridge one night. Benny was in the car, which his brother Charlie was driving. Charlie Leonard inadvertently sideswiped an auto in the adjacent lane. Both drivers stopped to see the extent of the damage. The driver of the other car, enraged, yelled, "Come out here and I'll kill you!"

"Benny stepped out," Groucho said. "The other driver recognized him and took off."

Hattie Timberg Weinstein, today the widow of a Chicago jeweler, said her part consisted of singing, dancing, and playing the violin. "Chico and I did a number together where he hypnotized me to play the violin, and Zeppo and I did the love scenes together."

Chico couldn't hypnotize Hattie, however, into advancing him any money. "Chico was very annoying," she recalled, "because every time he ran out of money he had to come to me for an advance. He was quite a gambler."

It was unusual for an act to have a female manager, and the brothers hadn't been exposed to one since Minnie's temporary retirement. "They didn't like it very much either," Hattie added.

The act toured New England for a month before opening at the Palace the week of March 14, 1921. In the orchestra pit directing the house band was the Timbergs' younger brother Sammy. Nepotism ran as rampant offstage as on. The *Variety* review of March 18 read: ·

> The Four Marx Brothers, closing the first half, are now a production. . . . It was a riot Monday night. The turn holds 11 people, carries a thread of a story, has an outstanding smack of smartness about it which, coupled with the Marx Brothers' low comedy clowning, constitutes a combination that's infalli-ble. . . . Arthur Marx, the silent comic of the family, hasn't as much to do in a comedy way as in the former Marx turn, the meat being more evenly distributed. Julius, the eldest, shines as usual with a constant flow of "wise cracks," apparently for the most part impromptu, but all distinctly funny. Arthur's harp solos won an ovation Monday night, and is a distinctive feature of one of the very best acts that has hit the Palace this or any other season. . . . It should lift the Marx family right onto Broadway.

Having been touted as potential Broadway stars for the first time, the brothers decided to live accordingly. When they played Keith's Bushwick in Brooklyn, they occupied the star's downstairs dressing room, much to the vexation of Hattie. She retaliated by wiping the floor with Harpo's red wig.

There was probably no malice intended or a desire for revenge when the Marxes decided to play a practical joke on Herman Timberg shortly thereafter. It was one they had pulled several times. They told him they were going to set him up with a whore. Timberg was agreeable, so Groucho gave him the address. The brothers got there before he did. A man answered Timberg's knock

110

at the door. "I came to fuck the girl," the plain-spoken Timberg said. "Do *what* with my wife?" the man roared. Timberg took off, not looking back, as the brothers, in consort with their "outraged" friend, threw lightbulbs against the pavement, simulating pistol shots.

Although Hattie Darling was in love with Leonard, her parents wouldn't let her marry a boxer. She joined *The Passing Show* of 1922 on its tour to Chicago, where she met Morris Weinstein, the man she would ultimately wed. The fighter had to be content with the substantial profits generated by the show over the next two seasons.

The brothers were playing Keith's Riverside in New York on July 21, 1921, when Groucho's son was born at Lenox Hill Hospital. The boy was named Arthur. The marriage of Ruth and Groucho could be said to have officially begun. Up to now, they hadn't set up an organized household, and Groucho had tended to look on Ruth as the latest in a long line of chorines sharing his hotel room on the road.

In later years, Groucho would say that the greasepaint mustache had its origin when, overstaying his hospital visit with Ruth one night, he arrived at the theater too late to paste on his mustache, and smeared on some greasepaint instead.

When I asked him about it, he exclaimed, "Not true! I was having dinner with some friends in a kosher restaurant on Twenty-ninth Street, and got back late. That's the way it really happened." At the time he told me that, however, he and Arthur hadn't seen each other in several years, and Groucho wasn't favorably disposed to his son. Arthur in *Son of Groucho* reported the former version, and judging from the joy Groucho took in having a son, it's not unlikely this is the way it actually happened. His refusal to allow his son even a footnote in the evolution of his persona revealed an unattractive side of Groucho's private character to me. It was one of the few times I found him to be harsh, petty, and unforgiving, and it indicated some of the pressures Arthur must have lived with while growing up.

When the evening's performance ended, Groucho was accosted by the theater manager, whose name was Quinn, and accused of playing bush league tricks. "You didn't do that at the Palace on

Monday," Quinn charged. The act had played there for one day at the beginning of the week. Groucho pointed out that the audience laughed just as hard, a fact Quinn conceded. There were no further complaints. The greasepaint mustache remained.

In evolving the latest touch to his makeup, Groucho had reverted to the old days of the mid-nineteenth century, when theaters were gas-lit and makeup was crudely applied. Bright vermillion greasepaint was applied to cheeks and noses with no shading whatsoever. Solid black was used for wrinkles, expression marks, eye shadows, and mustaches. With the advent of electricity, such makeup looked frightful, and more subtle shadings resulted. Mustaches were made of crepe hair and applied with gum mastic mixed with ether.

Groucho had now developed all the trademarks for which he would become famous. The first had been the cigar. He had begun smoking them in his late teens so as to look older and make it easier to pick up girls. When the brothers joined the act the twenty-year-old Groucho, playing a teacher in his seventies, had used a mustache to help with the characterization. The Groucho walk came out of the same role. An elderly man would walk with a slight stoop, which Groucho adopted, but he would never walk as fast as Groucho did. "I was just kidding around one day and started to walk funny," he explained. "The audience liked it, so I kept it in. I would try a line and leave it in too if it got a laugh. If it didn't, I'd take it out and put in another. Pretty soon I had a character."

Frenchy was still an intermittent salesman, and the butt of more jokes. On one trip, all the boys had come to see him off. They kissed him good-bye, as he left to catch a train. He returned at midnight.

"Well," Frenchy explained, "I was on my way to the train station and I passed a cigar store where they were having a game of pinochle, and they said come in for a hand. So I went in for one hand and before I knew it, it was late and I missed the train."

The boys had a great laugh. The following night they again wished Frenchy godspeed.

He returned home at eleven-thirty.

"For God's sake, Sam," Minnie said, "another pinochle game?"

"I wanted to get even," Sam quietly replied.

The third night, Minnie insisted the boys take Sam directly to the station and put him on the train. Frenchy was home by ten-thirty.

"What happened this time?" Minnie asked.

"Well, the boys got me on the train and I sat down. Then I fell asleep. I was sleeping and sleeping and when I woke up, there was a man cleaning up the train. I asked him, 'Are we in Detroit?' He said, 'No, you're still in Chicago.' 'But I left for Detroit,' I told him. The man said, 'You ain't left no place. This is a dead train.'"

Groucho and his family were living in an apartment at 161 East Seventy-ninth Street. If gambling was Chico's greatest compulsion, fatherhood was Groucho's. He took up his responsibilities with a vengeance, seeming to wreak it upon Ruth as he took full charge of Arthur's upbringing. He would come home between performances to bathe the baby, change his diapers, and envelop him with love. The affection he held back from others, because of his constant fear of rejection, was wholeheartedly tendered to his infant son. At last there was a human creature he could totally call his own. Ruth could only stand by helplessly, with her unexpressed thoughts that Groucho was usurping the traditional woman's role.

Ruth was being minimized and exploited, first as a wife and mother and secondly as a cut-rate chorine. The outward happiness of their son's birth disguised the seeds of disaster that were being planted.

Groucho said he never drank until Prohibition took effect in January, 1920, the month before he and Ruth married. "Then I started," he said. "It seemed the right thing to do."

Ruth thought so too unfortunately.

The brothers were now touring with "On the Balcony," a variation of "On the Mezzanine," but without the Timbergs. Benny Leonard appeared with the act on a few play dates in the West, giving a boxing exhibition, but he soon dropped out. Ruth, who was having "artistic differences" with Zeppo, her dancing partner, delivered an ultimatum: either Zeppo or she would have to go.

Groucho didn't think twice. Zeppo stayed. Chico's wife Betty left the act at about the same time as Ruth. Both would become full-time housewives.

The act was playing the last week of November, 1922, at the Shubert-Grand in Hartford when, in New York, Congressman-elect Samuel Marx died of a heart attack. The brothers weren't among the thousands of mourners clogging the streets around the Institutional Synagogue on West 116th Street. This outpouring of respect so impressed Tammany leaders that they soon named a nearby plot of land Samuel Marx Square. Family ties with the Tammany leader of the Thirty-first Assembly district, who would have represented the Nineteenth District in Congress, never had been strong. Groucho, in fact, couldn't confirm they were related at all. When he was informed that Marx had been arrested in October, 1915, for electioneering, Groucho said, "I guess we must have been related after all."

"On the Balcony" ended the 1921-1922 season at the State-Lake in Chicago. The appearance was anticlimactic for the brothers. They were looking ahead to summer.

Chico, always thinking about how the act could be made more marketable, decided more money could be commanded if a triumphant European appearance was part of its credits.

The William Morris Agency had recently come to represent the brothers. Chico discussed the idea with Abe Lastfogel, who proceeded to put together a six-week London tour, in which they would re-create "On the Balcony." New faces also had to be hired to fill the void left by the departure of two of the four chorus girls in the act. One of them was Helen Schroeder, a Bronx-born, brown-eyed brunette who was as cuddlesome as her voice.

"She put in the boop boop a doop later," Groucho recalled of the girl who would change her name to Helen Kane.

The brothers, anxious about expenses, decided to leave their mother behind. Minnie was incensed. She dashed off a letter. "I am a maker of men," she wrote, "and everything you are you owe to me." The brothers were determined to be firm. The "Sailings" column in *Variety* reported that boarding the *Mauretania* on June 6, from New York to London, would be Mr. and Mrs. Julius Marx, Mr. and Mrs. Leo Marx, *Mrs. Samuel Marx*, Arthur Marx, Herbert Marx, and Edward Metcalfe. Minnie had gotten her way.

114

The act opened June 19 at the London Coliseum. It wasn't an auspicious debut. VARYING RECEPTIONS FOR AMERICAN ACTS, the June 23, 1922, issue of *Variety* reported. Five minutes into the performance some rowdy members of the audience started throwing pennies at them. Then the hisses started.

"We've come a long way to entertain you," Groucho called out. "The least you could do is throw silver." That seemed to be the only laugh received that humiliating opening night.

Basically, the act had to be Anglicized if it were going to be accepted by an English music hall audience. Discussing the situation later with the Coliseum manager, all agreed to revert to the tried and tested "Home Again." The brothers got better as they got to know their audiences, and the tour ended on a high note.

Back in the United States, however, *Variety* reported on their dismal opening night. Groucho, knowing that the report could be extremely damaging to the act, felt constrained to write a letter to the trade paper from Manchester on July 19:

> We opened at the Coliseum, London, in fifth position, and were such a big hit we were switched that night to closing the show, switching the positions with the Russian dancers.
>
> Ardent admirers of the Russian dancers, sometimes known as a claque, took exception to the switching of their favorites, and were responsible for the pennies that were thrown. After they were ejected, the act ran smoothly and we finished to a terrific hail of applause.
>
> That the disorder was due to a claque was later substantiated by the stage manager, and Mr. Johns, the Stoll booking manager, who personally investigated the affair.
>
> Why your correspondent here gave such prominence to the penny throwing and none to the reasons thereof, I do not understand. Why he quoted our salary at $1,000 a week, when as an actual fact we received 400 pounds a week for showing is also a mystery to me. The statements he sent in were injurious to our professional reputation.

At the then current exchange rate of one British pound to almost five dollars, the act was making closer to $2,000 a week than the $1,000 alleged by *Variety*. Judging from the audience reaction, they were being overpaid, and there was no doubt the reaction was negative. Why else would the brothers change the production in the middle of the run? Groucho was seeking to save face by dissembling.

The performers sailed for home on the British ship *Cedric* on July 29, confident that they would resume performing in the United States at the same high level as before their trip.

Helen Kane had bought a parasol and kid boots while in England, and had taken to wearing lots more makeup. As she got off the boat, her mother screamed, "Go wash your face this instant! What did they do to you?"

Chico smiled knowingly.

Dillingham hadn't been able to put a Broadway production together for the brothers. Albee was mad because the act had gone to England without getting clearance from him, as he insisted their vaudeville contract with him stipulated. The brothers were only able to get two weeks of independent bookings in theaters around New York as a result.

What Chico had envisioned as a triumphant return had led to a dismal impasse in the brothers' career. What recourse was available to them? No, never the Shuberts!

Lee and J. J. Shubert had started producing legitimate plays in 1901, although their offerings were considered the bargain basement of Broadway. The bulk were musical productions. They started with Americanized versions of European operettas, then they turned to inanely plotted musical comedies. Now they were staging revues slightly better than the vaudeville being presented at the Palace.

They had been so successful with the latter that they decided to invade vaudeville head on, challenging Albee by fashioning a circuit of eighteen cities from St. Louis to New York to Boston.

The brothers were understandably leery of the Shuberts, who had signed Gallagher and Shean to a contract, ostensibly to star in a Broadway production that would have opened in the fall of 1922.

Hidden in the fine print was the fact the pair had actually signed to do a vaudeville tour on the new circuit. As they were commiserating with each other, they were offered leads in the *Ziegfeld Follies*, at $1,500 a week, double their Shubert salaries. The team, feeling Shubert had breached the contract, signed with Ziegfeld and started rehearsals. The Shuberts sued. They claimed through their attorney, Willie Klein, that the act was unique, extraordinary, and irreplaceable, and that the contract gave them the right to tour the team in vaudeville.

Gallagher and Shean were put in the position of having to downplay their stature. They brought in witnesses to attest to the fact they were *not* unique and extraordinary, but merely ordinary performers. Why their "mediocre" talents should be surrounded by a full-scale Broadway production neither Gallagher nor Shean chose to explain. The team won its case, but lost on appeal. The Shuberts quickly put them in the *Greenwich Village Follies*, and after a short Broadway run sent them on tour.

The Shuberts, however, weren't finding vaudeville as easy a new field to conquer as anticipated. *Hollywood Follies*, starring a singing team billed as Kranz and White, was floundering. The Marx Brothers were approached to lend their drawing power. The money was right, and there were no other alternatives. The Marxes signed a contract to perform in an act called *The 20th Century Revue*, which incorporated an olio skit called "The Theatre Manager's Office." Kranz and White remained on the bill.

It opened on October 9 at the Englewood Theatre in Chicago. The Shuberts, hedging their bets, had franchised it to the Minneapolis production firm of Finkelstein & Rubin. By the time it reached Worcester, Massachusetts in mid-November, the revue had fallen apart. Attendance had declined and the artists weren't being paid.

The top billed acts, Kranz and White and the Marx Brothers, took over control of the show and the act, fortunately, looked like a winner when it played the Central Theatre in New York the week of December 4. The *Variety* review was favorable:

It's their humor (actions and dialog) that gets the laughs. The laughs are almost continuous, for Julius Marx gets a lot out of dialog. He is also an action comedian now, kidding around on his feet and otherwise.

117

In a way the program at the Central this week may be devoured by the Marx boys' admirers, for it lists them individually, so you can now find out who is who among them . . . This unit should do business for the simple reason there are plenty of laughs in it. The Marx boys may greatly profit in one way or another at the lead of their own show in a Shubert theatre on Broadway. They are a versatile quartet of laughable funmakers.

The revue literally kept one step ahead of the sheriff for three months. It stumbled on Saturday, March 3, at the Murat Theatre in Indianapolis, and a deputy sheriff attached the box office receipts, scenery, and costumes. The disenchanted Kranz and White had sued themselves and their partners for $1,490 in back salaries.

It was now up to the owners of the Betty Amusement Company, named after Chico's wife, and owned by the brothers, to salvage what they could. They couldn't. Charles Moy, who owned a Chicago Chinese restaurant, put ten thousand dollars in the act for the brothers. The money was lost. If it was any consolation, the Shuberts lost $1,500,000 on their venture in vaudeville. They, however, had legitimate theater to fall back on.

The Marx Brothers were at liberty. Keith-Albee would have nothing to do with them, and the smaller circuits were afraid to book them, fearing possible reprisals from Keith-Albee.

With no vaudeville bookings, Chico again turned to Dillingham. The brothers wanted to work, and they offered themselves at a rock-bottom total of four hundred dollars a week. Much as Dillingham would have liked to help, he couldn't find a property for them. The brothers received a release from their contract with Dillingham.

Seventeen years after the brothers came into being as The Three Nightingales, they were back where they started . . . at the beginning.

CHAPTER SIX

We're four of the three musketeers
We've been together for years
Eenie, meenie, minee, (horn)
Four of the three musketeers.
    Bert Kalmar and Harry Ruby,
        Animal Crackers

Years later, as much as he would rail against Chico's selfishness and irresponsibility, Groucho would usually add that if it weren't for the eldest Marx Brother, they never would have made it. "He made us believe in ourselves," Groucho professed.

"They had the talent," Betty, Chico's first wife, said, "but there's always somebody to put the talent forward." That person was her first husband.

Chico would negotiate complicated contracts and get favorable terms for the team from the craftiest men in the world, then turn around and gamble his money away. This was the contradiction that made him the most fascinating of the Marx Brothers, an

119

opinion both Groucho and Harpo shared. They envied his reckless-ness. Groucho also envied Chico's success with women. Harpo was as active sexually, but being a bachelor, he was permitted to womanize, as was Zeppo. Groucho's morality denied any married man that privilege ... unless the infidelity was conducted with a discretion Chico so flagrantly avoided.

And yet, his daring and his refusal to worry about tomorrow stood the brothers in good stead. Chico never gave the impression of negotiating from a hungry position. His rakish charm was part of his arsenal. All the world loves a lover, but show business also loves a scamp. Chico was both.

The Marx Brothers, despite being a proven draw at the box office, couldn't get a booking. Vaudeville had killed them off, and not a moment too soon. It wasn't humanly possible for a headline act to perform five shows a day, three more than had been the norm in vaudeville's heyday. Material was eaten up almost as quickly as it is on television today. The jokes got staler and more vulgar. Movies and sports were the new favored pastimes. For a brief time, big time circuits tried a more elegant approach. Men in dinner jackets and formally gowned women appeared on stage, with frequent costume changes. Albee was largely responsible for dressing up vaudeville. But it was all in vain.

Joseph M. Gaites had in 1919 produced a show, *Love for Sale*, starring Kitty Gordon, which played a fast three weeks out of town and folded. Its successor, *Gimme a Thrill*, also a Gaites production, met the same untimely end.

After a month of negotiations, Chico reached an agreement with Gaites and the Shuberts. The original plan was to do a summer revue in Philadelphia, under the title of *You Must Come Over*. The show's name was changed to *I'll Say She Is*, and it was scheduled for a June 4, 1923, opening at the historic Walnut Street Theatre in Philadelphia, which had been owned in the nineteenth century by classical actor Edwin Booth (and would be the site of the first debate between Gerald Ford and Jimmy Carter during the 1976 presidential campaign).

The enterprise was an experiment to determine if Philadelphia could support a summer revue. Theater audiences hadn't yet shown an inclination to sit in the sweltering, humid theaters while the temperature outside was in the nineties.

120

Will and Tom Johnstone were hired to put sparks in the script, which hopefully would incorporate the better elements of two less than mediocre productions. The Marx Brothers proved to be the cohesive agents and the show was an enormous hit, playing three record-breaking months and grossing more than $10,000 weekly, impressive statistics for the slow summer season.

Harpo and Gaites's co-producer, a coal mine owner named James Beury, had something in common. They were sharing the favors of the same chorus girl. Chico was able to convince Beury to tour with the production, then bring it to New York for a Broadway opening. Along the way, he negotiated a substantial salary increase for the brothers. They were again able to indulge themselves.

Because Groucho had in the past spent a good part of his earnings on books, he had to be content driving secondhand cars. Groucho often told the story of "the first real car" he ever bought, a Studebaker, while playing in Philadelphia. The showroom salesman was French and called the car a "Stoo-duh-bay-care." Delighted with his first totally new car, Groucho decided to take it for a spin during the intermission of a matinee. The streets around the Walnut Street Theatre were narrow and hardly navigable. Groucho found himself caught in a traffic jam, and he didn't see how he could make the last act curtain on time. He decided to leave the car on the street, and thus created an even more mammoth traffic tie-up behind him.

Imagine a man with a greasepaint mustache running through the streets in a Napoleon costume, and you can gather the impression left on a cop patrolling his beat. He started running after Groucho. When the cop caught up with him, Groucho explained he was an actor, late for his curtain.

"He didn't believe I was an actor," Groucho said, "so I gave him two tickets for the evening performance. He came backstage afterwards to look me up. And you know what? He still didn't believe I was an actor."

From Philadelphia, the act went to Boston for the month of September and was indifferently received. The show's average weekly gross, of less than $10,000, was considered mediocre for the early fall period. The show moved to Chicago, where its grosses were respectable. From then on, I'll Say She Is picked up momentum as it worked its way to New York.

While in Kansas City, the act played at the Shubert-Missouri Theatre. The stage manager brought the drama critic from the *Kansas City Star* backstage to meet the brothers.

"This is Ace," the manager said.

Years later, Goodman Ace, who had been twenty-four years old at the time, didn't recall who said what, but he described the general conversation with the brothers.

"Jacks up is my name," one of them said.

"I'm as wild as deuces," added another.

"I'm the drawing card, though," said a third.

"Well," Ace said, "glad to know you. How long have you boys—"

"How do you like the newspaper game?"

"Fine, fine," Ace replied. "But how do you boys like the big production idea since your last vaudeville—"

"We know a lot of newspaper men. Know Benchley? Broun? Ashton Stevens?"

"Just by reputation," Ace said. "They're good critics too. Is your family a theatrical—"

"Benchley is doing a monologue in the *Music Box Revue*, you know. Yes. Gets five hundred a week and does reviews right after his seven minutes in the show. How long have you been in the game?"

Another brother took up the conversational ball. "Have a cigar? Go ahead."

"Have a drink?" offered another. "Who wouldn't?"

"What do you think of the newspaper business?" the first brother asked. "Do you think it is taking a change for the better or do you think the newspaper reading public is losing interest?"

Ace by this time was ready to leave, but the brothers stopped him. They explained they were bored with interviews and had thought they would turn the tables.

After the show, Ace and the brothers went to see the "Baltimore Revue" at a local nightclub. There was a specialty act on the bill, consisting of ten chorus girls who would page people in the audience.

"Call for Mr. Davidson," one of them sang.

"Did you say Mr. Davidson?" Julius called as he rose from his seat at the table.

"Sit down," Ace cautioned. "You'll be thrown out."

"I don't mind being thrown out under somebody else's name," Groucho snapped.

By the end of the three-week run, Ace could differentiate between the brothers, and became especially close to Groucho, a friendship which lasted until Groucho's death. The relationship was sealed when Groucho, as he left town, gave Ace a book by E. B. White and James Thurber, *Is Sex Necessary?*

Ace would go on to become one of the great comedy writers of radio and television and, with his wife Jane, one of radio's most warm and comic teams.

(Throughout his life, Groucho would make friends of writers who—through their own talents or because of his intercession on their behalf—would go on to greater prominence. It started with Jo Swerling, a friend of Nuck Sachs and Mike Mirantz, and extended to Dick Cavett, a writer on the Jack Paar show when the two first met.)

Groucho was vastly amused by the jacket blurb on Ace's *The Book of Little Knowledge:*

Before becoming involved with the mass media, Mr. Ace was a newspaperman in Kansas City, Missouri. And it might be interesting to note in passing that he gained some little fame as the only Kansas Citian extant who was not personally acquainted with Harry S. Truman when that distinguished gentleman was a haberdasher in that Midwest metropolis.

Groucho for his part claimed he had bought a tie from Truman when he played at the Shubert-Missouri. Actually, Truman and his partner had gone bankrupt in business two years previously, and by 1923 the future president had been elected to county court. The two men conceivably met on earlier vaudeville playdates, though Groucho persisted in placing the meeting at the time *I'll Say She Is* played in Kansas City.

The Four Marx Brothers, to their surprise, had toured with the show for almost a year before they returned to the Walnut Street Theatre in Philadelphia for a three-week shakedown prior to invading Broadway. The engagement was a holding pattern of sorts. The Shuberts were busily juggling productions at several theaters to try to accommodate the incoming show. Finally, the date was confirmed, and the brothers were ready to take on Broadway, even if it was the less fashionable part of the street.

The Casino Theatre, at Broadway and Thirty-ninth Street, had lost considerable luster since the Florodora Girls had opened there in 1900, introducing an intimate formality between the performers and the audience that had never been seen before on the stage. The girls, smiling and winking, had ten curtain calls that opening November night.

After 1904, legitimate theater had begun to inch its way uptown. The ornate, Moorish-turreted theater had often stood empty during the intervening nineteen years. Now it was being prepared for another opening.

Frenchy and Minnie were also preparing for the most important night of their lives. Unfortunately, Minnie, while standing on a stool having her dress fitted, fell and broke her leg. Not that it kept her from the opening. She was borne into the theater on a stretcher, ready to see her sons take their places on the Broadway stage.

The theater season her sons' show would soon be a part of was an extraordinary one. Being staged that year were *What Price Glory, The Show-Off, Beggar on Horseback, Rose Marie, The Student Prince, Lady Be Good* with Fred and Adele Astaire, *Charlot's Revue,* which introduced Jack Buchanan, Gertrude Lawrence, and Beatrice Lillie to America. Starring in Eugene O'Neill's ponderous *Desire Under the Elms* were Mary Morris and Walter Huston. (Huston had appeared on a vaudeville bill with the brothers when he was part of the Whipple-Huston Company. When they met as Broadway stars, Groucho greeted the now distinguished actor. "Do you remember the time we were all on the train, and you were fucking a girl in the lower berth and I was dropping coat hangers on you from the upper?")

One of the great fallacies in the Marx mythology revolves around their New York opening which made them overnight stars. Every book that touches on their early career, including those

124

written by the Marxes themselves, has reported that New York's first-string critics attended the opening only because the premiere of a more important production was postponed at the last minute.

The Marx Brothers weren't strangers to most critics, or to newspapermen in general. They had headlined in its prominent theaters for almost two years. Newspapermen would have had to be cloistered in a monastery not to have heard of them, and few members of the fraternity were notably monastic.

Mistinguette, the French music hall star, was scheduled to open in *Innocent Eyes* at the Winter Garden on May 19, the same night *I'll Say She Is* was set for the Casino. The maneuvering hands of the brothers Shubert could be seen. Both the Winter Garden and the Casino were Shubert theaters, and it was to management's benefit to postpone one of the openings. This was the tag end of the theatrical season, when few shows opened; thus the Shuberts would only be competing with themselves if they launched two productions on the same day. The Marx Brothers had their first-string critics not by accident but by calculation.

Alexander Woollcott, his biographers would tell us, had confused the Marx Brothers with a team of acrobats, and didn't want to go to the theater because it was a hot night. Charles MacArthur was said to have dragged him there against his will. His May 20 review in the *Sun* refutes this. At the same time the headline over the piece showed where his preferences lay: HARPO MARX AND SOME BROTHERS.

As one of the many who laughed immodestly throughout the greater part of the first performance given by a new musical show, entitled, if memory serves, "I'll Say She Is," it behooves your correspondent to report the most comical moments vouchsafed to the first-nighters in a month of Mondays. It is a bright colored and vehement setting for the goings on of those talented cutups, the Four Marx Brothers. In particular, it is a splendacious and reasonably tuneful excuse for going to see that silent brother, that shy, unexpected, magnificent comic among the Marxes, who is recorded somewhere on a birth certificate as Arthur, but who is known to the adoring two-a-day as Harpo Marx.

Surely there should be dancing in the streets when a great clown comic comes to town, and this man is a great clown. He is officially billed as a member of the Marx family, but truly he belongs to that greater family which includes Joe Jackson and Bert Melrose and Fratillini brothers, who fall over one another in so obliging a fashion at the Cirque Medrano in Paris. Harpo Marx, so styled, oddly enough, because he plays the harp, says never a word from first to last, but when by merely leaning against one's brother one can seem richly and irresistibly amusing, why should one speak?

The speaking is mostly attended to by Julius H. Marx. Julius H., who seems to be the oldest of this household, is a crafty comedian with a rather fresher and more whimsical assortment of quips than is the lot of most refugees from vaudeville. To be sure, he is not above having Napoleon request the band to strike up "The Mayonnaise." But then, it was in a music hall in Omaha in 1904 that a French scene was last played without someone referring to that inspiring anthem "The Mayonnaise." And, after all, the oldest Marx's vein is more fairly typified by faithless Josephine that she was as true as a $3 cornet.

Then Leonard Marx is more or less suppressed until the property man remembers to leave a piano on the stage. As for Herbert Marx, he is probably the property man. Strange to relate, the real names of these four are not Thompson, Oppenheimer, Timkins and Goldberg. Nor are they, respectively, Lemuel Beam, Roscoe Mortimer, Daniel Smith and Lionel Schwartz. They are, as it happens, brothers. And their real name, as opposed to the one they employ for stage purposes, is Marx.

To add to the kudos, Charlie Chaplin generously allowed his name to be used in advertising, stating this was "the best musical comedy revue I've ever seen."

"Overnight we became big stars," Groucho recalled. "But Chico wasn't the type to say, 'I told you so.' "

"Why not?" I asked.

"He was too busy fucking."

126

Woollcott persisted in rhapsodizing about these talents, especially Harpo. He had come to look on the Marx Brothers as his invention, and felt free to offer unsolicited advice.

"Why don't you use your nicknames on the program?" he once asked Harpo.

"Well," answered Harpo, "they're not dignified."

Woollcott sputtered. "Are you crazy? Dignified? Are *you* dignified?" He made them change their names on the billing.

In later years, friends from their youth would call them by their real names. Nick the Greek always called Chico Lenny, and George Jessel referred to Groucho as Julius. But to the rest of the world they would be known, as Joe Adamson put it in his overview of their work, *Groucho, Harpo, Chico and Sometimes Zeppo.*

Woollcott, shortly after the opening of *I'll Say She Is,* happened to sit next to Minnie, a cast still on her broken leg, at a dinner party. Apprehensive about all stage mothers, he was prepared to concede that the Marx Brothers were funnier than any other four living people, including Will Rogers, Al Jolson, Frank Tinney, and Ed Wynn. He was also prepared to endure Minnie's vicarious experience of stardom.

To Woollcott's surprise, Minnie mentioned neither her sons, the theater, nor her triumph-once-removed. Instead she started discussing the fact she was now in the ginger-ale business. Woollcott hadn't considered there might be a basic indifference to her sons in Minnie's makeup, taking her silence about them as a sign that Minnie now considered her work done as far as the Marx Brothers were concerned, and that it was time to move on.

Minnie had conquered another male, albeit one of dubious persuasion. The hyperbole was about to begin. The June 26 issue of the *Saturday Evening Post* carried a Woollcott article titled "A Mother of the Two-A-Day."

Shortly thereafter, Minnie's picture appeared in *Vanity Fair:*

Nominated for the Hall of Fame: 1925 . . . Because, as the daughter of a German magician, she felt inner promptings which bade her snatch her five sons from their boyhood occupations (bellhops and the like) and drive them onto the stage. She was not content until the Marx Brothers shone in

127

electric lights on Broadway. Then, feeling suddenly idle, she went into the ginger-ale business.

Minnie had become a celebrity in her own right, wearing her surrogate stardom with a charming insouciance.

With Woollcott's review acting like a trumpet's blare, Harpo easily moved into the set which his new friend and champion dominated. The barely literate Harpo was the most unlikely recruit to the hallowed Round Table. Though he was of equal, if not higher, stature as a celebrity, he certainly couldn't compete with the likes of Woollcott, Dorothy Parker, and Robert Benchley on a verbal level. But he was the world's most appreciative audience, eager to sit at their knees to listen and learn. Harpo brought a charm and style of his own to the Circle. Harpo's literary betters respected the spare eloquence of his art.

Woollcott was his mentor, and Harpo began receiving an education in his middle thirties. Their relationship was cause for great conjecture.

"A lot of rumors went around that weren't true," Harpo's sister-in-law, Betty, said. "Harpo received a great education from Woollcott."

Groucho often described Woollcott as a neuter. When Howard Teichmann's biography, Smart Aleck, was published in 1976, Groucho was repelled by a passage wherein Woollcott confessed that he was nature's accident, and that nothing would have pleased him more than to give birth to a child of his own. Groucho amended his assessment. "Woollcott was in love with Harpo," he concluded.

Chico preferred action to talk, and he was happier off on his own placing improbable bets instead of listening to improbable stories.

Groucho's verbal wit should have qualified him twice over to become a member of the group. But he was competition. Groucho's inventive mind wasn't entirely welcome.

Groucho occasionally joined the group for lunch, but he didn't feel at ease. Once, he placed his order and received it immediately. Woollcott had to wait half an hour before being attended to.

The waiter finally asked, "Mr. Woollcott, what will you have?"

Woollcott was livid. "Muffins, filled with pus."

The suddenly queasy Groucho left and didn't return to the

Algonquin for some time. He much preferred the company of his family on the West Side.

With his greater affluence, Groucho took a two-year lease on a comfortable, unpretentious two-bedroom apartment at 651 West 161st Street, at Riverside Drive, and began looking for ways to invest his money. With an eye to the future, and in partnership with Nuck Sachs, he invested in twenty-four shorefront bungalows at Far Rockaway. Otherwise, he continued his same frugal ways. It was a frustration to Ruth, who saw how other entertainers pampered their wives. Hers wasn't a distinguished background, but now that they were socially circulating among the nation's most famous names she understandably wanted to look as well as they did. She was certainly prettier than most, and possessed of a charming diffidence she would never lose.

"I think Ruth had one very bad fault," the former Betty Marx said. "If she had been smarter, she would have gotten everything out of Groucho she wanted. But she went about it the wrong way. She would say, 'Look at the big diamond ring Betty's wearing. Look at the mink coat Chico gave her.' She wouldn't mention that the diamond ring might have to go into hock next week."

Groucho once said to Betty, "I'd like my wife to say just once that we shouldn't buy it . . . we can't afford it . . . it's too much money."

"You're not being fair to Ruth," Betty replied. "You think and think many times before you spend your money, so she doesn't have to say it. Chico goes out and buys when he hasn't got the money, and he doesn't worry about where he's going to get it or who's going to pay for it. That's why I have to say, 'No, we can't have it.' It's not because I'm different than Ruth. I like nice things too. I just have to worry about it."

Betty recalls Ruth as loving to dance, enjoying a social drink, reveling in the crowded gaiety of night clubs. "None of the boys drank when I was married to Chico. Groucho liked his guitar and a few friends with whom he could discuss world affairs. He'd surround himself with writers and good books, and the girl was bored to tears with the whole bunch."

Further complicating their life was Groucho's reciprocated dislike of his mother-in-law, Josephine Delano, though he got on well with his father-in-law, Oscar Johnson, who was a Swedish immigrant and a carpenter. (Ruth's parents were divorced, and each had remarried.)

"Ruth's mother was a small-town bigot," Groucho told me. She apparently wasn't thrilled with the idea of a Jew for a son-in-law.

"My first wife's mother," Groucho once wrote Sidney Sheldon, "who is the essence of all objectionable mothers-in-law and certainly was the inspiration for most of the distasteful jokes that are said about mothers-in-law, never failed, when visiting us, to declare that she was as busy as a skunk in a hen house. I don't know about the hen house, but the first part was certainly accurate."

Ruth too was having her own in-law problems, even though she was the physical embodiment of everything Minnie would have wanted in a daughter-in-law. She was blonde, very pretty, and very Aryan. These were all qualities Minnie saw in herself. Yet she didn't disguise her dislike of Ruth.

The show ran for thirty-eight weeks at the Casino, averaging a weekly gross of twenty thousand dollars.

The Marxes had become certifiable characters around town. Were they suddenly liberated into new behavior patterns, acting in the same anarchic way on the streets as they did on the stage? It's hard to say. Groucho never told me, "And then I did this crazy thing." Few survivors are around to tell of their didoes during their youth, and what the brothers chose to laugh about was not the practical joke they might have played on some pompous windbag, but about the adversities they had to overcome.

The anecdotes Groucho recited usually had him acting as the onlooker, the straight man, or the butt of the joke. He told, for instance, of a time when he was standing in front of the Casino with Eddie Foy, father of the Seven Little Foys. A man approached them.

"Do you know how to get to Bellevue?" he asked.

"Yes," Foy answered. "Shout, To hell with the Irish."

The knights of the Round Table, in adopting the Marx Brothers as the greatest team since the Chicago Black Sox, subjected them to

130

a barrage of questions. One was why they hadn't made any films.

Groucho reluctantly admitted they had made a disaster called *Humorisk.* Woollcott insisted it should be shown to the group.

Al Posen was contacted. Did he still have the picture? Yes. A screening room was hired, and Posen showed up at the appointed time.

Present that evening, in addition to the brothers, were Woollcott, Benchley, Dorothy Parker, Herbert Bayard Swope, and others. The lights dimmed, but not for long. The projectionist came out of his booth.

"How can I show a movie," he asked, "when I've been handed a negative instead of a print?"

Instead of being irritated, the members of the Round Table were amused. A typical Marx Brothers maneuver. The group disbanded.

Woollcott, a few days later, adamantly insisted a print be struck from the negative. The brothers were having great misgivings about the whole idea of showing the film, but reluctantly agreed.

Posen was again called. To his embarrassment, he discovered that he had forgotten to retrieve the film. Maybe it was still in the projection booth. Posen went back to look for it, but there was no film nor any clues to its disappearance. It was no doubt thrown out with the trash, and lost to history.

The brothers started on a seventeen-week tour to Boston, Hartford, Chicago and Detroit, after closing at the Casino. An incident occurred in Detroit, that would forever color the relationship between Groucho and Chico. Their relationship had been marked by jealousy and resentment since Groucho's infancy. The show was due to close the night of Saturday, June 6. In the middle of the Napoleon scene, Chico left the stage complaining that he didn't feel well. He said he was going out for fresh air. After stopping at a nearby leather store to buy a small bag, he disappeared. Groucho had to play both his and Chico's part for the remainder of the show, sometimes having to talk to himself. The brothers had played 524 entire performances without a single member of the cast missing a performance. That Chico should walk out in the middle of the last one was unforgivable to Groucho.

A tremendous heat wave had swept the Eastern part of the

country, and box office receipts were down everywhere. Police called in to investigate theorized that Chico might have been crazed by the oppressive temperature. He was, in a manner of speaking.

Chico had collected his week's pay in fifty-dollar bills during intermission and vanished. His brothers and his wife Betty, who traveled with the show, spent the weekend consumed with worry.

Chico called Betty from Cleveland on Tuesday of the next week. He explained he had taken a boat to Buffalo and then taken a ride to Cleveland. He assured her he would be back in Detroit that same night.

Betty was very frank with the reporters. "He lost thirty thousand dollars in New York shooting craps at the Greek's joint just before the show left there and he had to borrow a lot of money. That has been worrying him. He just loves to gamble. When he failed to show up Saturday I got a taxicab and a wise driver and we went to every gambling house in Detroit and, believe me, there are plenty of them. I had a strong hunch that Chico was gambling again. He always tells mama the truth, and he has admitted it to me—and that's that."

"He shouldn't have done that to us," Groucho said. "He was running away from some gangsters who were coming for the money he owed them. I knew the gamblers were after him, and he could have told us something, instead of having us worrying that he was in a block of cement at the bottom of the lake."

The troupe disbanded, the brothers going to New York for the summer. All except Harpo. He was off to movieland to make a silent picture, *Too Many Kisses*, which was to star Richard Dix. That film has also been lost to history—mercifully, according to Groucho.

When the Marxes made Broadway their own, they were subject to a publicity barrage that had turned many a less sensible head. Harpo received the most favorable press, being the lovable man that he was and a member in good standing of the Round Table. Chico couldn't have cared less that his publicity was almost as minimal as Zeppo's, the fourth brother who had been dismissed as a fifth wheel. Groucho's image was a difficult one to handle. He was seen as suspicious and hostile, his voice had a sneering quality to it, and some found him arrogant and superior. At the time, his sardonic tone seemed interchangeable with that of George S. Kaufman's, a man he had yet to meet. Critic Percy Hammond in his column had already noticed their physical similarity, which Kaufman took exception to. Groucho got into the act:

Sir: While in a subway car this morning I picked up a *Herald Tribune* off the floor. It might have been thrown there by Samuel Shipman, since it was folded right on your column. At any rate, it had an article by Mr. George S. Kaufman, in which he expressed himself as being greatly annoyed because you said that he looked like me.

I have never seen Mr. Kaufman in the flesh, or the rough, or whatever you call it. I have seen a number of his plays, and I am not sure whether he has a mustache or not, although some authors find it advisable to wear something on the opening night.

My make-up is a sort of hit-and-miss proposition, and when I start putting it on I am never sure who or what I will look like when I get through. Some nights I resemble one author, some nights I look like another, and it is purely a coincidence that basically I happen to look like Mr. Kaufman.

If you can suggest any humorous get-up that wouldn't look like the aforementioned gentleman I would be only too glad to adopt it, but I think you will find that that is impossible.

It was also impossible to forestall the inevitable. Florenz Ziegfeld had sent for Chico after the success of *I'll Say She Is*, and offered to put the brothers in his next show. A weekly salary was agreed on, but the deal fell through when Chico insisted on a higher percentage of the gross than Ziegfeld was willing to pay.

"I left Ziegfeld's office and went up to see Max Winslow, who was then associated with Irving Berlin," Chico told Louis Sobol of the *New York Journal* in April of 1934. "Just to say hello. Irving Berlin came into the room. 'Here are the boys you should write a show for,' said Max. 'Now you're telling me,' answered Irving. I told him that we hadn't signed yet with Ziegfeld. Sam Harris signed us for *Cocoanuts* the same day."

Harris, being Kaufman's producer, thought his writing talents would mesh well with the brothers. "I'd rather write for the

Barbary apes," Kaufman reportedly said. Yet he couldn't deny the exuberant reception they received from audiences. When he wasn't playwrighting, Kaufman was on the drama desk of the *New York Times*. He took a leave of absence for several months to write the book based on the Florida land boom. It was a situation made for caricature, if not for the satire which the playwright claimed "closed on Saturday night." That year of 1925 saw hucksters bringing golden-tongued William Jennings Bryan to Coral Gables to lecture by a lagoon. The bubble wouldn't begin to burst until September of 1926, when a hurricane swamped Miami and investors reconsidered the advisability of putting their money in Florida real estate.

Berlin composed the score. There would be no hit songs coming out of the show, though Berlin composed "Always" during that period and sang it for Kaufman, who was unenthused. The song was not written specifically for the show, though it could have been incorporated into the score. "Thinking back," Berlin wrote Groucho, "if I had put it in the show, I wonder who could have sung it outside of yourself."

Kaufman reputedly was indifferent to music, which he thought interrupted the flow of his words.

The dialogue the playwright built up could have been spoken by Kaufman himself. For a long time it was popularly conceded that Groucho had borrowed his stage walk and talk from Kaufman, a misapprehension Groucho finally felt compelled to refute. Yet, they did have the same rapid delivery and either one could have spoken the lines Kaufman so cleverly constructed:

Eight hundred beautiful residences will be built right here. They are as good as up. You can have any kind of house you want to. You can even get stucco. Oh, how you can get stucco. Now is the time to buy, while the new boom is on. Remember, a new boom sweeps clean, and don't forget the guarantees. If these lots don't double themselves in a year, I don't know what you can do about it.

Kaufman conceded in an interview with Flora Merrill of the *World* that all his characters talked like him in his early plays.

"You could take a line of dialogue and give it to anybody in the cast. I had ancient grandmothers making wisecracks and children of three uttering observations on theatrical conditions—it made no difference." Apparently, he was well suited to write for the Marxes, a situation he appreciated. "All my time is taken up telephoning to ask if they are well and to tell them to be careful crossing the street and to wear their overshoes. I predict that in 150 years the American will have vanished and there will be nothing but Marx Brothers ... I have secretly hoped that somebody would fall sick at the last minute of every play that I have had anything to do with. I am always up in every male part, but I know very well I'll never act ... I am supposed to resemble Groucho Marx and am understudying him. He says he never misses a performance."

Playing a social climber in *The Four Flusher* was a majestic thirty-five-year-old actress named Margaret Dumont. Kaufman saw her in the performance and thought she would be fine for the part of the society leader in *The Cocoanuts*.

She was born Marguerite Baker, the daughter of an Irish father and a French mother. The latter had fostered her daughter's ambition to be an opera singer. Taking her mother's maiden name, she made her debut at the Casino de Paree, where she was discovered by J. J. Shubert and signed to appear with Lew Fields in *The Girl Behind the Counter*. She was featured in two other Fields shows before meeting John Moller, Jr., a sugar heir. She left the stage when they married.

When her husband died eight years later, Margaret Dumont returned to the theater, appearing in two shows with George M. Cohan before playing in *The Four Flusher*.

The first out of town tryout, during the three weeks of October 27 to November 14, 1925, took place at the Tremont Theatre in Boston.

Miss Dumont, though not of the comedian's knockabout world, nevertheless knew it well because of her previous association with Fields and Cohan. She had a formidable appearance, though in actuality she was a gracious and friendly woman who wanted only to be liked. She was also extremely sensitive, which the brothers were quick to seize on.

When the moment arrived for Miss Dumont's entrance the first

135

night in Boston, she peered out from the wings waiting for her cue. The brothers had long since forgotten the script and were performing their own variations. Being a professional, she knew the action had to be advanced. She entered without the cue and waited cautiously for the brothers' next move. When Chico and Harpo saw her they made an impromptu exit. Groucho approached. "Ah, Mrs. Potter!" he said. "Won't you—lie down?"

Harpo's role was pretty well set, as was Chico's, though he had slept through the rehearsals and hadn't learned his lines. Groucho agonized, trying to remember where the best laughs came. "Do you remember what I said when I tripped you?" he worriedly asked Miss Dumont. She had been too busy trying to break her unexpected fall to remember. For the rest of the run, a stenographer sat in the wings taking notes.

Because of the brothers' outrageous antics and Groucho's dissecting of the material, the show was different every night. Miss Dumont, however, could expect that sometime during the proceedings, Groucho would stage whisper in a voice that could be heard in the lobby behind the second balcony, "My cue! My cue!" Harpo or Chico would thrust a billiard stick from the wings, always managing to hit Miss Dumont with it.

The brothers' manhandling of her would always meet with the same outraged reaction, but Miss Dumont learned early to gird her loins for the inevitable fray. Her first piece of armor was a whalebone body corset. She instructed costume designer Charles Le Maire that dainty chiffon and lace garments wouldn't do. To this stricture she added dresses with loose sleeves after Harpo stuck his foot up her arm. Long trains were discarded because Groucho had a habit of following her off the stage, leaping from one side of the train to the other. One night, he leaped on the train itself and Miss Dumont found herself on the stage in her whalebone corset.

During the course of one of her scenes with Groucho, a blonde came running across the stage in front of them, the horn-tooting Harpo in hot pursuit. It stopped the show, and the piece of business would be added to the knife-dropping routine as part of Harpo's bag of tricks.

The Cocoanuts did capacity business during its three weeks in Boston, as it did for two weeks in Philadelphia. It opened in New

York on December 8, 1925, at the Lyric Theatre. With advance word being so positive, the management set an unheard of eleven-dollar top for the opening. Still the crowds came, and the theater added 140 more seats to try to keep up with the demand.

Groucho was singled out by most reviewers for his performance. Brooks Atkinson of the *New York Times* wrote:

> As formerly, the voluble Groucho keeps up a heavy musketry of puns and gibes, twisting everything into the vulgar, unimaginative jargon of the shopkeeper. To him the eyes of his love "shine like the pants of a blue serge suit." When he steps down to the local jail to bail out a $2,000 prisoner, he finds a sale in progress and captures his prey for $1,900. And to him "jail is no place for a young man. There is no advancement." There are puns on a "poultry" $1,000 and a request to the lovers that they transfer their caresses to the "mushroom." Nothing is more amusing than the rapidity with which Groucho reduces everything to the stale bromides of the serious-minded merchant; and the speed with which he twists a burlesque probe for a missing shirt into a tailoring shop where he is measuring the victim for a suit of clothes and trying to sell him a pair of socks. All this with the seriousness of the instinctive man of business, bent upon doing his job well, and with such baffling twists in allusion that the audience is frequently three steps behind him.

So was Kaufman, who didn't recognize any of his lines. Groucho later said he was the only actor Kaufman would allow to ad lib, but in his case, Kaufman's permission was like reluctantly giving the hand of a pregnant daughter in marriage.

Groucho took peculiar pride in the effect his extemporizing had on his understudy. "His name was Liebowitz, and he was trying to keep up with the switches I made with the jokes. He went crazy. They had to come and take him away."

The show was firmly blocked in for a long run. Groucho's shrewd investments had resulted in a healthy stock portfolio. He finally felt secure enough in his vocation to set his family up in greater style. Ruth convinced him to hire live-in help, and a

German couple was engaged. The problem with their two-bedroom apartment was there was no room for the couple to live in. Some of the Broadway and literary crowd—including Eddie Cantor, Ring Lardner, Al Jolson, F. Scott Fitzgerald, and Herbert Bayard Swope— had already discovered Great Neck, a few miles away from Long Island Sound. The Marxes found a two-story stucco house at 21 Lincoln Road. Groucho paid twenty-seven thousand dollars cash for the ten-room house on its wooded acre.

This was perhaps the happiest period of his life. He was a famed Broadway star, circulating among fascinating friends, married to a beautiful woman who at the moment was not placing any unreasonable demands on him, since the bulk of them had been satisfied.

The Cocoanuts broke box office records at the Lyric, and remained strong through May of 1926. The New York Building Department forced the theater to remove the 140 additional seats, but later rescinded the order. Weekly grosses at the outset were well over thirty thousand dollars, dipping below that figure in late April. The hot summer adversely affected all Broadway shows, but *The Cocoanuts* had a late surge of business when Berlin interpolated a few songs. It closed in New York on August 7.

Harpo and Chico, at the end of the Broadway run, decided to trade parts for one performance. They invited close friends to see what they thought of the switch. None of them caught it, and wouldn't believe the two had played each other's roles even when they were told.

Offstage the two brothers looked very much alike, and Chico capitalized on it as much as he could, claiming to be Harpo when he was committing his many infidelities. Betty didn't catch on for a while.

"Chico was one-sixteenth of an inch taller than Harpo," Maxine Marx said, "but Harpo had a better carriage. Chico and Harpo were constantly betting each other about who was taller. They would take off their shoes and socks, and Daddy always won. One day, after innumerable bets, Harpo bet him again. Chico said, 'Haven't you had enough? I'm taller than you are. Face it.' So they took off their shoes again and Harpo was half an inch taller. Chico went berserk. He made Harpo take off his socks. He wanted to see if

138

Harpo had something between his toes to make him taller. Nothing. He measured again and Harpo was still half an inch taller. Chico brought the brothers in. They agreed with Harpo. So Chico had to pay up. Harpo told him years later that he had gone to a chiropractor and had stretched himself for the past twenty-four hours."

After a summer layoff, the road tour of *The Cocoanuts* began at the National Theatre in Washington the week of September 22. Margaret Dumont was quickly made aware that the train ride south wasn't removing her from her *Torquemadas*. The first night on the train, Chico and Harpo fixed up a series of five alarm clocks and hid them in her berth, set so they would go off at hourly intervals. They drove her insane, and for the first time Groucho was on her side. He was a semi-insomniac and had also been awakened. "The next time you try that," he told Harpo and Chico, "there'll be only two brothers left in the act."

When they played in Chicago, she returned to her dressing room to find her street dress and hat gone. She rushed out the stage door, following a redheaded figure wearing her stolen clothes. She caught up with the thief, who turned out to be Harpo. "Please take off my clothes," she said coldly. "Why, Maggie," Harpo said, "I didn't know you cared." A bit flustered, she said, "You know what I mean. Why did you steal my clothes?"

It was Halloween night, and Harpo had been invited to a party. "I'm going to a masquerade," he explained. "I'll have them back the first thing in the morning."

Miss Dumont wouldn't wear her stage dress home. She compromised by wearing her undergarments under her fur coat.

She hadn't been swayed by Groucho's gallantry on the train, since it coincided with his own interests.

In one scene, with Groucho on his knees, trying to convince the dowager he was in love with her, Miss Dumont was to rise haughtily. "Oh, can you come down a little bit?" Groucho said. "Just think—tonight, tonight when the moon is sneaking around the clouds I'll be sneaking around you." As she tried to withdraw, Groucho grabbed at her ankles, trying to upend her. She wisely avoided the entanglement, until one night in San Francisco when she was distracted for a moment and wound up on the floor.

"That was bad enough," she later told an interviewer, "but it was worse when I tried to get up. The corset was so long that I couldn't bend my knees, so I just sort of rocked back and forth. Groucho was laughing so hard that he'd try to get me half up and then laugh some more and I'd go down again."

When they got offstage, Miss Dumont was so furious she wouldn't speak to Groucho. He ran after her. "Ah, Maggie," he pleaded. "Don't get sore. It wasn't my fault. It was these new shoes I'm wearing."

Shortly thereafter, Zeppo married actress Marion Benda, née Bimberg, at a traditional Jewish ceremony on April 12. Harpo wore red carpet slippers with his white tie and tails. The brothers were playing in Newark at the time, but would be moving over to the Century Theatre for a brief New York reprise of the show. They played there from May 16 to June 4 and, in line with their standing, were assigned dressing rooms on the uptown side of the theater.

During this run Ruth gave birth to a daughter, Miriam, at Mt. Morris Park Sanitarium, on May 19. Groucho would later say that day was one of the happiest of his life.

While they waited for the third Broadway show to be readied, the Marx Brothers agreed to take a short vaudeville tour West. It was to be called "Spanish Knights" and would incorporate the chorus from The Cocoanuts; it was a departure for the brothers. They were returning to their origins with an added member of the entourage, Margaret Dumont.

The summer layoff of 1928 was to be a pastoral one for Groucho and his family at their house in Great Neck. It was planned as a break before the brothers went into rehearsal for their new show, Animal Crackers, in late August.

Nearby, many of the great literary talents of the time were spending their social weekends. Although Groucho was occasionally included in these entertainments, Harpo was more of a regular.

At the house of Herbert Bayard Swope, the executive editor of the World, gambling and croquet were the most favored pastimes, the weekend culminating in lavish Sunday suppers at which

Swope's wife Margaret presided. Guests at Ring Lardner's spent the bulk of their time in conversation.

Marc Connelly was a regular at these weekends. He'd been George Kaufman's collaborator in seven plays in the early 1920s, and the men had remained friendly. Groucho quoted Kaufman, who would recall the times Connelly and his former partner would meet on the street. Kaufman would ask, "How's your play?" Connelly would invariably answer, "Finished one act." Kaufman and his associates came to call him One-Act Connelly.

"Groucho wasn't particularly chummy with the crowd," Connelly said. "Harpo was around a lot more. He was a very sweet guy, much more naive and ingenuous than Groucho. We respected them all. Back then we knew the work of the Marx Brothers would endure longer than ours."

That July, Ruth and Groucho gave a party for their son Arthur, who was celebrating his seventh birthday. Chico and Betty had leased a house downhill from Groucho's in Great Neck Estates. Their daughter Maxine was an only child, and her summer was proving to be a solitary one, since there were no children in the immediate neighborhood for her to play with. Charlotte, a maternal cousin, was brought to stay with Maxine.

Minnie arrived at the party with both Maxine and Charlotte in tow. Maxine soon discovered there weren't enough settings at the table for the total number of guests. She asked Ruth about this oversight, and was tactlessly informed she was the extra guest.

Maxine started to leave. Minnie asked her, "Where are you going?"

"I'm going home," her granddaughter replied, "because Aunt Ruth said she doesn't have enough room for me."

Minnie, drawing herself up to her full five feet, finally had occasion to give vent to her disapproval of Ruth.

"If you don't have room for my grandchild, you don't have room for me," she said. "Come, Maxine, we're not wanted."

Ruth stood there, shaken, as her mother-in-law and the two little girls left.

It was a hot day, and since Minnie suffered from hypertension, Maxine was fearful her grandmother would take sick as they walked down the hill. Fortunately, a taxi came along and they rode the rest of the way to Chico's. When they arrived, Minnie called Mrs. Karp—Maxine's "Jewish Grandma" as opposed to Minnie, who was "the regular one"—and expressed her indignation at such treatment.

In the meantime, Groucho had sent Gummo—often the family mediator—to bring his mother and the two girls back.

"Come on, Ma," Gummo said. "Groucho isn't talking to Ruth and she's in tears and you're ruining the party. For Christ's sake, come on back."

"I will not go anywhere my grandchild isn't welcome," Minnie stiffly responded.

"Ruth is sorry," Gummo persisted.

"I'm not going back unless Maxine does," she said defiantly.

"Grandma," Maxine said, "I don't want to go back." The little girl was aware that Ruth didn't get along with her mother, and whatever their differences, they extended to Maxine. She could also see there truly weren't enough settings at the table, which was at worst a matter of poor planning. That Ruth was too rattled by the incident to simply place an extra plate is indicative of the eggshells she had to walk on around Minnie or Groucho or both.

Minnie had made Maxine the issue, and only after her granddaughter adamantly refused to return did Minnie consent to be driven up the hill. The party never recovered from the incident, nor were Minnie and her daughter-in-law drawn any closer.

The late summer of 1928 was spent in rehearsals for the new show, to be called *Animal Crackers*. The producers planned a short three-week tryout in Philadelphia before bringing it to New York.

These were extraordinarily prosperous times. The bull market had begun in March, 1928. The theater was at its peak. That year, 140 productions would reach the boards. The road was strong for theater, even if vaudeville was gasping for life. Only four theaters were left offering vaudeville without films: the New York Palace, Keith's Philadelphia, Chicago's Palace, and the Orpheum in Los Angeles. The most successful theatrical productions in New York would be *Diamond Lil* starring Mae West; *The Front Page* by Charles MacArthur and Ben Hecht; *Whoopee* with Eddie Cantor; *Earl Carroll's Vanities* with W. C. Fields; and *Animal Crackers*.

The production was the most ambitious to date if the playwrights and composers are any indication. Kaufman was joined by Morrie Ryskind, with whom he would soon win a Pulitzer Prize for *Of Thee I Sing*. Bert Kalmar and Harry Ruby, two ex-vaudevillians who had moved on to song writing, composed the theme most closely associated with Groucho, "Hooray for Captain Spaulding."

Margaret Dumont was again in the cast, this time playing a nouveau riche hostess honoring the African explorer, Spaulding. Also in the cast as another society hostess was Margaret Irving. She had worked for Harris and Berlin in the *Music Box Revue*, and had recently completed a multi-season run in the *Desert Song*, when Harris approached her about appearing as a straight woman in the new show. If she at first thought this was descending from the sublime to the ridiculous, she would soon discover she much preferred this forerunner to the theater of the absurd.

"I went up to Sam's office to sign my contract," Margaret Irving said. "Girls were coming out of his office, screaming at the top of their lungs. There was a policeman on horseback on the street. 'What's going on?' I asked him. He said, 'They're auditioning the chorus for the new Marx Brothers show and the boys are goosing the girls.' That was for starters. When I talked to Sam, he said, 'Dress yourself in tin drawers and have some fun.'"

The cast went into rehearsal. "It was chaotic. Those little devils wouldn't rehearse. You could never get them together at the same time. Zeppo would be at his broker or Chico would be over at Jamaica Race Track."

The show was set to open out of town September 24, 1928, at the Shubert Theatre in Philadelphia. Maggie Irving hadn't yet rehearsed her scenes with Groucho.

"Now look," she told him, "we open in a few minutes. Don't you think we ought to rehearse these lines?"

Groucho replied, "You don't expect to get cues from me tonight, do you?"

Maggie had never gone on cold before. She tried appealing to Groucho's better side. "Groucho, what am I going to do?"

"Oh," he answered, not unsympathetically, "just go along with the gag and see what happens. We'll probably have a better show."

The dressing rooms of the theater were a floor above the stage, but there was a changing room downstairs, where the brothers later in the run would crouch beneath the makeup shelf to offer brutally frank evaluations about the semidressed figures making their quick changes.

"I had a change coming up," Maggie Irving said. "These boys were rough in rehearsal. They'd throw you all over the place. I wanted to be at least covered up and not have any bloomers split, or anything like that. So the costumes were constructed on leotards. I had to put on a beautiful lavender dress with a lot of net tiers sewn on. I went into the quick change room. First I tried to get into my shoes. They had stuck wet paper in the slippers. Then I tried to get into the dress, and they had sewn up all the openings. I couldn't get it on through the shoulders nor through my legs. My cue was coming up, so I just put the dress around me, across my bust, and held it on the back with a pin.

"I sidled on stage. Those four wrestled with me to get me to show my back to the audience. You might win against one, but against four? The audience was howling. I got through the scene. As soon as I got into my next costume, Sam came over. 'Mag, what was the matter with the last dress? I didn't like it. I saw your bloomers sticking out.' I replied, 'They sewed the dress up. I couldn't get it on and I did the best I could.' "

In the next scene, Harpo, who had stolen one of the paintings, which was part of the mixup of the plot, tried to conceal it by rolling the canvas up and sticking it in his costume. Maggie Irving, playing one of the hostesses of the house party, walked in. She figured Harpo had the painting, and tried to get it away from him. Harpo departed from the script and started hitting her with the rolled-up painting. He then proceeded to pitch oranges and apples at her. She pitched them back, and the routine deteriorated into an impromptu baseball game, Harpo batting at the fruit with the canvas.

"The two of us were now running for bases," she recalled. "He finally caught me, and started to hit me with the painting."

The last scene of the show was the garden party, a costume ball from the period of Louis the Fifteenth. It was based on the Napoleon scene from *I'll Say She Is*, but was now known as the

DuBarry scene, set up as a gag sequence to bring on the ballet for the finale.

"Now I was wise to these guys," said Maggie Irving, who was playing DuBarry in the play within the play. "I knew I had to keep covered. This costume was also built on a leotard, fixed beautifully with white satin and lace, pearls and brilliants. Over it was an enormous hoop. With all this I wore a white wig. The hoop was too big to get into the dressing room, so they hung it on a piece of scenery on the side. Just before I went on, I just stepped into it and buckled it. If it got knocked off, there were a lot of ruffles underneath. I walked on in the spotlight, feeling very regal. I was on a second or two, and I heard somebody in the audience giggle. Had I picked up a brassiere on the hoop, or a pair of pants or something? I walked around trying to get a look to see what it was. But I still couldn't see. Finally I decided I wasn't going to stand there, and I sat down on this chair wearing this big hoop. A pair of hands came out from under the hoop. The hoop was so big I hadn't sensed there was anyone under there before. It was Harpo."

Groucho asked, "What will you have to eat ... Dubarries?" Harpo's hand shot out from under the skirt, holding out a telephone. Groucho took it and said, "Waiter, will you bring some ice water up to ten?"

In the same scene, the four brothers were supposed to make a play for DuBarry. The couch in which they attempted their mass seduction was weighted down with iron so that it wouldn't tip over.

On that opening night, the brothers rushed at Maggie Irving, who was seated on the sofa, and knocked her over its back. While she struggled to get up, her hoop wedged between the sofa and the scenery. The brothers described to the audience the spectacle behind the divan.

"It looks like a full moon," Chico observed.

"No," Groucho corrected, "it's a couple of footballs."

The brothers would try to discompose Maggie in subsequent performances. If, when they rushed her, Maggie didn't topple over the sofa, they would pick her up by the feet and throw her over. The going got so rough that management had three hoop skirts made for Maggie during the show's run.

Kalmar and Ruby threw a party after the opening night performance in their suite at the Warwick Hotel. It deteriorated into another Marx Brothers production. The activity started when Groucho and Chico, after eating, tossed their plates out the window into a courtyard.

"Why should some poor guy spend all night washing dishes?" Groucho asked. He proceeded to collect all crockery in the room and toss it out. Harpo, who arrived later, was thwarted in his attempt to defenestrate the upright piano.

The party ended early the following morning. When Ruby went downstairs, he was stopped by the manager. "Mr. Ruby, I must tell you that another guest complained about all the racket in your suite last night. He said that if it continued he would take his business elsewhere."

Ruby promised he would be more quiet. The following morning he was accosted by the same manager, who reported that the other guest, a manufacturer, had complained that the noise from Ruby's room was unbearable and he was checking out. Since Ruby had been quiet all night, he asked what the guest looked like.

"He's a thin little man with glasses and a big nose."

The travails of Maggie continued. On a subsequent night Harpo leaned over to her behind the sofa and asked in a stage whisper, "What's better than home cooking?" The other brothers, in the manner of a Greek chorus, intoned, "He asked what's better than home cooking."

"Mag," Harpo repeated, "what's better than home cooking?"

The brothers droned, "He asked again what's better than home cooking?"

Maggie, struggling to get up from under the hoop, answered irritably, "I don't know."

"She said she doesn't know what's better than home cooking," the brothers chanted.

Harpo's next line was heard by the whole audience. "Home humping."

A few days after the opening, Margaret Irving discovered she had a boil where Harpo had been hitting her with the rolled-up painting. "Hey, look, Harpo," she said. "Take it easy when you hit me with the painting. I've got a boil and it's hard to sit down."

146

Harpo nodded sympathetically, and informed his brothers of her affliction. When she walked on stage for her first scene, the brothers walked her over to the footlights, and started to singsong, "Maggie's got a boil on her ass . . . Maggie's got a boil on her ass."

"I couldn't help laughing," she recalled. "In fact, I got hysterical."

By the end of the run, she too had laid aside the script, and went along with the brothers' whimsy. They were now giving notice how they would discomfit her during succeeding performances.

Harpo told her, "We're going to goose you tonight, Mag."

"Go ahead," she replied. "I love it. I *love* it!"

They moved on to torment others in the cast when they discovered how unruffled Maggie Irving was by their behavior.

Their next target was Nettie, a girl in the chorus. As Maggie put it, "If you pointed a finger at her she'd scream at the top of her lungs."

Russell Markert was the show's choreographer, and he would soon be taking the intricate routines he developed to Radio City Music Hall, where he would help found the Rockettes.

"These girls would line up backstage and come out with their knees kicking," Maggie Irving said. "Harpo would get behind the girl with a yardstick and goose this kid." For the rest of the show's run, the girl would come on stage, hands fore and aft, protecting her vitals. The inventive Harpo invariably broke through her guard and would elicit another scream.

"What's the matter with that girl?" the house manager asked about the nervous, twitching Nettie. "She makes a different kind of entrance every night."

Minnie and Frenchy proudly arrived in full evening clothes for the show's New York opening, October 23, 1928, at the Forty-fourth Street Theatre. Groucho, preferring not to stay in the dressing room, was mingling with the crowd in the lobby when he spotted his parents.

"Frenchy," he said, "I don't like the shirt you're wearing."

"It's a fine shirt," his father protested.

"Don't like it," Groucho repeated, as he somehow managed to

tear it off his father without removing the coat. Frenchy looked proudly at his son. "That's my Groucho."

Margaret Irving's mother always traveled with her daughter, and the brothers were fond of her. Mrs. Irving was hosting a theater party opening night, wearing a grand black gown with a full cape. Groucho wormed his way under the cape, pretending he was a photographer holding a black cloth over an imaginary camera. "Smile, please," he shouted into the back of Mrs. Irving's knees.

Backstage, a confrontation of another sort was going on. Walter Winchell, critic and columnist for the *Graphic*, had been barred from reviewing Shubert openings. "I don't mind missing the openings," Winchell wrote in his column. "I can always go the second night and see the closings."

On different occasions, as retaliation against real and imagined slights, the Shuberts had barred Percy Hammond and Charles Collins in Chicago; Philip Hale and George Holland in Boston; Goodman Ace in Kansas City; Heywood Broun, Woollcott, Leonard Lyons, and Gilbert Gabriel in New York.

Sam Harris requested the ban against Winchell be lifted. The Shuberts refused. Then the Marx Brothers issued an ultimatum. If Winchell weren't allowed to review the show, they wouldn't perform. The Shuberts answered by hiring detectives to patrol the theater to make sure Winchell didn't get in. Other critics had invited him to come as their guest, but he had refused such a simple solution.

George Holland had gotten around the Shubert edict by having himself appointed a Boston fire marshal, inspecting the Shubert theaters for fire violations only on opening nights.

The Marx Brothers smuggled Winchell in through a dressing room window, hid him in a shower bath, and made him up as a hunchback with crepe whiskers. One look at him and they knew the disguise wouldn't work. It was simply too obvious. They then made Winchell up to look like Harpo, and passed him off to the guards as a standby. Groucho explained, "Harpo sometimes throws a fit, and we need to keep an understudy ready at all times." The Shuberts never learned how Winchell had covered the opening.

The brothers had reached such a point of popularity that the opening of their third Broadway play had taken on the characteristics of a media happening. There was a great flow of human movement, with one destination in mind.

Brooks Atkinson, in his *New York Times* review the following day, analyzed it all:

> Here come the Marx brothers again with their uproarious, slapstick comedy in a new fury of puns and gibes by George S. Kaufman and Morrie Ryskind, entitled "Animal Crackers" and displayed at the Forty-fourth Street Theatre last evening. And here come their merry audiences who chuckle and roar at Groucho's sad, glib, shrapnel waggery, at Harpo's mummery, which is as broad as it is long, and at Chico's bare-faced jocosity. For if anything is more remarkable than the outrageous buffoonery of this team of cut-ups, it is their fabulous popularity.
>
> Speculators swore they could get as much as $100 for two tickets to the opening performance. And most of those who had squeezed into the bulging theatre last evening were obviously in the flattering mood of expecting the Marx brothers to redeem in one evening all the dullness of the current theatrical season. That would be a large order. However, those who remembered that the Marx brothers are not supermen but merely the maddest troupe of comedians of the day, limited in their vein, and compelled to appear in a routine musical comedy—those who were sane were not disappointed. . . . Delivering his mad-cap chronicle of an African exploration, Groucho touches on nearly every topic of the day and makes some of the most insane verbal transitions heard since his last appearance . . .
>
> They are nihilists—these Marx boys. And the virtue of their vulgar mountebankery is its bewildering, passing, stinging thrusts at everybody in general, including themselves. . . . Those who remember Groucho as the Little Corporal will know how comic he can be as the King.

Maggie Irving told of the constant undercurrent of excitement during the show's run, the expectation of the cast at every performance that something unexpected was about to happen. "In

149

New York, plays would get dull. But actors would be at the theater every night at seven, even if they didn't have to come on until ten. They were afraid they'd miss something. It was fun and laughter, and so spontaneous. It couldn't be manufactured."

Since the show was doing great business, Sam Harris had taken a month off in Florida. The day of his return, he arrived at the theater toward the end of a performance. Many thought the gentle Harris was standoffish, unaware that in fact he was merely hard of hearing. The Marx Brothers capitalized on his hearing problem.

The ballet was on with chorus girls strewing roses about them prior to the entrance of the Four Musketeers. Most of the stage was dark.

Above the music, the audience heard Groucho. "Sam, I think you should buy stock in Silver Rod Drug Stores." Harris's voice, like that of many deaf people, was equally loud. "I don't *want* any drug store stock." Then Harpo said, "Well now, you know there's a gold mine in Arizona." "You're crazy not to go into this," Chico said. "The gold is there on the ground just waiting to be picked up." To which Groucho added, "You didn't tell me you have to lean over to pick it up."

Gradually the brothers had pushed Sam onto the stage in the dark. The cue came on for the brothers' song and five men were now in the spotlight, four men in costumes from Louis the Fifteenth's court and a sunburned man in a Palm Beach suit.

"We're four of the three musketeers," they began to sing. Harris was forced to sing along with them, the fifth of the four of the three.

Their zaniness was contagious. Everyone wanted to get into the act. Maggie Irving, now Mrs. James, recalled the finale of the first act one matinee with the whole cast singing, "Hooray for Captain Spaulding."

During the song, Margaret Dumont was supposed to open a big chest the explorer, played by Groucho, had brought back from Africa. Then she would tell of the ivory and precious stones inside. When she opened the chest, a parade of Grouchos walked out of it. All the musicians and stage hands, unbeknownst to her, had been made up as Groucho, and the crew had cut a hole in the floor of the stage so that the trick could be played on her.

On another occasion, the brothers were playing cards backstage. Maggie Irving, who would later tend bar for the members of the Thanatopsis poker club in an upstairs room at the Algonquin Hotel, was nothing if not accommodating, and she would often sit with the brothers, usually rubbing Chico's neck.

The doorman interrupted the game one night. He addressed the brothers. "There's a gentleman outside who wants to see you."

Groucho said, "Bring him in."

In walked a little man straight out of Bond Street, sporting hat, cane and derby. He waited to be acknowledged, but nobody paid him any attention. Shuffling from one foot to the other, he tentatively cleared his throat. Still nobody paid any attention. Finally he spoke up.

"I beg your pardon, gentlemen."

The brothers gave him a dead-pan look.

"I represent Sir Oswald Stoll at the Palladium in London. Could you gentlemen open there, say January the fourth?"

The brothers nodded slightly to each other. Then, dropping their cards, they attacked the little man, stripping him of his shoes, pants, garters, socks, coat, tie, shirt, and derby. The puzzled victim, who'd placidly let them have their way with him, was unceremoniously dropped onto the floor wearing nothing but his drawers.

The boys were back at the card table. "What did you bid?" Harpo asked.

"One spade," said Chico.

The man picked himself up, put on his clothes, and again cleared his throat.

"I beg your pardon, gentlemen."

The brothers looked up again with equally dead-pan eyes. The man repeated the reason for his visit, whereupon the brothers laid down their cards, again undressed him, and dropped him to the floor. The man put his clothes on. "Good-bye, gentlemen," he said as he walked out.

Groucho worked another gag on backstage visitors. When anybody was introduced to him, he would ignore the name and talk to the person as if the man were an insurance agent.

"Now I want to buy a $50,000 double indemnity policy,"

Groucho would say. "How much will it cost?" No matter what the visitor answered, Groucho would continue with his line of questioning, inquiring about the benefits one insurance company offered over another.

Gummo, who often visited backstage, decided to get back at Groucho. He introduced him to a fellow named Moe Levinson.

When Groucho started on his routine, Levinson replied, "You're only kidding. You don't really want a policy."

"Sure I do," Groucho insisted.

Levinson took a policy out of his pocket which was already made out. "Just sign the form and you're all set."

"You son of a bitch!" Groucho yelled at Gummo. He took to the stage ahead of his cue, and stayed there. Every time he'd look in the wings, he'd see Levinson standing there, smiling, waving the policy at him. Groucho finally bought the policy.

The only time Groucho seemed to let up on propagating his frenetic, lunatic image was around children. With them, he was especially considerate. His niece, Maxine, recalls taking friends of hers backstage.

"I find myself saying the same things to children that Uncle Groucho said to my little friends. I still get the same kind of giggling response. The first thing he'd ask the kids if they were married or engaged. Then he'd ask, "How old are you—forty-five?"

"No," the child would laugh, "I'm *five.*" For some reason this would make Groucho laugh.

One night, when Minnie was visiting backstage, Chico was late for the performance. His disappearance in Detroit must have been uppermost in Minnie's mind when he finally appeared. She was enraged. For the first time in many years Minnie slapped Chico smartly across the face. "How dare you come in late!" she cried. "That's cheating."

Chico rubbed his jaw. "Minnie, that hurt." It's debatable whether the tiny woman could have inflicted much physical damage, but the emotional hurt in a man already in his forties must have been considerable.

He was Minnie's favorite, after all, and he had disappointed her again, not to mention his brothers. Margaret Irving, newly admitted to the Marx circle, discerned something in the relationships of the boys and their mother that others interviewed for this book never mentioned. "Harpo was more of a mother's boy than any of them," she recalled. "Not that he was her favorite. But he was awfully devoted to her, much more so than the others. I was always impressed by the united front they all showed to the world. They were a happy and loving family."

Chico's wife, Betty, recalled one occasion when the boys went from Philadelphia to see their parents, who were on holiday in Atlantic City. "There were these five brothers with their arms around their father and mother, kissing and hugging. This was typical of the boys. As old as they were, they still kissed their father."

Heartwarming as their displays of affection toward Frenchy might be, the way they kissed their mother revealed more about the brothers' characters. Harpo was joyful and exuberant, as he was with the whole world. Chico was casual and cavalier. Groucho was dutiful.

"Minnie lived in Jamaica," Betty said, "and Groucho lived in Great Neck, but he went to see her every day. He was a very good son. Chico wouldn't go. I'd have to remind him. 'You haven't seen your mother. Let's go see her.' When Chico went, if she made a touch, he'd pull out whatever he had in his pocket and give it to her, and not give it another thought. With Groucho it was different. If he gave her a hundred dollars, he'd give it with a lecture."

Minnie was now gambling for high stakes with the neighborhood ladies. "She was very cute about it," Betty recalled, "when she came to me one day and said she'd lost her pocketbook and she needed two hundred dollars. She'd lost the money gambling, but she didn't want to say that. I gave her the money."

The women she was playing with were very good poker players, and Minnie's major weakness was refusing to fold with mediocre cards and insisting on calling the other ladies' hands, "to keep them honest."

She didn't become as compulsive about gambling as her son Chico. Rather, sitting at the card table for hours was a way to pass the time. The ginger-ale business didn't have the appeal of show business, and she looked for other distractions. The Marx Brothers had hired a chauffeur for her and Frenchy, and in this family retainer she noted a raw talent which she thought she could nurture into stardom. She couldn't, perhaps because her heart wasn't in it.

Yet, Minnie Marx remained the eternal coquette, whose greatest artistry was in the con, which she continued to practice. The newspapermen she was exposed to through her sons were her biggest patsies. They manufactured her into the greatest stage mother of them all.

One wonders what value she placed on this role, or what she truly thought of her sons' accomplishments. One day, she walked into the jewelry store of George Davidoff, near her Richmond Hill house. She had brought a string of colored beads to be restrung.

After revealing her identity to Davidoff, she explained, "These beads have great value to me. I feel very sentimental about them. I don't think they cost more than a dollar. But my sons bought them for me, and I treasure them very much."

Davidoff said he would treat them as if they were the most precious diamonds. Minnie said she wanted them back as soon as possible. Months went by, and Minnie never returned to pick them up. After her death, Davidoff gave the beads to Aunt Hannah.

CHAPTER SEVEN

They made me sound as if I'd been castrated.
Tallulah Bankhead on talking pictures.

During their sixty-five years acquaintanceship, Groucho and Charles Chaplin may have seen each other a dozen times. On one of those occasions, Chaplin confessed, "I wish I could talk like you."

None of Chaplin's later pictures enjoyed the extraordinary success of his silent movies. The Little Tramp, through his comedy and his pathos, had moved the world. When Chaplin began to talk on screen, the audience wasn't as receptive. The self-pitying timbre in his voice gave the uneasy impression that no one felt sorrier for Chaplin than himself.

To compound the problem, Chaplin's social conscience as typified by the messages of his talking pictures was naive and simplistic. "When he found a voice to say what was on his mind," director Billy Wilder said, "he was like a child of eight writing lyrics for Beethoven's Ninth."

The Marx Brothers weren't silent picture comedians, as *Humorisk* so clearly proved. Their métier was the talkies, and they had no need to rely on the visual tricks their predecessors in the medium had performed. They were stage-trained performers, and voice was the most important component of the theater. Other stage actors had to modulate their voices for films. If the theater audience could move in on a stage actor like a movie camera, the acting would become unreal, the projection of the voice too loud, and the movement too broad to be believable. The Marx Brothers were purposely outlandish and outsize. They were the exception to the many recruits from Broadway. The medium was to adapt to them.

Variety in March of 1926 reported that the team was negotiating with First National to make a picture in New York, the screenplay to be written by Will Johnstone. Nothing came of it. Two years later, a test was made for United Artists, which planned to make a film of *The Cocoanuts.* The offer wasn't acceptable. The William Morris Agency then submitted the property and the brothers to Paramount for $75,000. Walter Wanger, a young Dartmouth graduate who represented the studio in New York, took the offer to Adolph Zukor. The studio head found the price excessive. A meeting was set up with Zukor, Chico, and the agent.

When they were introduced, Chico said, "Mr. Zukor, this is one of the greatest moments of my life. You're one of the great showmen of the world. When I think of what you've done for pictures . . . of what you did for Mary Pickford . . . I can't tell you what a thrill this is."

"So what's the trouble between Walter and you?" Zukor asked.

"All our lives," Chico continued, "we've worked to perfect this one show. The best things we've ever done are in it. We want to make a picture for you. We'll give you all our material and all our services for only $100,000."

"Walter," Zukor said to Wanger, "what's wrong with that?"

Wanger could only marvel at Chico's maneuvering. The meeting had been called to persuade him to lower his terms, and he'd walked off with $25,000 more than the amount Zukor originally found exorbitant.

The brothers were being paid $2,000 each a week during their current Broadway run in *Animal Crackers,* and now they would be getting more than twice that amount for a couple of months of moonlighting. Preparations were made to film at Paramount's studio in Astoria, Long Island. Built in 1919 as the original East Coast headquarters of Paramount's forerunner company, Famous Players-Lasky Corporation, the studio had recently been fitted for sound recording.

Paramount, coming late to sound pictures, was operating the studio at double time. Features were shot during the week on the single soundstage, tests filmed at night, short subjects were made on weekends. The brothers would be filming four days a week, taking Wednesdays off to play their matinee at the Forty-fourth Street Theatre. Other Broadway performers recruited to movies— Rudy Vallee, Eddie Cantor, and Alice Brady among others—were caught up in the same routine.

Paramount had scheduled fifteen talking pictures and fifty shorts for the calendar year of 1929, and *The Cocoanuts* was among the first to be filmed. *The Cocoanuts* was also to be among the first screen musicals, which explains in part its disjointedness. Oscar Shaw and Mary Eaton of the Broadway stage were billed above the Marx Brothers. Shooting time was limited to a month at most, because of Paramount's ambitious production plans for the year.

Robert Florey and Joseph Santley were hired as directors. Florey, who'd arrived in the United States from his native France in 1921, had been befriended by Charles Chaplin in 1927, who had been impressed by *The Death of a Hollywood Extra,* an experimental film Florey made with Slavko Vorkapich and Gregg Toland on a ninety-dollar budget. He would later recruit Florey to act as associate director for *Monsieur Verdoux.*

Santley was a former dancer who had gone on to stage several Broadway musicals. His primary duties were to rehearse the dialogue and to put the chorus girls through their paces. His choreography was reminiscent of Busby Berkeley's, who had worked in *Earl Carroll's Vanities* the previous season.

The first indication of Groucho's obstinacy came in reaction to Florey's request that he do away with the greasepaint mustache. Because of its high varnish content, the greasepaint was glossy and created a shiny spot on Groucho's face when photographed from certain angles. Groucho's only concession was to allow the makeup man to dust the mustache with talcum to remove the glare.

Florey wanted to take some background scenes in Florida, but he was overruled by producer Monta Bell, who was also the East Coast production head for Paramount. "Why use real backgrounds when one of the leading characters wears an obviously fake mustache?" Bell asked.

The upper floor of the two-story studio was converted into a beach. The rest of the building was taken up by the principals, show girls and chorus, and four dancing troupes who rehearsed simultaneously and rattled the walls of the drafty building.

Because of the loss of mobility, Florey had five cameras shooting scenes at the same time. One was for a master shot, another for medium shots, and the remaining three for closeups.

Since the brothers had performed their parts hundreds of times, Florey didn't rehearse them. The picture was to be a slightly enlarged interpretation of a stage musical, although much more static than any Broadway audience would permit from the Marx Brothers.

One of Florey's greatest frustrations was getting the brothers on the set at the same time. They were a bucket of unmanageable eels. Once they were gathered, however, the filming went smoothly, and the picture was finished within schedule.

The story line involved many maps, charts, newspapers, and other paper which crackled like a forest fire when recorded. The solution was to wet all these paper props, and they resembled Claes Oldenburg sculptures when they appeared on film.

Florey had developed overhead shots in his experimental films over the years, and as he saw the chorus in one of the routines form a circle of petals around a fountain, he instructed cameraman Joseph Ruttenberg to shoot the scene straight down.

Mordaunt Hall's review in the *New York Times* would take note of the "dainty dances . . . this sequence proved so engaging that it elicited plaudits from many in the jammed theatre" when the picture opened.

While the brothers were filming on weekdays and performing on the stage, Gummo was otherwise occupied. He had proved to be as adamant a holdout to marriage as Harpo. Now, at thirty-six, Gummo had decided to take the step. The brothers were playing a

Saturday matinee when he married Helen Von Tilzer on March 16. Press reports described the groom as being "in the dress business, being of the five Marx Brothers, four of whom are the three musketeers." The bride was identified as the niece of the prominent songwriting family, when she was in fact the widowed daughter-in-law of one of them. She had been pregnant when her first husband, R. Russell Von Tilzer, was killed in an accident. After their daughter.Kay was born in early 1927, the Von Tilzer family persuaded the girl to give up her baby and make a new unencumbered life for herself.

Shortly before the *The Cocoanuts* was released, the brothers returned to vaudeville, playing four weeks in New York houses. On April 14 they opened at the Palace for the astronomical sum of $7,000 a week, the highest salaried act ever to play the Palace.

On May 3, 1929, the world premiere of *The Cocoanuts* was held at the Rialto in New York. The brothers, playing at the Riverside in New York, were unable to attend. The feedback they received from Minnie was encouraging. The exhibitors were more subdued. The love team of Oscar Shaw and Mary Eaton didn't register. The musical numbers were an intrusion. Robert Florey's overhead photography of the dance routines was one bright spot. As for the brothers, they spoke too rapidly, and much of the dialogue was lost.

Two days passed before the brothers could see for themselves. Groucho took in the Sunday matinee, which left him disconsolate. The theater was merely half-filled, noisy children running up the aisles to the lobby in mid-picture to buy candy. He hadn't seen such an indifferent audience since his early days in vaudeville.

"We have to buy the picture back," Groucho told Chico. "It's going to ruin our careers."

By the time they consulted with Wanger, the first reviews were in and unanimously enthusiastic about the film. The exhibitors who formerly complained about the rapid talk of the brothers noticed they were getting repeat business. People were coming back two or three times to catch the dialogue.

The picture went on to play throughout the country, and proved to be one of the top grossers for Paramount that year.

Small matter that the picture was little more than a filmed

version of a stage play, and that the brothers were hamstrung by the lack of mobility. They were winners, and proven movie stars. Their mother had lived to see her sons triumph in yet another medium.

Groucho had ample reason to feel cocky as the summer of 1929 approached. He had almost $250,000 invested in the stock market. Playing golf one day with producer Max Gordon at a Long Island country club, the two men talked about their good fortune as they strolled down the fairway.

"This is the life," Gordon told him. "Here I am, a nobody. My real name is Salpeter, and I'm just a kid from Rivington Street. But I can spend a fine day playing golf because I already made three thousand dollars in the market this morning. Groucho, how long has this been going on?"

Although Groucho could count his blessings, he wasn't the type to recite them. He didn't offer a reply, content to share his friend's good feelings.

In those days, he had more than his quota of friends to share them with. There were great and intellectually stimulating men like Eddie Cantor, Ring Lardner, and George Kaufman. A newcomer in his circle at Great Neck was Nunnally Johnson, a Southern writer who was as droll as Groucho was wry.

Groucho had recently bought a 1929 Packard, a 6-40 Runabout, one of the classic cars of the period. "It was a pretty fancy car," he recalled. "Good for necking." Two passengers sat up front. The interior was upholstered in handcrushed leather, the flooring was carpeted in deep pile rugs, and the dashboard was of burled walnut. The luggage compartment was between the front and rumble seats, and on both sides of the auto were narrow lighted openings, each large enough to hold a golf bag.

Groucho would motor down to his broker's Great Neck branch and where he would spend hours monitoring the visible appreciation of his holdings.

His family life was reasonably happy, although Groucho made a much better father than he did a husband. Arthur was eight and growing like a weed, and Miriam at two was beginning to discover the world around her. Too soon, the summer would end and

Animal Crackers would go on an eight-month tour before the filming of their second picture for Paramount began.

Groucho went to see Minnie one day in late summer. He knew his mother was upset about the lawsuit Helen, Gummo's wife, had brought against the parents of her first husband to regain custody of Kay, now nineteen months old, claiming she had been unduly influenced when she gave the child to her former in-laws. Minnie was extremely critical of Helen for giving up the child in the first place. "You can't tell me she didn't know what she was doing," she told Chico's wife Betty. Minnie felt the publicity didn't reflect well on Helen's character. The long custody suit would end with Kay joining the Marx family and Gummo adopting her as his own. Minnie now had another daughter-in-law besides Ruth to give short shrift to.

Minnie seemed to have lost her vibrancy. She obviously wasn't feeling well.

"What's wrong?" Groucho asked her.

"I think I'm closing up shop soon," she said. "The show is almost over." The mixed euphemisms, an amalgam of Frenchy's tailoring days and her sons' career, nevertheless conveyed the point.

Minnie had never talked so explicitly about oncoming death and it made Groucho uneasy. "Don't be silly," he told her. "You'll outlive us all."

On Friday, September 13, Minnie and Frenchy dropped in on a rehearsal of *Animal Crackers*. The show was scheduled to open its road tour on September 22 at the Shubert Theatre in Boston. She playfully went up to Leo and asked for a job in the chorus.

"I'm sorry," Chico answered. "You're not old enough."

A reporter was at the theater. Overhearing the exchange, he asked Minnie if she were planning to travel with the show. "No," she replied, "I've done enough trouping. But I'll sneak in every once in a while to see that they give a good show."

Zeppo invited his parents to come home with him after rehearsal for an early dinner. The company turned out to be congenial and the food was delicious. Minnie had two helpings of everything. After dinner entertainment was a quick game of Ping-Pong.

Chico and Betty left the theater to spend an Indian summer

weekend at The Dells, Adolph Zukor's 760-acre estate north of New City, New York. To the public, Groucho might have been considered the central figure in the act, but a businessman like Zukor had different criteria. Chico was the team's wheeler and dealer, and the person to cultivate.

"Adolph's son Eugene took us up in his car," Betty said. "We were shown to a bedroom-sitting room, with a valet for Chico and a maid for me. It was a fascinating place. Everybody was given a dozen golf balls and a caddy. Zukor had his private zoo there too, and wild animals roamed the estate.

"When we met for dinner, there was a lackey standing behind every other chair. That's all they did. We passed the food among ourselves."

Meanwhile, Minnie and Frenchy had left Zeppo's. As their driver was crossing the Queensboro bridge on the way back to Great Neck, Minnie had a seizure.

"I'm having a stroke!" she told Frenchy. One side of her face felt numb. She asked her husband for a mirror, wanting to see what was happening to her. Frenchy instructed the driver to return to Zeppo's. After calling a doctor, Zeppo phoned his brothers.

Harpo was the first to arrive. Groucho, having to make the longer trip from Great Neck, reached the house somewhat later. Back at the Zukors', the group was watching a movie in the projection room. A page came in and whispered something to Chico, who left the room with him. He returned a short while later.

"What's wrong?" Betty asked.

"Mother took sick," he said. "I've got to go now. You come tomorrow."

Minnie died at ten that night. The cause of death, according to the attending physician, was a cerebral hemorrhage and apoplexy. She was sixty-five.

She was buried at Woodlawn Jewish Cemetery. Woollcott accompanied the family to the burial. On a nearby tombstone was the name of Tom O'Flaherty. "There's a spy in this cemetery," he told Groucho.

Minnie's boys left for Boston within the week, each with his own thoughts of what their mother had done for them . . . and to them.

162

* * *

The week after Minnie's funeral, the brothers opened their road tour at the Shubert Theatre in Boston. There had been a recession in stock prices in March and declines in certain stocks at various times throughout the spring and summer, but it hadn't affected the majority of investors. On Thursday, October 24, the market opened badly and prices plummeted. The bull market was broken.

Max Gordon called Groucho. "Marx? This is Salpeter. The jig is up."

Groucho quickly went to his attorney, Morris Ernst, with his investment list. He, like many others, had bought on margin. The stocks were inflated in value, and had been bought for as little as ten percent down, with the bulk of the purchase price financed by brokers' loans. As stock prices slumped, he was required to put up additional margin. He had to sell the stock he owned outright to cover the margin calls. Within two days he lost his total life's savings.

Groucho blamed part of the debacle on his friend Eddie Cantor, who advised him to invest in Goldman Sachs when Groucho visited him backstage at the Palace. Groucho bought two hundred shares for over $40,000. He wrote about it in *Groucho and Me* thirty years later.

Cantor read the book and declined the belated honor. In a letter to Groucho he said the only Goldman and Sachs he knew were partners in the rag business, until Goldman caught Sachs with his wife, which placed a strain on their relationship until Sachs caught Goldman with *his* wife. Cantor also disputed Groucho's version as to who was playing at the Palace. He insisted it was the Marx Brothers who were there, because he distinctly remembered seeing Zeppo in the prop room. He added that Zeppo was only a baby in his nurse's arms at the time, getting milk . . . not from the bottle.

Despite his recent affluence, Groucho had always scrimped, in marked contrast to the free-spending Chico. "He saved every nickel," Chico said, "and look what happened. I had fun, and he didn't, and now we're both the same. He's starting from scratch with me."

Groucho, personally insecure, was now financially insecure too.

163

It was a nerve-racking combination that turned him into a life-long insomniac.

That the brothers were able to open at the Maryland Theatre in Baltimore, three days after the crash, is a tribute to their resiliency. Groucho was deeply touched when Sam Harris offered to advance him money, though he rejected the kindness. He was still part of a headliner team and he would have to make do with the handsome salary he was getting. So on with the show.

Nettie, the chorus girl, was still screaming at the top of her lungs at Harpo's goosing attempts when *Animal Crackers* went on the road. She had, however, developed a fairly impenetrable defense mechanism simply by giving him a wide berth.

The company gave a midnight benefit performance in Kansas City for Actors Equity, which jammed the Shubert Theatre with townspeople and actors and vaudevillians playing the same city.

The chorus had high-kicked its way on stage when Harpo approached Margaret Irving, who was standing next to him in the wings. He was looking at the scenery flats, secured against a side wall by a steel-covered stage brace. A hook on the brace was attached to a steel ring firmly embedded on the back wall.

"Mag," Harpo said thoughtfully, "how far do you think that stage brace stretches out?"

"I don't know," she replied. "Probably forty or fifty feet."

"Well, I made a bet and I'm going to win it," Harpo said. He unsnapped the stage brace and handed one of the ends to Miss Irving. It was dark, and she realized that Harpo had pulled the hook on stage. Groucho was in the middle of one of his routines when the audience's laughter rose higher than ever. He might have thought he was being exceptionally funny, but in fact the audience was laughing at Harpo, who had stalked on stage holding the stage brace by the hook and was preparing his assault on the hapless Nettie.

Nettie spun around at the last moment. "Don't, for God's sake," she screamed, "it's for sweet charity!" Even at a benefit there would be no dispensation.

Margaret Dumont in real life matched the fastidiousness of her stage character. Every night after the performance, she would stay behind in her dressing room until the theater was deserted, brushing her costumes and wrapping them in tissue paper, so that they would be just so for the following day.

"She packed everything as if she were going to Europe every night," Margaret Irving recalled. "Then she'd be the first one at the theater the next day, to see that everything was perfect. She'd take great pains in making herself up and getting dressed, and she'd be ready to go on long before the performance actually started."

While on the road, Miss Irving and her mother took adjoining hotel rooms with Miss Dumont. "She was a charming woman," Maggie Irving recalled, "and my mother got along very well with her. So did I." The three women would frequently unwind together over coffee after a night's performance.

As they got into the elevator of the Indianapolis hotel they were staying at one night, they ran into Groucho. Wearing a tailored grey suit and without his mustache, he looked like a successful traveling salesman. He nodded to the three women, but didn't speak.

All four got off on the fifth floor, where their rooms were. Halfway down the corridor, a moose of a house detective stood against the wall, looking skeptically into an open door.

As the group passed him, Groucho asked, "What's going on here?"

Inside the hotel room was a group of four men playing cards. The detective said, "I'm watching these men to make sure nothing happens."

Groucho bristled. "Now look. It's very strange. You're so strict in some things and lax in others."

"What do you mean?" the cop asked, his temper rising.

"Here are four guys playing a very innocent game," Groucho said. "There are no women that I can see. They're not drinking. There's no loud talk. And you treat them like criminals. And yet you'll harbor the best-known hustler this side of the Atlantic Ocean."

"What did you say?"

"The best-known hustler this side of the Atlantic Ocean. She's known on every boat going between here and Europe."

By now the detective's ears were wiggling. The three women had gone on to their rooms.

"Now, look," Groucho said, "I have a suite in this hotel—my family and I—and I don't intend to stay in a hotel that harbors a woman of that character."

"Who is she?"

"Didn't you notice the three women in the hall just now?" Groucho asked. "She was the one in the middle, in the fur coat."

"She doesn't look like a hustler to me," the detective said.

"You haven't been around much," Groucho said. "These women look like queens. If you don't believe me, why don't you check with the Marx Brothers? They're staying here too."

"Marx Brothers?" the detective said. "Never heard of 'em."

"Then believe *me*. If that woman is still here tomorrow, I for one am going to check out."

The detective left the card game and camped outside Margaret Dumont's door until morning.

The next day was a matinee, and the two Margarets, Irving and Dumont, left the hotel with the former's mother at eleven-thirty in the morning for an early lunch. After the matinee, they shopped and had an early dinner before going back to the theater for the evening's performance. They had their usual cup of coffee afterwards.

They got off on the fifth floor and proceeded to their rooms. The detective was present, casting fish eyes at Miss Dumont.

"Good evening," she said.

The cop was silent.

"It's certainly a wonderful thing," she went on, "to get into a hotel where you can get a good night's rest."

The detective kept his silence his look distinctly unfriendly. Miss Dumont, it was apparent to Maggie Irving, was getting a touch nervous.

"I've been all over, you know," Miss Dumont rattled on, "Europe and all. This is one of the quietest and nicest places I've ever seen. It certainly shows that you know how to run a place."

The detective's expression didn't change.

Miss Dumont fumbled for her key, while Miss Irving and her mother looked on. The cop still hadn't said a word.

Miss Dumont managed to get the door open. Out walked Groucho in his stage makeup, wearing pajamas and carrying a douche bag.

"You sneak!" he snapped at Miss Dumont. "I don't know why I put up with this."

She flushed red with embarrassment. Turning to the detective, she fluttered, "Well, that's Groucho. He does these things." Her eyes started to water. "It just hurts me terribly."

Groucho, by this time, had pressed the elevator button and asked to be taken to the eighth floor. The elevator operator, seeing a man in his pajamas and carrying a douche bag, became suspicious. "There's something wrong here," he told Groucho. "I have to get the detective." He closed the elevator door without letting Groucho on, and rode down to the lobby, where the house detective usually sat.

As Miss Dumont opened the door, the detective noticed a man lying on the bed in his shorts, and reading the *Racing Form*, an Italian hat over his black wig. "Oh," Chico said, as he got up. "You got another guy. Well, I'll be back in half an hour." He passed Groucho in the hall. The elevator operator, having failed to find the house dick in the lobby, closed the door on Chico and went to get the housekeeper.

Now milling in the hall outside the open door were Groucho, Chico, Miss Irving, her mother, and several other hotel guests who had been drawn by the commotion. The closet door then opened and out walked a bare-chested Zeppo, a hotel towel wrapped around his middle, his thighs wrapped in paper laundry bags. He said to Miss Dumont, "Just because I'm the youngest, you take my money, but you never get around to me."

Miss Dumont turned to the detective. "Now that's Zeppo. He's right. He *is* the youngest. They're making him do these things. You know, there are four of them."

For the first time the detective spoke. "Where's the other one?"

"I don't know," Miss Dumont wailed, "and I don't care. I'm so unhappy I just want to go away." She cried and packed at the same time.

"I'll find him," the detective said. He could hear water running in the adjacent bathroom. He opened the door to see a man in a red wig with a bow tie wrapped around his neck, sitting in the claw-footed, bubble-filled bathtub.

"You can't stay in here," the detective said. Harpo shook his head and smiled.

"You gotta get out of here," the detective repeated. Harpo shook his head again.

The hotel employee went to the tub, reached down and picked Harpo up. Though naked, he was sporting the latest sartorial touch. The four-in-hand tied around his penis had a Windsor knot.

Miss Dumont was in the lobby, tears streaming down her face as she checked out. The housekeeper was mopping up the damage upstairs and instructing other hotel employees to wrap blankets around the naked people milling around.

Several hotel guests, recognizing the brothers, were quite vocal about "show business rubbish."

The detective was thus informed who the Marx Brothers were, the practical joke was explained, and everyone retired to their rooms.

The next morning, Groucho found Maggie at the railroad station, where she had spent the rest of the night waiting for the first train back to New York. She took one look at him and burst into tears.

"Ah, Maggie," he said soothingly. "Don't be mad. You know we'd never do anything to hurt you."

Miss Dumont allowed herself to be mollified. She needed the work.

"Maggie, bless her heart," Margaret Irving said, "she would quit the show every night of her life, and they'd coax her back. She couldn't get wise to these boys and the treatment she was getting. Because of them she got thrown out of so many hotels. I told her, 'Don't resent it. Tell them to do it some more and that you love it.' But she could never bring herself to say that."

The tour moved on. *Animal Crackers* was playing in Chicago when Groucho met Arthur Sheekman, a columnist for the *Chicago Times*, who had come by the theater for an interview. Somerset Maugham once wrote about those special male friendships, in which men immediately develop an animal liking for each other. Sheekman was a kindred spirit, albeit a gentler, softer spoken one. Groucho, instead of being interviewed, volunteered to write Sheekman's column for him. Before long the two men would be collaborating on books and comedy sketches. (Sheekman would ghostwrite *Beds*, Groucho's first book, which was published in 1930. It was a snicker-filled book studiously skirting man's favorite pastime. When I asked Groucho about the book, he said, "It was about people not fucking." He recalled that it took less than one week to write the book, parts of which had already appeared in *College Humor* magazine.)

The chartered train, carrying the troupe as well as scenery and costumes, ran between regular schedules. On closing nights, as each scene was played, the scenery would be taken by the grips and put on flat trucks. The whole show would be fairly well dismantled by the time the final scene was played. An additional two hours of hard work would be required before the gear was ready to be loaded onto the theater car.

Margaret Dumont was the first one on the train as the troupe prepared to leave for Cleveland. She quickly retired to her berth.

Harpo, as was his custom, took a compartment, where he would practice on his harp, lulling the nearby passengers to sleep. Minnie long ago had told him he'd be one of the world's finest harpists if he rehearsed, and this he continued to do.

Despite the fact that this was a chartered train, the conductor was required to collect so many tickets for so many cars. Railway employees traveling on theater trains were wise to the ways of show business and were rarely fazed by the hijinks of entertainers. The one in question came along in the middle of the morning and asked one of the brothers for the tickets. The three other Marxes were called, and they proceeded to take off the conductor's pants. He was rather amenable about the whole thing.

Margaret Dumont was sound asleep in her berth when the conductor, sans pants, was thrown on top of her by the brothers. "You never heard such screaming in your life," Maggie Irving recalled.

When the train reached Cleveland at mid-morning, most of the troupe was dressed and ready to be taken to their hotel. They were, as a class, well dressed and refined-looking people, in contrast to their outlandish behavior both onstage and off. Harpo this morning was among the missing. Maggie Irving went to look for him. "Don't worry," he called out from his compartment. "I'll make it."

The troupe was lined up at the check-in desk of the hotel at about noon. The lobby was beginning to fill up with business men, local gentry, and conventioneers.

"We were all looking very grand and elegant," Maggie Irving said. "Harpo hadn't arrived. Suddenly, through the revolving doors, there he came. He was in his red wig, wearing purple striped pajamas, carrying a golf bag on one shoulder and his harp on the other." Notice was given. The Marx Brothers were in town.

Catching the show for the third time (he'd paid for the first two admissions) was film director Victor Heerman, who had been sent to Cleveland by his studio.

The film career of the London-born Heerman, the son of theatrical costumers, began in 1914 at Mack Sennett's Keystone Company. He was now a contract director at Paramount.

His previous assignment, *Paramount on Parade*, was based on an idea by Elsie Janis that all the studio's stars be spotlighted in a sound picture structured like a vaudeville show, with comedians Leon Errol, Jack Oakie, and Skeets Gallagher acting as masters of ceremonies. Actors performing featured spots were Maurice Chevalier, Gary Cooper, Clara Bow, and Nancy Carroll. Also in the picture were "Buddy" Rogers and Lillian Roth, who sang a duet, "Anytime's the Time to Fall in Love."

The picture had been a winner. Not the least of Heerman's accomplishments was his taming of the temperamental Lillian Roth, who had signed a seven-year contract at the studio in 1928. Hers was an enormous if undisciplined singing talent. Studio heads felt she had a great future in talking pictures if she could learn to control her on-set tantrums.

B. P. Schulberg was sent to California to replace Jesse Lasky as West Coast production head of the studio. Lillian Roth was quickly made to understand that the new man would be less tolerant of her outbursts. At a party hosted by David O. Selznick, Schulberg said casually as they were dancing, "You haven't been easy to handle lately, have you, Lillian?"

He proceeded to enumerate her many displays of temperament.

"We're sending you back to New York to be kicked in the rear by the Marx Brothers until you learn how to behave," Schulberg concluded.

Heerman, who had effectively handled Miss Roth, was given the added burden of controlling the Marx Brothers when he was assigned as director of *Animal Crackers.*

Heerman was a long-time Marx Brothers fan and had seen the team's first film, *The Cocoanuts.* "You could see the picture going all over the place," he recalled. "There was nobody in charge."

The next day, after he saw the show in Cleveland, he stopped at the hotel where the brothers were staying, and called on Groucho.

"Here we expect a long lean Jew and instead we get a little fat Gentile," Groucho told him. Heerman was then introduced to Morrie Ryskind, who informed him that some changes were being made in the script.

"In place of the romantic lead being an artist," Ryskind told him, "we're going to make that fellow a newspaperman. Do you read Winchell?"

Walter Winchell was the widely read drama editor of the *New York Graphic,* and would soon be moving over to the *New York Mirror* to achieve even greater prominence.

"Who's Winchell?" Heerman asked. Since he lived in California, he wasn't aware of the huge following the columnist had in New York. Ryskind proceeded to read to him from eight or ten yellow pages. Heerman couldn't disguise his disinterest in the new concept. A fictional character based on a person unknown outside of New York wouldn't play in middle America.

"You have four reels and the Marx Brothers haven't shown up yet," he told Ryskind. "You're developing a whole new character."

Heerman returned to New York with the script. He kept every comedy scene and discarded the rest of the script. Now he had to tie the scenes together.

He discussed the situation with George Hall, the New York stage manager of the show. Hall told him that the brothers, three weeks prior to opening, had made notes of their scenes, timing every laugh. They had used musical scenes in between the comedy routines. Heerman thought they weren't needed, that one comedy routine could follow another. If the audience missed some of the laughs, they could always come back to see the picture a second time as they had for *The Cocoanuts*.

He discussed the idea with Ryskind. "The boys will never do this," he was told. The two men were at an impasse. "I knew damn well," Heerman said, "that I wasn't going to get involved with forty reels of film, which included musical numbers, only to cut them out."

Wanger asked him how things were going. "It's not coming at all," Heerman answered. The brothers had just finished their spring tour and were free for the summer. Wanger suggested they all come into Paramount's home office in New York for a story conference.

The brothers walked into the board room and moved the conference table out of the way. "We're going to set up a boxing ring," Groucho said. "Ryskind and Heerman are going to fight it out."

Heerman, ignoring the comment, went right into his main objection. "I already have ten reels of film with these funny scenes," he said. "We don't need the music." The brothers didn't agree. Berlin, Kalmar, and Ruby had taught them well.

After much give and take, the brothers finally agreed to an experiment. They would shoot five or six comedy scenes and screen them before an audience.

"I want a clean performance just the same as you do on the stage," Heerman instructed. A couple of routines were filmed each day. Three or four reels were shot. Heerman wrote a title frame: THESE ARE SCENES FROM THE FORTHCOMING *ANIMAL CRACKERS*. The film was taken to the Paramount Theatre at Broadway and Forty-third. The brothers arrived with Lou Holtz and George Jessel in tow, and the whole group was sequestered in an office at the top of the theater near the projection booth.

The house was half-full. When the film clip came on, it got a smattering of applause. Once it started, the audience never stopped laughing. The audience clapped again when the film ended.

The whole group went back to the Paramount office. Chico took Heerman aside. "Now listen," he said. "You know your business and we know our business. But we don't know your business and you do. If any of those goddamn Jews bother you, you come to me,

172

and I'll fix him." Groucho later told him virtually the same thing.

Heerman had long since learned that comedy films should be shorter than conventional ones. "You can only hold people up for a certain length of time," he said. "When you have to use footage to explain why something is funny, it's not a good thing."

He was to be proud of the picture, finding it less static than *The Cocoanuts*. "I think I was more sure of myself than the two directors on the first picture. Trouble is bound to happen when you have two directors."

The crew building the sets at the Astoria studio was a good one, although there would be a couple of slipups along the way. Two or three set designers were sent to watch the stage show. Then they returned to their studios and made a huge model of the sets, complete with carpets and paintings. The scale model, showing Art Deco and Art Moderne influences, almost filled a room. The home office quickly approved the handsome sets, and their construction began.

When Heerman saw the sets, he called the designers aside. "Did you see the play?" he asked.

"Six or eight times," one of them replied.

"Did you see the sequence where Groucho is making love to Mrs. Rittenhouse and Chico and Harpo steal the painting over the fireplace?"

"Yes," the set builder said.

"Where's the fireplace?" Heerman asked.

Oh.

"Also, do you remember the card game?" Heerman continued. "Where's the setting for that?"

These oversights were quickly remedied. The fireplace was built, and a platform was brought in on which the card table was placed.

In the meantime, the revised script was being written. "Morrie never said my approach was right," Heerman said, "but I never had anyone cooperate any more for those little scenes I needed."

The DuBarry scene was a long production number, and the picture was already over footage. Heerman suggested it be saved for another film. Groucho, who coauthored the scene, then known as the Napoleon scene, for *I'll Say She Is*, felt proprietary about it, and was more than agreeable to the suggestion.

The shooting went smoothly, although Heerman did have occasional trouble getting all four brothers on the set at the same time, as had the *Cocoanuts* directors.

"What time do you want me?" Chico would ask right before he disappeared.

"We'll be ready for you in about half an hour," Heerman might reply.

A stand-in was alerted to advise Chico when his time had come. Once, he wasn't to be found. An assistant asked Heerman, "Do you think he went over to the bridge club?" Heerman called Chico there. "I'll come back right after I finish this rubber," Chico said. He was back an hour later. Zeppo was getting a straight five hundred dollars a week, while the other brothers were on percentages. Heerman found him no trouble at all.

As for the story of long-standing that he finally had to lock them in a portable hoosegow near the set, Heerman denied it. "These were adult men," he said, "and they didn't have to be locked in. There was a jail left over from another picture, and we used it as a makeup room or for the actors to lie down in. It was never locked."

Groucho's entrance, "Hooray for Captain Spaulding," was filmed exactly as it had been done on the stage.

Lillian Roth's memory of the filming conflicted with Heerman's. "It was one step removed from the circus," she wrote in *I'll Cry Tomorrow*. First Zeppo, the youngest, sauntered into the studio, about 9:30. At 10 somebody remembered to telephone Chico and wake him. Harpo, meanwhile, popped in, saw that most of the cast was missing, and strolled off. Later they found him asleep in his dressing room. Chico arrived about this time. Groucho, who had been golfing, arrived somewhat later, his clubs slung over his shoulder. He came in with his knees-bent walk, pulled a cigar out of his mouth, and with a mad, sidewise glance, announced, 'Anybody for lunch?'

"Work resumed at mid-afternoon, and then it was five o'clock, and they were finished for the day . . . Every scene took longer than the director planned, for the ad libs came thick and fast, and the budget soared as the laughs increased."

Among the dress extras was a young actor named Robert Allen, who nearly thirty years later would be playing the boss in the play

Groucho wrote with Norman Krasna, *Time for Elizabeth*. "I'd just started in pictures," Allen said. "It was the depression and no one could get work, so I used to shuttle back and forth from the Warner's Vitagraph studio in Brooklyn to the Paramount studio in Astoria. Working as a dress extra meant between thirty-five and sixty dollars a day, depending on overtime. At the time you couldn't make eight dollars a week on Wall Street. *Animal Crackers* was more fun than work. You sat around with a lot of pretty girls watching the Marx Brothers perform. Everybody talked to everybody in those days, the stars with the extras. No one took himself seriously.

"The brothers were chasing a pretty blonde girl around the set, with Groucho in the lead. She was in the Texas Guinan scene as one of the dancers, and she was so beautiful. She didn't go out with any of them. The assistant director was luckier. He caught up with her and a few days later he came in to the set on crutches, with blue balls. They were so swollen he couldn't walk, so thank God the brothers didn't catch up with her."

Heerman, early in his career, had been making $150 a week as a film editor at Sennett, at a time when the weekly salary for directors was seventy dollars. Because of his editing credentials, Paramount gave him final cut on the picture.

"When I started cutting I got the shock of my life. Groucho had danced out of camera view in one scene. I'd asked the cameraman if he got it. He said he wasn't sure. We shot the scene again. I instructed them to print both scenes. When it came time to cut the scene, I was informed by the music department that the clarinet sounded much better in the first take. There was a ruling then that in any scenes with music, the music department had its choice of scenes. There was no way the scene could be corrected in the cutting. It was a full length scene, and I had to use the bad one."

The brothers' standing as film stars was considerably enhanced by the picture. Chico received an added bonus in the form of Lillian Roth's younger sister Ann, who was playing a bit part. The two girls had appeared in vaudeville as child actresses. Chico was smitten for the first time since his marriage to Betty. The hundreds of girls along the way had been playthings. His involvement with Ann was deeper and their relationship would seriously threaten Chico's marriage to Betty.

* * *

The same month that *Animal Crackers* was released, Heywood
Broun, a Socialist, was running for Congress in the Silk Stocking
District of New York. Frank Case, the owner of the Algonquin,
supplied Broun with free campaign headquarters in the hotel. The
Round Table hadn't been so politically committed since the Sacco
and Vanzetti trial, nor would they achieve lasting recognition for
possessing an effective social conscience.

All of Broadway seemed to line up behind the columnist-
candidate. His supporters included Minnie Maddern Fiske, Deems
Taylor, Walter Winchell, Eva Le Gallienne, George Jessel, Irving
Berlin, Lynn Fontanne, Alfred Lunt, Helen Morgan, Robert
Benchley, Edna Ferber, Fred Astaire, Ed Wynn, Irvin S. Cobb, Ina
Claire, Helen Hayes, Charles MacArthur, and the Marx Brothers.

A Broun rally was held at the Selwyn Theatre one Saturday
night. Woollcott presided as the theater world turned out to cheer
the candidate. The newspaper columnist was eulogized for two
hours. Woollcott was about to adjourn the meeting when Groucho
got up.

"The fine flower of the theater has met here tonight to honor
Heywood Broun," he said. "This is fitting and proper. But before
we leave, I'd like to ask a question. How many here live in Broun's
district?" Out of an audience of two thousand, three people raised
their hands.

Broun finished a distant third in a slate of three candidates. It
may have been this air of dilettantism that Groucho found offputting about the Round Table. Its members were witty and bright,
but they hadn't used their potential as opinion makers.

Groucho might well have summed up what he thought of the
Round Table when he repeated a self-deprecating story Dorothy
Parker had once told.

She ran into an acquaintance as she stepped into a cab one day.
"You must come to my house tomorrow night," Mrs. Parker said.

"Oh," the woman replied. "Are you entertaining?"

"Not very."

Later that month, the brothers set another salary record, signing
for $9,000 a week to play the Radio-Keith-Orpheum Circuit. They
would start at the Palace, then go to the Midwest for play dates
over the next eight weeks. .

Groucho was unable to perform when the show premiered in Chicago, having been rushed to a hospital for an emergency appendectomy shortly after arrival.

The *Chicago American* of November 10 reported the means by which the show went on:

> Well, imagine RKO's embarrassment Saturday morning when, with the biggest of all their Diamond Star attractions billed, and a theater jammed to the very rafters and overflowing clear out to the curb, they had only THREE Marx Brothers to present, instead of FOUR! Groucho was in the Michael Reese Hospital . . .

> Well, the curtain rose. And there to all appearances was Groucho . . . baggy pants, mustache and all. It was noticed that Harpo ran away with the act when usually the applause is a fifty-fifty proposition. But few people discovered until they got out on the street once more that they had only seen THREE of the brothers. Zeppo, the good-looking one . . . the straight man . . . had been missing.
>
> Where do you suppose he was, Philo? He was up there behind the footlights all decked out in Groucho's outfit, speaking Groucho's lines and doggoned if he didn't get away with it.

Groucho later said Zeppo did such a good job imitating him that he got out of the hospital as soon as he could. The words were uncommonly generous, but a more practical reason for his return was his realization of his worth to the act.

Behind the scenes in Chicago, the remaining brothers had a bitter argument with RKO management before agreeing to go on. They refused to perform unless they were paid the full $9,000 for the week. This was finally agreed to, but subsequent bookings were postponed until Groucho returned to the show. The tour resumed one week late. Though Groucho had assured RKO he was well enough to perform four shows a day, he only did two. The act was docked $800. Not until the tour's end in Detroit did he perform the full complement of shows. The finale was at the Michigan Theatre on December 18.

The S. S. *Paris* embarked one week later, on Christmas Eve of 1930, for Plymouth, England. None of the Marxes nor Margaret Dumont were on the ship's register as "society guests." The Four Hundred were tightening their belts at home, while the Marx Brothers were on their way to London to perform.

Maxine Marx was living on Long Island with Mike and Flo Mirantz, attending Woodmere Academy, when the Marx Brothers made their second tour of Europe.

"My mother thought it was a bad thing to take me out of school," she said. "I remember going down to the boat to see them off. There were Arthur and Miriam on the upper deck. I started to cry. Groucho never cared whether he took them out of school. He wouldn't go anywhere without them."

While the cousins were experiencing their emotional leave-taking, a group was meeting in Groucho's stateroom. The assemblage included lawyers from Paramount, the four brothers, and Max Gordon, who had negotiated a new contract for the team. There was no doubt how successful the first two pictures had been, judging by the new terms. The team signed a contract aboard ship for $200,000 for a third picture. The amount was twice their original salary, and the deal carried an option for two more features. The brothers would also be getting fifty percent of net profits, with the stipulation that this share was not to apply against the negative cost. S. J. Perelman and Will Johnstone were already writing the screenplay for the picture, with shooting slated to start in California in April. Coincidentally, the setting for the new picture was a ship.

Groucho booked three rooms for six hundred dollars. "This was the Depression," he recalled. "They were glad to get anybody. We had so much caviar you could throw it away."

The crossing wasn't a smooth one. "That boat rocked like Frisco during the quake," Groucho wrote Arthur Sheekman. "Sleeping was impossible as we were thrown from one side of the bed to another. It was always a surprise to find when morning came, that the hulk was still afloat, and our flag was still there."

About the upcoming opening at the Palace, Groucho wrote:

I think we will do well, although I don't think they will laugh at me, but they will laugh enough at Chico and Harpo to put the act over, and that's all I care about. We are billed here like Ringling's Circus, all over London electric signs, and no act could be as good as the advance billing. We were met at the pier by twenty newsmen and cameras and asked for our opinions on everything from the house of Parliament down to fish and chips at four and six. We are very important over here, our pictures having been sensational. *Animal Crackers* is still here in its ninth week at the Carlton and going big, and we are considered next to Chaplin as comics. Wait until they get a load of me at the Palace tomorrow night, they will revise their opinions.

The brothers' three-week stint at the London Palace was an amalgam of scenes from *The Cocoanuts* and *Animal Crackers*. The day after their January 5, 1931, opening the *New York Times* reported:

> The Four Marx Brothers scored an instantaneous success with a London audience when they appeared in Charles B. Cochran's International Vaudeville Show at the Palace Theatre. *The Daily Mail's* critic defied the most lugubrious theatregoer to keep a straight face for two minutes while these American comedians, who have "made an art of absurdity," are performing.
>
> The *London Times* gives the palm to Harpo whose "extreme facial expressions made a most direct assault on our gaiety."

Other critics raved about all the brothers, save Zeppo, though one thought Harpo's "business of lifting his leg as a mark of affection and confidence is not very funny."

The opening night audience was captivated. Groucho took advantage of the opportunity in his curtain speech after the show to remind the audience how rudely they had been treated during their first trip. The penny-throwing incident still rankled.

All of London was fascinated by the brothers. They were feted by many. "Groucho took Arthur and Miriam everywhere," Chico's first wife, Betty said. "When the Duke of Manchester invited us all out for an afternoon at his Sunday home, he certainly didn't expect Groucho to say he wanted his children around. Nobility didn't bring children. There were nurses to take care of them. Groucho

179

wouldn't go unless his children went. He spent the whole day with Arthur and Miriam, touring the grounds, and pointing out things he thought the children would find interesting."

It must have been a heady realization to his children that, as much as the Big World wanted to cultivate Groucho, he preferred the company of Arthur and Miriam.

CHAPTER EIGHT

You can take all the sincerity in Hollywood, stuff it in a flea's navel, add three caraway seeds, and still have room for an agent's heart.

Fred Allen

Seen from today's perspective, the brothers' first two talking pictures were rudimentary exercises. With the advent of sound, a whole new cinematic language had to be learned by the entire industry. The public, taken with the innovation, gladly paid to see this apprenticeship.

It was an era in which no sound pictures could fail. Paramount's net profits for 1930 were $18,000,000, the brothers accounting for a substantial percentage of this amount. Within a year after their arrival in Hollywood, they, along with Maurice Chevalier and Marlene Dietrich, would be Paramount's biggest money-making stars.

As their future studio publicist, Teet Carle, pointed out, "Those first two films swept the nation, creating a cult of fans that embraced millions. The folks insisted on quoting Groucho quips or chanting the hypnotic lyrics of 'Hooray for Captain Spaulding.'

"Idolizers saw the two movies again and again, and neighborhood theaters found bonanzas in return engagements. I recall being astounded at the marquee of a suburban theater, past which I drove to and from work at the studio, proclaiming, '28th Return Engagement of *The Cocoanuts.*' "

A large segment of today's audience can't gauge how comically innovative the brothers were. Too many imitators have sprung up in the meantime. This part of the public may have first been exposed to the humor of later comedians, so that when they were introduced to the creativity of the Marx Brothers, the originals seem—through a time warp— derivative of those who came later.

There could be no denying at the outset of their Hollywood career that the brothers were immediate box office stars. Studio executives weren't noted for their altruism, and they had closely guarded figures to justify the doubling of the team's salary in their third film.

Paramount, like every other major studio, was accelerating the construction of sound stages at its Hollywood plant. Pictures shot there in 1928 and 1929 were filmed on silent stages in the middle of the night, when the din of passing traffic was minimal.

Now, with new facilities, Paramount began to phase out the Astoria, Long Island, studio. Tallulah Bankhead's first three motion pictures were the most notable productions to be shot there during the early 1930s. Paramount insisted that the very verbal Groucho's art could best be captured in the California facilities, and the team was persuaded to come West. The plan was to be away for a few months, and then decide where to make their headquarters if the options on their next two pictures were picked up.

Groucho was about to take a long trip, so he decided to get his financial house in order. Through his accountant, he was introduced to a twenty-seven-year-old stockbroker with a Harvard Business School background named Salwyn Shufro. He had only been in business five years, but Shufro came highly recommended. Groucho would become his first show business client.

"We set up a luncheon meeting," Shufro said, "with Harpo and Zeppo too. There were two or three others at the table. It was quite an entourage. During lunch there was no real opportunity to discuss investment policies. The brothers were too busy topping each other. After lunch Groucho took me aside and asked if I would take a walk with him to Guaranty Trust Company, where he had his vault. He took his securities out of the vault and handed them to me. He said from there on they became my problem. I suppose some dissolution had been taken with whoever had represented him before. He had not opened an account, and whatever securities he had, he'd taken and put them in a vault."

Shufro noted that his new client had a great sense of insecurity about his financial future. "Having had this early start in life in a home on the poor side, and then making a lot of money and losing it, it wasn't unusual for him to have this insecurity.

"Groucho and Harpo were quite conservative. They were anxious to build up an estate for their protection. Groucho believed the life of an actor was short, and he didn't know when he would be out of favor. He'd been frugal all his life. He lived well. He never gave up anything he really wanted, but he tempered his wants with his general desire for security."

Financial anxiety may have motivated Groucho to turn to movies. Groucho didn't feel films were his true métier. He and his brothers placed too high a value on the response of a live audience to want to deliver their efforts to a group of distracted craftsmen on the set, artisans often too busy with their own work to offer even a token laugh. And how funny could a scene be after the tenth take? Such tiresome repetition would, of necessity, dissipate the spontaneity for which the brothers were famous. The team had been seduced by the big money, but they would often return to the stage, in spite of the fact that the financial compensation was less and the life much more rigorous.

The brothers, preparing to leave for California with their families in February of 1931, became the targets of promising writing talents who were trying, discreetly, to latch on to their rising stars. Two of them successfully captured their attention, and would later be numbered among Groucho's closest friends.

Bert Granet, then in his early twenties, had been submitting story ideas to George Kaufman and Morrie Ryskind, and the two older men had taken a shine to him. Kaufman sent him around to see

Groucho when the team was playing at the Albee Theatre in Brooklyn sometime in late 1930.

Granet was one of several young men Paramount had recruited from Yale. He was currently assigned to Western Electric as an assistant director and sound engineer. The job was beginning to look like a dead end. Clever measures were called for. A pretty blonde was in his company when he knocked on Groucho's dressing room door.

"May I come in?" Granet asked.

"No," Groucho replied, "but *she* can."

After learning that Kaufman had sent Granet to see him, Groucho became more hospitable. During the course of the meeting, Granet submitted two ideas for possible films. One was *The Seas Are All Wet*, revolving around the hijinks on a cruise ship, and the other was *College Daze*, obviously with a campus setting.

His concepts were to become the basis for *Monkey Business* and *Horse Feathers*, although Granet conceded "neither were totally the stories."

Granet was upset some months later when he discovered that his ideas were being adapted into screenplays without his participation, and that the brothers—already in California—would be starring in them. He had his father's attorney contact Paramount.

Leaving the Paramount office one day, Granet got into the same elevator with a company attorney, whose services had just been terminated by the studio. "Kid, you've got a good case," the lawyer told Granet. That he had. Paramount's settlement called for the hiring of Granet as a screenwriter with the stipulation that he be shipped off to the Coast for seasoning. One of his first assignments was to collaborate with Groucho's friend Arthur Sheekman on *The Big Broadcast*, an early Bing Crosby picture.

The ploy of the second young man was also cleverly plotted, and met with more immediate success than Granet's.

Nat Perrin had just graduated from Fordham law school and was preparing to take his bar examination the following week when he also went to the Albee Theatre in Brooklyn to submit a comedy sketch he'd written for the Marx Brothers.

He was armed with a phony letter of introduction, ostensibly from Moss Hart's agent, in which Perrin was introduced as a "bright young man." Groucho found him to be exactly that. What is more, he liked the sketch. He arranged for Chico to meet Perrin the following day.

"I had dealt with someone at Paramount some weeks before," Perrin said, "and I asked for some salary. They said it was too much, and they concluded their talks with me. I couldn't get them to reconsider. Chico asked what salary I wanted. I didn't want to gum it up. I just wanted to go West. 'Whatever you say, Mr. Marx,' I told him. 'I just want you to pay my expenses to get there.'

"Chico said one hundred dollars. That seemed like an enormous expense. 'Whatever is necessary,' I told him. 'I'll take less.' He repeated, 'One hundred dollars.'

"We kept arguing. I was asking for less, and he kept insisting that I should just leave it to him. I could see he was getting annoyed with me."

A studio representative approved the salary figure and Perrin was instructed to be ready to leave for California the following Wednesday.

On Monday and Tuesday of that week, Perrin took the bar examination. He was on the train the next day heading West with the Marx Brothers.

"All the brothers were nice to me," Perrin recalled. "I was very young, and it wasn't really a friendship on an equal level. But there was a total absence of snobbery among them. With Groucho especially, his attitude toward me was kind of paternal."

He arrived in California and discovered he had passed the bar. He also discovered that his hundred-dollar salary wasn't much higher than an office boy's. Although he worked with others on the script, he never received screen credit. "Had I known then what I know now, I would have," Perrin added.

If there was a basic contempt for writers, as various Hollywood histories have maintained, Perrin didn't notice it. "I didn't see that the writer was lower in the caste system. I remember Ben Hecht was getting $1,000 a day in cash for his work. Writers *were* respected, but once a script was finished the writer was kind of shunted aside, and another writer might be put on it before the producer would take over. Only on rare occasions would the original writer be called for. There was minimal actual involvement later. I don't think it was even customary to invite a writer to the first preview."

Perrin described the main entrance to the Paramount lot as resembling a college campus. It was a quadrangle around which dressing rooms were located. "It suddenly was like a dream world," he said. "I saw Jack Oakie passing a football to Skeets Gallagher." He saw the camaraderie of the actors but not the venality, maneuvering and back-stabbing rampant in Hollywood. The forged letter that had admitted him to the Marx circle would be a mild boyish prank in comparison. Everyone was on the make, jockeying for position and attention, be it at studios in Culver City, in the San Fernando Valley, or on Hollywood's Marathon Street, where Paramount Pictures was located.

A gang of uncultured ruffians, tough but fair, headed Paramount. On the next level was a group of aggressive executives incorporating the more negative qualities of Genghis Khan, the Mafia, and a Chinese tong. Pictures were made with the notorious "Paramount spirit." It was a call for unity, ostensibly for the common good, but under it a variety of high crimes and misdemeanors were self-servingly committed.

Ferenc Molnár, the great Hungarian playwright, often told a story about Adolph Zukor, the founder of the studio, which typified the actions of many other film executives.

Zukor had found a literary gold mine in his native Hungary, which staged perhaps the most avant garde and sophisticated theater in all of Europe, and he made yearly trips to his homeland to ferret out properties.

"On one of Mr. Zukor's trips to Hungary," Molnár would recall, "he was planning to choose between two candidates for the job of Paramount's mid-European representative. One of them offered to take him to the town where Zukor's mother was buried. It was a two-hour drive. When they arrived in this little village, they drove to the cemetery. They found a man at the mother's tombstone, crying as if his heart would break. It was the other rival for the job!"

Everyone but the actors seemed to be protecting his own interests. The performer offered his services on the outwardly

186

open, actually closed market, since there was a gentleman's agreement among studios that they wouldn't lure stars away with higher salaries. Agents were largely ineffective, and the primary loyalties of many were suspect. B. P. Schulberg, Paramount's creative head, for example, was the husband of Adeline Schulberg, one of the top actors' agents at the time. Her brother was Sam Jaffe, who would have the longest agent's career in Hollywood history. Agent Stanley Bergerman was married to Rosabelle Laemmle, the daughter of the head of Universal Pictures.

Then, in 1927, the actors found their first effective champion in agent Myron Selznick, who broke the studios' stranglehold by raiding Paramount for such stars as Kay Francis, Ruth Chatterton, and William Powell. He negotiated more favorable terms for them with Warner Brothers, which doubled their salaries. The studio was long on money from the blockbusting success of the talking pictures it had pioneered, but short on stars.

Paramount, because of the Warner talent raid and the diminished popularity of Clara Bow, was also in need of star material. Soon, Claudette Colbert, Nancy Carroll, Sylvia Sidney, Gary Cooper, and Bing Crosby would be part of the new wave at the studio.

Chico with the assistance of Max Gordon, succeeded in extracting one of the first participation contracts from any studio. However, he failed to take into consideration the very suspect bookkeeping methods by which the brothers' share of the profits would be determined.

Gordon, in addition to his percentage off the top, received a percentage of the profits of *Monkey Business,* and subsequently of *Horse Feathers.*

"Eighteen years later, these terms obliterated from memory," Gordon wrote in his autobiography, "Gummo Marx notified me that *Horse Feathers* was just one thousand dollars short and that it would not be long before I began collecting the money owed."

The two screenwriters who formed the framework of *Monkey Business* were Will Johnstone, the former cartoonist of the *New York Evening World,* who had been writing for the brothers since *I'll Say She Is,* and S. J. Perelman, a regular contributor to *Judge,* the humor

187

magazine. Perelman was also the author of *Dawn Ginsbergh's Revenge*, which was published in 1928. Groucho wrote a jacket blurb for the book: "From the moment I picked up your book until I laid it down, I was convulsed with laughter. Some day I intend reading it."

The two men met backstage during the production of *Animal Crackers*, and Groucho suggested Perelman and Johnstone collaborate on a radio series for the team. A network had approached the brothers about doing a weekly show.

The two writers developed a concept of the brothers as stowaways on an ocean liner, the same setting Bert Granet would later submit.

After discussing their presentation with his brothers, Groucho told the writers, "You fellows have stumbled on something big. This isn't any fly-by-night radio serial. It's our next picture."

Johnstone and Perelman wrote the script while the brothers were performing in England. They were already in California when the brothers arrived, having reported to Herman Mankiewicz, who would produce the picture.

A Teutonic, abrasive man, Mankiewicz was a compulsive gambler and a nonstop drinker. Even before he started working with the brothers, he told the writers, "They're mercurial, devious and ungrateful. I hate to depress you, but you'll rue the day you ever took the assignment. This is an ordeal by fire. Make sure you wear asbestos pants." Mankiewicz have been verbalizing his personal forebodings.

He would say after completion of the project, "I never knew what bicarbonate of soda was until I worked on a Marx Brothers picture."

Though Hollywood in the form of Mankiewicz wasn't giving the brothers a Chamber of Commerce welcome, the Marxes could take care of themselves.

Perelman, writing about the experience later, recalled having to read the entire screenplay to the Marxes and their entourage six weeks after he and Johnstone had started work on it.

A meeting was called at the Hollywood Roosevelt Hotel, owned by Chico's gambling crony Joseph Schenck (who two years later would co-found Twentieth Century-Fox with Darryl Zanuck).

"We [he and Johnstone] put in some intensive burnishing on the script," Perelman wrote in *Show* magazine in 1961, "though truth to tell, our handiwork already seemed to us to outshine the Kohinoor. To make it still more acceptable, we decided to salt our paper with as many technical movie phrases as we could, many of which we only half understood. We therefore went over the action line by line, panning, irising down, and dissolving, painstakingly sandwiched in Jackman and Dunning shots and even, at one point, specified that the cameras should vorkapich around the faces of the ballroom guests. Neither of us, of course, had the remotest notion of what this last meant, and it was years before I discovered that it derived from a special effects genius named Slavko Vorkapich. I still have no idea, between ourselves, whether his technique could be applied with impunity to the human race."

The meeting with the Marxes was called for eight-thirty on a Friday night. The first to arrive was Frenchy, who strolled in with a pinochle player. The time was nine-fifteen. Mankiewicz showed up next with his brother Joe (the latter was a screenwriter with an erratic income. Groucho got him a job as a counselor at the boys' camp his son Arthur attended. At least the employment gained him a regular salary). Then Zeppo and Marion arrived with a brace of afghans they had bought in England. Harpo made his appearance with a couple of blondes he had picked up at dinner, followed by Chico and Betty with their wirehaired terrier. A fight between the afghans and the terrier ensued, with Groucho and Ruth arriving in the midst of it. Perelman added that the brothers' own three gag men were also present. Presumably, they were Arthur Sheekman, Nat Perrin, and Solly Violinsky, all of whom eventually worked on the picture.

With a full complement of twenty-seven people and five dogs, Perelman nervously turned to the 126-page script.

"Go ahead, man," Groucho said. "Get a move on. As the donkey said, 'We're all ears.' "

Throughout the agonizing hour-and-a-half that it took to read the script, Perelman noticed that the original polite ripple of attention had turned to wariness, then to resentment.

After the reading, Groucho offered a two-word critique: "It stinks. Come on," he said, to no one in particular, and the group departed, leaving Perelman and Johnstone alone with their misery.

The next day, Groucho changed his mind. Perhaps something might be salvaged. Sheekman was brought in to work with Perelman, and Johnstone was assigned to develop some sight gags. Violinsky was hired for ten weeks by the brothers to insert some comic sparks. Also contributing was Nat Perrin, a very junior writing partner. After the picture was released, it was revealed that still another writer had added a dash of pepper to the stew.

Harry Evans, reviewing the film in the original *Life* (not the later news-picture magazine) told of studio gossip "concerning this picture that is one for the book. A famous comedian, whose name we will not mention, was hired at a fancy salary to write gags into the dialog, create comedy situations and generally brighten up the piece. In one scene a girl says, 'Ever since I have been married to this man I have lived a dog's life,' to which Groucho answers, 'Maybe he got a dog license instead of a marriage license.' You probably laughed at it the first time you heard it, if you can remember that far back. This line is the one and only contribution that the famous comedian made to the picture . . . and it cost the company *five thousand dollars.* Now you can understand where they got the idea for the title of the film."

The Marx Brothers didn't consider the joke so feeble; rather, they felt they had pulled a pretty good one on Paramount, with their uncle, Al Shean, as the beneficiary.

Groucho's main objection to Perelman's writing was that it was inaccessible to the masses. "Write for the people of Peru, Indiana," he instructed Perelman. (That Midwestern hamlet was Cole Porter's birthplace, where Sophistication's Pierian Spring might just be located. Groucho wouldn't have agreed had Perelman made that point. He'd made his own, and one the screenwriter had better understand.)

The Marx Brothers were new to films, but they understood where their appeal lay. If it took walking over people to get their point across, so be it.

Mankiewicz wasn't let off the hook. The brothers, with Groucho in the lead, disputed his every spoken thought and intruded on his silent ones. They reduced him to silence during story conferences. Whenever Mankiewicz offered a suggestion, he would be interrupted with questions about characterizations and motivations.

Groucho was the most persistent. "What am I supposed to be in this picture?" he asked at one point.

Mankiewicz, his patience worn thin, snapped, "Groucho, I have a new character for you. You're going to be a middle-aged Jew with bushy eyebrows, a painted-on mustache—and you smoke a cigar!"

Frank Tuttle was originally scheduled to direct the Marx Brothers' first Hollywood picture. When the starting date was pushed back because of the revisions in the script, he was replaced by Norman McLeod.

McLeod, as Groucho described him, was "inexperienced, but a good boxer." Apparently Mankiewicz felt the brothers might be intimidated by such a bruiser. McLeod had just finished co-directing an undistinguished effort, *Finn and Hattie*, for the studio, and *Monkey Business* was to be his first assignment as a solo director.

In flexing their collective muscles, the brothers were no doubt fighting their own insecurities. Their first two picture successes might be considered flukes, since they were among the first talkies. *Monkey Business* was to be the test of their staying power in films. It was the first picture with material that hadn't been tried hundreds of times before a live audience. Margaret Dumont, who had remained in New York, wasn't in the picture to serve as Groucho's foil and to symbolize the Establishment these anarchists were attempting to tickle to death. Thelma Todd was a luscious alternative, but whether the brothers' rowdy humor could bounce off her curvaceous figure as effectively as it had off Miss Dumont's more stately body had yet to be proven. Also, for the first time, Zeppo was being given something to do. He would be the love interest. Yet despite his blond good looks, Zeppo was the first to admit he was a wooden performer.

The squabbles with the studio left the brothers with a collective case of jangled nerves. Thus burdened, they began their Hollywood careers.

In his later years, reporters and photographers beat a regular path to Groucho's door. He suffered their banal, repetitious questions less than gladly.

191

Once an interviewer asked him, "What was it like making movies in the Thirties?"

"Hard work," Groucho tersely replied.

"How was that so?"

"We didn't have restrooms on the sound stages," Groucho said.

"How has that changed?" the reporter persisted.

"People don't piss anymore."

It *was* hard work and the movie industry was about to fall on hard times, but the filming of *Monkey Business* proceeded smoothly enough.

The brothers were rapidly assimilated into the studio's everyday workings, and their daily lunch table at the Paramount commissary was an impromptu extension of the scripted escapades on the set.

Every day, a foreigner would walk by their table and mutter, "Beware the Ides of Marx."

The brothers found the pun funny at first, but grew edgy as this sinister-looking man daily repeated the same line. The punster turned out to be Josef von Sternberg.

Frenchy had come West with his sons. Since Minnie's death he was lonely and lost. Then he met a woman. When he informed his sons of his plans to marry again, their response was negative. His remarrying, they felt, would be an affront to Minnie's memory. His sons, caught up in this newest Gold Rush, were supporting him and were calling the shots. He felt he had become an intrusion in their lives.

Frenchy was living with Zeppo and Marion when the brothers suggested he appear with them for the first time. He played an extra in a scene where people were disembarking from the ship. Frenchy was first seen on the boat. Then he was shown waiting on land for the ship to dock. Extras were paid fifteen dollars daily, and Frenchy received thirty dollars for his twin roles.

The cameo appearances excepted, their father was left pretty much to his own devices, and he quickly took up with an older pinochle-playing crowd. During the course of filming, Zeppo would retire early, since he had to be up at six every morning. There would be no one up to trade small talk with whenever Frenchy returned home.

The "Home Again" troupe from which the brothers emerged to become prominent vaudevillians. At center are Zeppo and Harpo, holding hands with Chico's daughter Maxine. Chico is kneeling. Directly behind him is wife Betty. (Maxine Marx Collection)

On the beach, 1924: Chico, an unidentified relative, Groucho's wife Ruth, Harpo, the immortal Minnie. Kneeling is Chico's wife Betty holding Groucho's son, Arthur. (Maxine Marx Collection)

The brothers as Broadway stars. (Maxine Marx Collection)

At the Richmond Hill house of Sam and Minnie Marx: Ruth, Sam, Chico's daughter Maxine, Harpo, Groucho, Arthur. (Maxine Marx Collection)

Two new Paramount players in 1931 were Groucho Marx, about to move to California to film *Monkey Business,* and Tallulah Bankhead, who filmed her first picture at the studio's Astoria facility. (Maxine Marx Collection)

Groucho with Thelma Todd in *Monkey Business*, the first picture filmed by the brothers in California. (John Tefteller Collection)

Sam (Frenchy) Marx made his show business debut at the age of 70 in *Monkey Business*. Here he is with actress Ruth Hall. (Bob Cooper Collection)

Our Meshpoche. The Marx and Schoenberg families held a reunion on January 8, 1932, at the Croydon Hotel in New York. Seated around the table, left to right, are Johanna Shean, Al's wife; their son Larry; Sam Marx; Tante Sarah; Chico; Tante Hannah Schickler; Uncle Al Shean; Harpo; another Tante Sarah; Maxine; Heinie Schoenberg; his son; Mrs. Sarah Karp, Betty Marx's mother; Cousin Polly Muller; her husband Sam; the hotel waiter, standing; five unidentified relatives; Zeppo; another unidentified relative; Beattie Muller, Polly's daughter; Groucho; Ruth; Zeppo's wife Marion; Betty; Gummo's wife Helen; Gummo; and four unidentified relatives. (Maxine Marx Collection)

Prior to the filming of the culminating football sequence in *Horse Feathers*. (Bob Cooper Collection)

Groucho in the opening scene of *Horse Feathers*, the Paramount film in which he portrayed Professor Quincy Adams Wagstaff. (John Tefteller Collection)

Another final sequence, in which the brothers played cards while the college burned down around them, was not used. (Bob Cooper Collection)

Zeppo and Chico at The Brown Derby. (John Tefteller Collection)

A costume party in September, 1933, in which Groucho was disguised as Rex the Wonder Horse. Others are Ruth and Mr. and Mrs. Charles Butterworth. Butterworth was one of the few actor-members of the West Side Writing and Asthma Club. (Paul Wesolowski Collection)

Groucho and chorus in a scene from *Duck Soup.* (Henry Golas Collection)

The brothers on the set of *Duck Soup*. From top to bottom: Groucho, Zeppo, Harpo, Chico, Gummo. (Henry Golas Collection)

A mirror scene with the four brothers, shortly before Zeppo left the act. (Maxine Marx Collection)

At the piano, prior to filming the classic mirror scene in *Duck Soup*. (John Tefteller Collection)

With Margaret Dumont. (Henry Golas Collection)

Groucho and Chico in August, 1934, as they prepared to inaugurate their radio careers with "Flywheel, Shyster, and Flywheel." (Henry Golas Collection)

(Bob Cooper Collection)

A panel of comedians got together in New York in mid-1934 to discuss the merits of live studio audiences. They were Jack Benny, Chico, Jack Pearl, Jimmy Durante and Groucho. (Maxine Marx Collection)

(John Tefteller Collection)

Seated on the set of *A Night at the Opera:* Groucho, Chico, director Sam Wood, screenwriter George S. Kaufman. (John Tefteller Collection)

A scene from *A Night at the Opera.* (John Tefteller Collection)

A scene from the road show version of *A Day at the Races.* (Maxine Marx Collection)

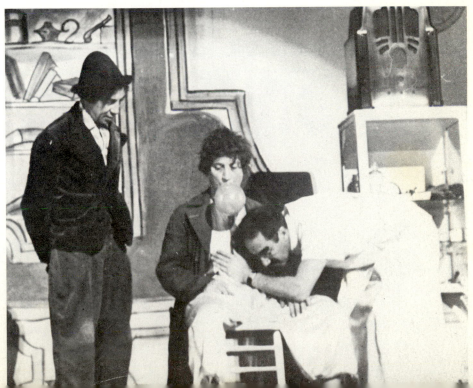

(Maxine Marx Collection)

With Esther Muir in *A Day at the Races*. (John Tefteller Collection)

One night, he rang the doorbell. A sleepy Zeppo stumbled to the door. "Pop, for Christ's sake, where's your key?"

"I must have lost it," Frenchy replied.

"All right," his son said, "I'm getting you another key. So stop ringing the bell and waking us up."

A couple of nights later, the doorbell rang again. Zeppo stumbled to the door of the darkened house and opened it. There stood his father. "Didn't I give you a key?" he asked.

"Sure," Frenchy said, holding it out, "here it is."

"Then why did you ring the bell?"

"I wanted to see if somebody was home," this funny-sad little man said. It was another story to be added to the family folklore.

In getting into the Hollywood swing, Frenchy would also become the subject of stories related by people outside the family. Gregory Ratoff, recently arrived in Hollywood, was introduced to the elder Marx.

Having noticed Ratoff's accent, Frenchy asked, "You're Cherman?"

"No, I'm not German," answered Ratoff.

"Hungarian?"

"No," said Ratoff.

"French?"

"No, I'm not French," Ratoff answered.

Frenchy listed all the European nationalities he could think of. Finally he asked, "You Russian?"

"Yes," said Ratoff, "I'm Russian."

"Mmm," said Marx, "I thought so."

Groucho and his family had stayed at the Garden of Allah when they first arrived in California. Although there seemed to be no cures for his chronic insomnia—he tried them all—it wasn't helped by the constant revelry of transplanted Easterners like Robert Benchley and Charles Butterworth, many of them Algonquin refugees, who lived there.

The family later moved to a rented house in the Hawthorne school district of Beverly Hills. Groucho still wasn't sure the team would remain in California, and he wanted to stay as flexible as possible.

During the course of the filming, he wrote Salwyn Shufro about his brokerage account:

> Just a line to let you know I received all the various swindle notes from you, and just for the sake of the record, I wish you would let me know how much I either lost or made on the various transactions ... I mean the total. I'm still paying off money I borrowed to clear myself at the bank, but a few weeks will see that clear, and then for those four per cent bonds I have been dreaming about all these years.
>
> The picture is coming along slowly, and I predict it will be the most colossal failure in the history of the movie industry. I hope the turn has arrived even though it is only the wrong turn.
>
> Yours,
> Groucho

Shooting progressed more smoothly than Groucho maintained, and the brothers were able to take the summer off, as they had during their stage career. They interrupted their film career secure in the knowledge that not only had they gotten Mankiewicz's goat, they'd stolen his secretary. Rachel Linden would work for them throughout the 1930s.

The studio prediction was that the box office slump affecting the theater would spread to motion pictures. Paramount's net profits of $18 million the year before would slip to $6 million in 1931. Overall film attendance, with all but 1,500 out of 22,000 film theaters in the country equipped for sound, would drop off forty percent. Soon, double features would be introduced, and audiences would be further enticed by bank nights and free dishes.

During that summer, however, it was the theater that was hardest hit. Its poor health, however, was contradicted by the big money dangled in front of the brothers to lure them back to the stage. Loew's State promised them $15,000 for a one-week engage-

194

ment. Earl Carroll offered them $10,000 a week if they would appear in his fall musical revue. Discussions were also held with Ziegfeld. They gave all the managers approaching them the same answer. If they returned to the stage, it would be in a vehicle they could later film. All the offers were turned down.

The militant Heywood Broun, in the meantime, had been carrying on a drunken conversation with Helen Morgan and Helen Kane in a New York speakeasy. The three, along with press agent Milton Raison, decided to put together a revue whose sole purpose was to employ, clothe, and feed out-of-work actors. It was called *Shoot the Works!*

Another great cause was unfurled under the sponsorship of the collapsing Round Table. Sketches were provided by Dorothy Parker, E. B. White, Peter Arno, Harry Hershfield, and Nunnally Johnson. George and Ira Gershwin and E. Y. Harburg supplied music and lyrics. The two Helens, Morgan and Kane, donated their services, appearing as guest stars along with Bill Robinson, Harry Richman, George Jessel, Al Jolson, Texas Guinan, Eddie Cantor, Sophie Tucker, and Morton Downey. Groucho, Harpo, and Chico agreed to be added to the list of stars.

The revue opened on July 21, with the brothers scheduled to appear on August 20 and 21. Margaret Dumont and Lou Sorin, their confrères from *Animal Crackers*, appeared with them in the DuBarry scene.

"At the conclusion of the number," the *New York Times* of August 21 reported, "and after several bows, Groucho attempted to quiet the audience with a sly curtain speech in which he expressed gratification that the three brothers could get along without the fourth. The capers concluded with the brothers combining to carry Mr. Broun bodily from the stage when he came to plead for silence in order that the next number could proceed without interruption."

Because of the brothers' appearance, the revue enjoyed its biggest weekly gross of the entire run. (The show would fold after eighty-nine performances.)

At the conclusion of their final performance, Broun came forward. As a token of his appreciation, he presented each brother with an early Broun—all of his amateurish paintings were called early Brouns.

Groucho accepted the touching token for the three brothers. "It was bad enough playing for nothing," he said.

Monkey Business opened nationally in September. An ad in *Variety* at the end of the month told the story:

HARPO, GROUCHO, CHICO, ZEPPO, SRO EVERYWHERE.

Box office records were broken in ten cities. Within a week, Paramount had taken up the option on the next picture, and Perelman was sent East to begin work on the screenplay.

It was originally thought *Horse Feathers* might be filmed at Astoria. The brothers had signed for a one-month vaudeville tour starting in late October on the midwestern RKO Circuit. They would be grossing $10,500 weekly. Harpo had taken a six-month lease on an East Fifty-first Street penthouse. Chico was planning to bring Betty and Maxine to New York for the Christmas season, when the brothers would have a month off, before winding up the tour at the Palace in New York and the Albee in Brooklyn. Groucho intended to go back to California until the script was ready.

While Groucho and Zeppo were enjoying a mild California Christmas, Harpo was braving the snowstorms of New York to mingle with his intellectual friends. Chico already had a heavily booked gambling schedule. He also had to fit in his family and his extracurricular activities, passing himself off as the unmarried Harpo to girls who didn't believe in sleeping with married men and being his natural self with those who had no such compunctions.

Betty understood that girls who acted so familiarly with her husband in public were even more familiar with him when alone. The excuse that he was being mistaken for Harpo had been exhausted.

"Even if I found Chico in bed with a woman, he would say it wasn't so," Betty said. "There was no woman there. She was the product of my imagination."

Later, as even his daughter began to understand the extent of his indiscriminate infidelities, Chico tried to explain the facts of life as he perceived them.

"There's no such thing as a faithful husband," he told Maxine.

"Oh, Daddy," she protested, "that's not true."

Chico insisted otherwise. "There is no man who doesn't cheat on his wife unless he's so broke he can't afford it, or he's so ugly nobody wants him."

During this same trip Betty discovered he had had a quick affair with yet another girl.

A few nights later, Betty and Chico were sitting at the theater. Nearby was an attractive woman who flashed a dazzling smile. "Hello, Chico," she called out. Chico smiled back, then turned to his wife. "Who's that?"

Betty answered, "That's the girl who nearly broke up our home last week."

Because Zeppo chose to pass the summer elsewhere while his three brothers were back East appearing in *Shoot the Works!* rumors again cropped up that he was quitting the act.

The talk originated early in 1929 when the name of the team was changed from The Four Marx Brothers to simply The Marx Brothers.

A story circulated along Broadway that Groucho, in the middle of the stage run of *Animal Crackers*, had gone to producer Sam Harris and said, "Sam, I have bad news for you. Zeppo has decided to leave the act."

"Well, Groucho," Harris replied, barely able to conceal his glee, "that's not terribly bad news."

"It is in a way," Groucho insisted, "because we're going to have to get more money."

Just as they were preparing to start their fourth picture, both Paramount and Groucho issued a denial that the brothers were splitting up. The denial notwithstanding, the breakup was only a matter of time.

The rest of the world might find amusement in his do-nothing image, and he himself was aware that his contributions to the act were minimal, but Zeppo couldn't laugh at the kind of joke he had become. He wasn't a particularly sensitive man, but he had great pride, and he got greater personal satisfaction out of the business deals he was putting together. Zeppo was getting less money than any of the brothers, and yet he lived better than any of them, indulging himself with a yacht and buying his wife furs and jewels which would later be impounded by burglars with monotonous regularity. The houses they lived in reflected Marion's exquisite good taste. At the time home was a handsome apartment, but they would soon begin trading up, finally settling in a San Fernando Valley house in Tarzana.

"It was the prettiest house I've ever seen," Maxine Marx said. "Marion designed it from a movie she saw. It wasn't ostentatious, but the house was totally charming."

Each brother had gone his own social way when the team first went to California. Harpo was adopted by the William Randolph Hearst-Marion Davies circle and was invited to the most distinguished homes of California. Chico was the most egalitarian of the brothers. He was at home with beggars and kings, mingling with gambling gangsters and cultivating studio moguls in order to make better deals. To his mind, the moguls were gamblers too, and playing for even greater stakes.

Chico would often cross the Mexican border to visit the racetrack and gambling casino at Agua Caliente, where Al Jolson, Clark Gable, Jack Dempsey, Babe Ruth, and Bing Crosby would often blow on each other's dice. The establishment, with its own golf course, was outside Tijuana, a border town littered with pimps, prostitutes, and cut-rate abortionists. It offered, in short, everything Chico required. Agua Caliente flourished from 1929 until 1935, when Mexico banned casino gambling and California racetracks began operations.

On one occasion, Chico received an urgent telegram on the studio wire from the Agua Caliente Jockey Club, demanding immediate payment to cover a bounced check. This didn't sit well with Paramount executives, but it didn't affect Chico's negotiating power when the contract for the new picture was to be signed.

Max Gordon came West to lend his expertise to the brothers, who had no official agent to represent them. The Morris Agency was suing the brothers, claiming they were owed a ten percent commission on the Marxes' $200,000 salary for *Monkey Business*. The brothers countersued, maintaining that their agency contract had expired before the deal for the third picture was signed. In addition, they asked for repayment of a $12,500 commission on the first two pictures, charging that Paramount had a half-interest in the commission and had received that amount as a kickback. The brothers eventually had to pay the commission.

The year of 1932 would be an all-time low for the film industry. Salaries were cut by forty percent at United Artists; by thirty-five percent at Metro; and the salaries of all Paramount employees making over one hundred dollars weekly were cut by five percent. Warner Brothers was even more drastically affected, losing $30,000,000 between 1930 and 1934.

Understandably, Paramount wanted the team to take less money for *Horse Feathers*. The brothers were proven winners, however, and were adamantly opposed to a cut. In the midst of the Depression, their $10,000 weekly salary was the highest in vaudeville. The studio had only to look at its ledgers to see how big a draw they were as film stars. The terms of the original contract stood.

The brothers had veto power on the hiring of writers for the new picture. Bert Kalmar and Harry Ruby were immediately recruited, as were S. J. Perelman, Arthur Sheekman, George Marion, Jr., and Harry Sweet. Norman McLeod would be directing again.

This would be Perelman's last collaboration with the brothers. In recent years, he has taken umbrage at being identified by film cultists as the screenwriter for the Marx Brothers, when his later accomplishments were more important. As a writer, his work should be read and not seen. His humor is so convoluted that several readings are often required to catch all its nuances. Groucho later gave Perelman stinted credit for his contributions.

The first four weeks of filming went smoothly. Though the names of their characters were different, the brothers played the same types, as they would in all their future movies. Harpo portrayed a dogcatcher to Groucho's college president and Chico's bootlegging ice man. Zeppo, as Groucho's student son, was the love interest again, playing opposite Thelma Todd in the role of the college widow. He revealed a good baritone voice, in a duet with Groucho, that sounded suspiciously like that of Bing Crosby, another Paramount player.

In the first week of April, Chico was severely injured in an automobile accident, suffering a fractured knee and several broken ribs.

The picture was shot around him for as long as possible, but the production had to take ten weeks off before Chico was well enough to participate in the climactic football sequence. Few people had noticed up to now how vital his contributions were to the act. Rarely did Harpo and Groucho appear without him in scenes. It was usually Harpo and Chico, Chico and Groucho, or all three. Chico was the bridge between Groucho's sharpie role and Harpo's impish innocent.

While Chico recuperated, and Harpo and Zeppo were otherwise occupied, Groucho was being installed as the president of the newly-formed West Side Writing and Asthma Club. Perelman coined the name for the group, which met weekly for lunch at Lyman's Restaurant, across the street from the Hollywood Brown Derby. There were fourteen writers in the club, including Robert Benchley and Donald Ogden Stewart, as well as Ben Hecht and Charles MacArthur whenever they were in town.

"Charlie Butterworth was the only actor in the group," Groucho told me. Significantly, he didn't place himself in that category as yet. He found Benchley to be the most extraordinary of them all. "He was the only one of them to laugh at other people's stuff."

Among the first items on the club's agenda was the devising of plans to continue weekly meetings at a beach club over the summer. Groucho made inquiries for the group. On one occasion he was informed he wasn't acceptable because of his religion, which prompted his now famous riposte: "Since my children are only half-Jewish, can they go into the water up to their knees?"

Finally, composer Buddy De Sylva was drafted by the group, and he gave the club permission to use his house in Malibu on weekends. "Just let my family use the house the other days," he told the members.

"So," Groucho observed, "he's high-hatting us."

Before long the members would be unintentionally high-hatting each other, as deadlines approached and they had to work through many nights to finish scripts on time.

In New York, Max Gordon was mounting a new show, *Flying*

Colors, when the Depression caught up with him. He lost his money and had a nervous breakdown.

Harpo, in New York at the time, visited Gordon in the sanitarium.

"Harpo spent an hour with me, humoring me, showing me the promise of the future," Gordon wrote in his autobiography. "As he rose to leave, he reached into his pocket and withdrew a roll of bills, threw it across the bed, and ran for the door. Four thousand dollars were strewn around—needed, helpful, reassuring. The following day Groucho called to tell me he knew what Harpo had done. 'I want you to know,' Groucho said, 'that I've got fifty percent and there is more where that came from.''

In mid-June, Chico was sufficiently recovered to resume filming. Shooting was finally completed a month later.

The brothers then announced they would wait a year before filming the fifth picture on their contract. In the interim they planned to make theatrical appearances. Harpo accepted an invitation to perform with the Moscow Art Theatre, and left in late summer for New York on Hal Roach's private plane.

Horse Feathers was sneak previewed in early August, and its reception was so enthusiastic that the studio called the brothers back to start immediately on the next picture. The personal appearance tour was cancelled, and Harpo had to postpone the trip to Russia. Paramount thought Ernst Lubitsch might burlesque one of his mythical kingdom films by placing the Marx Brothers in this operetta world. Pre-production commenced.

Any remaining doubts about the film stature of the Marx Brothers were dispelled with their appearance on the cover of *Time* magazine. They were in Hollywood to stay.

Groucho's goal of purchasing four percent bonds was further delayed. He wrote Shufro in August of 1932 that he bought a house but hoped to be able the following spring "to catch up with myself and be able to buy some bonds."

California, with its temperate year-round climate, worked its insidious seductiveness on the Marxes. It was an easy life, and, as Groucho later told me, the West Coast was "a wonderful place to raise kids." He was now in his early forties and no longer a youngster. He merely gave lip service to the need to return to the stage, the desire for public performing having lessened. That yearning, however, would never totally abate.

The family moved to the new house, situated on the block below Sunset Boulevard on Hillcrest Road, in October. It had been repossessed by the mortgage company after the contractor had gone bankrupt as a result of the Depression. Groucho bought the fourteen-room house—with seven baths, a billiard room, servants' quarters for three—for $44,000.

Groucho and Ruth had now been married for eleven years. On their tenth anniversary, just three months after being wiped out in the crash, he swept his innate frugality to the winds and bought his wife a diamond bracelet, more an award for her forbearance than a romantic symbol. Chico, of course, had been giving Betty similar baubles throughout their marriage out of a sense of guilt. Although Groucho never stopped having his one-shot sexual encounters during his marriage, he handled them with more discretion than his brothers. Any guilt he had about his infidelities would have to be added to the end of the long list of complexes with which he was already burdened.

Husband and wife took separate bedrooms in the new house, a tacit indication that his ardor for her had waned. Yet, content as the basic malcontent that he was could be, he had no desire to disrupt the familiar routine he had slipped into.

Much of his daily activity revolved around the Garden of Allah. Some of Hollywood's great characters were its habitués. Although Groucho was never much of a drinker, he often managed to make friends of men, writers mostly, whose legs were as hollow as their brains were creatively filled.

Arthur Sheekman was the friend Groucho loved most. Sheekman was shy, sensitive, and kind. In its way, their mutually giving relationship was one of Hollywood's greatest love stories. Groucho— the established star—promoted his friend's career with a fervor unmatched by the most selfless of agents. He nurtured Sheekman's talent, advised him on career goals to pursue, hired him to work on his screenplays, used him as a ghost writer. The humor and wit of the two men was complementary, Sheekman tempering Groucho's caustic bent with his own gentler viewpoint. In return, Sheekman offered Groucho a devotion that was profound and a loyalty that was unquestioning.

Yet, theirs wasn't an exclusive friendship. It could encompass anyone who fit Groucho's definition of "a nice man," his ultimate accolade. Many "nice men" frequented the Garden of Allah, and Groucho met them all. He was present at one afternoon party to meet yet another one, who would be immediately admitted into his life.

Screenwriter Arthur Caesar was in his cups that day, as was almost everyone else. Caesar, however, had gotten belligerent and was challenging everybody. A very young fellow blithely topped a few of his insults with a surprising combination of humor and tact. Groucho took an instant liking to him. Before the day was over, the young man was taken home by Groucho to dinner and had wormed his way into the whole Marx family's heart. His name was Norman Krasna.

Now twenty-two, he had written a play *Louder, Please!* starring Lee Tracy, which George Abbott directed on Broadway in 1931. He wasn't of age when terms were agreed to for the play's production, and his mother had to sign the necessary contracts for him.

The play was about a phony publicity stunt with a starlet riding off in a motor boat and being "lost" at sea. It was written when Krasna was a press agent for Warners-First National. A studio head named J. L. appeared in the play, and Jack L. Warner, assuming the initials were his, was offended at being unflatteringly depicted. Krasna explained that the real model had been one Jesse Lasky.

Before coming to California at the age of twenty, Krasna had been the drama editor of the *New York Graphic* and assistant film critic of the *New York World*. He also attended law school in his spare time. This wunderkind wasn't going places, he'd already been there.

Nevertheless, Krasna didn't feel like a somebody until he became Groucho's good friend. "I was in awe of this idol," he said. "What I owe him is inestimable. You can't imagine the effect it had on others to be seen with him. I'd later have publicity of my own and would be almost worthy of being his friend. The great obligation I have is that he liked me and took me around when I was a nobody.

... By comparison, everybody else was colorless. All the fun was around him, and everybody tried to gravitate around Groucho. He did it for a number of people. He was wonderful to Arthur Sheekman and Nat Perrin. But I wasn't married, and I think I was with him more than anybody."

Legend has it that before an audience of six people or more, Groucho felt compelled to perform. But, Krasna said, "You read about him, and it's an unbroken line of great cracks. You picture this as going on continuously, but the density was actually very, very slight."

Because of Groucho's deep convictions, serious talk about national and world conditions dominated his everyday conversation. He could never treat the foibles of politicians with the easygoing tolerance of Will Rogers, nor the prospect of Armageddon with the contemptuous humor of the later Mort Sahl. His intellect was too great to offer the simplistic one-liner, and he could hardly be sardonic in the face of mass disfigurement and death. He cared too much.

Krasna recalls that the household "wasn't pretentious and literary. Nobody was reading Proust, but everyone read, even Mama."

Being an only child, he took to Arthur and Miriam immediately. "Arthur was a nice kid, always playing practical jokes. I remember he'd make me jump. He'd have a toy buzzer in his hand, or something like that. He wanted to play tennis very badly. He was a hard-working fellow."

As for Miriam, "I was crazy about her. She'd sit on my lap, and I'd tell her bedtime stories. She was terribly bright."

She had sufficient insight, much as she adored Groucho, to ask him not to come to her fourth birthday party. "You'll scare my friends," she told him. Though it disturbed him that other children considered him a bit menacing, Groucho tried to laugh it off. He might even have been proud of his daughter's candid perception.

"I don't know if Miriam had more native intelligence than Arthur," Krasna said, "but I will say this. We always thought Miriam would do something."

His children, at the time, must have considered Groucho a wonderful father. He was totally supportive, totally permissive, and was with them constantly. He might have lunch with his friends, but at day's end, he wanted to be home with his children.

"Groucho would be the focal point of any group," Krasna said. "He would get many invitations. Maybe Ruth wanted to go to the party, but he wanted to stay home. The glamor set didn't impress him."

If there was a dark cloud in his relationship with Arthur and Miriam, it was in the baiting way he poked fun at them. The devastating humor that might liven any party traveled better than when it stayed in its natural habitat. His children overlooked the innate hostility of his words for as long as they could. As adults they would handle the psychic damage with varying degrees of success.

"I was so envious of Groucho's kids," Maxine Marx said. "They were so free. My mother censored everything I read and saw. Groucho never censored anything. Any book was open to his children, any movie they wanted to see. He said, 'There ain't nothing there that's going to spoil anything.' I read everything too, but I always had to hide it. I had to be careful my mother didn't know it. And yet some sixth sense told me it was better that I had my mother there. I could depend on her.

"That's how I was raised. Now Miriam and Arthur had none of that. On the other hand they didn't have a secure mother who stood behind them no matter what.

"My parents were indulgent in other ways. I never had to worry about money the way Groucho's kids did. I always had a good allowance. My mother had a taxi take me to school every day. Groucho's kids walked. I had lessons for everything. When I took tennis lessons, the ball would come across the net and I used to close my eyes and swing. Later I had riding lessons, and I'd ask for the gentlest horses.

"Arthur and Miriam grew up with absolutely no physical fears. Groucho never paid for lessons for them. He was too tight. Yet, they would get on horses and dash around, picking things off the ground. I looked at them and envied them so. Arthur once played Ping-Pong with me. He spotted me twenty points and played with his left hand, and still he beat me.

205

"If my parents thought of me as a hothouse flower, Groucho treated Arthur like a weed. Nobody realized I was very near-sighted, so I stumbled a lot and they thought I was clumsy. Everyone would say, 'Maxine, be careful, hold on.' I grew up petrified of everything. And Arthur was so strong and sturdy, and Groucho never pampered him."

And yet, as much as Maxine was sheltered and Arthur and Miriam were given free rein, Groucho didn't like leaving them with other people for even a day.

The end of the Jazz Age coincided with the rapid decline in drawing power of twenty-five-year-old Clara Bow, one of Paramount's most important stars. The actors B. P. Schulberg recruited from Broadway in 1929 and 1930—Fredric March, Claudette Colbert, Miriam Hopkins, Sylvia Sidney, Phillips Holmes—hadn't caught the public's fancy as yet. Cecil B. DeMille's socio-sexual comedies of the 1920s had given way to religio-sexual films, mammoth and expensive productions that took many months to make. He was currently filming *The Sign of the Cross* starring Claudette Colbert and Fredric March, but the picture wouldn't be released until December. Josef von Sternberg and Marlene Dietrich were so closely allied that they could be counted as only one talent. If each had a following, the studio couldn't split them up to work with other creative people and thus broaden their drawing power. Dietrich's pictures, like Chevalier's, were big box office in Europe, but much of the studio's profits had to stay on the Continent. It wasn't easy to get money out of Europe and many studios were forced to invest in unwanted foreign production facilities as a result.

It was now Paramount's turn in the barrel. The picture division had already lost $6,000,000 and the theater division $12,000,000 when the studio went into receivership in midyear.

B. P. Schulberg was ousted as head of production and Emanuel Cohen, who supervised the news and short feature program, was brought in to replace him. He in turn would be replaced three years later by the ubiquitous Ernst Lubitsch.

It was a confusing time for all Paramount players, since they didn't know if the studio would survive. Chevalier had already taken preventive measures by signing a $5,000 a week radio contract, bringing the star system to the comparatively new medium. Soon, Ed Wynn, Al Jolson, Ben Bernie, Jimmy Durante, and Jack Benny would make the transition from moribund vaudeville. For the Broadway actors now at Paramount, it was a case of *déjà vu*. They had seen the theater go into a deep recession, and they now saw the film industry caught up in the same dilemma.

The powers at Paramount shrewdly enticed the brothers back to Hollywood. They had to rush out a program picture to follow up the strong grosses of *Horse Feathers*. It was already apparent that with only one picture, the Marx Brothers would be the studio's box office leaders for the year, with Maurice Chevalier and Marlene Dietrich trailing behind. It should also have been obvious that no modestly budgeted comedy could salvage the situation.

There was no longer any talk of Lubitsch directing them in a Ruritanian operetta to be called *Oo La La*. During the year, the magic of his name would be lent to four other pictures, though the directing was farmed out to younger talents who were instructed to emulate the Lubitsch touch. The master director was kept busy supervising their efforts.

Sheekman, Kalmar, and Ruby were assigned to write the new film, *Cracked Ice*. No details were revealed about its plot, but it conceivably might have a Western setting, or perhaps it would be a sendup of Chaplin's *The Gold Rush*, or a jewel robbery caper. The script would have to be completed in two months if shooting were to start in December.

In the meantime, Standard Oil of New Jersey, Pennsylvania, and Louisiana approached Groucho and Chico, offering them $7,500 weekly to broadcast from New York.

Arthur Sheekman and Nat Perrin by this time had become writing partners, and the two men left for New York with Groucho and Chico to write the thirteen radio segments.

Shibboleths had already been set up in the infant radio medium. Sophistication was not its strong suit. Jokes acceptable on the stage were not permissible in puritanical living rooms. No fast gags, no wisecracks, no double entendres. On the face of it, Groucho and radio were like oil and water.

The series, "Beagle, Shyster and Beagle," was scheduled to air November 21. Groucho played an ambulance-chasing lawyer, and Chico was his assistant. Delays pushed the opening back a week. Zeppo was tentatively scheduled to participate in the broadcasts when Groucho and Chico returned to California for the filming of their Paramount picture, now called *Firecrackers*.

The "Radio Reports" column of *Variety* reviewed the debut of the brothers on radio in its December 6 issue:

> In aiming for their air debut as a part of the oil companies' new 5-Star Theatre broadcasting scheme, Groucho and Chico Marx seem to have considered everything but their audience. They have the material and of its kind very good, even though a little too fast. Opinion differed on their first broadcast ... Some said they were great, others thought they were about 50-50 and others couldn't see them at all. Of course, all these opinions come from New Yorkers, so they don't count. It could be said the Marxes did an average show for a first performance on the air.

Variety, while conceding radio listeners were basically a small-time vaudeville audience, and that the two Marxes knew the milieu well, was nevertheless critical of some of the gamier aspects of the show, concluding that Groucho and Chico had potential on radio if they chose their material more carefully.

The show was reasonably well accepted, except by an attorney named Beagle who resented the implication. The name of the show was changed to "Flywheel, Shyster and Flywheel." The story lines remained pretty much variations on their movie themes: playing stowaways on a boat; doing Chevalier imitations; Groucho impersonating Sir Roderick Mortimer, an African explorer. The show's highest rating was thirteenth, but it didn't match the appeal of the other ex-vaudevillians. Nevertheless, it was renewed for an additional thirteen weeks.

Meanwhile, back in California, trouble was brewing. Groucho and Chico decided to return for consultations with director Norman McLeod. There had been some talk that Kalmar and Ruby, along with Harpo and Zeppo, would come East to finish the screenplay. No one seemed satisfied with the script, however, the writers included, and drastic revisions were needed. Shooting was pushed back until February 15. Talk began to crop up that the picture, its name now changed to *Grasshoppers*, would be based on the radio characters and expanded to include Harpo and Zeppo. While the script problems were worked out, Standard Oil permitted Groucho and Chico to finish their commitment in California.

Compounding the problem was Paramount's continuing dismal profit and loss statement. The studio had offered a lot of talk thus far, plus some seed money, but the brothers didn't know if there would be any funds left to pay them should they act in the film.

In mid-February they publicly questioned the validity of the transfer of their contract from Paramount Pictures to Paramount-Publix to Paramount Productions, claiming their contract had no such assignment clause. The studio's receivers were consulted on the matter.

The matter was still pending during the first part of 1933, a record low period for all of show business, when Frenchy suffered a heart attack in March. It was his second in three months.

Frenchy had been living with Zeppo and Marion at their place on North Havenhurst. Marion had created a showplace environment of which she was justifiably proud. She was understandably upset when her father-in-law, a vain man to the end, spilled some hair dye on her curtains.

Frenchy moved to Harpo's unoccupied apartment at the Garden of Allah. It was there that he had suffered his first seizure the previous December 26.

On March 10, three days after Frenchy's hospitalization, the brothers walked out of the studio, claiming their contract had been breached for "non-payment of certain sums of money," as well as for the transfer of their contract from one corporation to another. They announced the formation of their own company with Sam Harris as a partner. Max Gordon and Sam Katz, it would later be revealed, were part of the group.

Chico, at home, told Betty and Maxine of the lawsuit. "We've never won a lawsuit yet," he pessimistically said, "and it looks like we're not going to win this one."

Back in New York, the fifth Marx Brother was also in trouble.

Gummo's dress business went bankrupt. His liabilities amounted to $105,868 and his assets to "none."

These demoralizing events didn't presage a prosperous, happy year for any of the brothers. Nevertheless, the four performers proceeded to incorporate. The Katz-Gordon-Harris combine had previously revealed it had financing for the brothers' new picture, which they made clear wouldn't be *Cracked Ice* or any of its aliases.

The film version of the Kaufman-Ryskind musical, *Of Thee I Sing*, was announced as the brothers' first picture for Producing Artists, the group controlled by Katz. Shooting was scheduled to start on June 1, with Norman McLeod leaving Paramount to direct. The brothers would receive, in lieu of salaries, fifty percent of the gross.

The brothers may have felt they were helping Gummo out by hiring him to become their business manager. But he proved astute, and within a few years he, along with Zeppo, would be one of the top agents in the industry. At the outset, he was assigned to assist Al Lichtman of the production office with distribution.

Kaufman and Ryskind were adapting their topical political commentary to the screen. Chico and Harpo were to join them in the East, Chico to iron out business details and Harpo to work out his interpretation of the mild-mannered Vice President who now literally didn't have a voice. Frenchy's illness required them to postpone the trip for a few weeks, but they finally left for New York to meet up with Groucho. Zeppo stayed behind to watch over Frenchy. His father would be sick for six months.

Frenchy died on May 11, 1933, at the age of seventy-two.

The New Deal of Franklin Delano Roosevelt sparked an upturn in the fortunes of the entertainment world as well as the nation's economy in general. It was a fitting contribution from a man who, because of his carefully staged orations, would be known as "The Barrymore in the White House." The repeal of Prohibition was looming. Recovery was on the way.

It hadn't come soon enough for the Marx Brothers. Producing Artists, when the chips had to be put up, was unable to finance the picture. Paramount in the meantime was quietly proceeding with preparations for a Marx Brothers picture, investing $100,000 in preproduction costs for a film to be known as *Duck Soup*. Additional financing had suddenly materialized for studio productions. Paramount reverted to the mythical kingdom setting originally announced when Lubitsch was being discussed as a possible director.

With no alternative—the radio show had ended for Groucho and Chico, and Harpo was spending most of his time seeing an actress named Susan Fleming and discussing a possible tour of Russia—a settlement with Paramount was reached. The brothers reserved the right to make new claims against the studio's bankrupt estate if an accounting of the profits from *Monkey Business* showed they had more money coming to them. By the end of the summer, Hollywood studios would sign 315 refugees from the stage to film contracts. Paramount's most notable recruit was Mae West. Her pictures over the next few years would save the studio from extinction.

The act gave Katz an option for a later picture, but it was currently committed to report to Paramount on June 19 for their fifth picture. Kalmar and Ruby were signed for the screenplay.

After six months of constant emergencies, Groucho should have been enjoying the leisure time before the start of the picture with his family. He evidently wasn't.

The years of nitpicking had finally caught up with Ruth. She had been dismissed as a woman and minimized as a mother and homemaker. She began looking forward to her evening drinks.

"This was the tag end of Groucho's golden years," Norman Krasna said. "From that point on, he never knew a tranquil home. His life was an unbroken line of unhappiness." That much of it was of Groucho's own doing didn't ease the pain.

Their children must have sensed the change, although life went on as before, but with an added fillip. Gus and Grace Kahn had moved to California earlier in the year, buying a house on Arden Drive, across the back alley from Groucho's house on Hillcrest.

The Marxes didn't have a swimming pool, and Arthur and Miriam would often scoot across the alley to join the Kahn children, Donald and Irene, in their pool.

A polio epidemic that summer necessitated the emptying of the water from the pool. The neighborhood children played in dry dock.

Grace Kahn remembered Groucho's calling her one day. "Why don't you Kahns put some water in your pool?" he asked. "Arthur keeps diving in and he's getting all chafed."

Margaret Dumont arrived in California to appear with the brothers in *Duck Soup*. She had agreed to appear in *Cracked Ice* when that aborted picture was in the talking stage, and made the move when *Duck Soup* went into production.

"I remember Groucho's elation at luring her to Hollywood," publicist Teet Carle worte in the February, 1974, issue of *Archives*. "Groucho may have considered her a good luck object inasmuch as critics were calling the Hollywood-made films 'descents from the heights' and the distribution department was grumbling."

Signed as director was Leo McCarey, whom Groucho would later describe as "the only great director we ever had . . . and a good drunk." Curiously, despite being a teetoler, Groucho placed a high value on drinkers, possibly because they were often convivial men. His assessment of McCarey as their greatest director came after film revisionists had upgraded the picture as among the Marx Brothers's best. *Duck Soup*, when originally released, didn't begin to approach the success of their four previous Paramount films.

Chico would later recall McCarey as a kindred soul, a great fellow for making bets. "I had lost a lot of bets to him," he wrote in the *New York Journal* in April of 1934, "so I decided to fix him.

"I came in one day with a bag of walnuts. 'How far do you think you can throw a walnut?' I said. 'Further than you, I bet,' he said, rising to the bait. 'I bet you a hundred,' said I. 'Done,' says he. He threw the first walnut and it went about a hundred feet. I threw a walnut and it went way off into the blue. Looked like a half mile. He never could understand it. He didn't know that my walnut was filled with lead."

Toward the end of shooting, a number of actors bolted from the Academy of Motion Picture Arts and Sciences and joined with a group of non-members to form the Screen Actors Guild. The Marx

Brothers were among the non-members of the Academy to join SAG, which had 501 original members. Their main reason for organizing was the flagrant practice of salary-fixing among studios. This most affected lesser players, but major stars spearheaded the drive. They included Adolphe Menjou, Fredric March, Paul Muni, James Cagney, Robert Montgomery, Gary Cooper, Ralph Bellamy, George Raft, Eddie Cantor, Spencer Tracy, and the Marx Brothers.

Cantor was elected the president of SAG; Menjou the first vice president; March, second vice president; Ann Harding, third vice president; and Groucho, treasurer.

"After the first meeting," Groucho said, "Robert Montgomery and Jimmy Gleason and I went to a whorehouse. It was the only safe place to go."

The question, after *Duck Soup* was completed, was where the team would go. The brothers had tied in with Sam Katz, primarily because Sam Harris was involved with the company. When Harris broke his ties with Katz, claiming Katz had dragged his heels in putting *Of Thee I Sing* together, the brothers had some serious thinking to do.

Duck Soup was indifferently received by both critics and the public. The brothers had become unpredictable in a rather predictable way.

Years later cinema cultists would single out the picture as one of the brothers' greatest films. It was cited for its anti-Fascist viewpoint, performed at such a breakneck pace.

"Pacing is always a problem," notes Woody Allen in Eric Lax's *On Being Funny*. "There are very few comedies in the world, and even the greatest have *langueur* in them. There's no way out. There are moments that you tolerate. Once in a while you hit on something like *Duck Soup* that has practically no dead spots in it. If you were asked to name the best comedies ever made, and you named *The Gold Rush* and *The General* and a half dozen others, *Duck Soup* is the only one that really doesn't have a dull spot." The Marx Brothers had given the public too much of a good thing.

Toward the end of 1933, Sam Harris and Max Gordon tried to revive *Of Thee I Sing* for the brothers. It didn't pan out. Harpo finally made his tour of Russia and was a spectacular hit. His six-minute pantomime at the Leningrad Music Hall drew a twenty-five minute ovation. Groucho announced that they were finished with Paramount and the movies, and that Harris would produce a musical for them in the fall of 1934, with either Irving Berlin or Moss Hart involved in its writing. The move wasn't entirely voluntary.

The motion picture industry would have its first profitable year in some time in 1934, attendance reaching a peak in August. Hollywood had spent a total of $800,000 for rights to Broadway hits.

As for the brothers' role in films, Edwin Schallert wrote on New Year's Day in the *Los Angeles Times:*

> Every indication points to the Marx Brothers being through with the movies for the time being. They played the game for what it was worth, but the screen is relentless in its exactions on comedians. It's their duty to be funnier in each succeeding picture, and that isn't anything easy.
>
> "Duck Soup" was scarcely a fade-out . . . but the same tricks can't be worked over and over again . . . the comedy quartet has a rather set routine.

Mae West had shot to the top as Paramount's greatest box office star, followed by Bing Crosby, Harold Lloyd, Fredric March, and the Marx Brothers. *Duck Soup* had been the brothers' most lavish production, yet the returns weren't as favorable as expected.

The brothers announced that Robert E. Sherwood, George Kaufman, and Morrie Ryskind might be contributors to the fall show. They confirmed that discussions were under way with Twentieth Century-Fox and United Artists for release of their next film. But the only work two of them—Groucho and Chico—could get was a radio series, "Marx of Time," sponsored by the American Oil Company on ABC.

After their first program in the new series, the *New York Post's* "Dialist" complimented Groucho and Chico "on the noble precedent they set . . . They barred from the studio not only any studio audience, but even their sponsor and agency representatives, we hear. They believe that radio programs are intended for radio listeners, and they did a show that the folk by the loud speakers could enjoy."

It's curious that the stage-trained two, who knew the contagion of laughter, should choose to speak into open microphones behind closed doors.

Groucho and Chico suggested radio comedians in New York should meet to discuss the subject. The meeting was set for Tuesday, April 3, at the Algonquin Hotel.

In the meantime, Groucho received a letter from Zeppo in California. He had finally decided to quit the act, and had bought a partnership in the Bren-Orsatti talent agency. George Kaufman and Moss Hart had already given him permission to use their names as clients, so that other writers would seriously consider Zeppo as a possible agent.

Groucho made public a letter from Zeppo explaining his defection from the act:

> I'm sick and tired of being a stooge. You know that anybody else would have done as well as I in the act. When the chance came for me to get into the business world I jumped at it.
>
> I have only stayed in the act until now because I knew that you, Chico and Harpo wanted me to. But I'm sure you understand why I have joined Frank Orsatti in his theatrical agency and that you forgive my action. Wish me luck.

"It's going to complicate things terribly for us," Groucho told the press, "particularly on sleeper jumps. In the old days there were four of us. Then we would split up peacefully, two to a berth. Now we're three, and there's bound to be hard feelings."

At the moment, however, there were only two, for Harpo was dallying elsewhere.

The April 3 meeting was at hand, and Jack Benny, Jimmy Durante, and Jack Pearl had arrived to discuss the subject of studio audiences with radio editors.

The meeting started out like a solo comedy routine, performed, of course, by Groucho, the self-appointed chairman.

"Only one guy should talk at a time," he ruled, "and, most of the time, not even him.

"I'm against studio audiences for several reasons. One is that you have to get tickets for all your relatives. It's bad enough to have relatives without seeing them out in front of you every Sunday night.

"It hampers our work greatly because all through the program we are wondering which door will be best for a quick escape before the relatives can assemble to congratulate us and make a touch.

"But right now we have decided to have a studio audience so the sponsor can hear the people laugh. That's the only way we can convince him we are funny."

The previous Sunday, Groucho and Chico, under sponsor pressure, had broadcast before a studio audience of over one thousand people.

"People have become accustomed to hear laughter," Jack Benny explained, "and if programs went on without it, the whole thing would sound flat. Groucho and Chico started without an audience, but their program last Sunday with an audience sounded better than any of their others. I don't want to get into personalities, though, so I wish you wouldn't quote me on that."

The discussion continued with other levities before Groucho concluded the meeting by saying he and Chico had put the matter to a vote. "We asked our listeners to write us about it and we got 500 letters—400 in favor of studio audiences and 100 against the Marx Brothers."

The matter became academic as far as the two Marx Brothers were concerned, because their show was cancelled after eight weeks.

Groucho, however, decided to stay on in New York to work with the writers on the new production. Sherwood and Hart agreed to write the book; Irving Berlin would compose the score.

He leased a ten-room suite at 1088 Park Avenue until the following September, and the family joined him for the summer. Miriam, now almost seven, was developing as quick a tongue as her father. One day, Ruth was trying to put her hair in Shirley Temple curls, but Miriam wanted nothing to do with it.

"Don't be like that," Groucho said. "Let your mother make your curls. Why, when I was a little boy I had curls right down to my shoulders."

"Yeah," his daughter replied, "and I bet everybody called you a sissy."

Having some time on his hands, Groucho decided to buy a new guitar and take lessons. He dropped into a musical studio, unrecognizable without his greasepaint mustache, and asked about the course of study.

"What kind of lessons are you interested in?" the teacher asked.

"Is there more than one kind?" Groucho asked in return. "I thought a guitar lesson was a guitar lesson."

"Oh, no," the teacher said, "there are several types of playing—symphonic, band, accompaniments, and so forth. If you would play for me, I could tell you the sort you want."

Groucho took the guitar out of the case and started strumming his best piece, running up the scale, adding some furbelows along the way.

"I see," the teacher said when he finished. "Hillbilly."

Throughout his career, Groucho would eat up comedy writers by the dozens, as he now seemed to be doing with the prospective production.

"Hecht, MacArthur, Kaufman, Moss Hart, Ryskind and Gene Fowler are working on a play for us," Groucho wrote Arthur Sheekman in mid-summer of 1934. "I am getting three more authors today, and I hope to have forty or fifty on the job by the end of the month. It's becoming as big a craze as Mah Jong, writing a show for the Marx Brothers, and I predict in time it will sweep the country."

Actually, MacArthur and Hecht were now writing the play, with Kaufman offering suggestions on staging. He was too busy collaborating with Moss Hart on *Merrily We Roll Along* and with Morrie Ryskind on *Bringing on the Girls* to offer any more substantive help.

Only Norman Krasna of all his close literary friends would never write for the team. He had rapidly become successful as a screenwriter and had priced himself out of the market.

"It certainly wouldn't have been a comedown for me to write for the Marx Brothers," he said, "but I was never somebody who collaborated and was never good enough—nor was anybody—to be a sole writer for them."

Groucho often stressed the strong connection between a good writer and a good comedian. He would like it believed that he was both. The world sings his praises as a great comedian, but a critical analysis of his seven books, most of which were ghostwritten with

Groucho having final literary control, reveals him to have been only a fair writer-editor. That he was willing to dim his luster as a performer, to admit only to being a "good comedian," so that he could proportionately upgrade himself to a "good writer," reveals something about his priorities.

None of the writers who worked with him denied Groucho's contributions to the final product, but all of them knew what they had created for him. The characters developed for him by writers made him a star; the resourcefulness and lightning wit he brought to his portrayals made him a legend.

"I always got the best writers I could," he told me. "They're very important. George Jessel is an example of a funny man who wouldn't spend money on writers. He wrote his show himself with a burlesque comedian. It only lasted thirteen weeks. I was an integral part of the writing. I'm essentially a writer who unfortunately went into show business."

Any comedian can go over his lines and tell the writer which ones won't play for him. If this makes a comedian a writer, then Groucho was a writer.

The summer ended with Groucho starring in the road production of *Twentieth Century*. He was staying at a house in Lakewood, Maine, and decided to trod the boards in a straight comedy acting role with the Lakewood Players in nearby Skowhegan. Any actor of lesser stature might have played the role without public notice, but *Time* magazine caught his act:

> Taking the part of Oscar Jaffe in the Ben Hecht-Charles MacArthur play, 'Twentieth Century,' he competed for honors with John Barrymore and Moffat Johnson who played the part in movie and Broadway presentations respectively. The audience agreed he compared creditably with his notable predecessors. This is one of the rare times when any one of the four Marx brothers has been seen on the stage without the others . . . Now, at 45, he sails alone.

Harpo, influenced by his brother, also decided to make his dramatic debut. He would play an "aged, crawly, filthy bag of old rags and bones," in *Tobacco Road*, who "finally wanders off into the bushes never to return."

The brothers were marking time, waiting for some project to fall into place. At this point they didn't know what form it would take.

During this limbo period Arthur Sheekman wired Groucho from California, telling him of his marriage to actress Gloria Stuart. The romantic that lurked beneath his caustic exterior surfaced when Groucho wrote them a loving note:

Dear Sheek and now Gloria too:
I wondered why you hadn't written, but now I understand, and someday I hope to be the best man, that is with the exception of you, Sheekie. Don't be so afraid of love, and ashamed of it. It's the only thing worthwhile, even though it isn't always permanent. I look forward to coming back, there now will be four of us, instead of the customary three, and we will have great times. We can take long motor trips in my Cadillac (with you paying half of the gasoline).

Groucho

CHAPTER NINE

His dark eyes . . . were kind, aloof and, though they often reasoned with you gently, somewhat superior. It was no fault of theirs if they saw so much. He darted in and out of the role of "one of the boys" with dexterity—but on the whole I should say he wasn't one of them. But he knew how to shut up, how to draw into the background, how to listen. From where he stood (and though he was not a tall man, it always seemed high up) he watched the multitudinous practicalities of the world like a proud young shepherd to whom night and day had never mattered. He was born sleepless, without a talent for rest or the desire for it.

F. Scott Fitzgerald, The Last Tycoon

One of the oldest of Hollywood bromides is, "You're only as good as your last picture." Artistic merit is not the main criterion by which "good" is judged. It is called the motion picture *industry*, after all, and profit is always its uppermost consideration. The business is heart-breaking and nerve-racking, as countless books have already shown, and possessed of a notoriously short memory and absolutely no sense of gratitude. The case histories of too many D. W. Griffiths and Buster Keatons are testimonies to its callousness.

No matter what face-saving statements were made to the contrary, the Marx Brothers were generally conceded to be through in films. They were now middle-aged, conspicuously so. Despite the genius and originality of their characterizations, honed over nearly thirty years, they were no longer credible as juvenile zanies. *Duck Soup* was a failure, the verdict of future students of film notwithstanding, and the new officers at Paramount weren't beating on the brothers' doors with a new offer. The team, however, had an advantage over other performers in similar circumstances in that Chico had cultivated the movie moguls over the years. Several were willing to enter discussions with them. Trade newspapers periodically reported a deal was brewing with one studio or another, yet none came to fruition.

Samuel Goldwyn was very fond of Harpo, and he made a halfhearted offer, which the team was just as halfheartedly considering.

Among Chico's bridge-playing friends was Irving Thalberg, who was head of production at Metro-Goldwyn-Mayer. He spearheaded such studio triumphs as *Anna Christie, Grand Hotel,* and *The Barretts of Wimpole Street.* His friend, Hal Roach, had once accused Thalberg of having no comedy sense, and the heavy dramas with which he was associated seemed to bear out Roach's contention.

Thalberg decided to prove him wrong. When Harpo told Goldwyn that the boy genius of MGM had approached the brothers, Goldwyn said, "If Irving wants you, go with him. He knows more in one finger than I know in my whole body." Goldwyn's praise of Thalberg may have been expedient. He would be off the hook.

"Thalberg was a strange man," Groucho said. "He was a Jew from a poor Brooklyn family. Yet he had elegance and good taste."

Thalberg also had some concepts he wanted to test with the brothers. "Men like your comedy, but women don't," he told them. "They don't have your kind of humor, so we'll give women a romance they can become interested in." He also presumed to suggest that the Marx Brothers weren't the greatest authorities in

222

the making of film comedies. They weren't sympathetic types, and didn't wear well. They also didn't seem to understand the importance of pace in films. The brothers could gauge audience reaction in the theater and "hold" their lines until the laughter died down. They weren't able to do this in pictures, and the result was frenetic and confusing, with the movie audiences laughing through their best lines. And now the public was no longer returning to see their movies for a second and third time to hear what it had missed during the original viewing.

Louis B. Mayer, the head of the studio, noting the brothers' unimpressive showing in their last picture, didn't find them worthy enough talents to join the existing roster of MGM stars: Greta Garbo, Joan Crawford, Clark Gable, Jeanette MacDonald, Nelson Eddy, William Powell, Jean Harlow, Myrna Loy, and Spencer Tracy among them. Thalberg not only succeeded in wearing Mayer down but was able to wrest an extraordinary concession from the studio: fifteen percent of the gross. The brothers turned down an offer from Max Gordon to appear in a Broadway musical and, on September 19, 1934, signed a three-picture deal with MGM.

Past percentage deals were usually based on net profits. Many actors found out too late that these net percentages turned out to be less than their normal salaries. They wouldn't have been surprised to find, in the catch-all below-the-line costs, that they had to absorb the expense of oats for Mayer's racehorses before they began receiving money. The Marx Brothers wouldn't suffer such an indignity; their money came off the top. Cinéastes later accused Thalberg of having a detrimental effect on their humor, adulterating their genius with "breathing spaces" of plot and song. Groucho, in defense of Thalberg, replied, "It doubled the gross." Consequently, it doubled the money the brothers made.

At the outset, Thalberg had opposition within the studio when he assigned dramatist James McGuinness to write the story for the picture, "a yarn concerned with the fortunes of a grand opera troupe." The brothers weren't taken with the idea, either. Thalberg felt time would be saved if McGuinness were assigned to develop the plot, with comedy writers being brought in later to develop the laughs.

As the original story took form, the brothers would play opposite an operatic diva, preferably blonde, with two juveniles playing the love interests.

While the story was taking shape, Zeppo called on Thalberg, ostensibly to sell a client. The studio executive resisted Zeppo's sales pitch. "I'll have to think it over," he said.

Zeppo threateningly pointed his finger at Thalberg. "If you don't sign him, I'll go back to the Marx Brothers!" In the next few weeks, his lot as an agent appreciably improved.

The brothers were understandably nervous about the material, since it was such a departure from their original films. Groucho went to see Thalberg.

"Our first two pictures were good because we played the gags hundreds of times on the stage," Groucho said. By "good" he too meant profitable, tending to forget that they weren't the greatest examples of cinematic art. "The three other pictures weren't as good because we never knew if the gags were going to work out. We don't know if they will in this picture, either."

Thalberg suggested the script might be played before an audience. As they discussed the possibility, the two men saw they could take several comedy scenes from the script and play them in vaudeville houses with connecting narrative projected on the screen. The brothers agreed to try out the concept.

In the meantime, George S. Kaufman joined the writing team. He had declined the studio's previous offer of $80,000, but when the ante was raised, he reconsidered, and came West from New York after the first of the year.

Groucho, knowing how distracting the New York expatriates could be, asked Kaufman why he chose to stay at the Garden of Allah.

"It reminds me of Hollywood," he replied.

His salary was also Hollywoodian. He had been lured out to California at five thousand dollars a week, with a minimum guarantee of $100,000, to rework the script with Morrie Ryskind. Ryskind was receiving a salary one-fifth the size of his partner's.

The film industry was beginning to revive early in 1935, and other talents were being similarly enticed. Higher prices were being paid for Broadway properties. Film budgets for the year would approach $100,000,000. There was a new surge of building activity for the theater divisions owned by the studios, for the purpose of showcasing the forthcoming products. No one was busier than Thalberg himself, who was producing three other films at the same time as *A Night at the Opera: Romeo and Juliet, Mutiny on the Bounty,* and *The Good Earth.*

Sam Marx, the brothers' distant cousin, was already at Metro in the creative department when Groucho and Company moved onto the lot. "At last I've got some relatives here," he told Groucho. The comedian wasn't amused. Nevertheless the friendship of the Marx cousins became stronger during their stay at MGM. Chico had always sought out the Marx cousins in New York. Now Sam became closer to the other brothers at the studio and began socializing with them and their wives.

"I went to dinner at Groucho's several times," he said, "but I found it a bit wearing. Each family member was always trying to top the other. You couldn't carry on a serious conversation, and I began looking on it as an ordeal."

Excessive laughter may have been a symptom of the family's incipient deterioration, but it wasn't totally unloving. The Marx family would become the models for Norman Krasna's *Dear Ruth,* which would be produced on Broadway ten years later.

"Miriam was one of the daughters and Ruth was the other," Krasna recalled. Their parents, patterned after Groucho and Ruth, were named Edith and Harry Wilkins. She was a "generous, sentimental woman, suspiciously like the backbone of the country," he was a Municipal Court judge in a blue suit, "forty-five, easy-going, and a fit companion for his nice wife."

Krasna created an impossibly wholesome image of the family in the play, as much a product of his own muse as it was a projection of Groucho's fantasy. The badinage he re-created reflected an underlying fondness between the principals. If read with a sarcastic intonation, however, it could create a totally different picture:

EDITH. How did you sleep, dear?
HARRY. Like a top. I spun all night. *(No reaction)* That's pretty good.
EDITH. Groucho Marx. We all heard it.
HARRY. That wasn't his joke at all.

MIRIAM. Slept like a baby. Cried all night.
EDITH. Would you like some Sanka?
HARRY. You're welcome.

Krasna was one of the few remaining bachelors in Groucho's circle, and as he virtually lived with the Marxes, he was privy to a more intimate view of the family than any of Groucho's other friends. The two men also collaborated on a screenplay, *Grand Passion*, (which would be optioned by Paramount in February of 1935) and Krasna was exposed to Groucho's basically warm outlook. It was a comedy about a king and a chorus girl, mixing romantic as well as screwball elements, which would become topical the following year with the revelations of a love affair between the King of England and a Mrs. Simpson.

"It had a simple elemental Cinderella basis," Krasna recalled. As such it reflected Groucho's sentimental nature, a facet of his character generally well-hidden. "Unless you were really close," Krasna said, "you might think he was quite selfish. He wasn't afraid to show you his intolerance. Then he would turn around and do these enormous things. What he wouldn't do for himself, he'd do for a friend."

He could have callously turned his back on his friends Harry Ruby and Bert Kalmar, who wrote the screenplay for the failed *Duck Soup;* instead, he insisted that they be the first additions to the writing staff after McGuinness completed the original concept for *A Night at the Opera.* Afterwards, Kaufman and Ryskind would doctor and polish the material.

The two Broadway expatriates worked out of a suite with an adjoining sun porch at the Beverly Wilshire Hotel. Kaufman, in agreeing to take on the assignment, had specified the studio couldn't call him for six weeks while he and Ryskind thrashed out the rewrite. They were clearly visible during the day from the Beverly Hills Brown Derby across the street, pacing and screaming and, presumably, writing.

The road tour was set to open at the Orpheum Theatre in Salt Lake City the week of April 13, and was to be followed by week-long engagements at the Paramount Theaters in Seattle and Portland. The show was scheduled to end on May 9 after a week's run at the Orpheum in San Francisco.

Just before the brothers left for Salt Lake City, Thalberg called Groucho into his office to inform him that an additional writer would be joining them on the tour. His name was Al Boasberg. He also informed Groucho that the director of the picture would be Sam Wood, who would be catching the tag end of the road tour to see how the comedy played.

Groucho knew Boasberg's work quite well, and was glad to have him along. The writer was a roly poly eccentric, the son of a Buffalo jeweler, who had first been hired in 1923 by George Burns and Gracie Allen, and had created their well-known "Lamb Chops" routine.

"Now, as far as writing went," Burns wrote in *Living It Up; Or, They Still Love Me in Altoona,* "Boasey wouldn't sit down and put together a script. But if somebody else wrote the script, you'd give it to Boasey and he'd punch it up for you. He was sort of a doctor of comedy, and he was great at it. His lines always made the script funnier."

Boasberg's writing was so facile that he had developed a weekly service in the late 1920s to wire different jokes to his clients, which numbered half of the comedians on the Loew's vaudeville circuit as well as in legitimate revues mounted by Ziegfeld, Earl Carroll, and the Shuberts.

He had made an extraordinarily easy transition to the cinema, first in silent films and then in talking pictures. His contributions proved to be significant. Groucho, though he was never personally close to him, continued singing Boasberg's praises long after the writer's death.

When Canada celebrated its centennial in 1967, the Canadian Film Archives polled critics of forty countries to determine the greatest all-time movie comedies. The films were to be shown at an Ottawa film festival in April of that year. Their consensus: Chaplin's *The Gold Rush,* Buster Keaton's *The General,* and the Marx Brothers' *A Night at the Opera.* These were singular achievements, each film involving totally different casts before and behind the cameras.

Only one person could claim to be involved with more than one of these pictures: Al Boasberg. As a comedy writer under contract to MGM, he was one of the four screenwriters involved in *The General.* Many versions were later offered about the germination of

227

the stateroom scene in *A Night at the Opera*, each giving a different person credit for the inspiration. Yet, there was a definite forerunner to the scene in *The General*, a setting on a train with a big shoving around of people, which Boasberg helped create. At the outset, however, Groucho gravitated to Boasberg because of a legendary Hollywood story in which the writer was involved. He reportedly visited Keaton on a cold, wind-swept outdoor set and started a bonfire from small scraps of lumber to keep warm. The winds fanned the flames until the entire set was engulfed.

Boasberg had worked closely with Wood in 1929 and 1930, and had just finished work on a Charlie Ruggles picture, *Murder in the Private Car*.

Thalberg, in explaining the assignment of Wood, told Groucho, "Sam hasn't been doing very well lately. I think he can supply a different approach. He'll also take suggestions better."

The assignment of Wood didn't sit well with the chronically insecure Groucho. It seemed as if Thalberg, while claiming to be mounting a first-rate production, had nevertheless given the brothers less than the best in the persons of McGuinness and Wood. Groucho, however, refrained from voicing any objection to Thalberg; instead, over the next few months, he complained directly to Wood and McGuinness.

In the case of McGuinness, Groucho's criticisms seemed to have spread all over town. When the overblown talk got back to Groucho, he realized he might have been unfair to the writer. He invited the maligned party to his house for dinner.

"I'm sorry," McGuinness replied, "but I have a previous engagement which I will make as soon as possible."

When the company went on tour, the writers' secretaries came along. A last-minute addition to the cast was singer Allan Jones.

"I never thought I was coming on as Zeppo's replacement," he said. "I knew they had to have a love interest and they brought me on to do it. But I knew I was going on to other things. I often saw Zeppo at parties in Las Vegas whenever I played there, but we never discussed the fact I'd taken his place."

Soon after Jones was announced as the romantic interest in the production, he was contacted by composers Arthur Freed and Nacio Herb Brown, who knew he needed a signature song. They opened their piano bench and dusted off the sheet music to "Alone," a previously unpublished song. Jones liked it and thought it should go into the picture. His influence, however, wasn't overpowering at the time.

Jones's previous film credit was in a Jean Harlow picture, in which the platinum blonde was required to dance to a song number. Since her movements were clumsy, Jones was placed by a piano on the stage,. and whenever Harlow's turns were less than graceful, the camera would cut to him singing.

This incidental exposure hardly qualified him to discuss music theory with Irving Thalberg, but Jones brashly brought up the subject. Thalberg allowed him to try the song out on the road tour.

Jones stayed in the same hotels as the brothers, and quickly fell into the habit of walking over to the nearby theaters with them.

"I was scared to death we were going to be run in by the cops in Salt Lake City," Jones recalled, "because Harpo would see some pretty girls coming toward us, and he'd run and jump and wrap his legs around their waists, and kiss them. Fortunately, they were so famous that people accepted their antics."

To make sure that their stage performances were equally acceptable, the writers' secretaries sat in a box, timing the laughs. Lines would be changed for the four daily shows, to determine which ones were the best received.

The stateroom scene didn't work on the road tour, according to Jones, so the writers decided to delete it. They were overruled by Thalberg. "Leave it in," he advised them by phone. "Just because it doesn't work in the theater doesn't mean it won't work in films. You see a flat drop that's supposed to be a stateroom, and you can't make it look like it's crowded. In pictures, it will have an entirely different perspective."

More was added to the scene as the troupe moved on to Seattle and Portland. Clifton Fadiman described the process in the January, 1936, issue of *Stage:*

> I went to see Harpo about one thing and another, and he told me that in its original form, the sequence, while comical, was not comical enough. It seemed to go a bit flat. Then one day ... Chico had an idea. In the first part of the sequence,

Groucho is outside giving a breakfast order to the steward. As he finished the order, Chico thought of adding, in stentorian tones, "And two hard-boiled eggs"—and Harpo, not to be outdone, blew his horn. For some reason or other, this gag, properly worked up, of course, made the whole scene jell. It turned something merely funny into something almost pitilessly hilarious. Harpo doesn't know exactly why, but that's the way it happened.

The original filmed script called for the opera house to be set ablaze through the misguided efforts of the local fire department. Boasberg objected, predicting that a movie audience would not be moved to laughter by such a scene. Boasberg won out.

The brothers were receiving $7,500 weekly for their stage tour on the Fanchon and Marco circuit, and the script was falling gradually into place as they prepared to move on from Portland to San Francisco. Suddenly, the Orpheum wasn't available to them, since Fanchon and Marco didn't want to alter their continuous-run movie policy. The show was offered to Fox West Coast, which operated the Warfield Theatre there, but the theater managers wanted the brothers to come into the smaller house at a proportionately smaller salary. The brothers declined and the act played its final week in Santa Barbara.

With the tour-tested gags fairly well set, shooting was scheduled to start in the late spring. Kaufman was persuaded to stay on as dialogue director for the picture. Groucho would often say that he was the only one Kaufman would allow to ad-lib, but that was on the stage and not in this minutely plotted film.

The blonde diva the brothers had been looking for had long since evolved into the society dowager, as played by Margaret Dumont. The soprano playing the romantic lead opposite Allan Jones was unexpectedly cast on one of those crazy Sundays Fitzgerald wrote about, when Oscar Levant brought Kitty Carlisle to the Thalbergs' beach house. Kitty had starred as a teen-ager in *Champagne, Sec* on Broadway in 1933 before signing a contract with Paramount Pictures, where she had played ingenue roles in two Bing Crosby movies.

"I had been studying opera very hard, and I felt I was ready," Miss Carlisle recalled. "Irving promised me I could sing opera seriously in the picture. I had reservations about being a serious singer in a movie with the Marx Brothers. The contrast is ludicrous. It seems churlish, unnice to say so, but at that time I had no idea that the movie would be so good and turn out to be a classic.

"I didn't see the script beforehand, not until the rehearsals. My reaction then was that it was wonderful. Something I always tell youngsters when they ask me about *cinema verité* is that you don't make classics that way. You make classics the way the Marx Brothers made *A Night at the Opera*. You get the best writers possible, then have the best possible rehearsals. It's only now, so many years later, that I fully realize the talented writers we had.

"On the set, the Marx Brothers performed very seriously. What I recall most about Groucho is that he used to come up to me between breaks, and he would do lines of dialogue, reciting jokes to me, *very* seriously. In that deadpan voice of his, he would ask, 'Is that funny?' I'd have to reply, 'No, Groucho, it's not funny.' And he'd slink away, terribly crushed, and come back later and try it again."

The first day of shooting, two dozen roses were sent to her dressing room. The card was signed "Allan Jones" and the bouquet came C. O. D.

A few days later, as the brothers were sitting on the set, Jones mentioned he was looking for a cocker spaniel for his daughter. When he got home that night, he found a Great Dane tied to his front door.

The practical jokes didn't have the stamp of cruelty that had typified those the brothers had played on their stage co-stars. Yet, in their own way, the brothers told both Allan Jones and Kitty Carlisle that they had arrived.

Sam Wood never got a similar message. Norman Krasna would later co-produce *The Devil in Miss Jones* with Frank Ross, and with Wood directing.

"I found Wood to be a marvelous movie mechanic," Krasna said. "Groucho's differences with him were political, I suspect. Wood was humorless in business, an arch conservative. Groucho's political philosophy was that of a man of great good will. He attracted the noble people of the world. Groucho couldn't bear to see injustice of any kind."

(In the late 1940s, when Communists allegedly dominated Hollywood, Wood was one of the right-wingers who regularly found anarchic dogma in any screenplay making a social statement.)

Allan Jones didn't like Wood either. "He was a disagreeable guy, very insecure. He wasn't the great director people thought he was. He was only good because he had good cutters around. He'd get about thirty takes, and then his cutters would pick the best ones when he ran the dailies. He wasn't a very sensitive man, nor was he a joy to work with. Although he had a great reputation as far as his pictures were concerned, he wasn't the type you'd think would direct a comedy."

In Wood's defense, he was following Thalberg's instructions in shooting many takes. A stolid, dignified man with no sense of humor about himself, he was a likely target of the Marxes. He simply couldn't see anything funny about the adolescent hijinks of grown men.

Chico was the leading miscreant. He flagrantly lifted five dollars from Wood's wallet. The director demanded that the money be returned. Chico delivered a sack filled with five hundred pennies.

Two weeks into the shooting, a bewhiskered messenger boy riding a creaky bicycle delivered a telegram to Wood. "Have decided to take a short vacation in Honolulu," it read. "Hope to be back in a month." It was signed by Groucho, Harpo, and Chico. Wood literally staggered at the news. The messenger boy then removed his whiskers to reveal himself as Chico, the practical joker.

Because he suffered from a queasy stomach, and possibly ulcers, Wood always had milk with his lunch, which would be delivered by a nearby grocery. One day the milk came in a baby's nursing bottle. Chico soon after brought a doctor and nurse onto the set.

"Where is the crazy man you called about?" the doctor asked.

Chico and Harpo grabbed Wood. "This is-a him," Chico said. "He's-a think he's a baby again. It's-a too bad, doc."

Wood could stand it no longer. "Don't you people have any

sense of dignity?" he bellowed. For some reason, the brothers were silent.

As shooting was completed the following evening, a dilapidated carriage drawn by a plowhorse drew up to the set. A coachman in livery was at the reins. The brothers came out of their dressing rooms, wearing white tie and tails and high silk hats. Groucho and Chico, with great pomp, seated themselves in the carriage. Harpo jumped on the horse's back and pulled a short pole from his pocket from which a carrot dangled on a string. The coachman called "Tallyho!" Harpo thrust the carrot in front of the horse and they were off.

Wood threatened to resign several times from the picture, but Thalberg always talked him out of it. Chico, when asked by a reporter about the brothers' differences with Wood, was indignant, denying that there was any friction between them.

"I can't imagine where anyone got an idea like that," he said, "because even if we're hard to get along with, anyone can get along with Wood. He's the top. Furthermore, there's not a truth to the whole thing. Wood is very fond of us. Why, only today, he's so fond of us, he told us that if the picture is a success, he's going to invite us to his house."

If Wood were going to place the credit where due, he would also have to be inviting Boasberg, Ryskind, and Kaufman. The studio was getting its money's worth out of the latter, having assigned him to doctor the screenplays of *Marie Antoinette* and *The Good Earth*. Kaufman arrived on the Marx Brothers set one day for another stint as dialogue coach. Groucho asked him about his other work for the studio.

"Don't be surprised," Kaufman replied, "if, when I hand in the final scene on this, you find you're guillotined for not planting rice in China."

In addition to his work for MGM, Kaufman was carrying on clandestinely with actress Mary Astor, an affair that would soon be revealed in sensational newspaper headlines.

Contrary to the popular folklore about Kaufman's distaste for music in his plays, it was the Marx Brothers themselves who decided "Alone" wouldn't work in the picture. Jones was informed

233

by composers Freed and Brown to this effect. He went to Thalberg.

"I don't pretend to know that this song will be a hit," he said, "but it's a beautiful song and I love singing it. I think it's a mistake not to have it in the picture."

"The brothers know their comedy," Thalberg replied, "and you should know your music. Let's put it back in."

"Alone" went on to become one of the top songs of 1936, being Number One for seventeen consecutive weeks on radio's "Hit Parade." It would be the only hit song ever to be associated with a Marx Brothers picture.

Although he was contravening the brothers' wishes by putting the song back into the picture, this was a short-term move and not indicative of the relationship Thalberg was anticipating with them over the long haul.

While shooting was nearing completion, Thalberg was concluding negotiations with Loew's, Inc., MGM's parent company, for the I. G. Thalberg Corporation, a new company which he would head, free of any subservience to MGM, whose films would be distributed by Loew's. Mayer bitterly fought the move, rightly seeing it as a threat to his autonomy. But Thalberg was too valuable to the studio. Rather than risk losing him to another company, Loew's agreed to finance and release the films of the new company when it came into being in 1939. Until then, Thalberg would have control of any talent he might employ over the next four years. He asked that Norma Shearer, Charles Laughton, and the Marx Brothers be put under personal contract to him, to which Loew's also agreed.

The brothers were now irrevocably tied to Thalberg. Not only did he want to make more movies with them, he was also discussing the possibility of producing, in collaboration with Max Gordon and Sam Harris, a separate Broadway play for them. His plans called for the comedy to be made as a film after its stage run. No studio executive had ever expressed such a tangible, all-encompassing belief in their potential, and it was reassuring that this trust should come from a man they all liked, rather than from the dreaded Mayer.

"I hated Mayer," Groucho said, "and Mayer hated me. He once asked me how the picture was going. I said, 'It's no concern of yours.' He didn't say anything . . . just walked away."

Mayer stored the affront for future reference. When the picture was previewed, it seemed like his vengeance was nearer than he had anticipated. The studio brass attended en masse. The laughter was scattered and far from the uproarious sort the brothers had come to expect. Thalberg's pacing had apparently left too much breathing space between the laughs.

Thalberg assured the brothers that it was not a Marx Brothers audience, and he would prove the comedy was a good one by running the film at the theater across the street. While underlings were preparing for the second screening, Groucho was especially jocular, unaware of Mayer's ill-concealed delight at the prospect of an impending catastrophe. Thalberg, the writers, and the brothers took in the second showing of the picture. The audience reaction was again tepid.

Groucho's mood had turned almost suicidal by the time the long evening was over. Thalberg reassured him, as he had hundreds of times before. Everything would be fine. The next morning, Thalberg began a three-day session with film editor William Levanway, tightening the movie until it achieved its final form.

The picture turned out to be the best and most profitable to date of the Marx Brothers comedies, both to the distributing studio and to the stars themselves.

Of all the huzzahs and hosannas tendered the picture, Groucho derived the greatest pleasure from a postcard the brothers received from a fan in Iowa:

> Mrs. King was telling me about a little boy who was spending Thanksgiving at the Emrie Hatchery near depot, and Mrs. Emrie took him to see Marx Bros. in the picture, and he laughed so much he wet his pants.
> This occurred in Humboldt, Iowa, and it seems to me that the best thing for you to do would be to send the boy a new pair of pants for the advertising is well worth the price.
> From Fair Play Movie Fan

With *A Night at the Opera*, the brothers became the first comedy team to reach the heights in talking pictures. The jump from silent pictures had been made successfully. The brothers were a true

235

symbol of show business's transition from vaudeville to silent pictures to sound. Chico, with his Italian accent, had his roots in vaudeville. Harpo, the last of the great pantomimists, though never a star in silent pictures, represented its highly expressive tradition. Groucho was the first of the fast-talking masters of insult, the style-setter who would be imitated by radio comics of the 1930s and 1940s. Together the three represented all the great American comedy styles. What made them unique, and mirrors of their time, was the national need they supplied by impertinently putting down the System, education, politics, sex, culture, and authority.

A Night at the Opera was quickly recognized as a minor classic, and its status has grown with every passing year. Without its enormous acceptance, the brothers' earlier pictures might literally not have stood the test of time. The highly perishable acetate negatives probably would have been destroyed had their first picture at MGM failed.

Many years after *A Night at the Opera* was released, director Mike Nichols approached Groucho at a Beverly Hills party and introduced himself.

"Groucho," he said, "I must tell you. I've seen *A Night at the Opera* seventeen times."

Groucho smiled. "Really?"

"Yes," Nichols replied, "I just couldn't get over that love story between Allan Jones and Kitty Carlisle!"

Modern audiences may agree with Nichols that the romance was a banal intrusion in the film, but it was extraordinarily well accepted by film audiences of the time, and gave a boost to the careers of the principals. On the strength of his performance, Jones was lent to Universal Pictures to play the showy Gaylord Ravenal role opposite Irene Dunne in the 1936 production of *Show Boat.*

Moss Hart and Cole Porter recruited Kitty Carlisle to star in their Broadway musical, *Jubilee,* ending her Hollywood career, for she then chose to stay on in New York and become Mrs. Moss Hart.

A Night at the Opera would prove to be Kitty Carlisle's sole claim to film immortality. Recently she recalled being invited to dinner at the White House when Lyndon Johnson was president. She was seated at the same table as Johnson and presidential advisor Walt Whitman Rostow.

"During dinner, I could see Mr. Rostow asking his dinner partner who I was. After she explained, he reached out his arms to me and said, 'Oh, darling! You're my favorite!' And I said, 'Don't tell me ... *A Night at the Opera.*' And that's the way it's always been. It's my claim to fame with my children and their friends. I had no idea it would become such a classic."

Hollywood in the mid-1930s was producing films of high sophistication and subtlety despite—or perhaps because of—the strict censorship of the period. With so many taboos in picture-making, visual euphemisms were employed to suggest things that could not be portrayed. Many students of film feel the eroticism and sensuality achieved by these means are not matched by today's more graphic pictures. Curiously, the inventive creators were plunked down in the middle of a generally naive and socially backward culture. As Tallulah Bankhead had put it when she arrived in Hollywood two years previously, "In Hollywood, a debutante is any girl who's a high school graduate."

Norman Krasna, the debonair bachelor, often entertained. A local morning newspaper passed on to its readers the guest list he supplied them for one party: H. G. Wells, Karl and Harpo Marx, Jennie Gerhardt, and Ethan Frome.

In the light of such provincialism, social cliques developed as a defense against the local Philistines. Few actors were accepted socially by Old Guard Los Angeles, yet two cliques in particular couldn't have cared less. First there were actors of the English colony, who could have taught the natives a lesson in snobbery. They tended to treat the city as one of the British Empire's more backward outposts, rigidly adhering to their stiff-upper-lip traditions, creating an exclusive enclave beyond the reach of the locals. Then there were the hard-drinking literati, most of them transplanted New Yorkers aching to get away from the torpid lotus-eaters at the same time as they itched for the top dollars they were receiving from them. They looked down their noses at the local citizenry, just as the studio moguls who hired them looked down their noses at them. Morrie and Mary Ryskind—Groucho had been the best man at their wedding—often had writers as dinner guests. On one occasion, playwright Marc Connelly and screenwriters Manny Seff and Edward Childs Carpenter were at the gathering. Mrs. Ryskind went upstairs for a moment and was accosted by her children's governess. "Mrs. Ryskind," she asked, "are all writers bald?"

Many of them, of course, had full heads of hair. Some of them even had a passing knowledge of English grammar. Krasna was the first to admit he wasn't among them. In doing so, he would regale guests at dinner parties about the great three-piece-suit-and electric-toaster caper he shared with Groucho.

Krasna was at home at his typewriter when Groucho called him one day.

"Somebody on the radio is advertising an offer of a three-piece suit, shirt, tie, and choice of a topcoat or electric toaster for $17.50," Groucho said. "I think his name is Smiling Jack. This I gotta see. Put on your cheapest clothes and I'll pick you up."

Krasna was in what he now calls his Beau Brummell and Rolls-Royce period, so he had trouble looking properly ragged. Naturally, Groucho had an extensive wardrobe of shabby clothes to draw from.

When the two men arrived at the block-long store, they succeeded in passing as a pair of indigents.

"Smiling Jack sent me," Groucho told a salesman, as the radio commercial had advised him to do. The pair were passed distastefully to the back of the store, the price of suits diminishing by ten dollars as they passed each section. When they finally located the merchandise on sale, it was apparent the dozen suits that were part of the $17.50 deal were being used as come-ons, and were virtually nailed to the floor. No one had any intention of selling anything that cheap.

Groucho, however, insisted on buying the advertised package, trying on misshapen coats and offering asides that so overwhelmed Krasna with laughter he could not stand up. The salesman, apparently having had a great deal of experience with stumbling derelicts who frequented the area, bent over Krasna and said, "We don't allow that in this store."

Groucho meanwhile took his time picking out his ensemble. Next came the decision of the topcoat or electric toaster.

"Does the toaster meet the voltage requirements in Beverly

Hills?" he asked the salesman. This was the final straw. The salesman pointed imperiously to the front door. "Out!" he ordered.

The two men marched the length of the store. At the entrance, displayed on a Bakelite stand, was an electric razor, a novelty in those days. Groucho asked a salesman how it worked, and the store employee proceeded to shave Groucho with the display model.

Groucho was satisfied. "I'll take it," he said. He threw his arms around the whole display stand. "This is the one I want."

"I'm sorry, sir," the salesman said. "The display isn't for sale, and the magnifying mirror isn't part of the price."

"Smiling Jack isn't going to like this," Groucho said as he and Krasna, to the whole store's relief, departed.

On their way back to Groucho's car, they passed a bookstore and went in. Krasna bought a pamphlet on simplified grammar for twenty-five cents.

"You mean," Groucho said, "that you are one of the highest paid writers in Hollywood and you are buying a twenty-five-cent book on grammar?"

"If you will lower your voice," Krasna said, "I will remain one of the highest priced writers in Hollywood. I'm sorry I don't know conjunctions and participles. If I knew enough about grammar I would write novels. Scenario writers and playwrights don't need grammar because their mistakes are the mistakes of the characters and lend verisimilitude, which is a word I throw in every once in a while and makes up for my uncertainty in grammar."

All the way back to Beverly Hills, Groucho kept shaking his head. "Three thousand dollars a week and he buys a twenty-five-cent book on grammar."

While Groucho was reflecting on the state of screenwriting, his brothers went East on a working vacation. Plans were pending for the Broadway show in which Thalberg would be involved. George Kaufman would soon be following them to New York to begin work on it.

One night Harpo went to see the new Broadway production of *Pride and Prejudice* with Chico, Betty, and Maxine. Coming out of the theater they ran into an acquaintance, who asked Harpo. "Did you like the play as much as the book?"

Harpo turned to Chico and asked, "Is that the book I read?"

Bill Marx, Harpo's son, confirmed to me years later that his father never had been much of a reader. "Dad had a complete collection of Maugham's works. The only thing he read out of them was Maugham's inscription to him."

As it turned out there wouldn't be anything by Kaufman for the two more literate of the Marx Brothers to read because early in October the plans for the Broadway production were scratched, and the studio agreed to mount a ten-week road tryout for their new picture, just as it had done with *A Night at the Opera*. That film had just gone into general release and the reception by the national press confirmed the earlier raves that had come from regional reviews.

Douglas W. Churchill wrote in the *New York Times* of October 20:

> The tour developed a new regard for the comedians. In past shows they always have been heartless clowns, perpetrating their gags on innocent and helpless victims. Movie audiences differ from stage audiences in mental attitude and demands. They didn't like it ... So the Marxes and their writers reversed the players' personalities. They became sympathetic souls in the manner of Chaplin and Lloyd. The chill that had met them was dissipated and the picture audience liked them.

Churchill concluded that the success of the experiment would lead to other studios also trying out their scripts on the road.

Harpo had only a few days to spend at Woollcott's sanctuary, the talk-ridden, cribbage-infested Neshobe Island, before heading back to Hollywood to prepare for the new picture.

While he waited for the brothers to return, Groucho dawdled away the Indian summer days at the Beverly Hills Tennis Club which he and his family had recently joined. The club had been formed in 1930 in the city's commercial district, and many of Hollywood's top stars could be seen playing on its six courts.

Groucho bought a $200 membership for the whole family, and tennis soon became a favorite form of recreation for all the Marxes.

Never had he gotten so much out of an investment, and yet its ultimate cost in emotional wear would prove quite dear.

At first, the club gave him an opportunity to spend time with his children, while still trading barbs with his contemporaries in the clubhouse. He became one of the "in" members very quickly. Fred Perry, the English tennis professional, was sitting with a group one day. "Say," he said, "I read a very funny story in an English magazine this morning."

"Well," said Groucho, "it's about time." Perry was still scratching his head the next day over the remark, which had been met with great laughter. Was it a dig at his alleged illiteracy or a comment on the lowly state of English humor?

His children were similarly shell-shocked. They were now past the ages where they were inordinately coddled. As thinking creatures, they were currently in a position to pass harsh judgments on their father, and the spontaneous displays of affection were abruptly withdrawn, to be replaced by his digging, sniping, and fault-finding. Groucho still maintained a residue of affection but it had been wrapped in many defensive layers.

When interviewed about his family life in the 1930s, few of Groucho's friends came up with as much telling information about his son Arthur as about Miriam. Artie was a polite boy, they conceded, and deeply attached to his mother. Groucho's mistreatment of Ruth, they agreed, probably began the alienation of father and son.

"Groucho was crazy about both his children," Betty, Chico's first wife, recalled. "He greatly respected writers, so they both decided to become writers. He liked to play tennis, so Arthur became a tennis player and went on to become one of the Top Ten.

"I noticed that Groucho always tried to butt in with Arthur, and they'd have fights. I heard later that he didn't stop doing it when Arthur became a man. It's too bad. Oh, how he loved that boy!"

Being the daughter of a famous star was an inescapable burden for Miriam, particularly at status-conscious Hawthorne Grammar School in Beverly Hills, which she was now attending. Like many young girls, she had developed an intense, tell-all friendship with a classmate named Sunny Sauber, the daughter of a producer at

Columbia Studios. A third girl told Miriam that Sunny was cultivating her only because she was the daughter of Groucho Marx.

She came home and disconsolately told Groucho what the girl had told her.

"That's not true," Groucho assured her. With one phone call, he set straight the relationship of the two girls. They would be the closest of friends throughout their school years.

"Miriam was a real tomboy," her friend, now Sunny Nadel, said. "She didn't dress like other girls. Her hair was short when it wasn't in fashion. She wore blue jeans when girls didn't wear them. This was the only area Groucho was cheap about. He wasn't easy about spending money for clothes. Groucho also played rough with her. He lashed out at her. I don't ever remember Miriam doing anything that would put Groucho down, or answering him back. Everything Miriam did was for his approval and love. Groucho, in return, made her feel kind of klutzy. He made me feel that way too."

It was Ruth, however, who got most of his venom. The tennis club became her haven and escape valve, and she gradually lost interest in keeping up the house or watching over the children.

When Chico and his family came to dinner one night, Ruth wasn't present to play hostess.

"She knows what we're having for dinner," Groucho told them, "so it's no wonder she doesn't want to be here."

By this time, Groucho had completely taken over supervision of the household. The group was seated at the table when Ruth joined them. Instead of sparkling dinner table dialogue of the sort Krasna had created for *Dear Ruth*, they were treated to a sour Groucho soliloquy.

As the soup course was served, Groucho commented, "Oh. Concentration camp fare again, eh, Ruth?"

His wife sat quietly as their children started to titter. Throughout the meal, Groucho bombarded Ruth with devastating comments: "What prison sent you the recipe for this?" "I suppose the meat could be tougher, but will someone tell me how?" "I'll bet you've never had vegetables like these before. But then who has?"

By the end of the meal, Ruth was decimated. Groucho had again humiliated her, and their children laughed at his cruelty.

Groucho had married an unsophisticated girl, then refused to let her grow with him. In truth, she didn't share any of his interests. She was bored by his friends, no matter how witty the rest of the world found them. She came to hate the Gilbert and Sullivan operettas he persisted in playing at home. Her youth was passing. She had married at nineteen a man of thirty with the reflective interests of a man twice his age. The gulf between them had grown wider over the last fifteen years. Seemingly, no one at home desired or enjoyed her company. There were men at the tennis club who did, and who were happy to buy her a drink after a couple of sets in the afternoon.

"Almost everyone at the tennis club found her nice and like-able," Nat Perrin said. He had married Helen Schorr, the secretary of George Burns and Gracie Allen. "Ruth was very beautiful. There was something very wholesome and athletic about her . . . something so daytime-y. I never saw Ruth drunk. It wasn't until years after they were divorced that I began to hear about her drinking. She was the last person I would have figured would become an alcoholic."

"The boys weren't drinkers," Betty recalled. "Later in life, I understand Gummo and Zeppo drank, but I wasn't around. Harpo didn't touch it. He wasn't well, and he wasn't supposed to drink. Nobody knew it. He would pick up a glass of White Rock or ginger ale and pretend it was a cocktail.

"Ruth wasn't drinking heavily early in the marriage. She always liked a drink or two. She became an alcoholic later. Her drinking became uncontrollable. Sometimes she'd smash the car in the driveway of their house."

That it took Ruth so long to crack was a tribute to her hardy Swedish background. Ruth was essentially a simple girl—perhaps with a strong streak of latent masochism—trapped in a hopeless situation.

Where, in the final analysis, Groucho was supportive of his children, Ruth never had that assurance from him. She also rarely saw the humor in Groucho's words, knowing the bitter roots from which they sprang. And when she occasionally attempted to imitate his humor, her words came out hostile, heavy-handed, and not very funny.

Betty and Chico were once at a nightclub, when Groucho and Ruth danced by. "What a pretty necklace, Betty," Ruth exclaimed. "Did you just get it out of hock?"

Groucho exploded. "I wish I could say that you would hock something for me if I were ever in trouble."

Ruth was silent. That she had few jewels or furs with which she might prove her similar devotion was beside the point. Yet, when her indiscretions began receiving wide notice, it was Betty—the target of her malice—to whom she confided.

Ruth had thus far exhibited her regard for Groucho by not talking about their sexual maladjustment. Groucho, in lashing out at her, was also raging at himself. He feared he couldn't sexually satisfy any woman. Feeling himself less than a man, he had developed a self-hatred which he projected by hating others.

Premature ejaculation is one of the most common of sexual dysfunctions. Psychologists identify its most common cause as an innate rage against women. In Groucho's case it no doubt stemmed from his mother's rejection of him. He was afraid of emotional closeness, because caring involved vulnerability. At some deep level of his being Groucho seems to have said, "Sooner or later I'm going to be hurt by the woman I love. I must hurt her first."

"Instead of saving his money, he should have spent some of it on a psychiatrist," Betty says. A well-adjusted Groucho might not have become one of the great comedians of his time, but he might have spared himself and those close to him immeasurable heartache.

And so, as the Hollywood gossip factory began churning out stories about his wearing the cuckold's horns, Groucho attempted to go about his everyday life. "Even then," Betty says, "he told Ruth, 'You go your way and I'll go mine, but let's stay married.' "

Gummo was now working in Zeppo's East Coast office where the agency was making plans to go into legitimate stage productions. The performing brothers, splitting a base annual salary of $100,000, would soon be dividing up an additional $600,000 as their fifteen percent of the gross of their first MGM picture. In late December of 1935, MGM and Irving Thalberg picked up their option for a second and third picture. Al Boasberg, Robert Pirosh, and George Seaton were at work on an original story about a racetrack, while Gus Kahn was to write lyrics to three songs, the music to which would be composed by Bronislau Kaper and Walter Jurmann. At the same time, Bert Kalmar and Harry Ruby were working on a second screenplay with a Western setting.

Harpo was vacillating about marrying Susan Fleming, a pretty brunette actress who was under contract to Paramount Pictures. Groucho, with his new open marriage, chose to spend his time with his cronies. Friends noticed he exhibited a new indifference in his behavior, shunting off responsibility to others. It was a pattern that would continue for the rest of his life.

He began entertaining more at his house in Beverly Hills, whether Ruth was there or not. He met with friends daily for lunch.

Norman Krasna says that through Groucho he met some of the great people of the world. He received a telephone call from Groucho one morning. "I'm having lunch with an idol of yours," Groucho said. "Meet us at Romanov's."

His curiosity piqued, Krasna arrived at the restaurant to discover the other guest was Noel Coward.

"I was pop-eyed," he recalled. "I was wearing a white sweater vest, which Noel admired. I took it off and gave it to him." The two men became such close friends that, before his death, the only people Coward would see were his friend Adrian Allan and Norman and Erle Krasna.

Another time, Krasna arrived at Groucho's for a simple dinner to find that the other guest was Arthur Rubinstein.

"Mr. Rubinstein," Groucho said, "I'd like you to meet Norman Krasna, another piano player."

"Mr. Krasna," the great man replied, "I'm always happy to meet a fellow musician."

Though he knew Groucho was capable of saying anything, Norman was nonetheless startled.

"Mr. Rubinstein," he said, "I can't let this terrible lie go on one moment longer. I'm not only not a musician, I'm the most tone deaf person in the whole world."

Rubinstein smiled graciously. "Young man, don't be arrogant. The most tone deaf man in the world is an intimate friend of mine, Alfonso of Spain, who from the time he was four years old had a man employed to nudge him whenever the national anthem was played. I might concede, however, that you're the second most tone deaf man in the world."

Occasional meetings of such eminent men couldn't be called friendships. "On that level," Krasna said, "people don't have the time. I'm sure Rubinstein saw Groucho as an original, and was happy to know him. It's a kind of homage they paid each other. But of all people, Rubinstein was just as witty. The way I look at it, Rubinstein could have operated as a gag man. His sense of humor was something extraordinary. I'm sure Groucho would have felt the same way about Picasso. But Groucho never sought anybody out. I don't know specifically how he met Rubinstein. They probably were introduced at somebody else's house and they took a shine to each other."

Groucho still frequented the tennis club, and often encountered Ruth there. They were more cordial with each other among others than they were at home.

Arthur, in his mid-teens, had developed into a fine tennis player. Zeppo was a touch better at the time. He bet Groucho that he could beat Arthur. The match went to set point several times with Arthur on the brink of a victory, but Zeppo rallied and bested his nephew.

Sam Marx, sitting next to Groucho said, "I bet you beat the hell out of him when you get him home."

"No," Groucho corrected, "halfway home."

Miriam was nine and passionately in love with her father who, despite his bark, remained totally permissive with her . . . as long as it didn't cost money. She had been casually exposed to her parents' nudity since she was born. Common sense might have told him the time had come to stop taking showers with his daughter. To Groucho, it was a totally innocent pastime and anyone who thought otherwise had a perverted mind.

"Where parents have unfulfilled and perhaps unrecognized sexual needs," Marshall Bryant Hodge wrote in *Your Fear of Love*, "this may involve exhibitionistic and unconsciously seductive behavior that is not conducive to healthy development of sexual feelings in the child. When we attempt to deny our fears about sex, we simply find new ways to pass them on to our children in disguised and perhaps more subtle forms."

There were many girls about town—compliant, undemanding—who understood his need for discretion. He often turned to them as sexual outlets. During the road tour of *A Day at the Races*, Groucho managed to carry on a short affair with one of the dancers of the company.

Of the principal actors who would appear in the picture, only Margaret Dumont was along on the tour. Allan Jones was still on loan to Universal for *Show Boat*, while Maureen O'Sullivan was finishing up her role in *Tarzan Escapes* with Johnny Weismuller. However, facilities for the touring company, in keeping with the renewed standing of the brothers as major film stars, were lavish.

The tour opened July 14, 1936, at the Lyceum Theatre in Duluth. It was there that Hi-Hat, the trained horse touring with them, fell into the orchestra pit. "He knew where the horse players were," Groucho observed. From there they moved on for one-week runs at the Minnesota Theatre in Minneapolis and the Palace in Chicago before closing on August 18, 1936, after a week at the Golden Gate Theatre in San Francisco.

One hundred gags were tested in each town and members of the audience filled out all 30,000 ballot cards taken along by the troupe. By trial and error, 175 laughs were selected, with the seventy-five which got the best reaction scheduled to be used in the picture.

Technicians built props as they were needed to accommodate the constantly revised script. Some were discarded after one appearance. At one point, Harpo didn't like one of the props he was required to bring out from beneath his capacious cloak.

"Throw it out," he instructed.

"But it cost several hundred dollars," the propman protested. "We can't do that."

Groucho stepped in. "He's right, Harpo. You can't waste money like that." Turning to the propman, he ordered, "Have it silver-plated, and then throw it out."

There were enough props that weren't discarded along the way to fill four trucks when the troupe returned to Hollywood.

While the brothers were breaking Eddie Cantor's attendance record in Chicago, Harpo was breaking down a girl's resistance backstage. Earlier in the run a man had made the rounds of the dressing rooms selling exotica and erotica. Harpo bought a teakwood penis. A dressing room with a bare bulb in the ceiling was hardly the most conducive spot for romance, but Harpo was always adaptable. The two were soon out of their clothes. Came the crucial moment and Harpo employed the teakwood penis. Then it seemed a sudden thought came upon him. "Gee, it's drafty here," he told the girl. "I think I'll close the window." Without removing the wooden dildo, he got off the couch and closed the window. The girl fainted.

The brothers didn't break Cantor's record in San Francisco, as they had in Chicago, perhaps because of the boost in admission from forty to fifty-five cents for evening performances. They grossed $28,000, about $6,000 less than Cantor had the previous week.

"They played twenty-eight shows that week," Maxine said, "and I went to every single one. During one show, the performance ran over the total allotted time of one hour. It was a good audience and everyone was having a great time. There was a set routine in making transitions. Daddy would play the piano, then Harpo would come out, and he and Daddy would go off and Harpo would play. The stage manager decided to cut the duets. Groucho was supposed to pick up right when Daddy finished playing. Groucho started to talk, and the audience started stomping and applauding. They wanted Chico to keep playing. Groucho kept on talking, and they booed him, which I don't think happened to him very frequently. The way he handled it was great. He waited until they got kind of quiet and he said, 'I have to stay here. They pay me, but nobody's keeping you.' That broke the audience up, and then they started laughing, and he was able to go on with the show. But instead of saving time, it made the show much longer."

Earlier in the tour, Chico told a newspaper reporter that Chicago audiences were the most receptive in the world. He revised his opinion in San Francisco.

"San Francisco audiences are too easy," he told a reporter from the *Chronicle.* "They're pushovers for laughs. They see more laughs in the show than we put there."

Irving Thalberg and Norma Shearer arrived on closing day to confirm how enthusiastic the brothers' reception had been.

The final shooting script had yet to be written. The brothers would be sitting in on several of the sessions before filming started in mid-September.

Teet Carle, their former publicist at Paramount, was recruited by MGM to help Sam Wood time the laughs in the upcoming film. Observing a rehearsal, he came to realize the arduous work involved in building a laugh. One scene had Groucho washing his hands in a basin. When Groucho caught Siegfried Rumann eyeing his wristwatch, he took it off and threw it into the water. "I'd rather have it rusty than gone," he said.

Groucho then turned to Al Boasberg. "Is that the right final word?" he asked.

It was not. Boasberg made notes throughout 140 stage performances in four cities. Three words—*gone, disappear,* and *missing*—had been tried nearly fifty times each. Groucho was informed which word caused the most laughs, and when it came time to film the scene, he said, "I'd rather have it rusty than missing."

Teet Carle wrote in the February, 1974, issue of *Archives:*

Pin-pointing word values in comedy was a must with the comedy stars and helped make whole scenes more effective. Groucho lambasted Chico with, "That's the most nauseating proposition I've ever had." Just how ideal for the line is the word *nauseating?* That's what I asked the Marxmen and their writers. I wondered if it was universally understood—by kiddies at Saturday matinees as well as the oldsters at the early evening show and the lovers who cuddled up during the late screening.

I was told that among other words tried out were *obnoxious, revolting, disgusting, offensive, repulsive, disagreeable,* and *distasteful.* The last two of these words never got more than titters. The others elicited various degrees of ha-has. But *nauseating* drew roars. I asked Groucho why that was so. "I don't know. I really don't care. I only know the audiences told us it was funny."

Another fact pointed out to me was that while the Marx comedy usually was utterly insane, it never was impossible. They made a point of sticking to realism. For example, in *Races,* Harpo got his hands on a bottle of fizz-water and began spraying the villains. By intercutting, the dousing could have gone on and on, but Harpo said it must not be ridiculously long in spouting. A bottle was tested. The jet lasted two minutes. That is as long as the scene was permitted to last.

The script was rapidly taking shape when the company disbanded for the long Labor Day weekend. Chico and Betty spent the holiday with the Thalbergs and several friends at Del Monte Lodge on the Monterey peninsula. The group passed an afternoon on an outside veranda playing bridge. When the weather turned chilly, Thalberg insisted Betty put on his sweater. The next day, he came down with a head cold.

Over the next ten days, the cold took a serious turn, developing into lobar pneumonia. Thalberg died on Monday, September 14, at the age of thirty-seven.

In November, 1976, Sheilah Graham wrote in the *New York Times* about her contributions to F. Scott Fitzgerald's *The Last Tycoon:* "I had told him of the Marx Brothers sobbing their eyes out on the day Thalberg died—always making sure they were within crying distance of the 'right' people. Scott was going to have Stahr's spirit say 'Trash!' " Thalberg, the inspiration for the Stahr character, would have instead understood the venting of honest emotion.

Her gratuitous comment revealed her lack of discernment and understanding about intense male friendships. If the brothers cried openly, it was hardly the politic thing to do now that Mayer would be in sole charge of the studio. An equally cynical but more plausible observation might have been that they were crying over this setback to their careers, since as far as they were concerned, the only "right" person at MGM was now dead.

The death of Thalberg was a double loss to Chico and Betty,

who were close to him and Norma Shearer. The friendship of the two men had started at the bridge table, and extended into a deeper friendship of two married couples often sharing happy talk at small dinners.

Harpo was a close friend too. Within two weeks, he would secretly marry Susan Fleming, the death of his friend perhaps intimating his own mortality. He was now nearly fifty and after a lifetime of casual affairs with hundreds of women, he would become a passionately devoted family man. He and Susan would, over the next few years, adopt four children, "all of whom they raised successfully," as Groucho often put it.

Norman Krasna once talked to Harpo about his adoption of the children at a relatively late age. "I wanted to have a child at every window, waving to me when I came home," Harpo said.

Back at the studio, Mayer was reasserting his authority. His actions, Groucho felt, were turning a golden career into dross. Within two weeks, Laurence Weingarten—Thalberg's brother-in-law—was assigned to produce *A Day at the Races* in tandem with director Sam Wood. Kalmar and Ruby were instructed to stop their work on *Go West*, the brothers' third scheduled picture, and were reassigned to write *The Life of the Party*.

"I think Mayer wanted us to bomb," Groucho told me. Thalberg, however, had so carefully crafted the film that it couldn't fail. All his successors had to do was follow his instructions. Yet they didn't seem clear to the less gifted Weingarten, for the making of the picture stretched over seven months. Its scheduled March 12, 1937, opening had to be pushed back two months because the film wasn't completed until April 20.

Another reason for going over schedule was the movie's cumbersome 109-minute running time, the longest of any Marx Brothers film. The actors also seemed to resist any suggestion that didn't coincide with the concept originally laid down by Thalberg.

Maureen O'Sullivan, who played the ingenue, had been married for two years to director John Farrow. Married or not, Groucho had fallen in love with her. "I knew he had a crush on me," she said. "A girl always knows when a fellow is interested. There was nothing between us. But even if John wasn't around, Groucho was not the type I'd be interested in. I don't like funny men . . . at least not the type that crack jokes all the time. Groucho never stopped. It went on all day. He and I would go out for lunch. After a while your face starts to crack. I was tired of it after the third day. I told him, 'Please, Groucho, stop! Let's have a nice quiet normal conversation.' Groucho never knew how to talk normally. His life was his jokes. I hope I don't sound hard on him. He was such a darling man."

Miss O'Sullivan admitted that if it hadn't been for his machine gun chatter and the fact that they were both married, she would have gone out with him. "I found Groucho very sexy. He had physical presence and a good build. I always regretted that I didn't tell him."

Groucho told me, "I was crazy about her. I didn't like her husband. He was a mean man." He thought Farrow was being physically abusive to his exquisite wife, causing Groucho to love her all the more. (Miss O'Sullivan denied that her husband beat her.)

Groucho, however, reserved his greatest dislike for Sam Wood. He was still shooting take after take, driving the actors to exhaustion and near violence. None of them could know that the picture would ultimately be among their most successful, grossing $4,000,000 during its original run, the brothers taking home $600,000 of that amount.

Groucho's insecurity possessed him. "There were twelve women working as extras in the movie who had once earned $1,000 a week or more," he said. "I was so terrified that someday I, too, might have to work as an extra, that I took all the spare money I had at the time—$25,000—and put it into an annuity which would pay me eighty dollars a week when I reached fifty-five."

He was also trying to persuade Chico to set aside a certain percentage of his income with which to create an account with Salwyn Shufro. Chico resisted the idea. He wasn't as afraid of the future as his younger brother. Problems always worked themselves out, so he believed.

At Warner Brothers, Mervyn LeRoy bought *Grand Passion* after the Paramount option expired, and changed the title of Groucho's collaboration with Norman Krasna to *The King and the Chorus Girl*. Shooting had started on the picture, which starred a French actor named Fernand Gravet and Joan Blondell. Similarities between the screenplay and the life of the King of England who had abdicated were already being pointed out, although Norman and Groucho began work on the screenplay long before that historic event.

Once they completed the final shooting script, neither Groucho nor Norman had anything more to do with the picture, being occupied with other projects. Groucho's friend, Arthur Sheekman, however, was hired on to supply additional dialogue.

In this, his first picture as a producer-director, LeRoy presumed to insert a line about Coney Island that wasn't in the writers' script.

"Mervyn was waiting at the bottom of the stairs as we came down from the preview," Norman said. "Groucho was so offended that anybody would tamper with his lines—and look who's talking—he was the world's greatest tamperer. Mervyn was waiting to hear something nice said. It's a tradition in the theater. Groucho just looked at him and said, 'Coney Island.' He continued walking. He left Mervyn shattered."

Back at MGM, another director was having his differences with Groucho. Wood couldn't get him to follow the script. Groucho's wild improvisations were in decided contrast to the tight ensemble playing of their previous picture together. During one particularly bothersome scene, Wood said in exasperation, "You can't make an actor out of clay." Groucho snapped back, "Nor a director out of Wood."

Harpo, in a slapdash wallpaper hanging scene, was required to carry a bucket of paste on his head while climbing a ladder. Wood made him do it at least twenty times, finding fault with each take. Finally, Harpo became fed up. "What time is it?" he asked an assistant director. "Twenty past ten," he was told.

With that, Harpo fell off the ladder and lay in a "coma" for almost an hour, refusing to rise for Wood, Mayer, God, or country.

While making *A Night at the Opera*, Thalberg made the brothers aware of the need for several takes, but under Wood's direction they seemed endless. The brothers saw Mayer's devious hand behind Wood's petty harassment and intimidation. Wood was nothing if not a company man. "He never had an original thought in his life," Groucho once told me.

Somehow spontaneity was preserved. Maureen O'Sullivan recalled sitting with Margaret Dumont between takes. "The script only showed her lines, and never the setups," she said. "For example, she was to deliver some lines in the boat scene. They never told her they would capsize the boat and nearly drown her. And that worked so well, because the camera always caught her reaction, so dignified and furious at their pranks."

They also unexpectedly upended her in the scene where she was lying on the operating table. Miss Dumont was so embarrassed by this unseemly fall that she left the set and refused to come back until the following day.

At the time the picture was released, Miss Dumont was featured in a *Collier's* magazine piece. She wistfully talked about the serious character parts Thalberg was promising her shortly before his death.

"He understood about comedy, and always insisted that the Marx Brothers stories should have a real plot. The only thing that ever hurt me about my job was being called a stooge. I resent that. Playing comedy in the movies is a hard job. You just can't stand still and wait for the laughs, but they do have to be timed so that the laughter won't wash out the next lines. When the wait comes, it is necessary to be doing something all the time and not just something haphazard. That's what is called acting."

The brothers claimed she never knew what was funny, but apparently Miss Dumont devised her own approach to playing opposite them. No matter what indignities befell her, she reacted to them like an actress in a drawing room comedy. If the brothers chose to act as less than gentlemen, then that was a frailty in their character she, a lady, would nobly—if not silently—bear.

Nevertheless, there was a decided gallantry in the way she was treated in her films with the brothers, as Andrew Sarris astutely pointed out in the July 23, 1964, issue of the *Village Voice:* "Groucho always treated Miss Dumont shamefully, too shamefully, in fact, for realism to intrude on comic fantasy. Deep down we have always known that Groucho is too much of a gentleman and Miss Dumont too much of a lady for anything irrevocably sordid to occur. Groucho's excessive rudeness is actually a form of gallantry, enabling Miss Dumont to withdraw from his bedroom without being deeply humiliated. Groucho takes the burden of outrageousness upon himself because he can afford to let people see through him. He has nothing to hide; his transparency is merely the means by which he deflates the pomposity of others."

No sooner had the film been completed than the brothers began fretting about the future. Mayer's scrapping of the *Go West* screenplay indicated a decided lack of studio interest in them, although they still had a contract for a third picture. Groucho and Chico couldn't go into radio, because a studio policy prohibited such a move without their consent. After Mayer had let them swing slowly in the wind, the studio agreed to a termination of the contract.

Groucho's personal life was similarly at the crossroads. Maureen O'Sullivan remained cool to him and his occasional flings with girls about town had a decided lack of romance. Believing a change of scene might prove beneficial, he and his wife decided to visit Hawaii. Groucho acquiesced to Ruth's request that Arthur and Miriam be left behind. She wanted their vacation to be free of any responsibilities. The trip was to be their last effort to hold their marriage together.

"Going to Hawaii," Groucho told me, "I remember there were hundreds of people waving to those on the shore on one end of the boat. On the other end, I was vomiting."

It wasn't an auspicious start to the trip for the chronically seasick Groucho, nor did it bode well for Ruth, sharing a stateroom with her foul-tempered husband, who would have to do without his lingering, temper-saving visits to the Beverly Hills Tennis Club.

After arriving in Hawaii, Groucho learned that he and Chico had been indicted by a federal grand jury on a misdemeanor charge of violating national copyright laws. They were accused of broadcasting a radio skit the previous September without permission of the writers, Garrett and Carroll Graham. A $26,000 civil suit had already been filed by the Grahams against the brothers, the Columbia Broadcasting System, Don Lee Broadcasting Company, and the R. J. Reynolds Tobacco Company. Attorneys told the brothers it was a typical nuisance suit, and in answering it, declared that the script in question, "Mr. Diffle and Mr. Daffle," had been written by Boasberg with the Graham brothers and that Boasberg had authorized their use of it.

255

Chico, during his arraignment in Los Angeles, initially tried to treat the matter lightly. "Do I have to get my head shaved too?" he asked reporters. As he was being fingerprinted, Chico realized the seriousness of the situation. "I've been on the stage and screen twenty years," he said. "This is the first time I have ever been accused of stealing anything. Many other actors have used our stuff and we've never said a word." The case was held over until Groucho returned from Hawaii.

Throughout the three-week vacation, Groucho was irritable. Ruth, in sharing the vacation with him, thought the embers of their dying love might be rekindled. Groucho was more realistic. There was no way the marriage could be saved. Their son Arthur wrote that his father caught Ruth in a passionate embrace with a dance instructor the night before they docked on the mainland. "After this vacation together," Groucho wrote in *The Groucho Phile*, "we knew divorce was just a matter of time."

Paramount, RKO, and Columbia had made firm offers to the brothers. Like a man who has discarded his mistress only to find her more attractive when she is being courted by another man, MGM suddenly did a turnabout. They entered into discussions with the brothers about a possible three-picture deal.

A Day at the Races was released in mid-June to an extraordinary reception. The Marx Brothers wound up among the studio's top box office stars for 1937. They ranked behind the team of William Powell and Myrna Loy, Powell individually, Jeanette MacDonald, Clark Gable, Greta Garbo, Robert Taylor, Spencer Tracy, Norma Shearer, Miss Loy individually, Joan Crawford, Luise Rainer, Jean Harlow, and Lionel Barrymore. But their Number Fourteen rating was based on only one picture during the year of 1937, while the others had made from two to four—with the exception of Miss Shearer who, inexplicably, was listed despite the fact that she hadn't made any. Trailing behind the brothers were such reputedly greater stars as Freddie Bartholomew, Eleanor Powell, Wallace Beery, Robert Montgomery, Nelson Eddy, Rosalind Russell, Leslie Howard, and Edward G. Robinson.

Mayer, looking at the box office returns, chose to forgive the brothers. They airily replied that they would probably forsake pictures for radio for a couple of years. Now they were in a position to leisurely sort out the offers coming their way.

On June 16, RKO announced it had bought George Abbott's smash comedy, *Room Service*, which would go on to run for sixty-one weeks on Broadway, for $255,000. Every major studio had sought the property. Paramount and Metro had dropped out of the bidding at $200,000. For a while it looked like Warner's bid of $225,000 would prevail, but RKO topped it at the last minute. It was a new high for film rights to a stage play, the previous record being $235,000 for *Broadway* in 1929.

On June 18, Al Boasberg, who the day before had renewed his first-year contract for the Jack Benny radio program, died of a heart attack. He was to be the defense witness for Groucho and Chico on the plagiarism charge. More importantly, an inspired writing talent was lost, and his passing was mourned by Benny, Burns and Allen, and the Marx Brothers.

Zeppo was now representing the team, and since RKO had a property in *Room Service* that could be adapted to fit the brothers' talents, he negotiated a deal of $250,000 plus a percentage for them to appear in the upcoming film. The production budget would top $1,500,000, one of the highest ever for a comedy film.

When the deal was announced, Mayer's representatives tried to repair the situation by getting a commitment for a future film. Mayer wouldn't let his personal feelings get in the way of a money-making proposition and the team responded in kind, agreeing to the terms, which included the possibility that MGM would offer the brothers to radio networks as part of the studio's new activities in that medium. MGM also agreed that the brothers could borrow Bill Bacher, a newly hired studio executive, to produce a pending radio series sponsored by Sinclair Oil Company. Ken Englund, collaborating with Groucho on a screenplay, *Madcap Mary Mooney*, would write the show.

The brothers, once burned, hedged their bet at MGM by also signing with RKO for two more pictures, the first perhaps *Of Thee I Sing*, which that studio now owned. MGM, in a tit-for-tat move, announced it was building Buddy Ebsen, Buster Keaton, and Ted Healy as a comedy trio to replace the brothers, in the event of their defection.

The success of the Marx Brothers had spawned other comedy trios. The Ritz Brothers were already functioning at Twentieth Century-Fox and The Three Stooges at Columbia.

Morrie Ryskind was assigned to adapt *Room Service* for the brothers. While the script was being readied, Groucho was at the center of several lawsuits. Already a defendant in one criminal case, he agonized as two other suits were filed. The brothers, their writers, and MGM were sued for $150,000, charged with plagiarism in *A Day at the Races*. A second suit asked $250,000 of writer Robert Pirosh and the studio for allegedly plagiarizing the work of another writer on the same film. (Both suits would be dismissed eventually.)

Columnist Irving Hoffman of the *Hollywood Reporter* cracked, "It seems to us that nine men were originally credited with scripting the Marx Brothers' 'A Day at the Races,' but since that plagiarism suit, the number has dwindled to one." That one, no doubt, was the dead, defenseless Boasberg.

On October 30, a United States District Court jury, after deliberating forty-seven minutes, found Groucho and Chico guilty of a copyright law violation in connection with the Graham brothers' sketch, marking the first time anyone in Hollywood had been convicted on a criminal plagiarism charge. The brothers had already made a $7,500 settlement on the $26,000 civil suit. They were each fined an additional $1,000 on the misdemeanor conviction. Attorneys representing them filed an oral notice of appeal.

While Federal Judge George Dosgrave said there was some question of the validity of the indictment, he was convinced there had been moral offense.

The brothers issued a statement:

We, after twenty-eight years of honest endeavor in the theatrical field, in which we hope we have brought to our public entertainment and happiness, are faced with the indignity of being convicted of a misdemeanor. We know we are innocent of ever intentionally taking anyone's property. So much has been written for stage, screen and radio broadcasts that original plots are difficult to obtain and exceedingly unusual. That we should have been singled out during negotiations to settle a civil suit, indicted and then found guilty on evidence which we consciously believe could not, by wildest stretch of imagination, be construed as holding us guilty of wilfully taking another's property, is, to say the least, very humiliating.

The conviction was upheld the following April, and the brothers quietly paid the fine.

Both Groucho and Harpo had been unable to convince Chico that he should adopt a more conservative way of life. The criminal conviction may have shown him just how tenuous a performer's career could be. Any further scandal might ruin him. He came around to his brothers' way of thinking.

"Hold your seat now, boys," Groucho wrote Salwyn Shufro in December of 1937, "here comes the big punch. I'm enclosing a check for Chico, sometimes known as Nick the Greek or Nicko the Chick. By strategy, force and persuasion we've withheld this much from him, and this is the beginning of a nest egg for that all-time sucker. Harpo and I will take good care that he doesn't get his mitts on the securities. They are to be sent to me at my home address. I still have hopes of coming to New York sometime this winter and if I do we'll warn you in time."

In 1938, Hollywood adopted an industry theme: *Movies Are Your Best Entertainment.* The line was dropped when the acronym of its first letters was discovered: MAYBE. It may have been moot whether motion pictures were the best form of entertainment, but it was indisputable that they were the most expensive. Thirty-five films, an all-time high, would be budgeted at over $1,000,000 that year. Lavish productions were needed to bring out the stay-at-home audiences who were listening to Bob Hope, Edgar Bergen and Charlie McCarthy, Rudy Vallee, Amos 'n' Andy, Jack Benny, Eddie Cantor, Burns and Allen, Easy Aces, and Bing Crosby on the nation's 35,000,000 radio sets.

The brothers, in preproduction for *Room Service,* were experimenting again. They would be playing established stage characters, and not ones that were variations on the public personalities George Kaufman had created for them in *The Cocoanuts.*

259

The trio had been assigned offices on the RKO lot which had been made to resemble the sets of the picture. They would spend a leisurely six months offering advice on the script before shooting started. Gregory La Cava, who had just directed *Stage Door*, would reportedly be directing them on the new film.

On the domestic scene Groucho's relationship with Ruth was alternately civil and contemptuous. He was sympathetic about her condition, but refused to take any blame for it. "No one made her an alcoholic but herself," he later wrote.

When I asked him to amplify on that, Groucho said, "When I married Ruth, she was a dancer . . . just a kid. We used to think it was funny to go up to Canada during Prohibition and sneak back liquor in Arthur's diaper. It was Prohibition that killed her . . . the defiance of the laws that killed her."

Ruth would live for nearly thirty-five more years, so it wasn't she who was dying in 1938. It was her marriage.

"What do you think when you think about Ruth?" I asked Groucho.

"I feel very helpless and very sad."

Arthur also couldn't cope with the problem, judging from what he wrote about it in *Son of Groucho*. It was impossible to revere his mother's memory and at the same time strive for objectivity. In the book, he recollects being called out of school to pick up his mother in a rundown part of Los Angeles where she had just undergone an abortion. Ruth, he wrote, told him Groucho had talked her into getting pregnant, but she couldn't bear the thought of assuming responsibility for another child. Arthur must have had a strong suspicion Groucho wasn't responsible for the pregnancy, although he didn't mention it in the book.

"Arthur let me read a short story he had written," his cousin Maxine said. "It was a bitter denunciation of women who are unfaithful in marriage. In its way, it was both the most passionate and the most sensitive thing Arthur ever wrote."

Arthur had celebrated his sixteenth birthday the previous July, and Groucho had given him his own car. The two were as personally close as they ever would be. In April, they won the round-robin tournament at the Beverly Hills Tennis Club. Later that month, Arthur drove to the Forty-Third Annual Ojai Valley

Tennis Championships. He upset Jack Kramer in the tournament and was well on his way to becoming a nationally ranked amateur. Groucho was understandably proud.

He would also be understandably pleased, after the sour experience of the last picture at MGM, that *Room Service* would be shot, under William A. Seiter's direction, in the amazingly short period of five weeks.

Appearing as supporting actresses in the picture were two young women who would later have long and noted careers: dancer Ann Miller, who claimed she was only fourteen when the film was shot, and Lucille Ball, who had signed a long-term RKO contract the previous year. In light of Miss Ball's later eminence as one of television's most durable comedy stars, it is interesting that Groucho had no lasting impression of her at the time, other than to find her young and beautiful.

"Didn't you see her potential as a comedienne?" I asked.

"She's an actress, not a comedienne," Groucho replied. "There's a difference. I've never found Lucille Ball to be funny on her own. She's always needed a script."

Room Service was released at about the same time that the brothers were signing a three-picture contract at MGM. Despite generally favorable reviews, the picture wasn't successful. The brothers played against their types in a film that was being released during a generally poor box office year.

The slump in movie receipts in 1938, which had prompted the head of a national association of theater owners to label Hollywood's biggest stars "Box Office Poison," led to gimmicks and giveaways to increase theater attendance.

Sam Marx was at the movies with Groucho one night when a card flashed on the screen: COMING ATTRACTION: A SET OF DISHES FOR ANYONE BRINGING THREE FRIENDS. Groucho, in a voice heard throughout the theater, said, "They won't need to give away a dish. Nobody's got three friends."

The brothers were allowed, under their new MGM contract, to do outside work. They announced plans to mount a burlesque version of *The Three Musketeers* in the late spring or early summer of 1938 if RKO gave them permission. With the disclosure that one of RKO's highest budgeted pictures of the year, *Room Service*, earned only ninety-three percent as much as the studio's average picture, RKO gladly allowed them to perform in anything they wanted, so long as it wasn't another RKO picture. But their plans for a return to the stage were abruptly dropped in favor of a French tour, in preparation for which they decided to take French lessons. Their studies ended with the cancellation of the tour, leaving Groucho with only a one-sentence vocabulary: *Voulez-vous coucher avec moi?*

Groucho and Chico also received several offers for network radio shows.

"I'm really not interested in radio," Groucho told a reporter for the *New York Post.* "I'm waiting for the smellies or the tasties. I want to crash through to the unseen audience in six assorted perfumes or flavors."

Nevertheless, Groucho and Chico agreed to be part of what *Time* magazine described as the "most revolutionary radio idea since Charlie McCarthy," a colossal one-hour Sunday evening production with a $2,000,000 annual budget called "The Circle." Sponsored by Kellogg's and produced by its advertising agency, J. Walter Thompson, the program was an all-star round-table discussion, touching on such subjects as poetry, music, death, taxes, and fur coats. Of the mammoth budget, $25,000 weekly was allotted to the stars themselves.

Carole Lombard and Cary Grant had already been announced as the first stars at $5,000 and $4,000 weekly when Groucho and Chico joined the group, splitting an additional $4,000 a week. Ronald Colman and Lawrence Tibbett would soon sign on for $5,000 each.

The show had its premiere on January 15, 1939. Reaction was mixed. "A legitimate criticism will, of course, be raised as to whether such a show is over their heads and whether it is ideally adjusted to the peddling of corn flakes," Bob Landry wrote in *Variety.* "A strange contrast is the smartness of the production in general and the extreme corniness of the Kellogg commercials, which are fired point-blank out of a slightly rusty 1926 howitzer."

Within a month, both Colman and Miss Lombard would walk off the program, complaining that the quality of the scripts was uneven. Groucho and Chico had brought their own writers with them and they were consistently singled out by reviewers as highlights of the series. Basil Rathbone was rushed in as a regular, and Madeleine Carroll was signed as a guest star on several segments. The program continued until July with Groucho and Chico as one of its few constants, trading verbal darts with such guest stars as Noel Coward, Jose Iturbi, Alexander Woollcott, Merle Oberon, and Boris Karloff.

Both Groucho and Chico liked the easy money in radio, a moonlighting effort since they were concurrently shooting *At the Circus*, the first of a three-film contract at MGM. Their co-stars, however, didn't like their domination of the program, nor their departures from prepared scripts—on one occasion they expanded their six-minute spot to eleven minutes. Basil Rathbone announced he would not return to the program because of Groucho's ad-libbing.

Their allegedly overbearing behavior notwithstanding, Groucho and Chico received vague assurances that they could make it as radio stars on their own program. They had already been approached about starring in a scaled-down version of the show, a half-hour program to air on a weekday night.

Arthur by this time had graduated from high school. Over the next three summers he would travel the country, participating in junior tennis tournaments.

Meanwhile, Miriam, attempting to compensate for an absentee mother, began to develop crushes on older women. They included Ruth Frazee, who would marry Norman Krasna the following year, and Helen Perrin. Sunny Sauber was still a close companion, and Eddie Cantor's daughter Janet soon joined their ranks.

"We were all total misfits," Sunny Sauber recalled, "but somehow Janet had more sense. Miriam was the ringleader, and Janet never seemed to be around whenever Miriam and I got into situations." In retrospect, their escapades are endearing.

They were about twelve years old when Groucho had to bail them out of jail. The two girls had been jumping on a sandpile at a building site on Beverly Drive, throwing caution and sand to the winds, when a woman yelled at them, "You ragamuffins! Get off my property!"

As she approached them, the woman tripped and fell into a mud puddle. Enraged, she went to a telephone and called the police, who ran the trespassers in. The complainant was later revealed to be actress Mary Boland. Groucho, outwardly unperturbed by his daughter's actions, may even have admired her unspoiled brashness.

Since Miriam rarely had any pocket money, she would bill store charges to her father. Sunny recalls one instance when the owner of an ice cream parlor refused to put their sodas on the tab. He was neither amused nor impressed with the fact she was Groucho's daughter, holding Miriam and Sunny captive until Arthur disgustedly arrived with the ransom of twenty cents.

Much of the girls' extra time was spent at the Marxes. "Miriam was never at our house," Sunny said, "and I didn't object. Our house wasn't as much fun. I think Miriam didn't want to leave Groucho alone. She was very worried whenever Groucho had to fly anywhere. She was always putting sugar in his sleeping capsules, which Groucho took for his insomnia, because she thought he might take an overdose.

"I remember Groucho putting Ruth down all the time. She wasn't around the house much. I don't recall her being around a lot even when Groucho entertained. People like Moss Hart, George Kaufman, and Max Gordon didn't interest her at all. I thought it was strange that Miriam's mother didn't run the house. She was at the tennis club a lot. Groucho would order the food and do the marketing. When Ruth came home, the rest of the family would sing, 'Everybody Works But Mother.' Groucho was always close and warm to the help, and despite his caustic way, he was always considerate of us. Being involved with Groucho, nobody thought of us as kids. He included you in conversations and treated you like an adult.

"Groucho would advise us on books to read. He was the first adult I ever knew who said he read *Alice in Wonderland* once a year. He introduced me to all kinds of classical music . . . also to Gilbert and Sullivan . . . he'd play the D'Oyly Carte albums and we'd each sing a part. I remember he once told us, 'Someday we're going to have a flying boat that will take us to the moon.' Miriam and I laughed."

If Groucho's waspish tongue tended to mercilessly bat down his children, he was supportive in other ways their schoolmates could well envy.

Miriam inherited his social conscience, and she wasn't even into her teens when she became a militant, highly vocal backer of various liberal causes, which often didn't sit well with the gentry of Beverly Hills.

Norman Krasna had built a house on Rodeo Drive. One day, Miriam, accompanied by her German shepherd, Duke, rang Krasna's door bell.

"How much money are you giving to the coal miners?" she asked, before the door was barely open.

Krasna replied, "You first say, 'Good morning' or 'Hello' or 'Would you like to give—' "

"You Fascist!" Miriam exclaimed.

"She kissed me before she went to bed every night," Krasna recalled, "and now I was being called a Fascist ... on Rodeo Drive."

The character modeled after Miriam in *Dear Ruth* was similarly passionate about noble causes.

"I was crazy about Miriam," Krasna said. "I wouldn't say she was unique, but she was certainly representative of the best."

Miriam, to a greater degree than Arthur, inherited Groucho's irreverent, cut-to-the-bone humor. Her cousin Maxine recalled that when Miriam went into a local hospital for an appendectomy, she was required to fill out a form. In the space after Religion, Miriam wrote "Druid."

Although Miriam said she wanted to be an actress, Maxine recalls, "She was writing short stories even then, and I found her quite talented. They were terribly sad stories."

A particularly ugly incident was the poisoning of the family dog. A gruff and unfriendly Protestant banker lived next door to the Marxes, and Miriam and Sunny were convinced he was the villain. They had already seen signs of anti-Semitism in him.

One day, the two stationed themselves on Groucho's back porch, and in retaliation, shot out some windows of the neighbor's house with a BB gun.

"Your daughter and her friend shot out eight of our windows," the banker told Groucho when he got him on the phone. "That will be eighty dollars."

Groucho apologized for the girls' behavior, and hurriedly paid for the damage. Then he called the girls to his room for a lecture. "You can do it once a month," he told them, "but no more."

Where his own property was concerned, he was less tolerant of the girls' high spirits. "Groucho was very possessive about his pool table," Sunny said. "He was afraid we'd rip the felt cover. We would sneak in the billiard room when he wasn't there. He also wouldn't let us near his Capehart record player. One time, Miriam broke it. When he confronted us, she told him I'd done it. Groucho yelled at me to keep my hands off things that didn't belong to me. Miriam later said she was sorry, but it was easier for me to take the blame."

The Capehart, a big console with an automatic changer, played 78 rpm records.

"It was probably the most expensive piece of furniture in the house," Mrs. Lenny Atkins, the former Irene Kahn, recalled. Irene, who grew up with Arthur, would later become the first Mrs. Arthur Marx.

"I was terribly afraid of Groucho at the time. He would always tease you. Arthur would pick me up and take me over to his house. We listened to records or played anagrams. Groucho really was a stay-at-home. He wouldn't go to nightclubs, although he liked to go to movies. Ruth liked to go out. I suppose there was a conflict."

The road tours used to perfect *A Night at the Opera* and *A Day at Races* were done away with. The studio thought them too expensive. Chico had a different explanation. He told a reporter from the *Brooklyn Daily Eagle* that the team decided not to tour because, "the elapsed time between the personal appearances and the picture's release was too long. In previous pictures many of the gags no longer were new stuff. They were grabbed by radio acts and other laugh-hunters."

Mervyn LeRoy, who produced *The King and The Chorus Girl,* was assigned to the Marx Brothers picture. He had recently completed production on *Wizard of Oz.*

Eddie Buzzell, the director, had shared Orpheum billings with the brothers, performing an extravaganza act called "Man of Affairs." He had just finished directing Burns and Allen in *Honolulu,* and had supervised a dozen previous pictures, the majority of them undistinguished. As far as Groucho was concerned, the verdict was still out on Buzzell, but he would accept him on the recommendation of LeRoy and other friends whose opinions he respected.

Buster Keaton, who had spent the previous year in a psychiatric clinic, was back at MGM thinking up visual gags for Harpo to perform. In the next few years, his lot would be further reduced to creating comedy bits for Red Skelton to perform in remakes of Keaton's classic comedies.

E. Y. (Yip) Harburg and Harold Arlen were engaged to compose four songs for the picture.

"Of course we had to tailor the music for their style," Yip Harburg said. "I knew that Groucho had a great love for words and word play. It was a fascinating gift he had, and don't belittle it. It was terrific. I had gone to his house many times, on nights when he had Gilbert and Sullivan evenings. He would gather us there, play complete operas and sing along with them. He knew all the words. He liked light verse and humor.

"I was also a Gilbert and Sullivan fan. I owe a lot of my background to Gilbert. When we wrote the score we put all those elements together. I tried to get as near to Gilbert and Sullivan as possible for 'Lydia the Tattooed Lady,' both in the rhyming scheme and the verbal juggling. Of course the idea had to be funny and had to pertain to a circus."

For the first time in the brothers' film career, a sole screenwriter would be involved. He was Irving Brecher, who was brought over from Warner Brothers by LeRoy, to whom he was under personal contract, in January of 1938. He had gotten his start as a comedy

267

writer, according to Hollywood folklore, by taking out a $15 ad in *Variety*:

> *Berle-proof jokes for sale. Jokes so bad even Milton Berle wouldn't steal them.*

Berle immediately hired him as a gag writer. Brecher had already contributed some uncredited material to *Wizard of Oz* and in four years would collaborate on the screenplay of another classic, *Meet Me in St. Louis.*

Though Brecher came to love Groucho, he always found him somewhat trying. "He had a quality of doing things when you were in public, such as in a restaurant or even in somebody's home for dinner. He would very often bug the help and ride them. I recall one night when one of our maids who was serving the dinner party became so upset by the things he was saying that she dropped a big tray and exited in tears. I always felt, and I told him a couple of times, that they were not fair game for him. He admitted this was true, but he couldn't resist going after the underlings."

Brecher also noted the contemptuous way he treated his wives. "He was pretty rough socially on Ruth. He would not let her talk. ... He made her feel she wasn't equal of holding her own in fast company. It upset my wife. ... Ruth was outwardly rather good about it. How she felt inside, I think we could all suspect. Ruth was a very delightful, attractive woman."

Brecher would also be the sole screenwriter on their next picture, *Go West.* "I guess I win the prize for endurance. Nobody ever did one alone and I did two, so I had a lot of sessions with the brothers. Mostly the sessions were with Groucho in the early stages of preparation. Groucho was a little more concerned with the overall story and script. Harpo trusted Groucho's judgment enough so that he could concentrate on his own scenes. Chico was interested in making any picture, so long as he got paid, so I never had any problems with him.

"Harpo and I were very good friends. I loved doing pantomime comedy and I was able to come up with a lot of things he loved. He encouraged me in terms of his reaction to them and his public utterances about what I was doing. The sessions I had with all of them were very minimal. Groucho did most of the talking, and as I said, Harpo kind of went along. He wasn't story-minded, but scene-minded.

"I never saw them unpleasant to each other. They were very sweet, I thought. I don't recall any backbiting by any of them. Groucho might be impatient with Chico's money-squandering or betting and he would expose certain irritations. But they were generally not too harsh."

The first day of shooting, Buzzell attempted to assert his authority by asking the brothers to "really act this scene."

"The Marx Brothers will do anything but act," Groucho answered. "If you want dramatics, hire our stand-ins."

The three then proceeded to display all the high-spirited juvenility that men in their fifties are capable of. Buzzell came up with another directorial approach. "Personally, I think the Marx Brothers are among the funniest people in the world, but, like all laugh seekers of their type, they are always 'working' and if I was to prove a good audience to them during rehearsals and between scenes, I would be sunk. So, I never laughed at their cracks and never tried to match repartee with them. . . .

"I would say to Groucho, 'You need new makeup on your nose.' He would crack back, 'Don't quibble, what I need is a new nose.'

"Or: 'Chico, look at Harpo and not at the camera!' He would crack back, 'Personally, I'd rather look at the camera than his mug.' "

His tactics must have worked. Groucho, in the midst of filming, wrote a letter to Arthur Sheekman:

Our picture is progressing quite rapidly considering that it's our picture and we'll almost finish on schedule. Buzzell is quite bright, smarter than I imagined, but in a way a sort of Norman McLeod . . . I think the picture will be better than I thought. This isn't saying a hell of a lot, but, really, I think the scenes are going to be pretty funny, although I must admit, in establishing an alibi, that I have seen very little of the rushes. I'm getting too old for rushes—the projection rooms, or at least the ones they give us, are either always a long climb or in an air-conditioned cellar, and I've decided to wait until the picture plays the Marquis before seeing it. [The Marquis was a small theater on the edge of Beverly Hills which later became the headquarters of the Academy of Motion Picture Arts and Sciences and most recently has been taken over by the Writers Guild] At least if I don't like it, I might win a Chevrolet! There's some talk of the Ritz Theatre raffling off a Buick, and if they do, I might not see the picture at all.

Postproduction was completed in mid-July. Buzzell planned to leave immediately for a leisurely European vacation. "Revealing my plans was not too wise," he later stated. "Groucho, Chico, and Harpo threw a dinner for me. It started at the Trocadero, from which they stormed out in a huff, then halted for soup at tables on a sidewalk, moved to a café, then to the ring of the 10,000-seat Hollywood American Legion Stadium, where we had dessert while two wrestlers tumbled around us. We wound up having coffee in a mortuary."

Joe Adamson, in his delightful *Groucho, Harpo, Chico and Sometimes Zeppo,* found the "deathless, mythical clowns" of the earlier pictures "hereby pummeled and subdued into a pack of sniveling, weaseling nitwits who get in the way and mess things up a lot" in their three final Marx Brothers pictures at MGM. "What comes between the punchlines of *At the Circus, Go West* and *The Big Store,* even the best punchlines," he wrote, "are pretty plain old ordinary 1940s movies."

The Age of Heroic Comedy, as Adamson described it, had ended. Buster Keaton was working at MGM as a $100-a-week gagman. Harry Langdon was performing similar duties at the Hal Roach studios. Chaplin, Harold Lloyd, and Laurel and Hardy were showing the same tired signs as the Marx Brothers. W. C. Fields, in 1940, was breathing his last creative gasp in *The Bank Dick.*

"Twenty-five years of brilliant gags, incisive characterization, and dynamic, subversive comedy had come to an end," Adamson wrote. "There was nothing left but disintegration, demoralization, heartbreak, and Abbott and Costello." The American audience in 1940 was no longer so eager for comedy. What moviegoers sought out was the epic grandeur of a *Gone with the Wind* or the inspira-

270

tional, down-home values of a Frank Capra. The Marx Brothers were not among nature's heroic figures, nor did they espouse noble, self-sacrificing gestures. They were tired and dated.

Special measures were called for. The studio entrusted the next picture to producer Jack Cummings, whose main qualification for the job was that he was Louis B. Mayer's nephew.

Groucho wrote Arthur and Gloria Sheekman in October of 1939, after the mediocre reception of *At the Circus:*

> The boys at the studio have lined up another turkey for us, and there's a strong likelihood that we'll be shooting in about three or four weeks. I'm not looking forward to it but I guess it's just as well to get it over with. I saw the present one the other day and didn't care much for it. I realize I'm not much of a judge but I'm kind of sick of the whole thing, and on leaving the theater, vowed that I'd never see it again. I don't feel this way about all our pictures: "A Night at the Opera," for example, I always enjoyed looking at, and to lesser degree, "A Day at the Races," but the rest sicken me and I'll stay clear of them in the future.

Bert Kalmar and Harry Ruby were reassigned to the *Go West* screenplay, but their efforts, revolving around the doings at a rodeo, were unacceptable to the studio. Seven more months would elapse before the final script by Irving Brecher was ready to try out on the road. The brothers insisted on returning to the Thalberg-developed concept this time around. A troupe of forty, playing four-a-day and five on Saturdays and Sundays—a total of 103 performances—would split a week in Joliet and Toledo before playing full weeks in Detroit, Chicago, and Los Angeles.

Prior to their departure, they had a picture-taking session with Alexander Woollcott, who was on a lecture tour, alternating his talks with appearances in *The Man Who Came to Dinner.* Woollcott sat like a pasha in a big chair, around which the brothers stood to pay him honor. Harpo did so in a typically mischievous way, as James Thurber later wrote in a letter to Groucho. "... *Les vêtements de Harpo étaient dérangés,* deliberately, and in such impish fashion

271

that his what's-its-name was clearly visible." The picture would not wind up in Woollcott's photo album.

Arthur Sheekman was living in Connecticut while working on a play during 1940. The many letters Groucho wrote him, few of which were answered, served as a safety valve. They revealed some of his greatest preoccupations during this time, although the most important one—the state of his marriage—went unmentioned.

Groucho wrote Sheekman in March:

Our picture is moving slowly. We hope to start rehearsing in a couple of weeks and baring it to the natives in about five. The amount of work, politics, intrigue and chicanery involved in assembling even as unimportant a triviality as a Marx Brothers' comedy is appalling! It's really unbelievable—all the meetings, conversation and arguments that have to be gone through with before one of these turkeys is completed! If I were to take it seriously, I'd probably kill myself, but once I get away from the meeting and the studio, it all recedes into a shadowy insignificance and I play the guitar and think of other things.

The two men were collaborating on Groucho's second book, *Many Happy Returns*, a draft of which was sent to Groucho at the Paramount Theatre in Chicago, while he was on the road tour, and he planned to inject some of his comedy style into it, but "I've been doing four a day and rehearsing between shows and I just haven't had strength to do anything about it."

The Allies suffered severe reverses in Europe during this period. "I am really bushed from this trip," Groucho wrote, "perhaps more from the front page news than from the actual trip, but, at any rate, I am fagged out and I can just about make my feet navigate. The trip was successful insofar as we were able to get many laughs that we didn't have when the trip started. How the picture will be, I don't know and I really don't care much, as it all seems so unimportant now. I'm going away next week and will try to get back some of my nervous energy for those eight weeks on the back lot arguing with Buzzell on how the jokes should be said."

Nat Perrin was supplying unbilled contributions to the script.

While playing in Chicago, he was recruited to act as a prompter for a new scene with Groucho and Chico which he and Sheekman had written.

"I was behind them, hidden by a piece of scenery," Perrin recalled. "Groucho always had a little trouble with his hearing. I whispered the cue. All I heard from Groucho was, 'Ah? What? Louder!' Up went the decibels. Every time I'd supply another line, we'd have the same thing. Groucho and Chico finally struggled through the performance. I went backstage, and just as I got there, I ran into Irwin Gelsey, who was then the story editor at Columbia. He had been asking the doorman for me. I went up to him and said, 'How did you know I was here?' He said, 'How did I know? I was sitting in the last row and the only one I heard was you.' "

Before the company left Chicago, Groucho wrote Sheekman another letter. "I'm not able to sleep any more. I thought you would like to know—I have to tell it to someone, and apparently, no one out here gives a damn and I don't blame them! There's nothing that will put me to sleep as quickly as someone else telling about not being able to sleep. That gives me a bright idea—I think I'll make a couple of records, telling about my problems as an insomniac. Then at night when I'm seeing things and little men keep running up and down my back, all I'll have to do is play the records and I'll be off in a cloud of talcum powder! You probably ask, 'Why can't he sleep? He has money, beauty, talent, vigor and many teeth'—but the possession of all of these riches has nothing to do with it. I see Bund members dropping down my chimney, Commies under my bed, Fifth Columnists in my closets, a bearded dwarf, called Surtax, doing a gavotte on my desk with a little lady known as Confiscation. I'm setting aside a small sum for poison which I'm secreting in a little sack under my mattress."

Groucho's son was seriously considering becoming a writer, and Sheekman was asked his opinion of Arthur's potential. It apparently was positive, for Groucho wrote in one letter:

I am glad you are enthusiastic about Arthur's literary future. His letters had always struck me as being amusing but I was suspicious of my own judgment. Being a parent yourself, you know how it is—we like almost anything our children do.

However, many people, including Ed Sullivan, Morrie Ryskind, Dore Schary, Brecher and yourself, have told me that they think Arthur has an incipient talent for writing and who am I to back my opinion against all of yours?

Later in the letter, he referred to "the most wonderful publicity item in the history of American journalism," which had occurred the previous week in Louella Parsons's column:

> You remember that we went on the road and played four weeks—one hundred performances—to weed out the debris in the comedy scenes and to fatten them up. At the expiration of those haunted weeks we felt (even though we were all ready for a sanitarium) that we had accomplished our purpose. Since we have been back, two people have been engaged for the picture—one is Lynn Carver, who by the damnedest coincidence turns out to be Nick Nayfack's wife—(Mr. Nayfack happens also by coincidence to be the nephew of Nick Schenck); the other is Lee Bowman, the other end of the love interest. Well, this was the item in Louella's column: "Lynn Carver and Lee Bowman have just returned from a vaudeville tour where they tried out the material to be used in their next picture, *Gone West* [sic]." This, I think, is the most magnificent piece of columnar inaccuracy that has appeared in print!

Louella Parsons proved even more inaccurate than Groucho first claimed since neither Miss Carver nor Bowman appeared in the finished picture.

Postscripts to almost every letter Groucho wrote Sheekman during the period were the parenthetical requests for employment for Margaret Dumont. "She's at liberty," he wrote in one of them, "not an unusual condition for her, and I imagine she'd be very appreciative of anything that fitted her, and wouldn't expect too much of a salary."

Later in the year, as the presidential election which would pit Franklin Delano Roosevelt against Wendell Willkie loomed, he talked about one of their friends' politicking:

Morris Ryskind has become (as only Ryskind could) the most militant Willkie booster in the United States. He wears a Willkie button on his lapel and acts like a freshman rooting for his football team—he is so adult in some ways and so juvenile in others! He has spoiled three different dinner parties for me by denouncing any of the guests who had the effrontery to admit that they intended to vote for Roosevelt. At the last steak dinner, I asked him to please postpone the denouncements until after the customers had eaten, but he just couldn't control himself and halfway through the meal he began. The meal ended in a sort of conversational free-for-all and just on the edge of blows. Over the phone the next day, I told him that I was not asking him to dinner again until after the election ... I imagine he'll kill himself if Willkie is defeated, and with his present attitude, I don't think that would be much of a loss.

Nevertheless, Groucho cast his ballot for Willkie during the election, the only time in his life he didn't vote the straight Democratic ticket. He believed electing Roosevelt to a third term would set an unhealthy precedent.

Even before the release of *Go West* late in 1940, Groucho was predicting the film would be poorly received. With this in mind, he sought out other opportunities. He got together with Irving Brecher, at his agent brother Gummo's suggestion, to discuss the possibility of a radio situation comedy to be called "The Flotsam Family."

"I'm shaping my ambitions in other directions and discussing a radio show that I might do with Irving Brecher," Groucho wrote Sheekman. "It's a kind of Aldrich family except that we hope to make it a little funnier. By that I don't mean joke, joke, joke, but a kind of human interest story with a slightly wacky father, who, of course, would be me.

"We are going to make a record of it as soon as it's written. We even have two or three suckers who claim they can hardly wait until they hear it. This statement, as you know, could lead to all kinds of funny answers, but I'll just leave them to you. I'm pretty sick of having the answers. My idea of an ideal program would be a show where I would have all the questions and some other bastard would have to figure out the funny answers. Of course, I wouldn't like the salary a man gets for asking the questions but why go on—there's no one going to offer me anything as attractive as that. In addition to the radio show, I have a deal on with Krasna to write a play."

The radio pilot never sold, and it was later adapted by Brecher into a vehicle for William Bendix called "Life of Riley," which Jackie Gleason would originally star in when it moved from radio to television.

The play the letter alluded to was *Time for Elizabeth*. "It took us twelve years to finish it, though we probably worked on it for only a few months," Norman Krasna said.

Miriam had always wanted to be an actress and her friend Sunny planned to be a writer. "We'd seen a movie where characters meet four years later," Sunny said. "In our fantasy we would meet at the corner of Palm Drive, halfway between our houses on Maple and Hillcrest. If she were in a Broadway show, she would send a man, whom I would fall in love with and marry. And vice versa. Something was wrong with our arithmetic, because we were seniors in high school when the time was up. The dumbness of it!"

Arthur, in his first year at the University of Southern California, had managed to win the National Freshman Intercollegiate tennis title. He fared less well in the classroom, flunking botany. When Groucho drove with him and Miriam to New York during the Christmas holidays, Arthur informed him of his intention to leave school and become a screenwriter. The three had taken many motor trips together, often leaving Ruth behind. This time, she took the train and met them at their destination. When they returned to California, all said that they had had a wonderful time, a blatant untruth inspired by their desire to preserve the image of a happy family.

Irene Kahn knew that Arthur's mother liked to take a drink, but although she virtually grew up with the young man she was now dating steadily, she hadn't been aware of the seriousness of the problem. The two later were at a party, held in Beverly Hills. Arthur and Irene were older than the rest of the group, who were still in high school. Drinks were being served, and as the crowd became progressively drunker, the revelers started pushing each other and the garden furniture into the pool. Arthur turned to Irene. His eyes misted. "I can't stand this sort of thing. My mother's an alcoholic. Let's get out of here."

On December 18, 1940, *Variety* set forth the new order:

> Although the three Marx brothers will make one more film for Metro next spring, following release of their "Go West," which has just been previewed, Groucho states that the trio will be no more thereafter. He himself has self authored straight comedy (with Norman Krasna) he plans to produce and star in on Broadway in a year or so.
>
> Harpo Marx and Oscar Levant, in a gag pantomusical routine, are primed for a concert tour, and Chico Marx isn't kidding about heading his own band.

If no show business offers were forthcoming after the final picture at MGM, *The Big Store*, Groucho was resigned to retiring to the eight acres he had bought in the San Fernando Valley, near Clark Gable's ranch. He declared that he would spend the rest of his days as a chicken farmer and swore he would do a better job of it than the brothers had at the farm in LaGrange.

Go West was released the same week as *Gone With the Wind* was showing at popular prices. The former was no competition for the Southern epic.

Because of the mild reception to the picture, there was no talk about a road tour for the one they were currently preparing. Everyone wanted to finish the studio commitment as quickly as possible.

Nat Perrin supplied the story idea for the third film, while the screenplay would be the responsibility of a trio of writers. Charles Reisner—who directed such great movie comedians as Laurel and Hardy, Buster Keaton, Marie Dressler, Polly Moran, and Chester Conklin—would be directing. The picture's title changed from *Bargain Basement* to *Step This Way* to *The Big Store*. There was some talk of filming it in 3-D, as had previously been done by the studio in a Pete Smith short subject.

Four years after Thalberg's death, no one at MGM had come forward to equal his creativity. Mayer, for one, would never understand the brothers.

According to Groucho in a *Playboy* interview, he "took things too seriously. Nobody else took us seriously in Hollywood. One day he was having a conference with a censor about Lana Turner showing too much cleavage in her last film and Mayer was trying to convince the censor that MGM was a highly moral studio. So Harpo hired a stripper for the afternoon and chased her around the room while Mayer was talking to the censor."

That year, Greta Garbo also made her final film at MGM, retiring after her unsuccessful *Two Faced Woman.* Groucho often told about getting on an elevator with her in the Thalberg building and tipping her wide-brimmed hat over her head. When she turned in anger, Groucho said, "I beg your pardon. I thought you were a fellow I once knew in Kansas City."

Nat Perrin was with him that day. "Groucho was at my right, and in front of his shoulder was this woman, wearing sloppy blue slacks and a cheap little hand-knitted pullover sweater that came down about to her navel. She was wearing a floppy brimmed straw hat, like something you wear out on a farm. When he tipped her hat, she gave him a terrible look. After she got off the elevator, the elevator operator turned to us and said, 'Did you know who that was?' We didn't. When he told us, Groucho went white, absolutely speechless. If he'd known it was Garbo, he never would have done it."

Salwyn Shufro, Groucho's stockbroker, had begun making yearly business trips to California in 1938 and always stayed at the Marxes, sharing Arthur's bedroom. He eventually met many of Groucho's friends at Hillcrest Country Club, and would be handling the portfolios of virtually all the comedians who lunched there.

"Arthur told me he would be very happy to have you as a roommate again," Groucho wrote him in February prior to Shufro's 1941 trip. "The last time you were here you lost an overcoat, two pairs of gloves, a pair of field glasses and a cigarette case, and he's been living on the spoils ever since. On this trip I hope you won't leave such a trail of disorder. When you arrive at my house, just knock loudly on the brass knocker on the door, and I'm sure no one will answer. In that case, go around to the servants' entrance, and sneak up to Arthur's room and start forgetting things."

"Everybody I did business with was directly or indirectly through Groucho," he said. "He introduced me to people practically every time I came out. They in turn introduced me to others. It finally ended up that I had to see fifty or sixty people each time I came out. It began to be quite a job to cover that much territory."

Groucho would give one dinner party for Shufro during his trip. Generally, they would have breakfast together; thereafter, Shufro would leave for his appointments and Groucho would spend another irritating day at the studio.

"We are starting our picture next week and it stinks!" Groucho wrote Sheekman on March 11, 1941. "Fortunately, for my frame of mind, this will ring down my Marx Brothers' career. I am firm about disbanding, as is Harpo, and from now on I'm strictly on my own. I am going on the Vallee show the 27th of March, provided I like the material. I have a contractual clause that if I don't find it satisfactory, I don't have to appear. I have a kind of vague and hazy deal on for around September, I think, for J. Walter Thompson, and I want to be sure not to jeopardize it in any way."

The picture was finished in mid-June. Chico, who previously announced the formation of his own orchestra, had to postpone his plans until he concluded a radio series, "Chico's Barber Shop." Harpo was making his speaking debut in a Bucks County Playhouse production of *The Man Who Came to Dinner*, co-starring with George Kaufman and Moss Hart. Other than two radio appearances, one on a U. S. Defense Bond program and the second on Rudy Vallee's Sealtest show, Groucho was professionally inactive. He was marking time both professionally and in his personal life. Ruth's drinking remained uncontrollable.

That summer Miriam graduated from grammar school. Groucho took her and Sunny to visit Clark Gable at his Encino ranch. Both girls, now about to enter high school, had enormous crushes on the film star. He proved to be the first man to come between them.

"We were both trying to impress him," Sunny said. "He offered to give us a ride on his tractor. Miriam immediately jumped on the hood before I could. I had to stand on the running board. Gable put his arm around me so that I wouldn't fall off. Miriam looked back. She was, of course, quite jealous."

That fall, now students at Beverly Hills High School, the two girls skipped school on Yom Kippur and hiked around Beverly Hills. It was a hot September day, and they decided, impulsively, to take a dip in a park fountain. In the midst of their ablutions, a police car drove up and they were carted off to jail. Groucho arrived at the station house and bailed out both girls, now two-time losers.

Groucho stayed close to home, half-heartedly threatening to retire. Shufro had succeeded in building up his stock portfolio so that he would never have to work again, should he so choose. The progress of the play he and Norman Krasna were working on was further slowed when Krasna accepted a more tangible commitment. Groucho was approached about writing a newspaper column, and flattered as he was by the implicit trust placed in him as a writer, he knew he couldn't deliver columns with any great regularity.

Groucho agreed to make an appearance in late November of 1941 at New York's Madison Square Garden at a benefit for the United Jewish Appeal. While in New York, a gossip columnist reported he had been seen in the company of a woman not his wife. He returned home to find Ruth outraged and humiliated. Amazingly, he didn't understand why.

Arthur had been in New York at the same time, and stayed on hoping to find work. He hadn't been having much luck finding a job in California, and he saw his father's hand in this, for Groucho thought he was getting too serious about Irene Kahn.

Miriam and Sunny were spending the day with Groucho, and Ruth was otherwise occupied at the tennis club, on Sunday, December 7, when the news broke of the Japanese surprise attack on Pearl Harbor.

CHAPTER TEN

Maybe I can be funny after the war, but nobody who has seen this war can be cute about it while it's going on. The only way I can try to be a little funny is to make something out of the humorous situations which come up even when you don't think life could be any more miserable.

                                        Bill Mauldin, Up Front

With the United States at war with Germany and Italy, battles would soon be fought on two fronts. At home, Groucho was waging a domestic battle of his own.

He implied it was business as usual in a letter to Sheekman on December 19, mentioning that he and Krasna were making headway with their play, before alluding to the inevitable:

This is beautiful weather for a divorce—the sun has been shining all morning and no matter how much artificial fertilizer or heat you use, it's not nearly as effective as the sun's natural rays. I'm having some window boxes made and I think the divorce papers will do very nicely in them. Of course, I'd like to have them fully grown for the Easter season.

Now that he had dropped the bombshell, he returned to their recent collaboration:

Simon and Schuster wired me that they're using the title "Many Happy Returns." I agree with you that there should be some recognition in the book to the current situation. Perhaps even a word about Defense Stamps—maybe coupling it with the Stamp Act of 1776. You might say that the Stamp Act was: Two fellows came out and stamped on the stage and finished with a song.

The book, a comic indictment of the income tax system, wouldn't have great success, partly because of poor timing. Americans were pledging their allegiance to the cause by supporting the passage in Congress of a $10,077,077,005 defense budget. The book sold about 5,000 copies. "I write nothing but first editions," Groucho cracked.

Four days after Christmas, on December 29, 1941, Ruth walked out of the Marx house and took her own apartment. Terms of the divorce had been worked out. Years previously, realizing that because of his dysfunction he couldn't sexually satisfy her, Groucho told Ruth she could take lovers if she were discreet. Her prudence had been long destroyed by alcohol.

The action was Ruth's desperate attempt to regain emotional equilibrium. Groucho didn't press the issue. He considered contesting Ruth's alimony claim. He could have offered her infidelities as proof of her unfitness, but the idea was quickly dismissed. He would spare his children an unsavory public airing of the differences between himself and Ruth. He also had no need to add to his already enormous burden of guilt.

"Ruth was the one who wanted the divorce," Betty said. "She knew that in California you get half your husband's assets. Groucho never hid them. He was an honest man. They divided everything down to the silver in the house. That's how honest he was."

Betty and Chico also separated in 1941. They would have celebrated their Silver Anniversary the following year, but, as Betty put it, "I gave him one year off for bad behavior."

Groucho called on Betty soon after the separation and tossed $300,000 worth of securities in her lap. "Then he started to berate Chico," she said. "That didn't console me, because I was still in love with Chico. It's very hard when you love somebody to let go. But I saw the handwriting on the wall. I had to protect my daughter and myself."

That Groucho gave the securities to Betty and not to Chico is indicative of his basic decency. "He knew if he gave them to Chico I would never get a nickel. Groucho was embarrassed about the whole thing. He knew I wasn't to blame. He was a very fair man, but he did it in a bad way. I didn't want to hear any criticism of Chico, who had a great deal of love in him. I don't doubt that until he died Chico still loved me. And he should have. I was a damn good wife. I never regretted marrying him. I thought later that I should have let go sooner. But you can only let go when you can. Groucho didn't have the same kind of love in him as Chico. He was basically a bitter man.

"Groucho wrote me a letter soon after the visit. He said he knew he was abrupt and didn't mean it. In the letter, he berated Chico all over again. He said if I wanted a divorce I could show the letter to a judge and I'd get it right away."

Her share of the securities, which appreciated considerably with Salwyn Shufro as her broker, has supported her in great comfort during the intervening years. As for Chico, he lost his half of the money within three months.

There was a basic difference in the two broken marriages. Chico's wife was still in love with him and Groucho's wife was not. He wondered if Ruth had ever loved him at all.

Groucho awoke one day to find himself fifty percent poorer, with middle age upon him and old age not far beyond. It was a bitter irony that the two brothers, one a profligate and the other a saver, should find themselves in the same precarious financial position again. This had previously occurred after the 1929 market crash.

Newsweek magazine, on February 23, 1942, reported the shelving of Groucho's sketchy retirement plans: "Although he supposedly retired from the scene last summer, Groucho Marx now plans a comeback—but without his mustache, slouch clothes, or Harpo and Chico."

Chico was already on tour, fronting as a bandleader. Harpo, in the meantime, was comfortably fixed, and could afford to take his time sifting through his many offers.

Groucho was offered an appearance in Irving Berlin's *Music Box Revue* for the following season, but there were no immediate bookings in the offing.

All of Hollywood was swept up in a patriotic fervor, and zealously looked for ways in which to aid the war effort. Groucho wasn't a noted altruist, but he would never equal Bob Hope or even his brother Harpo in the giving of his talent for charitable causes. Had he been more generous in support of the liberal, leftist causes he believed in, chances are that the postwar Communist witch-hunt in Hollywood would have blacklisted the Hollywood Eleven instead of the Hollywood Ten.

He, along with many other stars, agreed to participate in a cross-country tour to sell war bonds. It was a welcome distraction from the problems at home.

The Hollywood Victory Caravan opened at the Capitol Theatre in Washington, D.C., on April 30, 1942. It played fifteen cities across the country by the time it closed on May 19 at the Civic Auditorium in San Francisco.

The train was outfitted with a barbershop, a dining room, and an observation car where performers passed the early morning hours. Each performer was given a separate compartment, with chaperones separating the men's section from the women's.

Performers starting out on the tour included Bing Crosby, Laurel and Hardy, Cary Grant, Bob Hope, James Cagney, Pat O'Brien, Desi Arnaz, Charles Boyer, Merle Oberon, Claudette Colbert, Joan Blondell, Joan Bennett, and Bert Lahr. Other stars joined them along the way.

Groucho took an informal poll of the actresses. Despite the romantic leading men on the Caravan—Cary Grant, Charles Boyer, even Groucho himself—the women were most attracted to James Cagney.

One of them had eyes for neither Cagney nor Groucho, however. Olivia de Havilland was performing with Groucho in a comedy sketch written by Hal Kanter, "Who's Olive?" She was a young woman of refined beauty, and Groucho fell in love with her. "She was very beautiful," Groucho recalled. "A lot of men had a case on her." Much to his frustration, she was obviously fascinated with another man.

"I was in the second section with a certain officer," Miss de Havilland recalled. The man was director John Huston. "I told him, 'I've got to be in the first section with the other performers.' He said he would desert if I wasn't on the second section with him. When we got to Washington, I showed up twenty-five minutes later than the rest of them. I was careful that no one saw me. Instead of asking 'Who's Olive?' they were asking *'Where's Olive?'* "

She was quite surprised to hear thirty-five years later that Groucho was in love with her. "He never told me. I just thought he enjoyed my company. I was so flattered that such a great comedian would find me amusing."

Claudette Colbert had been joined en route to Washington by her husband, Joel Pressman, a doctor in the Navy. The couple hibernated in their compartment for two days. They finally emerged to go to the dining car, and found a note from Groucho, the love-sick Pagliacci, on their return: "Isn't this carrying naval relief too far?"

Bob Hope, in a 1963 radio salute to Groucho on his birthday, reminisced on the National Broadcasting Company's "Monitor" show about the Caravan's arrival in Washington:

At the train station, a tremendous crowd was cheering everyone. When Groucho got off, nobody recognized him because he didn't have his mustache or cigar. He climbed down and got on at the other end of the car, put on his mustache, cigar in his mouth, got down in a crouch and got a tremendous hand. He sat in the back of a limousine with a Washington society leader. As Charlotte Greenwood, the eccentric dancer, got off the train, she did a big kick. Groucho nudged the leader. He said, "You can do that too if you put your mind to it."

Later, at a White House garden party, the actors went through a receiving line to shake hands with the First Lady. They were trying to maintain a measure of decorum. Groucho, however, was his irrepressibly irreverent self.

"I'm very happy to meet you, Mr. Marx," Eleanor Roosevelt said as they met.

"Are we late for dinner?" Groucho asked. The gathering had rather specifically been scheduled between lunch and dinner, so he knew they wouldn't be fed.

Mrs. Roosevelt smiled, then nodded in time to the playing of the Marine Band, composed of men with dismally small musical gifts. Commenting on the quality of the music, Groucho told her, "Now I know why you travel so much."

A general later came up to Groucho and asked about Mrs. Roosevelt's whereabouts. "She's upstairs filing her teeth," Groucho responded. The general walked away.

The most convivial member of the Hollywood Caravan was Pat O'Brien. "You son of a bitch," Bing Crosby told him, "you play Father Duffy all day and Sherman Billingsley all night."

The one anecdote about the Caravan which Groucho repeated more often than any other involved O'Brien and Desi Arnaz. The Cuban singer came back to the train one night. "My 'Baba Lu,' " he said. "The people can't get enough of my 'Baba Lu.' "

O'Brien snarled, "We beat you in ninety-eight and we can do it again!"

The Caravan disbanded in Glendale in an atmosphere of good feeling. The participants promised to keep in touch with each other, but for the most part lost contact thereafter.

On June 22, 1942, Ruth filed for divorce against Groucho, charging that he "inflicted physical pain and mental anguish" upon her. The interlocutory decree was awarded on July 15.

Groucho, years later, still bristled at the accusation that he had physically abused Ruth. The subject came up when we were discussing Humphrey Bogart. "He was a close friend," Groucho told me, "but he really hated women. He was sitting once at

Chasen's with his wife, Mayo Methot. She said something he didn't approve of and he hauled off and hit her on the chin. He was a great actor, but a coward. Only a coward hits women. Bacall was a funny dame and a good actress. She handled him well."

When I mentioned Ruth's charge in the divorce suit, Groucho quickly said, "I've never hit a woman except in self-defense."

Norman Krasna said, "When people have their biggest troubles, and where I would go running to Groucho and where you'd go running to a friend, Groucho wouldn't confide his problems in others. You'd know it was going on, and yet he was the funniest man in the world. How do you separate that? How do you put your mind and disposition to it? The divorce was agonizing. You may build humor on it, but don't think that coming out of divorce court, with all the expense and embarrassment, didn't affect him terribly. It might be conducive for him to say something rude, but not necessarily funny."

Miriam now became the lady of the house. She would act as Groucho's hostess, and on nights when he wasn't wearing a pretty woman on his arm, fill in as his date. She had never seriously considered staying with Ruth, even if her mother had wanted her to. She didn't exactly turn her back on her mother, although she regarded her visits to Ruth more as an obligation than a pleasure. That she couldn't offer her helpless mother a modicum of affection would cause enormous guilt later.

"It was too bad that Groucho kept Miriam after the divorce," Betty, Chico's first wife, said. "It was no place for a fifteen-year-old girl. She was acting as hostess to these sophisticated men and women, sitting around and hearing a lot of remarks that weren't suitable for a girl her age."

Miriam was supplying a few of her own. Groucho invited a blonde nurse he was dating to dinner at his house. With all the intimidating talk and snappy comebacks of the other guests, the young woman was afraid to open her mouth during the entire evening. When Miriam was asked her impression of the girl, she commented, "Harpo in drag."

Groucho, having previously shipped off Arthur to New York because he feared his son and Irene Kahn would marry at too young an age, now wanted to keep him in California. Mannie

Manheim, the head writer of the Milton Berle radio show, owed Groucho a favor. He hired Arthur as a gag writer for $50 a week, a job that lasted until the summer of 1942 when Arthur went into the Coast Guard.

Professionally, Groucho's only commitment during the summer was as a semiregular on the Rudy Vallee Sealtest show. During his many off hours, he continued listening to Gilbert and Sullivan and worrying about the state of the world and his bank account, not necessarily in that order. During the day, he would bicycle to the brothers' office in downtown Beverly Hills. Much of his leisure time was spent with Miriam and her friends.

Groucho was uneasy around sick or old people, and visits to hospitals depressed him. He asked Miriam and Sunny to accompany him when he went to see Harry Ruby, who was convalescing from minor surgery, at Cedars of Lebanon Hospital. As they got in the elevator, Groucho requested, "Men's tonsils, please."

After thirty-five years before the public, Groucho was now at liberty. Given a larger stock portfolio, he might not have minded.

"I had an offer from the New Opera Company to appear in an Offenbach operetta, called *La Vie Parisienne*," he wrote Sheekman in September, "and the book was just about as good as the title. It had a very novel idea in it—it was all about a rich American who goes to Paris—well, you wouldn't want anything better than that, would you? Oh, yes, he also gets mixed up with a French girl, or a girl who does French. I just don't remember what it was. The second act is a race between a number of horses, and although I'm supposed to lose, my horse wins and the girl turns out to be extremely wealthy in her own right and not really an adventuress at all. It's a little hazy, but in the last act, I believe the girl marries the horse and she becomes the most popular brood mare in Antibes. I don't think I'll do this play unless they give me the horse's part—I would take the part of the horse, if I could get the part I need most. Well, these are my plans and for the balance of the week, you can reach me at Gilmore Stadium between Harry Ruby and first base."

Sheekman could also have caught him at the Marquis Theatre, whose facilities Groucho often slandered. Yet, he preferred going there with Miriam and her friends because the manager allowed him to smoke cigars in the small balcony. He saw virtually every film that played there from that vantage point, talking back to the screen to the amusement of Miriam and her friends. Many of his *bons mots* are lost to memory, but Sunny recalled a choice one. They had gone to see the new Bette Davis picture, *Now Voyager.* The movie opened with raindrops pelting a window pane. "My God," Groucho exclaimed, "she's crying already!"

Groucho began seeing Virginia Schulberg, the ex-wife of writer Budd Schulberg. "She used to read scripts for Goldwyn," Groucho told me. "We'd go to a party, and she was so beautiful, so bright, and so funny that there would be six men standing around her. I was crazy about her." Arthur theorized in *Son of Groucho* that they drifted apart because Groucho felt threatened by Mrs. Schulberg's intellect and her insistence on maintaining her individuality.

Her tragic death in a fire, Groucho implied to me, ended the relationship, when actually they hadn't seen each other for some years and both had been emotionally involved with others. She was to be one of a small list of women Groucho voiced great regrets about, mourning relationships that never developed. None of the women he discussed in this light were his ex-wives.

"These years were the lowest point in his life," Bert Granet, a neighbor of his at the time said. Granet's screenplay treatments had formed the basis for *Monkey Business* and *Horse Feathers.*

"It was obvious he was so lonely," Granet's wife Charlotte added. "He'd walk the dog back and forth in front of our house." Groucho seemed to be begging for an invitation. The Granets, only too gladly, complied. His hosts introduced him to a younger generation of writers—Sidney Sheldon, Norman Panama, Mel Frank, Julius Epstein—who would replace many of his older friends who had moved elsewhere.

The dining table at the Granets seated sixteen. Groucho would sit at the head. "I'm the oldest," he would explain. He held court and the Granets let him . . . five or six nights a week. He proved to be the man who came to dinner.

In February of 1943, Arthur and Irene Kahn were married while he was home on leave from the Coast Guard. They were both twenty-one. "Groucho said that he married at thirty," Irene said. "To him, this was the ideal age. He wasn't thrilled about our marriage."

It was a small wedding, held at the Kahn residence, and Ruth was present. Groucho was reasonably cordial with her, though Irene recalled that Groucho insulted the rabbi after the ceremony.

Evidently, he was sharpening his tongue for his imminent return to show business as the star of a radio variety show being sponsored by Pabst Blue Ribbon Beer. Gummo had obtained the job for him. The half-hour show premiered on Saturday, March 27, on the Columbia Broadcasting System.

A review in *Newsweek* on April 5 typified the general reception to the program:

When the Marx Brothers in 1941 quit movies "in anticipation of public demand," Groucho ... wiped off his phony mustache and optimistically set out to write, produce, and star in a legitimate play ... His drama reached the manuscript stage but not the Broadway one. Hence the public got nothing from the former Mr. Otis P. Driftwood but an occasional magazine article until he popped up last week, mustache, leer, and all, as the star of a new radio series.

Blue Ribbon (beer) *Town* is put on in Hollywood and goes out over the formerly dry CBS network Saturday evenings from 10:15 to 10:45 EST. During this half hour, for a reputed $2,500 a week, the predatory Groucho leeringly quips with his vocalists, Virginia O'Brien and Donald Dickson. As host of a full-fledged variety show, he also has command of announcer Dick Joy, Robert Armbruster's orchestra and any guest star who has the stamina to stand up under a half-hour of Marxist dialectics. Among those already committed to the ordeal are Joan Bennett, Hedda Hopper, Lucille Ball, and Charles Laughton.

Listeners who have harked back as long as nine years will recall Groucho and Chico on the air as the disreputable Flywheel and Ravelli. The new series, however, is the first to star a solitary Marx. To keep it from getting monotonous, Groucho will undergo frequent personality changes, becoming successively a mad scientist, a mad lawyer, a mad banker, a mad doctor, etc., maintaining his identity if not his sanity through his continued connection with the Pabst Brewing Co.

Newsweek erred in stating Groucho wore the greasepaint mustache while broadcasting. He dabbed it on for publicity pictures, but when he performed before the studio audience he stood before them in his everyday guise. He no longer felt he had to rely on his props and shticks.

After several previous tries on radio, Groucho was finally a success . . . and on his own. The format had been developed that would feature his love of word play.

Comedy writer Fred Fox recalls that twelve writers were originally assigned to the show, but producer Dick Mack—who himself had been a writer on the Kellogg show—reduced the number to four. "It wasn't that hard to write for Groucho," Fox said. "We all loved to write his kind of stuff."

Several of the shows were broadcast from the Naval Training Station in San Diego. Actress Carole Landis appeared on one such program. "When she came out on stage in that white sheath dinner dress," Groucho told the writers, "there was probably the greatest exhibition of mental masturbation in the history of the military."

Fox observed, "You mean the audience was made of soldiers, marines, and semen?" Groucho looked at him with added respect.

"As far as my relationship with Groucho was concerned," Fox said, "I found him a very gentle person. Dick Mack was a Napoleonic guy in terms of his shortness and overcompensating. He wore thick glasses, had a nervous tic, but a booming voice. Whenever Dick lay into a writer, which he did often, Groucho was always very uncomfortable. It was like he was saying, 'I want to get out of here.' I think this was an indication of the fundamental gentleness of the guy."

Fox noticed that one of Groucho's greatest frustrations, ironically, was his quick mind. "I think he couldn't put stuff on paper fast enough. He could drive us crazy with his ad-libbing. Once we were eating at the Brown Derby. A busboy dropped a tray of dishes, and there was a terrific shattering noise. Almost before the echoes died away, Groucho stood up and addressed the jam-packed restaurant. 'Ladies and gentlemen, that was Johnny stepping out of store windows all over the country.' "

A device created on the show, which comedian Gabriel Kaplan used thirty years later on "Welcome Back, Kotter," was the invention of a fictitious uncle. One was Uncle Peg Leg Marx, whose leg was bitten off by an angry blonde. "One night before a big naval battle," Groucho said, "he was pondering strategy. He paced the deck and got his peg leg in a knothole. He walked around himself all night."

Or, "My uncle was a very famous man. When the admiral said, 'You may fire, Gridley, when you are ready,' my uncle was ready, so he fired Gridley."

Or, "One night my uncle was on watch. He fell asleep inside a sixteen-inch gun and he was dishonorably discharged."

Fox recalled with less than pleasure the many script conferences he, Mack, and writers Artie Stander and Selma Diamond attended at Groucho's house. They often continued through dinner and into the night. "We were subject to many hours of Gilbert and Sullivan. He gave us all librettos and we had to sit there and be interested. Here we all were, fidgeting and wondering when we could go home. But this was the guy we were working for."

Miriam often took her friends backstage after each broadcast. Since she was a friendly girl, she made a point of meeting everyone involved with the show. Leo Gorcey, one of the Dead End Kids, was appearing on some of the broadcasts when she met his beautiful wife.

"Kay was exquisite," Maxine Marx recalled, "a Dresden china doll. She was delicate, with cornflower blue eyes and a beautiful little body. She'd been working as an entertainer from the time she was twelve."

Gorcey was a surly, quick-tempered wife beater, and Kay was terrified of him. She wanted to leave him, but she had no place to go. Miriam persuaded Groucho to take her in, and in so doing, pushed the girl into Groucho's arms.

Miriam was finding it increasingly difficult to cope with her conflicting feelings about her father.

"I did detect, as Miriam started getting older, that there was something strange in the relationship," Nat Perrin said. "It wasn't lack of love. It was too much love. She would call him everywhere. We had this very small poker game. Miriam would call Groucho five or six times during the evening. The attachment seemed a little unhealthy to me. But certainly there was attachment and not the lack of it."

To others, Miriam remained the girl whose offbeat personality matched her appearance.

When Miriam reached her sixteenth year, Groucho bought her a dilapidated convertible. She and Sunny would drive around with Miriam's dog, Shep, a German shepherd. Sometimes they would go to the tennis club, where Miriam could sign the tab for lunch. One night, they drove to Romeo Salta's Restaurant. "Is my father here yet?" Miriam blithely asked. The headwaiter said he wasn't expected. "I don't understand," she said. "It's my birthday and he said to meet him here for dinner." The two girls got a free dinner as a result, and the headwaiter was left with the impression that Groucho, if he was not insensitive and uncaring, was at best forgetful.

Their delinquencies seemed innocent at the time. They sneaked an occasional cigarette and took Dexedrine pills—in Miriam's case perhaps too many—to help keep their weight down.

Miriam was intellectually ahead of her fellow students, the world of reading having been opened for her by Groucho. The token attention she gave to her studies led to consistently mediocre grades.

"Why can't you be like Peter Swerling?" Groucho asked his daughter. The brilliant son of screenwriter Jo Swerling was receiving straight A's. Talking was the only art the boy couldn't seem to master, since he was plagued by an embarrassing stammer.

"All right," her father's daughter replied. "I'll s-s-s-s-tart r-r-r-r-r-right n-n-n-n-n-ow."

Inevitably, Miriam was called before the student council for continually ditching the last period of the day. "Of course I'm ditching school," she said in her own defense. "My mother is going through menopause, and the doctor has to leave at three every day. I have to go home to take care of her." The excuse made sense to the council, which didn't bother to ask why Ruth would need round-the-clock care for such a minor affliction, if menopause can

293

be called that. Nor did they bother to determine if Ruth actually lived at home with Miriam.

It was Kay Gorcey who was actually living at home with her and Groucho. "She was Miriam's friend first," Sunny said, "and mine too. One morning Miriam told me Kay wasn't sleeping in her bed, but in Groucho's. She was upset. Miriam missed not having Kay as a friend. She'd seemed like one of us kids. Miriam was very jealous at that point." Yet resentment must have been tempered with relief.

When Pabst Blue Ribbon celebrated its 100th anniversary in January of 1944, Kay went along with Groucho for the festivities in Milwaukee. A story, of dubious origin, later circulated concerning this trip. Groucho had been invited to his sponsor's house and the two were playing pool in the basement. His host's son was constantly underfoot. It brought to mind one of Groucho's lines from the radio show: "That boy is going far. I wish he'd get started." Groucho in this instance reportedly used blunter language: "Fuck off, kid." The sponsor was appalled. Groucho's contract wasn't renewed when it expired the following June and Danny Kaye was named to succeed him on the show. According to Groucho, he was dropped because he had taken out an elderly member of the Pabst family and gotten him drunk on Miller's High Life beer.

Despite uniformly good reviews for the show during the rest of its run, Groucho sensed that his sponsors had cooled toward him. If the story involving the boy was true, he may have regretted his sharp tongue. What he regretted even more was the loss of the vehicle that had quickly made him a radio star, then just as quickly dropped him.

At home, Groucho and Kay were talking about getting married when her divorce was final. Miriam may have felt in the way. She was obviously no longer uppermost in Groucho's thoughts.

Miriam had developed a schoolgirl crush on Katharine Hepburn. "She used to follow Hepburn all over Beverly Hills," Maxine Marx recalled. "She'd take binoculars and watch her play tennis. She was insanely crazy about her. Stars usually didn't get to Miriam like that."

Groucho arranged a meeting between the two. "I didn't know

what to say," Miriam told Maxine, "but there she was, and there I was."

Miss Hepburn asked Miriam about her plans for college. The girl said she didn't have any. Miss Hepburn was appalled. "Why not? You're obviously a girl with great intelligence. What kind of career are you planning?" Miriam replied she would like to become a writer.

Miss Hepburn, who had attended Bryn Mawr, suggested that the liberal atmosphere at Bennington would be ideal. Miriam had never heard of the school, but Miss Hepburn made her promise she would consider enrolling. On the strength of this recommendation, Miriam's mind was made up.

Later, the two talked about people they loved who were alcoholics. "She knew I was talking about my mother," Miriam told Sunny, "and I knew she was talking about Spencer Tracy."

Miriam was in her freshman year at Bennington when Krasna's *Dear Ruth* opened at Henry Miller's Theatre on December 13, 1944. His play would prove enormously successful, spawning off a movie version starring William Holden and Joan Caulfield and two movie sequels, *Dear Wife* and *Dear Brat.*

At play's end, the Miriam-inspired character drunkenly recites one of her favorite Edna St. Vincent Millay poems, beginning

My candle burns at both ends . . .

Within a few years, life would tragically be imitating art.

Although he was the father of two grown children and nearly fifty-five, Groucho nevertheless wanted a child by Kay. She also wanted children, and Groucho went to see geneticists and experts on fertility, who assured him that he was still capable of fathering a child. Thereafter, the wedding date was definitely set.

While Groucho and Kay were waiting for her divorce to become final, he contracted to appear on several segments of Dinah Shore's "Bird's Eye Open House" in the spring of 1945.

"I was getting three thousand dollars a week for every appearance," he told me. "The day Roosevelt died, we didn't have a show. I got paid anyhow. They buried him the day of the next show. I got another three thousand dollars. I never saw that kind of easy money. I thought to myself, there are not enough people dying."

The same week that the nation was mourning Roosevelt's death, the Marx Brothers were lured again into making another picture by producer David Loew. It was to be called *A Night in Casablanca,* a sendup of the Humphrey Bogart-Ingrid Bergman classic which Warner Brothers had produced two years previously. The star characters were to be named Humphrey Bogus and Lowan Behold. Plans were announced for a road tour prior to filming to test the script.

Groucho bypassed the tour in favor of a honeymoon after his marriage on July 21 to the twenty-four-year-old Catherine Mavis Gorcey. The groom was thirty years older. Arthur Sheekman was his best man and his wife Gloria gave the bride away.

Miriam came home after her freshman year at Bennington and Arthur was discharged from the service soon after as the war ended. The fragmented family was more or less together again.

Arthur and Irene moved in with Grace Kahn, with whom they would live for nine years while he tried to establish himself as a writer.

Groucho, now that he was starting a second family, bought a Mediterranean-style two-story house in the flatlands of Beverly Hills. He installed a two-passenger Inclinator on the staircase of the house on Foothill Road, half a block below Sunset Boulevard, in order to preserve his energies for more fruitful pursuits. So many friends wanted to try out the contraption that Groucho told Sunny and Miriam, "I'm thinking of hiring a hostess for it."

Filming on *A Night in Casablanca* started in November, after resolution of a minor flap with Warner Brothers, who were threatening legal action over the satirizing of their previously released film. Groucho headed them off with a series of now classic comic letters that have been reprinted in books and anthologies and every major periodical save *Popular Mechanics.*

Archie Mayo was assigned as director of the picture, which would eventually be released by United Artists. He was less noted

296

for the distinction of the numerous pictures he had directed than for his favorite catch phrase whenever he got a satisfactory take: "Give it to the hungry public."

During the course of filming, Groucho was again called into court by Ruth. Their property settlement gave her twenty-five percent of Groucho's income until her remarriage or death. Ruth wanted to remarry, but didn't like the idea of giving up her alimony. Ruth did not handle money well, having had no experience with the finances during her marriage to Groucho. Aware of this, Groucho insisted on stipulating that Ruth re-invest $50,000 of her divorce settlement with Salwyn Shufro. No matter how prodigal she might be with her money in the future, Ruth was assured of a modest nest egg because of this investment. In agreeing to the amended property settlement, which gave Ruth twelve-and-a-half percent of his income whether she remarried or not, Groucho revealed his presentiment about his marriage to Kay. He insisted that the payments to Ruth would end in the event of his own divorce. Ruth agreed to this, provided that the payments would continue for at least four years. The agreement was signed on May 1, 1946. Six days later, Ruth married a distant relation, John J. Garrity, whose father was a well-known stage manager for the Shuberts and who had himself worked at the craft for many years.

At about the same time, the Marx Brothers' latest epic was released. Missing from the eighty-five-minute film was a scene in which Harpo would scream, "Murder!" He'd turned down a $55,000 offer to break his long public silence.

James Agee, in his review in *The Nation*, observed, "It is . . . beside the point to add that it isn't one of their best movies, for the worst they might ever make would be better worth seeing than most other things I can think of . . . after all these years the Brothers are tired."

About Groucho, Agee said:

He is not, I suppose, one of the great comedians, but I can't think of anyone who has given me greater pleasure. My only regret is that, so far as I have seen, he has never yet been in a position to use everything I think he has. Most good comedians, probably all the great ones, require a very broad audience; Groucho, working with extremely sophisticated wit rather than with comedy, has always been slowed and burdened by his audience, even on the stage . . . because there is no sufficient audience for use of the brain for fun's sake, I suspect that we lose, in Groucho, the funniest satirist of the century.

The general reception to the film was dispiriting. Mayo's hungry public chose to be fed elsewhere. With the picture, the brothers didn't begin to re-enlist a vast corps of admirers . . . as yet.

The film opened in New York the second week of August. In California, Kay gave birth to a daughter at about the same time.

Over the years the brothers had adopted the practice of naming their daughters, like the three sisters described by the Dormouse in *Alice's Adventures in Wonderland*, "with everything that begins with an M." If Alice had asked Groucho, one of her most ardent admirers, why, he would have answered, like the March Hare, "Why not?" Maxine, Miriam, and Minnie had come before. Joan Bennett's daughter was named Melinda Markey and Kay liked the truncated sound of the name Melinda Marx.

Miriam was outwardly delighted with the birth of her half-sister. Yet, in that part of her being where emotions rule the intellect, she felt she'd lost a father in Groucho and a good friend in Kay. Their attentions had been diverted elsewhere.

The birth would prove to be the turning point in her life. A girl of such high intelligence knew that a feeling of sibling rivalry was unseemly for a girl of nineteen. She'd never felt such jealousy with Arthur. The two were genuinely fond of each other. But now she was competing for Groucho's love with yet another female.

Groucho was still receptive to her passionate beliefs and amused by her impertinence. He also continued to tease her. But somehow, things were not the same.

Maxine Marx was now married to Shamus Culhane, and on one occasion when the couple came to visit the discussion turned to one of the great headline stories of the day: the dynamiting of a wealthy man on his yacht and the subsequent trial of his daughter and her lover for the murder.

Miriam violently protested their innocence and threatened to lead a demonstration of equally fervent believers. "I'd better lock myself in my room tonight," Groucho cracked. The line was funny enough, but for some reason Miriam was no longer laughing. Miriam was in her room when Groucho turned to Maxine and asked, "Where's Lizzie Borden?"

In March of 1947, Chico suffered a heart attack in Las Vegas, where he and his band were appearing. Now about sixty, he announced his retirement. The decision, which marked the end of the three Marx Brothers, caused no extended heartfelt cries of protest or regret.

The other brothers were receiving job offers with less frequency. Groucho was happy to appear in a Walgreen radio special with Bob Hope in April. When Hope, in mid-performance, dropped the script, Groucho followed suit and the two men went off on a marvelously funny tangent. The show went over schedule because of the exchange.

John Guedel, the producer of the Art Linkletter show, was sitting in the audience. He came backstage and introduced himself to Groucho. Would he be interested in starring in a comedy quiz series of his own, in which he could ad-lib in the same way with contestants? Groucho agreed to try out the idea. Guedel worked on the concept for several months, but none of the networks were interested.

In the meantime, desperate for work, Groucho agreed to co-star with Carmen Miranda in a musical, *Copacabana*, in which Kay had a small part. It is notable only for the fact that for the first time in his film career, Groucho appeared in a motion picture without his brothers. "I played second banana to the fruit on Carmen Miranda's head," he observed.

Later, he auditioned for the master of ceremonies role on radio's "Take It or Leave It." He flunked.

Why, I asked him, did he even consider a job that was so beneath him? "I needed the work," he said. "I knew I probably wouldn't make it as a quizmaster. I didn't look the type. But have you seen the men on quiz shows today? They all look alike . . . like dress dummies."

There was still the Guedel project that might come through, although word thus far was discouraging. Everyone, as Jimmy Durante was currently saying, wanted to get into the act. *Newsweek* in September of 1947 reported, "Top-rank comics are mapping new-type audience participation shows. Groucho Marx has one called *Betcha Life* in the audition stage and . . ."

CHAPTER ELEVEN

GEORGE FENNEMAN: Now here he is, the one, the only—
STUDIO AUDIENCE: Groucho!

Those knowledgeable in the ways of show business theorize that a new mass audience comes into being every seven years. That is the rationale behind the re-release of blockbuster road show attractions like *Gone with the Wind* and *The Sound of Music* at seven-year intervals.

Hollywood hypothesizes that the careers of entertainers are governed by a similar seven-year cycle, enjoying peak stardom for seven golden years. The Marx Brothers up to now had proven the formula and then some. Milestones in their career had been marked in seven-year increments. They were established vaudeville performers in 1910. They became two-a-day headliners in 1917. They conquered the Broadway stage in 1924, and moved on to become film stars in 1931.

By 1938, after enjoying three unprecedented generations of seven-year stardom in as many media, their collective career was on the descendant. They had been making essentially the same movie time after time, and there seemed to be few surprises left in them. Now, in 1947, they were caught up in a frustrating undercurrent. They had been trying to tread water for nine years, World War II having added a two-year holding pattern to their careers, as it had to the careers of all male entertainers.

Offers were still sporadically tendered, and dispiritedly discussed. Neither Chico nor Harpo would ever rise again to their past prominence. Groucho, in contrast, was destined to have even greater triumphs. He had the foresight to age before the public eye, while his brothers were still playing Puck and the Rapscallion. They looked and acted tired, and though they were still loved, the ardor had waned.

One project, however, held common interest. *Newsweek* reported in September of 1947 that the four original members of the team would star in a film biography, *The Life of the Marx Brothers*, incorporating the best routines from their vaudeville days. This presumably meant Zeppo would be rejoining his three performer brothers, although Gummo in actuality had been the original member of the team. It was an academic point, however, because the film was never made and the two non-performing Marx Brothers were otherwise occupied. Zeppo, in addition to the talent agency, had also founded a company, the world's largest manufacturer of coupling devices, which now employed five hundred people. It had manufactured the clamping devices that carried the atomic bombs over Japan.

Gummo and Zeppo's brother-in-law, Alan Miller, virtually ran the agency. Gummo, in addition, was acting as the unofficial agent for the brothers, supplementing the efforts of the William Morris Company.

The downturn in the team's career was a greater tragedy in Chico's case, for he needed the big money to continue supporting half of the nation's bookies. Harpo had been more careful with his earnings, however, and he welcomed his semienforced semiretirement.

"Dad performed only when he had the urge," his son Bill said. "Later in life he'd do benefits. He'd work his ass off for a day or an evening. At the end of it, he'd say, 'I feel better. I had to get out in front of people again.' "

Despite the assessment of many that he was the heart of the Marx Brothers act, his abrupt dismissal by Pabst a few seasons back tended to confirm Groucho's belief that he hadn't established himself as a star in his own right. Full self-assurance that he could stand on his own would not come until his sixtieth year—three years in the future—when "You Bet Your Life," about to make the move to television, was the subject of a hotly disputed bidding war between the National Broadcasting Company and the Columbia Broadcasting System. "I'm being wooed for the first time in my life," Groucho then cracked about his sudden desirability. "I'm like a dame hot out of Vassar."

Newsweek would later liken his recruitment as a quizmaster to the selling of Citation, the greatest racehorse of the era, to a glue factory. Yet there was no immediate alternative available to him. Had "You Bet Your Life" not come along, Groucho might well have spent the rest of his performing career making special appearances and guest-star shots, as his brothers would do. He would, however, be compelled to make them with greater frequency. "Groucho was the only one of the brothers who required that constant ego gratification," Bill Marx said. "He *had* to be in the public eye."

Fortunately, Groucho became associated with John Guedel, a showman who combined the imagination of Barnum with the integrity of Sam Harris. During the course of his broadcasting career, Guedel would invent the singing commercial and introduce the rerun to television. The radio package Guedel was putting together would prove to have two seven-year lifetimes, lasting fourteen years on radio and television, making Groucho a truly wealthy man.

Guedel was attempting to modify the quintessential anti-Establishmentarian created by George S. Kaufman nearly a quarter of a century before so that Groucho would be more palatable to the American public. He was well aware that an unleashed Groucho wouldn't have much staying power on radio, a more intimate medium than films or the stage.

Groucho resisted this moderation of his personality at first, but he eventually came around to Guedel's way of thinking. He would show the public his warmth, deeply submerged as it might be, but there was one thing he adamantly refused to do. He would not stoop to maudlin displays of sentimentality to prove that he was, after all the vitriol, the nicest of men. He had too much pride.

After much give and take, he also agreed to grow his own mustache instead of daubing on the greasepaint, and he would appear in coat and tie in the guise of the businessman next door.

His ego asserted itself in a major respect. Groucho's reputation for rapid retorts often gave the impression that his mind was shallow and lacked profundity, whereas he would rather have those few men whose opinions he respected believe he possessed a ponderous and more deliberate intellect. Yet he had established the reputation among many as being the most reflexive of all wits, a tribute Bob Hope had originally paid him and which had been echoed by others. He wanted it both ways, and perhaps he got it. By the time he moved to television, the public thought all his humor was ad-lib. His writers had long been disguised among the show's credits in the catchall "program staff" category. The badinage would be considerably more crafted and structured than the public would ever know. Groucho was always a quick study, and he could convincingly read off his prepared lines as if they were springing directly from his mind, a considerable talent in itself.

Very little in the carefully designed package was being left to chance, other than the most important consideration of selling the show. The major networks weren't enthusiastic about the demonstration record. Guedel had sold Art Linkletter's "People Are Funny" to advertiser-clients, and he decided to do the same with "You Bet Your Life." Reading in *Daily Variety* that Al Gellman, the president of the Elgin-American Compact Company, was imminently due in Beverly Hills to sign Phil Baker for a new quiz show, "Everybody Wins," Guedel pounced. He approached Gellman with his own package, and sold it only five weeks after the audition program was recorded.

Gummo split the agency commission with the Morris office. "Groucho was good to Dad," Gummo's son Bob said. "He protected him and made sure Dad was in on every deal. Even if

William Morris was in the picture, Dad still got his. They had a very good relationship. Each of them gave as much as they took. Gummo loved Groucho all his life. My mother did not."

With the program sold, Guedel began gearing up the new operation. He recruited Robert Dwan from the Linkletter talent stable and also hired a "People Are Funny" contributor, writer Bernie Smith, to supply comedy and dash to the enterprise. Smith devised the introduction collectively voiced by the studio audience. Within a few years, the whole world would come to realize that when it came to inspired lunacy and trenchant wit, there was no match for the one, the only Groucho.

The year of 1947, which introduced fashion's New Look, was offering a somewhat dated term—the New Deal—to Groucho. There was no assurance, however, that his re-entry into radio would be more successful than his previous efforts in the medium. The malaise extended to his personal life as well. Kay, his artless child bride of two years, was finding it difficult to adjust to being the wife of this extremely complicated man. Groucho could joke about Kay's efforts to win him as a husband, as he did to his daughter-in-law Irene. "When Kay was going out with me, she claimed to love baseball," he told her, "but the minute we got married, she didn't go anymore."

Groucho and his brothers were among many in the entertainment industry who regularly trouped to Gillmore Stadium to follow the fortunes of the Hollywood Stars of the Pacific Coast League. "Groucho was there almost every night," Nat Perrin recalled. "He was a real ball fan. He was fun to be around, but he had one weakness. He never stopped with the jokes. It was hard to have a serious discussion with him . . . it had to be joke, joke, joke. If you were interested in a tight ball game, and Groucho was yammering away, you had to shut him up. Sometimes he missed, but he swung at the ball an awful lot and he made some wonderful jokes. The Stars had a second baseman named Lou Springer, and he was one of the weakest hitters in the league. One night, he suddenly hit a double. Groucho said, 'That's the first time I ever saw him on second base without his glove.'"

Inevitably, the many celebrities who frequented Gillmore Stadium were recruited to come down from the stands to play a charity match. Groucho was elected manager of The Comedians, who were playing The Actors. As Jack Benny, the lead-off man, tapped his spikes with his bat, Groucho called out, "All right, Benny, get up there and hit a home run." He struck out instead. Groucho huffily resigned from the team. "I refuse to manage a team," he said, "that won't follow instructions."

Wives and women friends had come out to see the celebrities play, and they were welcomed to join their men at the more traditional games, but the gatherings were basically male enclaves which couldn't have been of much interest to Kay. Groucho could see the humor in the oldest ploy of all, that of a man who chases a girl until she catches him.

But Groucho's young wife hadn't misled him about her desire to stop performing after their marriage. Groucho, however, wanted to show her off.

"Kay came to see me once," Chico's first wife, Betty, said. "She was just a kid. . . . Groucho wanted her to go on the Bing Crosby show with him. . . . He was pushing her. Kay was talented, but she didn't want to do that work any longer."

His diffident wife was prepared to bask in her husband's reflection, to be a beautiful, silent ornament in the drawing room if he would only allow her to function as a housewife. (The wives of all the brothers were expected to play the same role of silent, adoring onlooker. "I know lots of people must have thought me a very stupid girl," Betty said. "Unless I got to know people very well I wouldn't talk, and when you sit around and don't talk, they're bound to say, 'Jesus, she's dumb.' ")

His insecurity wouldn't permit Groucho to accept the idea that a woman as young and beautiful as Kay would be content to stay at home. He could never be sure of any woman's devotion, and greatly underestimated the extent of his charm. "Although he could be a little scary," Charlotte Granet said, "all the women who knew him were a little in love with Groucho."

Kay had willingly signed a prenuptial agreement before their marriage, and if Groucho still had doubts about her constancy, their friends did not. "Kay was very much in love with Groucho," Mrs. Granet said. "She was a sweet girl and a very nice person.

When they had the baby, Kay was ecstatically happy. But she couldn't cope with Groucho for long. She was minimized in several ways. He used to love to do the marketing. Kay might plan a menu of pot roast, potato pancakes, and green beans. When the cook put the meal on the table, it would be pot roast, mashed potatoes, and lima beans. Groucho loved lima beans."

His friends found his concern for Melinda heartwarming. Her birth had rejuvenated Groucho. He would terminate professional meetings and social engagements to get home in time to gurgle with Melinda during her daily bath and regular feedings. His lack of trust in Kay's ability as a mother, however, was implicit in his overly solicitous behavior with their daughter.

When Miriam arrived in Southern California with her college roommate for a visit, her old friend Sunny perceived that she had turned into a heavy drinker. "Thinking back on it," she recalled, "Miriam was already far gone when I discovered she had a problem."

Sunny was an appalled witness to an exchange between Groucho and Kay during Miriam's visit. Kay had ventured a housewife's opinion about some workaday matter. Groucho, snarling, said, "If you don't shut up, I'm going to throw you back in the gutter where you came from!"

Kay had ended a miserable marriage to Leo Gorcey because of his physical abuse, and now this bruised and delicate creature was subject to her second husband's verbal thrashings, which were having a no less devastating effect on her fragile hold on reason. That she deserved better goes without saying.

Throughout his life, Groucho's behavioral pattern was to give the impression he cared too little when in actuality he may have cared too much. It may have been a defense against inevitable rejection, but his often brutal, inexcusable behavior would inexorably drive the people he most cared about away.

Arthur's wife Irene was always a little afraid of her father-in-law, but she found a basic decency in him. She was thoroughly confused by his indifference when her first son Steve was born at Cedars of Lebanon Hospital in Los Angeles the previous May.

"Everyone came to see the baby but Groucho," she recalled. "I was a little hurt that he hadn't taken any interest in seeing his first grandchild. Finally Arthur said, 'I have to tell you Father has a thing about Cedars. He hates it because a friend of his died here.' I asked, 'Why didn't you tell me?' As soon as I got home, Groucho came over, talking baby talk to Steve. He was totally delighted with his grandson."

His refusal to become involved left the general impression of insensitivity when it was actually due to his aversion to personal discomfort and inconvenience. When it came to life's many difficulties, he would spare no one except himself. Only with the very young would he make the effort. Melinda and her nephew Steve, ten months younger, would be virtually brought up together. Their happiest memories of Groucho go back to these fledgling years. His love for them was unconditional, and it was expressed without embarrassment or inhibition.

Such magnanimity, however, did not now extend to his older children. Groucho could have helped Arthur in immeasurable ways. He offered little more than token financial assistance, and even less encouragement, in his son's ambition to establish himself as a writer. Arthur was beginning to sell articles to national magazines and Mannie Manheim got him some work as a radio comedy writer. Although he would later work for his father as a writer-consultant, this association would last for only a year.

Groucho would on occasion give his son cash gifts, but the greatest benefactor for the younger Marxes was proving to be Grace Kahn, with whom Arthur, his wife, and son lived.

"I can't fault Groucho for the lack of money," his former daughter-in-law, Irene, said. "If he gave too much he would be accused of indulging his children. If not enough, it was proof he didn't love them. It's difficult to strike a happy medium." Groucho hardly even tried to create the proper balance, Arthur and Miriam more often than not being subjected to a neglect that was less than benign.

There had been a long-standing rivalry between father and son, but Arthur, who had a fairly stable emotional base, managed to cope with his father's indifference. Arthur had also tempered his harsh opinion of his mother, Ruth. He was now an adult and could better understand the frustrations Groucho had visited upon her.

Miriam, however, was less equipped to handle the change in her father's feelings. Melinda was enveloped in Groucho's all-consuming love, and he seemed to have only a set amount to offer at any given time. Miriam looked for affection elsewhere, throwing herself into emotional quagmires with the same fervor she expended on unpopular causes.

In October, 1947, the same month that the House Committee on UnAmerican Activities opened an investigation into purported Communist infiltration of the movie industry, "You Bet Your Life" made its radio debut. The McCarthy Era and a different brand of Marxian rhetoric were being ushered into the nation's living rooms at the same time, and it initially seemed as if the senator from Wisconsin would have a longer run. Within a few years, the political ramifications of the witch-hunt would be so pervasive that even an innocuous comedy quiz show would feel its effects.

The first radio show was completely scripted. Groucho would spend considerable time before each program getting acquainted with the contestants. He soon perceived that this practice was at the expense of immediacy. Jack Gould's review in the *New York Times* told him as much:

> Among radio's unresolved problems is the full utilization of the talents of Groucho Marx, a man of brains and capital comic ability. Over the years he has been subjected to virtually every type of format but none really has worked out too well. Unfortunately, that state of affairs still exists apropos his current effort, "You Bet Your Life."
>
> What the Hollywood minds have done this time is to try to take Mr. Marx and cast him in the Art Linkletter-Phil Baker-John Reed King mold. His assignment is to make with the usual inanities in the guise of asking questions of eager quizzees, thereafter doling out dollars to those smart enough to know Washington's first name was George.
>
> Trouper that he is, Mr. Marx works hard and does his best, but the show never really comes off. Somewhere along the

309

line the delightful silliness of Mr. Marx's act has been confused with the exhibitionistic absurdity of the average radio quiz. Radio Row to the contrary, the two are not the same thing.

One happy day Mr. Marx will break into radio; he will be assigned a program without a stylized format.

To Groucho, the *Times* was omniscient. Later refinements of the show were to disprove Gould's assessment, but at the time his critique confirmed Groucho's opinion that changes had to be made. From that point on, he declined to meet the contestants before the show. Serendipitously, an innovation introduced by Dwan allowed Groucho to break away from the script. The program was originally supposed to be broadcast live, but the day before the first show was aired, some faint heart decided Groucho's spontaneous wit might need censoring. The show would be recorded instead. Dwan discovered that Armed Forces Radio was using big acetate discs that could be edited. In requisitioning them for the show, Dwan was able to record Groucho for as long as he wanted, and this could be pruned to twenty-six choice minutes every week.

Groucho might be prompted on his lines and the contestants would know approximately how they would respond, having been carefully coached by the program staff, but neither knew which way the interviews would go. They could spend up to an hour-and-a-half deciding. The show was achieving a polish no other quiz program could emulate. They didn't have as inventive a performer as Groucho, who was able to carry off the illusion that *all* his lines were ad-lib, even as he was reading many of them cold before millions. Groucho's frenetic, laugh-upon-laugh delivery had to be slowed down if the radio audience was to mine all the comedic nuggets. As a result, his resources were being only fractionally taxed. After nearly forty years as the catalyst of the Marx Brothers, Groucho in his new show was not so much an actor as a reactor. The contestants were carrying the conversational ball and, to a large degree, Groucho was being cast as the world's funniest straight man. He could now put breathing space around his lines. Despite the preshow jitters which would plague him throughout the run of "You Bet Your Life," it was a breeze.

It took time for the formula to evolve. Subsequent quiz shows found it impossible to duplicate its loose and casual construction, unaware that it involved much preproduction work. The talk shows that began proliferating some ten years later were better able to adapt and improve on the concept.

If the national ratings were any criterion, the radio audience didn't immediately take to "You Bet Your Life." The ratings, however, proved to be misleading, since the show was being broadcast on the American Broadcasting Company, the weakest of the three networks. ABC had come into existence in 1943 when the Federal Trade Commission forced the National Broadcasting Company to divest itself of its Blue Network. Edward J. Noble, the Lifesaver tycoon, bought the secondary network for eight million dollars, leaving NBC with its larger and more profitable Red Network. Up to this time, one of ABC's few top-rated programs was the Bing Crosby show. "You Bet Your Life" was serving as its Wednesday night lead-in. Groucho's show would never match the Crosby show in the ratings, but audience acceptance was being felt in an equally vital area. Elgin-American would be forced to terminate its first season sponsorship five weeks before the end of the traditional broadcasting year. The show had created such a demand for the sponsor's product that its entire line was sold out.

In the midst of the first season of the radio show, announcement was made by producers Mary Pickford and Lester Cowan that the brothers would be appearing in yet another farewell film, *Diamonds in the Sidewalk*. The film was originally planned as a showcase for Harpo's treasure trove of visual ideas, in which he would play a theatrical Robin Hood. Ben Hecht was writing the screenplay. It was rumored that René Clair, the Frenchman in the vanguard of surrealistic fantasies, would direct. Financing, however, could not be obtained until Harpo's two brothers consented to appear in the picture. Groucho agreed to put in a cameo appearance, at the beginning and the end of the film.

In the meantime, *Time for Elizabeth* was being readied for a Broadway opening after a twelve-year gestation period. A ludicrous message on a magazine advertisement had inspired Groucho and

Norman Krasna to write the play. It showed an elderly man standing with a young girl near a huge yacht. The caption read, "You too can live like this on $200 a month." They had intended, over the many years it took them to put the final script together, for their collaboration to be a star vehicle for Groucho. But he was unable to appear now that he was committed to the weekly discipline of a radio show. Paul Lukas was brought in to play his alter ego. He was soon replaced by Otto Kruger. Both men were better actors than Groucho, but they didn't have the comedic image needed to pre-sell an enterprise as frothy as *Time for Elizabeth*.

Rehearsals began for the play, which Norman Krasna was directing, when Groucho traveled to New York to guest star on Edgar Bergen's radio show. Putting a production together is difficult at best, and Krasna was finding it nearly impossible to cope with the artistic temperaments involved. Groucho was apprised of the situation.

"You don't have to take that," he told Krasna.

"Groucho," Krasna replied, "we have twenty six thousand dollars invested in this show. Do we drop thirteen thousand each?"

"If we have to," Groucho said. He wasn't annoyed for himself. What irritated him was the indignity Krasna was being subjected to.

He felt he was being subjected to some of it himself. Over lunch with Abel Green, the editor of *Variety*, he scathingly put down the overall state of comedy that June of 1948.

"I'm pretty fucking sore," he told Green and Harry Martin of the *Memphis Commercial Appeal*, "so don't expect any good humor stuff out of me. I come back here from my home in California and find everything shot to blazes. I should have stayed home."

"What's eating you, Groucho?" Green asked.

"I've been making the rounds of the nightclubs here the past week or so, and I'm telling you ... the state of comedy at this moment is lower than Truman's chances of re-election. I've never heard such lousy comics in all my life. I mean dirty. Now don't get me wrong. I like a good naughty laugh myself, and I suppose I've contributed my share in my time, but these characters around today are strictly from cesspools. Why, I saw a certain brother act pull stuff so crude in one of the plush joints the other night that Mae West would have blushed. These guys are a disgrace to the profession."

His diatribe also included a laceration of ethnic humor, as typified by the Mrs. Nussbaum character on the Fred Allen radio show. "Do you realize that every time she goes into that routine a lot of prejudiced sons of bitches get a special kick out of it, just because she makes the Jews look silly?"

Now that he had made his point, he was free to return to California in time for the August starting date of the next Marx Brothers picture, *Love Happy,* which *Diamonds in the Sidewalk* was now called.

Through trial and travail, *Time for Elizabeth* opened on September 27, 1948, at New York's Fulton Theatre. Critical reaction was underwhelming. Newspaper headlines told the general story: the *Daily News:* " 'Time for Elizabeth' an Ordinary Little Family-Entrance Comedy;" the *Journal American:* "An Aimless Comedy Neither Good Nor Bad;" the *World Telegram:* " 'Time for Elizabeth' Suffers from Anemia;" the *Post:* " 'Time for Elizabeth' A Very Mild Comedy."

John Lardner, writing in the *New York Star* gave an insight into the basic conventionality of Groucho's mind. He was, according to Lardner, a man of endless tortured complications, and yet, when it came to treating a prevalent dilemma, Groucho offered a simplistic, rosy-hued solution:

It looks as though Groucho Marx, beneath the salacious smear of black grease on his kisser, has been pining all these years to do something noble, something different. What was on his mind, you ask? Hamlet? Well, maybe next time. Meanwhile, to judge by what happened Monday night at the Fulton, he has settled for Dickens and written a play in the philosophical mood of *A Christmas Carol,* sprinkled—but tenderly—with gags.

The play is called *Time for Elizabeth,* a title with a hint of whimsy which I will decode in a moment. . . . It goes to show that all great clowns, from Pagliaccio to Marx, are hard to figure out. Who would have thought that Groucho was Tiny Tim with a mustache?

Lardner went on to describe the plot of the play: the general manager of a washing machine company, tiring of paying a substantial part of his income in taxes, decides it is *Time for Elizabeth*, his euphemism for retirement. After telling off his boss, he and his wife move to Florida, where they discover that a life of leisure bores them to distraction. At the end of the play, the hero is re-installed in his old job. His boss has apologized, curiously, for his former and future employee's unseemly outburst. All the problems are neatly if unrealistically solved.

Time for Elizabeth couldn't overcome the tepid reviews, and it folded in a week. Krasna, who enjoyed great successes on the stage with *Dear Ruth* and *John Loves Mary*, regarded *Elizabeth* much as a father feels about an errant favorite child. "We liked the idea and we did it as well as we could," he said. "Maybe we should have done it under better auspices. I've written other plays that have become dated, but this one holds up."

Groucho took refuge from the calamity by resuming his radio broadcasts and performing his cameo role in United Artist's *Love Happy*. Groucho was beginning to be notably more successful on the radio show than he was in the current movie. "You Bet Your Life" in its first season hovered near the bottom of the ratings, although Elgin-American continued enjoying record sales as a result of its sponsorship of the show. A hard-core nucleus of Groucho fans was building, one of the first indications that his star power was about to shine brighter than ever.

The great majority of critics and students of film still looked on the Marx Brothers as popular entertainers and not artists. The first reassessment came the same month that *Time for Elizabeth* folded and "You Bet Your Life" started its second season. Richard Rowland authored an article, "American Classic," in the *Penguin Film Review*, a British journal, which predated the hosannas of the French cinéastes by some twenty years.

Film devotees the world over had been bemoaning the lack of comedy classics in American films. Rowland offered the following reply:

> There is one series of films to which a little circle of devotees throughout the world return again and again to find pleasure not antiquarian, not in the least dominated by the technical progress of recent years. This is, of course, the series of some twelve films which feature the Marx Brothers, made

under various banners over a period of fifteen years. Almost nothing has been lost from them; when Groucho makes his sway-backed entrance into the regal palace in *Duck Soup* the audience stirs with excitement, with the knowledge that an important personage has suddenly appeared on a screen usually inhabited by pallid phantoms . . .

It is not hard to find an explanation of the endless appeal of these films. They deal with the gravest question with which comedy can deal. They ask us, at least the successful ones do, intermittently but irresistibly, "What is reality?"

Politics? Football? Universities? All of them evaporate before the onslaught of the Brothers. Even sex, the sacred subject about which Hollywood must be serious, becomes a joke in these films.

Groucho leers, the siren wears the most outrageously revealing clothes, there is a bed obviously built for sin, there is the predatory lope, the last word in carnality. Will Hays may have flinched now and again, but even he did not remove the ogles and the double entendres; and for once he was right, for sex, too, collapses into nothingness. No one was ever more lecherous in a movie than Groucho is; no movie, save Rin-Tin-Tin's, was ever less erotic than these.

. . . The Marx Brothers offer a pure escape; they do not falsify the world as does the world in which Portia Faces Life; but they show us another world, a moon world, a world which illuminates our own, revealing our famous surroundings as so much nonsense. We realise that we all behave with a solemnity too vulnerable to the attack of the Marx Brothers, who exclaim with the naiveté of wisdom, "But the emperor has nothing on at all!" And we may remain a little less willing to be crushed by solemnity, aware of our own vulnerability, aware that nonsense has a poetry which sense has not, aware in the most profound way that perhaps—who knows?—this world is, if not worthless, worth less than we had thought, being perhaps less real than we had thought.

Had Groucho read the piece, he would have been pleased with the reappraisal. But he didn't quite trust the rampant intellectualism Rowland's well-chosen words would be ushering in. Nor would he become fully aware of his standing among the intelligentsia until he was in his early eighties. In 1972, he became the first native-born American to receive the honorific *Commandeur des Arts et Lettres* from the French government . . . the accolade coming at an age when some friends believed he wasn't fully aware at all.

In the fall of 1948, James C. Petrillo, the president of the American Federation of Musicians, issued a waiver which allowed network radio shows to be recorded. Since the discs were used only once, they did not raise the same union problems as a record played repeatedly for commercial profit. As a result, a rash of radio's variety and comedy stars began taping their shows instead of broadcasting them live. Groucho had already pioneered the concept.

"All this cry and hullabaloo for tape," Jack Hellman wrote in *Daily Variety*, "can be traced to one show—Groucho Marx's 'You Bet Your Life.' Freely admitted the best show of the year, it owes much of its success to the editing made possible through the use of ribbon. We use the word 'much' advisedly, as Groucho and John Guedel are a pair of pretty fair showmen and you can't tape that . . ."

The show was hitting its stride. "Say the secret word," had become part of the national lexicon. A twenty-six-year-old transplanted San Franciscan was now performing triple duty as the show's announcer, audience warmer-upper, and Groucho's straight man. He had gotten a raise of almost twenty percent for his second season on the show, when his salary was increased from $55 to $65 a week. His name was George Fenneman.

"Many shows don't use the announcer to do the warmup anymore," he said. "In the early days there were a lot of poor announcers who had no business doing warmups. They were assigned to read a script, not get out there and do shtick. Some very good announcers were absolutely at a loss. They were stuck out there if they didn't have an affinity for working with an audience.

"At the beginning I did a lot of bum jokes. I'd talk about applause, tell them their seats were wired . . . terrible things. I made them applaud. I felt like a damn fool doing it, but it was

316

important that the applause be loud, and that they laugh. I'd say, 'If anything funny happens tonight, you will laugh. You will laugh here. You will figure out if it's funny at home, but you will laugh here.' They laughed.

"I'd make them do corny things, like tell them to turn around at the count of three and say hello to the guy behind you. Everybody would turn around and see the back of everybody's head."

The audience cottoned to the courtly young man, and Groucho benefited from the warmth Fenneman generated. "Groucho was of a stature in the business and with an aura that surrounded him of being different. He played by different rules. He was allowed to get away with rudeness that I would not countenance in a friend. I found myself defending him to people who said what a terrible man he was. I had to say he really wasn't that bad. I never felt he was evil or cruel, although he could be rude and gutsy and fearless. He was a person I would never want to emulate, because I couldn't. But I looked forward to going in to do the show every week, and I certainly wouldn't have felt that way if I hated Groucho or my job. It was an adventure. Was I going to parry or take it or defend myself so that I would get a laugh?

"At the beginning I was young and resilient, and I didn't have the good sense to know I was being insulted. When I realized that, I was hurt because I didn't realize that, in one way or another, he called a lot of people stupid. It was no more than he gave General Bradley or whoever else was on the air. It was part of the character he was building for me that became wonderfully saleable in years to come. I'd have to be a clod to badmouth the man who made it possible. Just 'Fenneman!' shouted to the wings got a laugh. The audience knew he was going to embarrass me. He didn't have to lie awake at nights thinking how he would do that. Groucho seemed to get me in at least once a show. I hit upon a way to coexist. There was no way to top him. He could keep going until he got you. And yet, with all this, I was the underdog and he was the villain. My confusion and gentlemanliness were in contrast to his confidence and rudeness. I was sometimes shocked at the things he said to other people, and yet I never heard anyone say he was badly treated.

"Groucho was amazingly gallant when he wanted to be. Yet after

317

he would do something nice, he would do something I thought was in bad taste. He'd have to immediately counteract that nice gesture. He also had that half-kidding thing that allowed him to pat a lot of fannies. I once commented to him that the ladies must have understood he didn't really mean it. Groucho said, 'How do you know I didn't?' "

He was becoming the caustic quizmaster in everyday life as well. Norman Krasna would often spend time with Groucho prior to the show. Despite their long friendship, which should have inured him to Groucho's scatter-shot insults, Krasna would often be embarrassed by this "middle-aged Jewish man saying dreadful things" to people who crossed his path. He would sometimes ask Groucho to refrain from these comments.

"You don't understand," Groucho told him. "For example, that waitress will go home and say, 'Do you know what Groucho said to me?' And she treasures it."

"Now, he wasn't making a living doing this," Krasna said. "He was doing what was expected of him. He'd make ten or twelve cracks, and then somebody would get offended. He understood when he went over the line."

Groucho was intolerant of strangers who tried to impress him with their own humor. "Why is it that when people recognize me, they feel obliged to come up and say something funny?" he once asked Fenneman. "I can't abide people who try to tell me a joke."

He did abide, if only barely, the promotional spots he was required to do for the show. Fenneman recalled one line that always broke Groucho up. As a lead-in to the Elgin-American commercial, he was obliged to ask one of the world's less urgent questions, "Have you looked at your compact lately?" There was only so much Groucho would do for his sponsor, as perfectionists who asked him to record take after take soon found out. "I used to love it," Fenneman recalled, somewhat enviously, "when he would say, 'That's it! No more takes.' "

Similarly, there were to be no more takes on *Love Happy*, but not because of Groucho's recalcitrance. The production values of the picture were of the cheapest sort. The first impact of Marilyn Monroe on the movie-going public was to be its sole future distinction.

Box office stars are rarely caught in the humbling position currently faced by the brothers. That the producers had constant financing problems throughout the shooting of the picture was an unsettling harbinger of their future in films. Producer Lester Cowan, having run out of money to finish the shooting, was forced to scramble to keep the project afloat when United Artists withdrew its agreement to release the picture. A chase scene was devised on rooftops, with Harpo scampering from one neon sign to another, from Bulova watches to Kool cigarettes to the sign of the Flying Red Horse. The sequence was one long commercial, the manufacturers of the products having paid for the advertising space.

As shooting resumed, word came from New York that the brothers' uncle, Al Shean, had died at the Ansonia Hotel, where he had lived for many years. The brothers had supported him in his old age, Uncle Al never having recovered from the stock market crash of 1929. None of the Marxes was able to leave California for their uncle's funeral.

As for Groucho, his last visit with Uncle Al had taken place almost three years previously. "He was crazy about the circus. I tried to get him good seats, but I couldn't, so I took him to *Life with Father* instead. He fell asleep in the first act and didn't wake up until it was almost over. Come to think of it, life with *my* father affected Uncle Al in the same way."

When the Shean estate was probated, it was revealed that his entire estate was left to his nephews. Groucho's share might barely cover his weekly cigar bill.

When shooting of *Love Happy* was completed, Cowan was forced to borrow an additional $75,000 from the Chemical Bank of New York to complete scoring, dubbing, and other postproduction work on the film.

In the light of such a shabby experience, the brothers resolved they would make no more pictures together. Groucho was the most vocal about it. He told United Press correspondent Virginia McPherson that Chico had been brought back from an Australian tour and Harpo from cross-country appearances to appear in the picture, and all for naught. "We're sick of the movies," he said, "and the people are about to get sick of us. Our stuff is going stale.

And so are we. We don't need each other. We can all make more money if we go our own way." To prove this, Chico soon left for England on tour and Harpo began weighing several television offers.

Groucho was convinced he had personally made the best decision when, in April of 1949, he won the prestigious Peabody Award for best entertainer on radio. A *Newsweek* cover story followed:

> Unlike some other celebrated ad libbers, Marx works without script writers. His preparation for the program consists simply of learning the occupations of his contestants—plumbers, tree surgeons, dentists—and thumbing through his mind for appropriate gags. Thus armed, he marches out on stage usually dressed in a two-tone tan sports outfit ("No matter how badly I dress," he flipped, "I look as good as the audience.") and sporting a heavy black mustache he cultivated two years ago to replace the old grease-paint job. Peering through rimless glasses at his guests, Marx resembles a biology student contemplating a frog in formaldehyde. The attitude prevails throughout the program, and rare is the contestant who fails to inspire some wisecrack. To a test pilot: "I could never be a test pilot. I get dizzy licking an airmail stamp." To a baseball umpire: "I've wondered why umpires don't wear the chest protector on the other side. That's where the danger is." To elderly newlyweds: "I'll never forget my wedding. They threw vitamin pills."
>
> If anybody had any doubt why Marx beat out the Bennys, Hopes, and Allens for the Peabody Award, he set them straight. And he did so in the best satiric fashion. In accepting the award he said: "You know, it came as quite a surprise being named for the comedy award. I can't recall making a single joke about the snow in California, Pyramid clubs, Rita Hayworth, or capital gains on other networks."

"You Bet Your Life" had gone as far as it could on the American Broadcasting Company. Its ratings were at the optimum for the smallest of the three networks, although nationally they weren't impressive when competing against NBC and CBS, each of which had many more affiliated radio stations than ABC. John Guedel started pressing for a move to a major network. Coincidentally, the Bing Crosby show would be moving over to CBS when Chesterfield Cigarettes supplanted Philco as its sponsor. Crosby wanted Groucho's show to move along with him. Groucho's sponsor, committed to only thirty-five weeks on ABC, would have to run a forty-five-week season on CBS, and Elgin-American's agency was hesitant about the greater financial commitment. Sponsorship of "You Bet Your Life" spelled such an extraordinary success for Elgin-American, however, that eventually it agreed to move.

Matters were not running as smoothly elsewhere, and some of Groucho's general unhappiness at this time was not of his own doing. For the first time in his life, he was pictured as having serious differences with Harpo. During the checkered evolution of *Love Happy*, the producer had gradually enticed Groucho into playing a larger part than the cameo originally called for. Cowan's agreement with Harpo specified that Groucho would be kept in a subordinate role, which Groucho went along with, agreeing to appear only at the beginning and end of the picture. After *Love Happy* was sneak previewed, Cowan and executives at United Artists, who were on again as the picture's distributors, felt more footage of Groucho was needed. Harpo's contract permitted only a limited amount of Groucho in the picture, so Groucho's scenes had to be shifted around so that his irreverent commentary ran throughout the picture. This did little to help the already muddled continuity. The re-editing, as well as Cowan's continuing differences with United Artists, delayed release of the picture some seven months. Chico was not involved in the contretemps, and didn't care who prevailed, but Harpo saw his concept and design go up like the smoke in the neon Kool cigarette sign on the rooftop in the movie's culminating chase scene.

All three brothers might well have rued the misadventure. They may have professed relief that this was their last picture, but they would have preferred to go out on a stronger, more harmonious note. Within a few months, they would be consigned to the ranks of comedy's also-rans. Dr. George Gallup's American Institute of Public Opinion took a poll of adults in September of 1949 to determine America's fifteen favorite comedians. The Marx Brothers came in thirteenth, behind Bob Hope, Milton Berle, Jack Benny, Red Skelton, Fibber McGee and Molly, Abbott and Costello, Fred Allen, Amos 'n' Andy, Arthur Godfrey, Eddie Cantor, Jimmy Durante, and Danny Kaye. (Only Henry Morgan and Charles Chaplin were less favored, the latter no doubt because of his highly vocal and controversial politics.) Significantly, by this time Groucho had been the star of his own radio show for two years, and yet the public still regarded him as part of the Marx Brothers and not as a star in his own right.

Groucho's second grandchild was due that spring. Because she was a diabetic, Irene's children had to be delivered by Caesarean section. The infant girl lived less than twenty-four hours. Groucho forced himself to go to the hospital.

"I barely learned the baby had died when Groucho was at my bedside," Irene recalled. "He had come to pay a condolence call. He was in tears. He was so heart-broken that it ended up with my consoling him."

During these times, when he might have turned to his wife for comfort, he resolutely turned his back on Kay. The distractions he was finding at the Hillcrest Country Club helped him get over the heartache, which acquaintances, given Groucho's hard-boiled exterior, found surprisingly disproportionate. He had joined the Jewish country club when he first moved to California, but resigned a few years later. Over the years, he had come back as a guest, sitting at the Round Table in the Comedians' Corner frequented by such members as Jack Benny, George Burns, Danny Kaye, George Jessel, Harpo, Chico, and The Ritz Brothers, most of whom also held boxes at Gillmore Stadium. Eventually, the other comedians insisted he rejoin the club. Frugal Groucho, who sold his membership for $350, now had to pay $6,000 to rejoin. Understandably, he hesitated.

In the meantime, he came to the club as Gummo's guest, setting up a folding card table in his self-imposed limbo near the Comedians' Corner, lobbing verbal darts at this most unlikely Establishment. The battle of wills lasted for weeks, until Groucho was finally shamed into joining. The comedians threatened to pay his initiation fee, then take out a trade paper ad announcing their act of charity. Soon after he formally joined Hillcrest, Groucho led a drive to accept gentile members, having no patience for reverse discrimination. The few Christians who joined, Danny Thomas among them, were delighted to discover that Hillcrest had the best food of all the area's country clubs. As for Groucho, as the years went by, he too was delighted, for the price of his $6,000 membership appreciated to $20,000.

Their efforts to get him as an official member should not be taken to mean that the comedians regarded Groucho as the most convivial of men. "He became his character frequently without benefit of writers," Bert Granet said. "Some of his humor was not always par. Consequently it came out very abrasive."

Groucho was finding the give and take at the lunch table more challenging and enervating than the exchanges with the civilians on the quiz show.

One day, he called Charlotte Granet. "Will you come over for dinner?" he asked. "Then Bert and I can go to a ball game and you and Kay can go to a movie."

When the Granets arrived at the house on Foothill, it was apparent their hosts had been quarreling. "We sat through a miserable dinner," Mrs. Granet recalled. "After Bert and Groucho left, Kay and I sat in the living room. She started to cry. 'You know, Charlotte,' she said. 'I get so mad at Groucho. He goes to Hillcrest for lunch. Jack Benny tells a joke. Then Groucho tops him. Harpo tells a joke. Groucho tells one funnier. George Jessel tells a joke. Groucho tops him too. At the end of the day, do you know how I get him? He's gasping for breath!'"

When Jack Benny consequently approached Groucho about trading appearances on each other's programs, Groucho agreed to be a guest star on his friend's program, but declined Benny's offer to appear on "You Bet Your Life." "I can get funnier comedians out of the audience," he told Benny. The putdown may have been prompted by insecurity. He would have been risking his exalted ad-lib reputation by trading insults with another of the great

323

comedians of the time. In spite of the prevalent Hollywood folklore that Benny was dead without a script, Groucho, from his experiences at Hillcrest, may have known otherwise.

He may also have realized, to a lesser degree, the inaccuracy of the picture of him as a doting father, as painted by Eddie Cantor in an article for *This Week* magazine.

Once I asked him, "Groucho, why do you do the shopping? Are you afraid your family won't buy the best?" He answered, "On the allowance I give them, they couldn't afford it." He punches hard so you won't think he's soft.

Several weeks ago I had to pick up a package for one of my five daughters in a department store and heard much laughing and carrying on. I found Groucho, wearing a beret, slacks, and a loud checked coat, chasing his two-and-a-half-year-old girl Melinda up and down the escalators. His wisecracks through the chase had the other customers roaring.

Recently, in the midst of a discussion concerning a new contract, Groucho suddenly jumped up and asked, "What time is it?" Someone told him, "It's ten minutes to six." He grabbed his hat and left. His lawyers and his sponsor couldn't figure out what was more important than this meeting. Had they followed the comic home, they would have seen him beaming as he watched little Melinda get her daily bath.

At night baseball games in Hollywood you will find Groucho sitting with his 26-year-old son Arthur, a writer at one of the major studios.

Arthur's always been fast on the comebacks. Once when he was 11 he begged Groucho for an air rifle. Papa Marx was afraid the boy might hurt himself and when he grew tired of the lad's pleading, he snapped angrily, "Look, Arthur, as long as I'm head of this house you won't get a rifle." Said the chip off the old block: "Get me a rifle and you won't be head of this house . . ."

Groucho's 21-year-old daughter, Miriam, is at Bennington College in Vermont, and editor of the school paper. Groucho's terribly proud of Miriam. She was offered a writing contract by Amos 'n' Andy. She turned it down because she had a feeling that Papa had something to do with it.

He phones Miriam every day. When a friend kidded him about retiring, Groucho answered, "I can't until Miriam comes back to California. Right now I'm working for Uncle Sam and the phone company."

He makes three telephone calls one minute after his program is off the air: one to Arthur, another to Miriam, and a third to his wife. He asks the same question: "How did you like it?" He would rather have their okay than the highest Hooper rating in the world. And speaking of Hooper—with whom I'm not on speaking terms—that office actually once called Groucho's home. When the question was put to him—"What have you got on your radio?"—Groucho replied, "My brother Harpo's picture."

"No one could deny Groucho's devotion to Melinda. She was a doll of a little girl," Nunnally Johnson's wife Dorris recalled. "She was a charmer, and Groucho was an adoring father."

A cursory look at his relationship with his older children might suggest he was a benevolent, supportive parent. Arthur, however, would have difficulty reconciling Cantor's description with the actuality.

"As Arthur reached manhood and chose writing as a profession," Dorris Johnson said, "I observed that it touched a hostile nerve in Groucho. I was more and more aware of it in things he said. Groucho, as with performers or actors I've known, had a longing to be a writer. He wanted to create the building blocks of thoughts into words. The fact he wasn't a true writer was a source of annoyance to him, I always felt. And when Arthur became a published writer, I think there was a kind of father envy there that I don't think Groucho could openly admit. Sometimes, if remarks were made in the presence of several people, he would talk about Arthur with some pride. If he made the remarks privately, he would sometimes denigrate Arthur's writing skills. That was to me the first giveaway. Arthur said that it was his father's resentment

325

that he was a writer which created a lot of the estrangement between them."

Groucho's ambivalence was still very evident even at the end of his life. While conceding that he had been a difficult father, he still wouldn't admit that Arthur might have been his literary superior.

"Being my son has been a hard burden on Arthur," he told me. "I've always tried to help him. The books he's written about me are pretty good. But he's not as good a writer as I am."

In Miriam's case, the Cantor article was ironic, for as it was being prepared for publication, she was unceremoniously expelled from Bennington, only weeks before she was due to graduate.

"They kicked her out for drinking," Groucho told me.

"How did you react to that?" I asked.

"Of course, I was embarrassed," he replied. Groucho again stuck his head in the sand, ignoring, as before, all the danger signals, unwilling to admit even at that late date the other factors which lead to Miriam's expulsion.

Around this time, she had driven her car off the road at a railroad crossing near Charlemont, Massachusetts. She and a girl companion barely escaped before a freight train hit the car. News stories about the incident didn't state whether Miriam had been drinking.

Groucho could sadly concede that alcohol might have been a problem, but he found it impossible to admit there might have been another factor. Administrators at the college discovered Miriam was having one affair too many—at that time even one affair was too many—and this was as responsible as her drinking for her enforced departure.

"Miriam felt the expulsion was totally unfair," her friend Sunny recalled. "There had to be a certain amount of malice involved." Her fellow students were equally angered by L'Affaire Marx, as they termed it, as were two faculty members, who resigned in protest.

Shortly after her expulsion, Miriam went to New York. Her experience in writing a humor column for the Bennington *Beacon*, "Re-Marx," and as editor of the campus literary magazine, *The Silo*, helped her get a job as college editor for a national magazine. She settled in Greenwich Village, transforming herself into one of its more eccentric sights, a carelessly dressed young woman lugging a baseball bat with her whenever she went to the corner store, as protection from imaginary marauding elements. The girl on her own had to cope with the emotional pain of feeling unloved by her father and of being found unworthy by her peers. Goodman Ace would periodically check in with Miriam during the time she lived in New York, serving as her father substitute.

Neither Miriam nor Kay, who desperately needed Groucho's assurance, received her adequate share. His daughter, since she was now three thousand miles removed, didn't experience the immediate, everyday neglect, however, that her stepmother and former close friend did.

Kay was a simple girl with few personal resources of her own, and in being exposed to Groucho's friends had been thrown into a pool of sophisticated, much older people. She had to sink or swim.

"Of all of Groucho's wives," Dorris Johnson said, "my favorite was Kay. I thought she was the most sensitive. It was almost as if Kay were a little sister to me. Groucho was a woman-eater. He seemed to destroy women, and I thought I could see some of the reasons why. I wanted to help that girl so much. I felt she had such a frustration that was beyond her handling or comprehension, and she was so vulnerable and had too much stress throughout her life. Now the generation gap with Kay was considerably greater than with any of the others of us. There was a pretty sizeable difference in Nunnally's and my age, but nothing like the difference between Groucho and Kay. She moved, as I did when I married, into the circle of her husband's friends, rather than bringing her age peers into the social circle."

In September of 1949 "You Bet Your Life" started its third season on CBS, in tandem with the Bing Crosby show. Within a matter of weeks, Groucho's show shot to seventh in the national Hooper ratings. Its previous Nielsen rating at ABC was seventy-fifth. In addition to his Peabody Award, the nation's radio editors had recently named Groucho the best quizmaster on radio. The momentum toward an extraordinarily successful transition to television had begun.

Opportunities also began opening up for George Fenneman, who was now a free lance. He gave up his ABC contract, and its attendant fringe benefits, to move with "You Bet Your Life" to CBS. Fenneman's voice, altered to give it an ominous intonation, could already be heard on radio's "Dragnet": "The story you are about to hear is true. The names have been changed to protect the innocent."

"A mutual friend talked me into hiring a press agent named Russell Birdwell," he recalled. "He was a charming son of a gun. I was impressed with his office and his monogrammed shirts. Right away Birdwell ordered $400 worth of pictures. He did it all. My name was in the trades every day. I'm not sure they're read today like they were then. He got my name everywhere: 'George Fenneman, emcee of the Groucho Marx show.' Groucho came up to me in the hall after one show and said, 'Why don't you fire whoever's doing your publicity for you?' I asked him if it bothered him. 'No,' he said, 'it doesn't bother me. But you don't need it. All you need is the show.'"

Eventually, Fenneman did drop Birdwell, but not as a direct result of Groucho's urging. The publicity campaign was leading Fenneman into a motion picture career, one field he had no intention of conquering.

By this time, Fenneman too was in the big money, the William Morris Agency taking over the stewardship of his career, and he would soon be the highest paid announcer in either radio or television. Because of this new popularity, ABC, his former employer, put together a five-day-a-week package for Fenneman called "The Perfect Husband." "It was like a male 'Queen for a Day,' only more fun," he said. "The women and their husbands would appear on the show and I would interview them. Groucho got me aside and told me, 'I wish you wouldn't do that show. It's too much like mine.' I was hurt and flattered at the same time, that he thought I was competing. I said I wouldn't quit, because I had to live up to the contract. Here was this man who was king, and he was worried about my little daytime show. Groucho heard it a few times, and he saw it was really no competition. The show was not a hit. It was cancelled one year later."

A spate of national magazine articles were trumpeting Groucho's progress, paying homage to his unbridled wit, while perpetuating the belief that all his lines were ad-lib. Negotiations were currently under way with the DeSoto division of the Chrysler Corporation for sale of the show, with the larger budget provided for in the transaction promising to finally place "You Bet Your Life" in the biggest of the Big Times.

Celebrations were in order. Two years previously, Groucho and Kay had hosted a Halloween party at which many of the guests came in the guise of their host. Another Halloween party was planned.

"Kay sent out invitations with the happy exuberance of a child," Dorris Johnson said, "inviting us to come in costume. Some of us who gathered there had children, as did Nunnally and I. Halloween is an occasion that puts a big work load on parents. The trick or treat things were big in those days, and getting the kids in costumes and taking them around was an exhausting experience . . .

"Kay saw her party that she dreamed of, I believe, in the way Kay *needed* to have a party. It was the fulfillment of a young girl's idea of a fun party. I expect her childhood was so barren of joy that she carried into her mature years a longing for these experiences. And I think she had worked very hard with a little girl's dream of an exciting Halloween party. She had gotten favors, she had worked out games, she had planned things, and all of this surfeited Hollywood group had little interest in doing those things. I saw Kay grow more and more tense, and her face set almost in a mask of unhappiness, and presently she went over to the mantelpiece and grabbed a whole basket of favors. She walked around and began to just toss them at the people. She would throw them in their laps. 'Here! Here!' People wouldn't play. She had planned games, and these were not games-type people. She wanted people to win prizes that she searched for and gathered, with the anticipation of an exciting party, and nobody was cooperating with her. The party broke up fairly soon. . . . Kay said something like, 'Oh, take the prizes or something—do *any*thing!' She was like a person who verged on hysteria.

"I know Kay was having a rough time. I felt so bad about that night that the next morning when I awoke, I wanted to apologize to her. I called rather early, and got her on the phone. I said, 'Kay, I want to explain about last night.' She said, 'Here! Here! Explain to Groucho. You don't have to explain *anything* to me.' She handed the phone to him and said, 'It's *your* friends.'

"I knew what she meant. The night before, she had felt the schism grow between her and Groucho's friends, and I believe she felt *she* was the outsider. She knew she'd never be a part of Groucho's *real* life: the contact with his friends. She was not one of that group. We had all made her feel that way, and I think it was quite inadvertent. I believe most of the people around Groucho felt very tenderly toward Kay. I never heard an unkind word said of her by any of his friends.

"Groucho took the phone. Clearly there had been a turbulent scene between the two. He began to apologize. He said, 'Kay's very upset. She felt the party didn't go, and really feels out of control this morning. I'll talk to you another time.' I could see the whole scene. The next time I saw Groucho, he said, 'Kay is having psychiatric therapy. She's very much in need.' "

Kay had told Groucho of her need for professional help that same day. "I think he felt very sympathetic about Kay," Dorris Johnson said. "He actually felt very paternal toward her . . . and I think he was loving. But Groucho didn't have a very effective way of showing tolerance. One of the things he did that I felt undermined and weakened whatever problem his wives had was to take more and more of the female role away from the female. He insisted on running the house, on being very absolute about money. Groucho was quite chintzy until the later days. But he removed all responsibility from them. He failed to let them grow in the sense of performing their role. So he exacerbated their insecurities more and more. And yet, he was always attracted to girls that had *grave* insecurities. That was a continuing Groucho syndrome. The girl that had problems, who was young, who was pretty, was the girl Groucho was attracted to. And it's my opinion that when he took on the girls as wives, he removed their chance to grow and mature in self-reliance."

While his wife was making a commitment to a regimen of extensive therapy, Groucho was making a lasting commitment of his own. The deal with DeSoto was consummated, with Groucho to be paid three thousand dollars a week starting on January 1, 1950. In light of his daughter's expulsion from Bennington a few months previously and his wife's deteriorating mental condition, Groucho sounded surprisingly ebullient when he was quoted in *Time* magazine about the state of his career:

> In the old days they almost threw me off the air if I deviated from the script. I had to sign a written pledge that I would read only what was before me. But now I'm doing what comes naturally. It's like stealing money to get paid for this.

His chipper attitude continued, at least in public, when he made a guest appearance late that year in *Mr. Music*, a Paramount film starring Bing Crosby. "It was embarrassing," Groucho said of his stint before the cameras, "because I sing better than Bing. Otherwise we get along fine together . . . I usually wait until he gets off the set before I start singing, because I don't want to embarrass him. We appear as a couple of ancient vaudevillians. I require very little makeup."

The mid-century milestone was personally marked with Kay still in therapy and Groucho coming to the realization that their marriage was at an end. Professionally, his life couldn't be rosier, however, since the television networks were courting him and even bigger money was in the offing.

His performing brothers weren't doing as well. Harpo, having returned from his joint European tour with Chico, was persuaded to appear with Jack Benny and Danny Kaye at the February, 1950, opening of the Shamrock Hotel in Houston. The three entertainers agreed to be paid in oil-rich lands. The underground oil deposits must have taken an incongruous turn, because no oil was struck on the lands deeded to the entertainers. This was one of the few instances where someone got the better of the financially conservative Harpo.

As for Chico, he was getting the business, as usual, while performing in Great Britain on the Empire Circuit. He ran into Allan Jones in Leeds, as Chico was checking out of the hotel suite that Jones as the next star act would occupy. Mary Dee, Chico's traveling companion, told Jones that her future husband had already gambled away his salary for the rest of the tour.

Groucho continued the weekly routine of the radio show. Few of his associates noticed any difference in his behavior, despite the personal turmoil he must have been experiencing. The clues to his unhappiness were nevertheless there, as George Fenneman soon discerned. "Groucho was somewhat hypochondriacal. When he said, 'I seem to be getting a cold,' it was a sign something was not going well in his life. The way the show was done, he couldn't look bad. And yet it wasn't an easy show to do. Before going on the air, his moods would vacillate from night to night. It was fun to have dinner with him afterwards. His mood was lighter, and he was often generous with his praise."

Taping for the season was almost over when Groucho announced that he and Kay would divorce. He filed the suit on April 14, alleging extreme cruelty without specifying instances. When reporters asked him to comment, he answered, "We're just plain unhappy."

Ten days later, he went to New York, where Miriam was still living, to take in the opening of the baseball season with Goodman Ace and his wife Jane. A *New York Times* reporter approached them during the game, having noticed that Groucho was rooting against the Yankees. "I don't like any club that has ninety farm teams," he said. "I hate all cartels and monopolies."

Jane Ace, a rabid Yankee fan, didn't appreciate his comments. Groucho didn't let up. "They're a cartel," he told Ace, "and they should be broken up."

After the game, Groucho dropped the Aces off in front of their Ritz Tower apartment. Instead of saying good-bye, Jane Ace spat at Groucho, "Communist!"

A bewildered Groucho took the cab on to his hotel.

"I wouldn't have minded so much being called a Communist," he told Ace over the telephone the following day, "but when I'm wearing a six-hundred dollar vicuña coat?"

"Which you probably got for nothing," Ace countered, "by endorsing something." Groucho conceded this was true.

He was back in California in mid-May for the divorce decree

from his twenty-nine-year-old second wife. Groucho, during their marriage, had made substantial amounts of money, and living in a community property state, Kay might have demanded half. Instead, she lived to the letter the terms of their prenuptial agreement, accepting $134,215 in alimony over the next ten and a half years. One of the few items of value that she took to the Westwood house Groucho paid for was the piano that the likes of George Gershwin, Arthur Rubinstein, and Oscar Levant had performed on. She took something even more precious in Groucho's eyes: Melinda. It was a difficult concession for him to make since he had grave doubts about Kay's ability to raise a child, doubts which were mildly absurd in light of his own paternal track record. He, however, had no doubts about his most recent ex-wife's basic decency, and Groucho retained enough regard for her to assure Kay he would take care of her modest financial needs should she never remarry. This he did until the last year of his life, more than twenty-five years later, long after his legal commitment to do so had ended.

CHAPTER TWELVE

A tart tongue never mellows with age, and a sharp tongue is the only edged tool that grows keener with constant use.
                                    Washington Irving, Rip Van Winkle

William S. Paley, chairman of the board of CBS, had, over the previous year, been making a systematic raid of NBC's prestigious roster of radio stars. Jack Benny, Burns and Allen, Amos 'n' Andy, Red Skelton, and Edgar Bergen would be the nucleus of NBC defectors around which CBS was to build television network supremacy over the next twenty years.

Since Groucho was already at CBS, Paley had every confidence that "You Bet Your Life" would be making the transition to television on his network. Consequently, the pilot television program was shot at CBS in the spring of 1950. Ralph Levy, who would ultimately direct both the Jack Benny and Burns and Allen programs, was assigned to supervise the original filming of "You Bet Your Life." He was then producing and directing the Alan Young show.

Levy noticed a great deal of insecurity among all comedians making the transition from radio to television. They had spent years building up their "mostest" characters in the audience's imagination and they would now have to adapt to a visual medium. "Jimmy Durante had the mostest nose in the world," Levy said, "and the worst vocabulary. Jack Benny was the tightest man. Ed Wynn was not a fool . . . he was The *Perfect* Fool. Groucho was the mostest too . . . the most irreverent person in the world, destroying authority, snobbery, and pretension."

The physical setup of the show was not complicated. "I remember a lot of cue cards, which was surprising. More was written for Groucho than I knew. I suppose I was as naive as the next person about certain elements."

Television in those early days did not extensively use editing facilities. "It was just kinescope, and there was no way to cut away to another shot," Levy said. "The only way I figured to solve the problem was to take an extra piece of film, in a long shot, which could be spliced in. I said to Groucho, 'Just keep talking. We're not recording anything but I want your lips moving. We can put in whatever sound we need later.' He didn't understand what I was saying. He asked, 'What'll I say?' I said, 'Anything. Sing some patter from Gilbert or Sullivan. That way your lips will be moving.' So he started to sing, and he forgot the words. Without trying to be rude, I cued him on the loudspeaker. He was a little annoyed somebody else knew the patter-song lyrics."

It was almost as foregone a conclusion in the minds of Groucho and his associates, as it was with network brass, that "You Bet Your Life" would be on CBS television. To assure receiving the most favorable deal, however, the show's principals decided the property should be put on the auction block. They were pleased to discover that NBC was also greatly interested in buying the show.

The bids were to be received at Gummo's house, who was still sharing the Groucho account with the William Morris Agency. To everyone's surprise, Paley flew in from New York on the deadline date to present his bid in person.

"We were sitting at Gummo's house being sociable," Groucho wrote in *The Secret Word Is Groucho.* "I rose and excused myself. Paley rose and followed me into the guest bath and locked the door.

" 'Look,' he said to me, 'you're a Jew and I'm a Jew. We should stick together. You can't afford to sign with NBC.'

"But there were a couple of fellows at NBC named Sarnoff, who were also Jews, though they'd never tried to drill the fact into me.

"I told Paley I wasn't pleased with his conversation."

Groucho was incensed by what he considered Paley's breach of decorum. His outburst drove the visitor out of Gummo's house and onto the front steps. Paley sat there, in a tuxedo, waiting for the NBC bid to arrive. Finally, Guedel talked him into going on to his dinner engagement at the house of Charles Correll, the Andy of Amos 'n' Andy.

NBC president Joe McConnell and his associates arrived around midnight, their plane from New York having been delayed by an electrical storm. Fortunately for Groucho, he wasn't forced to accept the offer of the insensitive Paley. NBC's offer for forty-nine percent of the show was three million dollars over an eight-year period, substantially higher than the CBS bid. The first two million dollars were to be paid over the first five years, with an option for the additional one million over the next three years. Groucho retained thirty-eight percent ownership of the show, and Guedel kept thirteen percent, the two men together retaining majority ownership. In addition, NBC agreed to pay Groucho $4,800 weekly for a thirty-nine week season. Guedel would get $1,800 weekly for the same period. The network, as a lagniappe, picked up the legal fees for Groucho and Guedel. In gearing up for television, NBC's operating losses for 1950 would total $18,000,000, the same year that Groucho benefited in more ways than one. He got the big money that accounted for a sizable part of that loss, and as one of the few comedy stars on the network, he also received an inordinate amount of attention and promotion from the network.

DeSoto had three years remaining on its current sponsorship contract, and its executives agreed to the increased budget, provided it could simultaneously broadcast and telecast the show at its usual Wednesday night slot. Bristol-Myers was currently sponsoring the television version of "Break the Bank" at that time, and some negotiating was in order. It was to no avail. Bristol-Myers head Lee Bristol refused to budge, and the television version of "You Bet Your Life" was consequently held over one day, being broadcast on Thursdays.

On Tuesday, October 3, the same week the show's fourth season was to begin, Groucho was sued by his first wife Ruth and her husband of four years, John Garrity, acting as his wife's managing agent. Groucho believed his divorce from Kay released him from making further alimony payments to his first wife. This provision was part of the 1943 amendment to his property settlement, which also allowed Ruth to remarry.

To surmise that Groucho had deliberately divorced Kay so as not to have to make further alimony payments to Ruth would be ludicrous. Nevertheless, a public ignorant of Groucho's well-defined code of integrity might interpret Ruth's suit as a distasteful indictment of a man trying to project a warmer image to the public. The suit was settled the following June, with Groucho agreeing to pay Ruth a lump sum of $49,500 in full satisfaction of her claim. The settlement also called for each party to assume individual attorney costs.

Otherwise, Groucho's mind was honed and ready for his foray into television . . . if you discount the turmoil of his second divorce, the apprehension over the quality of care Melinda would receive, the sad realization that Miriam's mental condition was deteriorating, the acrimony that was developing with his son Arthur, and the resignation that in all his affairs of the heart he had loved neither wisely nor well.

Chico preceded Groucho's television debut by two days, starring in "The College Bowl" on ABC. He was cast as the owner of a soda fountain on a college campus. The low-budget show afforded him an opportunity to practice his Italian dialect but denied him much of a chance to sit down at the piano. Although it introduced singer Andy Williams to a national audience, the show was not a success.

The same Jack Gould of the *New York Times* who had previously judged the quiz show format unsuitable for Groucho now found it, with minor reservations, admirably tailored to his talents. In his review of October 5 he wrote:

> Groucho Marx, who is a match for anybody when it comes to thinking on his feet, joined the list of new faces on television last night on N.B.C. He was amusing, indeed, providing you don't listen to radio any more.

338

In its anxiety to kill two media with one payment, Groucho's sponsor presented on television the identical show it had offered only twenty-four hours earlier on N.B.C. radio. On Wednesday a listener heard all the gags; on Thursday there came the pictures. Electronic fission, it might be called.

As a matter of fact, the duplication of Groucho's show on radio and television represents the first time that N.B.C. has conceded publicly that the televiewer is not apt to turn on his radio. Boy, there's going to be a conference this morning at 30 Rockefeller Plaza!

The reasoning in Groucho's case, however, is faulty. If there is one reason to still keep a radio, Mr. Marx is it.

On his program, called "You Bet Your Life," he is displaying his usual trigger wit. His attitude of disbelief and unconcern makes for constant hilarity as he leads the quiz contestants down the path of utter confusion. With his ad-libbing, he is a real relief to ears jaded by the comics who are helpless without a script.

The television version, which this season is being filmed in advance at the same time that the radio show is being recorded, provides further evidence of Mr. Marx's instinctive flair for comedy.

Before the camera he sits in shirtsleeves and leisurely smokes a cigar, meanwhile lifting an eyebrow and puffing smoke to give added meaning to his quips. To Mr. Marx's credit, his is probably the first radio show that without material change holds interest on television.

A more reflective overview which supplemented Gould's early assessment was provided by Groucho's friend Hal Kanter, who was quoted in Max Wilk's 1976 book, *The Golden Age of Television:*

> ... it was Groucho Marx, who first proved the philosophy, which at the time was very unfashionable, that if people were laughing at you in radio, they'd continue to laugh at you in TV, without any embellishments. Groucho merely took his radio show, *You Bet Your Life,* and transferred it to TV intact. And he proved his point—that the only thing you had on TV

that you hadn't had on radio was the sight of Groucho sitting on a plain stool, puffing his cigar and waggling his eyebrows as he leered at pretty girls. That's all he added, and the show was a big hit.

Subsequently, on TV shows, especially variety shows, everybody took to sitting on stools and singing and talking to people. Maybe doing a few sight gags, but with no real use of the visual aspects of TV.

The pioneer was Groucho. And does anybody need to remind you that all those episodes of *You Bet Your Life* are running on your home screen tonight—while all the other wildly "inventive" TV concepts of the fifties and sixties have long since been forgotten?

The transition to television was considerably more complicated than described by Kanter, and Groucho gladly left its arduous mysteries to the experts working for and with him. They would be devoting their waking hours for the betterment of the show, so that Groucho could come in for a few hours every Wednesday evening to pull it all together. He had recruited one of these talents, Virgil Miller, previously the head of Paramount's camera department, as head cameraman.

Miller reminisced with Robert S. Birchard for an Oral History commissioned by the American Film Institute. He said that Gummo, before shooting, often brought a different coat for Groucho to wear. A member of the studio audience asked Groucho during the warmup why he changed his coat.

"Well, I don't know just why," he replied. "Its color or something. But I'll let the cameraman tell you."

"Well, Lord," Miller said, "he caught me with my pants down . . . so I haggled through something. I don't know what it was now. But I decided that if he did that again I was going to be prepared for him. So I came home and wrote this thing . . . and I suppose people must have thought I was crazy, 'cause they'd see me drive around in my car, repeating this and trying to learn it and all that; and sure enough he said, 'Well, my cameraman will explain that.' "

And so Miller explained, "The concentric demands of the image orthocon, when subjected to the equalizing pulses of the synchronizing generator, induces a radiant light flex that modulates the electron beam, forcing the black blacks and the white whites into a mutual video differential."

Groucho, his mouth agape, looked at Miller. Then he turned to the audience. "Any questions?" His cameraman repeated the same line for the next five years.

Head writer Bernie Smith, whose activities would be disguised with his being billed as the show's co-director, supervised pre-production. Robert Dwan, the actual director, took over when filming started, supervising thousands of feet of film during his six-day work weeks, until it was edited into final shape. Often, the radio and television versions of the show would be substantially different, particularly when there were visual aspects which wouldn't play on radio. In addition, he often combined footage of contestants from different shows to make a more entertaining program, carefully checking the sound track to determine that the secret word originally announced by Fenneman had not been spoken by contestants on a different date. If it was, and the footage could not be edited, Fenneman would be called back to the studio to shoot a pickup scene, to announce another secret word which none of the pairs of contestants had spoken.

Norman Colbert worked as head film editor of the show. "The problem he had to solve," Dwan said, "was how to deal with this mass of film. It required ingenuity. Essentially the editor and his assistants had to work very steadily and very carefully. The sound would be recorded several blocks away. It would be piped by line to the recording studio and the editor would have to synchronize it to the film. We were using an optical sound track, since this was just before the invention of audio magnetic tape. After that our objective was to make it look live, to make it look as unedited as possible. Norman did it very well. The show had an immediate look."

Groucho's prepared ad libs were now smoothly functioning, thanks to the development of an overhead projection system with an acetate sheet over it, similar to the device used to project scores in bowling alleys, on which his lines were written. It was placed so that Groucho appeared to be looking at the contestants as he read from it, instead of just behind them.

341

And yet, Groucho had every opportunity to offer his spontaneous zingers. John Guedel, in his interview for *The Secret Word Is Groucho*, likened the written construction to the building of a wall. "The scaffolding is the written material. Then you put up the wall, and then often you tear down the scaffolding."

Bernie Smith, who should know better than anyone, agreed. "Groucho didn't want to get that closely involved in the preparation. He wanted to be fresh when he went out there. We had a pretty good idea, but time after time Groucho would come out there, and be wild, and we had no idea what was happening. That's when we had the great shows. When he was at his peak you could never write for this man. He was much better than any writer could ever be."

Despite its fail-safe format, Groucho's nervousness before every show never left him. Gummo's son Bob would be joining the program staff within a few years, after he got out of the service. "Part of my duties was to have dinner with Groucho at the Brown Derby before every show. He was so nervous that all he could manage was a bowl of chicken soup. We'd talk about current events . . . anything to distract him. The minute he was in makeup he would cut you out."

The extensive preparation made "You Bet Your Life" the most expensive of the quiz shows, even the big money ones that came in the mid-1950s. Groucho was receiving a substantial portion—at times almost half—of the show's budget.

Jerry Fielding, who was the show's musical conductor from 1949 to 1953, said, "I think that although he felt the show was easy and worth a lot of money to him, it really wasn't what he would have preferred to do. He was miserably unhappy. When I first went on the show he was having marital trouble. You'd go to a party at his house at the end of the season and he'd never come out from behind the bar. He didn't want to talk to anybody.

"Groucho had a much higher intellectual level than most people who do quiz shows, and I'm sure he had a vile inner contempt for what he was doing and for half of the idiots that appeared on the show. That's why he appeared to be mean to some of them. He could get away with it because they never believed it."

I can believe that Groucho's self-contempt was there, but in the dozens of hours I spent in his company, I rarely heard him denigrate the contestants. He was, in fact, laudatory of the great majority of them, and delighted in reporting on the progress of their careers. Any entertainer who got a start on his show was automatically a singular talent. Phyllis Diller was a prime example. Only with provocation would he alter his opinion of a former contestant.

While the whole world seemed to be singing Groucho's praises as he made the transition to television star, Chico's own television fortunes were dwindling and Harpo's national concert tour was marked by cancellations due to poor advance sales. The only negative aspect of Groucho's professional career was the recent *Love Happy* misadventure, and he had already brought suit against its producers for $35,000 in moneys owed him. The suit was resolved in his favor within a few months.

Groucho was flattered, although he didn't take the report seriously, when Blanche Patch's book *Thirty Years with G.B.S.* was published in early 1951. George Bernard Shaw's secretary quoted the great man as telling Sir Cedric Hardwicke that he was the third greatest actor of the age, adding that Groucho and British music hall entertainer Lew Lake ranked first and second.

In February, the Academy of Television Arts and Sciences, in its third annual awards, named Groucho the Outstanding Television Personality of 1950. "I deserve it," Groucho commented. "I've been a good father to all my children and a good husband to all my wives." NBC felt he deserved it for another reason. "You Bet Your Life" was its top-rated television show for the first four seasons, and was in the Top Ten for its entire eleven-season run.

Groucho had agreed to appear with Tallulah Bankhead on "The Big Show," NBC Radio's last stand against television. In a letter to his friend Goodman Ace, the show's head writer, he explained the circumstances that led up to one of the network's tokens of appreciation for his contribution. He wrote in April of 1951:

> My second ex-wife, Kay, has a mother who is a piano teacher. At one time she was married to a combination janitor and taffy puller in a minor candy factory in the deep South. Between the bonbons he stole from the factory and her piano lessons they eked out a modest and dreary living.
>
> Eventually, like all mothers, she dragged her daughter Kay

to Hollywood. Apparently she had grown weary of the part-time confectioner's chocolate drops and yearned for greener and more lucrative pastures. At any rate, Kay grew up and then married in quick succession one of the Dead End Kids and your correspondent. During these marriages her mother had been teaching juvenile delinquents in San Fernando Valley how to mutilate the piano.

Describing his former mother-in-law's marriage and subsequent divorce from a plasterer, he went on:

One of the things that Kay sequestered in the divorce proceedings was my piano, and one of the things that her mother held on to when she booted out the plasterer was her practice piano . . . both of the girls now being without men, they decided to live together in the little house I had paid for in Westwood. Since it's difficult to house two pianos in what is the equivalent of a Quonset hut, Kay's mother suggested that she stable one of the pianos in my house . . .

Shortly after this . . . the mother . . . decided to move out on Kay and rejoin her ex-lover in a plastered house of their own. This meant she wanted her piano back. The score was now Kay with one piano, her mother with one, and me, of course, with none.

Gummo, on being apprised of the situation, naturally was horrified and immediately went to N.B.C. and demanded a showdown. In effect he said, here was one of their brightest stars, a brilliant musician, with nothing to play on except an occasional girl, and what did the network intend to do about it. However, he added, this star, talented and wealthy though he was, would deign to appear with the glamorous and slightly venereal Tallulah if N.B.C. would loan, not give, mind you, merely loan Groucho one of its many pianos. N.B.C., having even more pianos than Kay's family, was delighted with the simplicity of Gummo's demands and even offered to send two pianos in case Groucho should decide to get married again. And so thus ends the tale of my love life and the two

344

pianos. Soon I will have a new piano and if I'm lucky, perhaps some day some new tail.

Groucho was not a mass of seething passions. "My sex life is negligible," he wrote Abe Burrows around the same time as the letter to Ace. "The only time I get real excited about a dame is when I am flying through the air and ... watch the hostesses wiggle their ways up and down the aisles. Since there's nothing more remote sexually than a hostess on an airliner (at least while she's on the plane), I always arrive at LaGuardia lustful and eager for a call girl. However this condition soon disappears as the Seconal taken twelve hours earlier begins taking effect."

The final divorce decree was entered in May. Groucho, in addition to the pre-established alimony, also agreed to pay Kay an additional $1,300 a year for Melinda's support. He was now able to play the field.

At the moment, Groucho was more concerned with the scheduled June birth of Arthur and Irene's child. "He was so apprehensive during my entire pregnancy," his former daughter-in-law said. "When Andy was born he weighed more than eleven pounds. He was one of the largest babies ever born at Cedars of Lebanon Hospital. Groucho was at the hospital the moment he was allowed to visit. He'd come to see Andy, but he also put on a whole show for the nurses. He did the Hackenbush routine up and down the halls."

Soon after, he embarked on his "mangy lover" phase, a self-coined description which graced the title of a memoir published in 1964. The girls he began bringing around were considerably younger than the wives of his good friends, and even less worldly. "We would try to bring them into the group," Charlotte Granet said, "but it was very difficult."

Groucho himself, when it came to female company, often preferred to spend his leisure time with his friends' wives: Charlotte Granet, Helen Perrin, Dorris Johnson.

"I think for a time," Mrs. Johnson recalled, "I was very close to Groucho. He used to talk to me and, strange, he would talk in a confidential way that he would *never* use with Nunnally. Groucho and I talked business, we talked about his problems with the children and with either girlfriends or wives. He never went into these confidences with Nunnally. As Nunnally told me, their relationship was on a very different level.... He was always serious with me. Once in a while, if we were at a social gathering, he would carry on banter in the usual Groucho ... manner. But if we'd stand and talk privately, he was always quite serious. I don't know whether he had confidential exchanges with other friends or not. Maybe it was because I was a relaxed person and untaxing for him. I was in no way a challenge, and he could talk more easily to me."

However, he never discussed with Mrs. Johnson, as he had with her husband, his crush on Ava Gardner. They'd never met, but this urbane sixty-year-old man turned into a mass of adolescent frustration just looking at her picture.

"I never even knew about his crush on Ava," Mrs. Johnson said. "They came and went so fast. But it certainly sounds right. Ava was a gorgeous girl. She was fun, high-spirited, outspoken—the things that would attract—also she was celebrated. I think Groucho was sometimes attracted to girls with identities. He would take them out with great pride. He loved entering a gathering with a beautiful star, somebody who had distinguished herself in some way that gave her a strong identity."

Dorris went on to explain that Groucho also liked nameless girls who were merely beautiful. "He once said to me, 'I'm an eternal romantic. I'll never be anything else. I always fall in love. And I fall in love with beautiful young girls. I get a crush on them. I'll never outgrow it.' "

He soon began keeping company with a young actress who'd recently arrived in Hollywood. Within a matter of months, Audrey Hepburn became one of the industry's biggest stars. Groucho simply couldn't compete with younger men who began flocking around her.

One can gather that there was no particular type of woman who appealed to Groucho. Friends never knew what to expect, a librarian or a girl about town.

"One night, I picked up a girl with big tits at the Garden of

Allah," Groucho told me. "I took her to Bogey's. 'Who's the broad?' he asked. 'She's my secretary,' I told him. Bogey took her around the room and introduced her as my secretary. Later this bimbo met the heir to a motor company and married him. Bogey said, 'You must be sorry you lost such a good secretary.'"

Norman Krasna, Groucho's friend and writing partner, was now acting as production head at RKO in tandem with Jerry Wald. In the middle of his second season on television, two films in which Groucho starred, *Double Dynamite* and *A Girl in Every Port*, were released by the studio. The first, co-starring Frank Sinatra and Jane Russell, was three years in the making. It was so named in glorification of the actress's endowments, part of Howard Hughes's continuing campaign to harness the talents he'd previously introduced in *The Outlaw*. The second, which co-starred William Bendix and chesty Marie Wilson, continued to mine the mother lode.

Groucho could in the future afford to be choosy about other movie offers. He was now firmly identified, according to one critic, as television's King Leer. No pun could be more sadly fitting, for he was playing a modern-day Shakespearean drama backstage. Groucho, unlike King Lear, had no doubt which child loved him the most. In Miriam, now returned from New York and working on the program staff of the show, he had his Cordelia, albeit a rebellious one. She wasn't a daughter of sweet reason. Hers were brooding silences. Her love for him, which had driven her to a dependence on alcohol and drugs, was threatening to consume her.

"Even when I first met her," George Fenneman recalled, "it was evident she was brilliant, despite all her problems. It was her choice of words and her interest in things. Some people you know are bright even if they don't talk. I can remember Miriam being absolutely silent. But I knew she liked me. I later ran into her a couple of times with Groucho in New York. She'd pinch my cheek and hug me. We'd never had that relationship before, but she seemed to light up when she saw me."

To Groucho's discredit, he continued to ignore Miriam's very obvious problems, and resolutely refused to acknowledge his contributions to them. Although he willingly paid thousands of dollars for psychiatric treatment, he tended to think of it as money

347

down the drain, since he had no faith in psychiatry. Rather than shoulder further responsibilities for her, he attempted to foist her off on others. Once he tried to talk Goodman Ace, who was fond of Miriam, into marrying her. "Much as I'd like to," Ace replied, "I don't think Jane would approve."

He tried to act as matchmaker between his daughter and Bernie Smith. When neither showed any romantic interest in the other, he asked Marion Pollock, the contestant coordinator on the program, if she and Miriam might possibly become roommates.

A young woman as perceptive as Miriam could see through her father's stratagems. She had every right to resent them. She was also intelligent enough to analyze her own problem. Why would she, who had seen drink destroy her mother, become an alcoholic too? Through many hours of therapy, she came up with an answer. "I do everything to fulfill my father's feelings about women," she told her friend Sunny. "He hates them, and I prove him right."

Hatred may have been too strong a word, although none of the females he was involved with would deny there was a basic mistrust of all women in Groucho's makeup. Despite the immediate example within his social group of happily married couples, he found it impossible to think of his lovers as friends. Friends would extend themselves for no other reason than friendship itself. Women always had an ulterior motive.

One such friend, Norman Krasna, caught Groucho's first appearance in the play the two men had written at La Jolla Playhouse in July of 1952. When he went backstage, Krasna told Groucho about his performance in *Time for Elizabeth,* "You're playing Walter Huston. It's fine, but not what the audience wants."

The review in *Variety* somewhat supported Krasna's opinion:

Since revised extensively, the play remains a flimsy soufflé with too many laughless lines to be a first-rate comedy and insufficient penetration for a study in irony. Nonetheless, it has moments of sharp wit in which truths are well stated and the perverseness of human desire is effectively put into focus ... Faced with an unreasonable handicap, Groucho's performance is all the more remarkable for its dogged devotion to his acting intent.

From that point on, his dogged performance was livened by the Groucho mannerisms. He had taken the cue from *Variety* and Krasna.

"Choose an author as you choose a friend," Wentworth Dillon, the Earl of Roscommon, wrote in the seventeenth century. Groucho, time after time, did him one better, choosing authors themselves as friends.

Charlotte's Web, a children's book by E. B. White, had recently been published. It told about the spider Charlotte and her friend Wilbur the Pig. Her web spelled out messages that ultimately saved Wilbur's life, and Charlotte herself died after leaving an egg sac of descendants. From that point on, every time he was asked, Groucho said *Charlotte's Web* was his favorite book. Its philosophy was akin to his own:

> Wilbur never forgot Charlotte. Although he loved her children and grandchildren dearly, none of the new spiders ever quite took her place in his heart. She was in a class by herself. It is not often that someone comes along who is a true friend and a good writer. Charlotte was both.

The affinity Groucho felt for writers extended to other men he considered to have equally great intellects. Goddard Lieberson was a case in point. He had started out as a pianist, composer, and music teacher. When Groucho met him, Lieberson was in charge of the Masterworks classical library for Columbia Records. He later became president of the company. Those who knew him described Lieberson as one of the great gentlemen of his time . . . and one of the least stuffy. His social circle was one of the broadest in the business, ranging from the grandes dames of Park Avenue to comedians in burlesque houses.

"I met Groucho with Phil Silvers and Irwin Allen," Lieberson said in December, 1976, only months before his own death. "We had a lot of mutual friends . . . George Kaufman, Goodman Ace, Harry Ruby, Oscar Levant. We became good friends through music. I play the piano and he sings. I see him whenever I'm in California. When he made out his will, he named me as executor. He looks on me as an intellectual, and he feels that intellectuals won't be crooks. That's no total guarantee, of course. But he thinks I'll be honest with everyone involved. He knows I have no personal involvement in money.

"One of my attractions for Groucho is that he thinks I look like his father. I also make him laugh, and that's not an easy thing to do. As for me, I love him. I rush in and kiss him whenever I see him. He's the witty old grandfather everybody would love to have.

"If he'd had a conventional education, Groucho could have been a teacher. He's professorial, and he reads. His knowledge of literature is good."

Lieberson, while agreeing that Groucho had a basic mistrust of women, said, "I don't think Groucho could be without a woman in his life. And this wasn't always necessarily a sexual thing. What he might have needed was an unusual combination: a hooker with an M.A."

Groucho did not know that was his need, for rarely did he seek out brainy voluptuaries. I often heard him tell Erin Fleming, "You're the only woman I've ever met with any brains." That he truly believed it—despite the immediate example of his daughter Miriam—was indicative of the male chauvinistic thinking that the women in his life were unable to cope with. The happiness they savored early in the relationship inevitably ended, leaving an extended, bitter aftertaste. That was certainly how it was with his second wife Kay.

"I believe Kay had need for a crutch," Dorris Johnson said, "for shoring up her unstable psyche. She turned to drink for it, which is the most familiar pattern. Maybe now, drugs would be just as familiar or commonplace, but at that time it was much easier to just soothe your agitation with drinking. I think that's what Kay had to do, as did Ruth, as did Miriam."

Kay's cousin, Virginia Seamon, stepped in to care for Melinda when the inevitable neglect ensued. The situation was untenable. Groucho knew something had to be done. Yet, even as his six-year-old daughter was being neglected by one parent she was being exploited by the other. For Groucho was using her as an emotional shill on the show. John Guedel had advised him to talk about Melinda during the show warmups, so that the audience would feel greater empathy toward their host. It was logical that she should next appear on the show, which she first did on October 18, 1952. Thereafter Melinda appeared at least once every season until "You Bet Your Life" ended its run in 1961.

"I remember very well being put out in front of the entire television world and being expected to come up with a marvelous performance," Melinda said in *The Secret Word Is Groucho.* "I remember on this first performance that I sang a song and did a little dance with my feet. When I was very little I had fun singing and dancing, and I would have done it in an alley. But I quickly became aware of tremendous pressure. During later times it became very intense and uncomfortable and something I didn't want to do at all. Groucho has his own fantasy about it, which is fine, but he never asked me if I enjoyed it or wanted it. He'll deny that he was a stage mother, but I'm afraid it's true. It was something that was expected of me: clean your room, do well in school, and give a good performance on the television show."

George Fenneman sat backstage with Melinda before her appearances on the show. "I can remember Melinda trembling backstage. I used to sit with her and hold her hand. She certainly didn't want to make any of these appearances. She was a cute, nice little girl, but she never wanted to be in show business. Groucho desperately wanted her to, so she did it to please him."

On November 21, a month after her first appearance, Groucho went to court to gain custody of Melinda. This too he desperately wanted, although he couldn't have been pleased with the circumstances that took him before Superior Court Judge Mildred Lillie. He was granted temporary custody, pending Kay's recovery from her various illnesses. Because of her ongoing delicate condition, the custody order in effect became permanent, and Melinda lived with Groucho from then on.

The following summer, "The Best of Groucho" had its first seasonal run, a thirteen-week series which retelecast the best "You Bet Your Life" programs of the previous season. Goodman Ace was a houseguest during its run, shortly after Melinda turned six. He heard Groucho telling his daughter a story: "Tommy was a poor little boy. He got up one morning and his mother said, 'There is no food in the house, so you better go out and get some money.' Tommy went out and he was hungry. As he was walking along he saw a little girl run across the street just as a car was coming along. He dashed out on the street and saved the little girl's life. The little girl's nurse said, 'Oh, you have saved the little girl's life. Her father is rich and he will reward you.' So they went to the little girl's house and the nurse told the father that Tommy had saved the little girl's life. And the father said to Tommy, 'You have saved my little girl's life and I will reward you. Here is four thousand dollars.' And Tommy said, 'Oh good, now I can buy some food. I have not eaten anything all day.' And the father said, 'Wait a minute. Here are some cookies and a glass of milk.' So Tommy drank the whole glass of milk and ate all the cookies. He was really hungry. When he finished, the father said, 'You better go home now and here is your money: thirty-five hundred dollars.' He had reconsidered."

Groucho looked up to see that Ace had joined them. "She's got to learn sometime," he explained.

At about the same time that Melinda came to live with her father, Arthur too was changing his living arrangements. Warner Brothers bought the movie rights to the life of Gus and Grace Kahn—the film would be *I'll See You in My Dreams*, starring Danny Thomas and Doris Day—and Arthur's mother-in-law had split the proceeds of the sale with her two children. Irene's share went for a down payment on a house in Pacific Palisades, and the Arthur Marx family moved out of Grace Kahn's house in Beverly Hills.

Shortly before each week's taping of "You Bet Your Life" Groucho would take a scrap of paper from the pocket of his jacket. (He wore the same coat and tie every week, so that Bob Dwan could combine pairs of contestants from two different evenings on the same program. The jacket was tailored so that it wouldn't bunch at the back of the collar when Groucho assumed his usual seated position before the cameras.) On the paper was a reminder: "F.E.U . . . Prod . . . Look Ahead." Once it was committed to mind, Groucho could go on with the show.

Dwan deciphered its meaning. "F.E.U. stood for 'Foul 'em up'. That meant to get the contestants mixed up, to see how he could get them confused. 'Prod' meant that if he knew the contestant had the capacity, he should be on watch for something more than the

simple answer indicated. 'Look ahead' warned Groucho to antici-
pate the direction the interview was heading."

Groucho would tuck the paper back into his pocket, to be taken
out again the following week. With the words written thereon as
his guide, and with the help of the projection device, Groucho was
able to weave hilarious, convoluted exchanges week after week by
playing the slightly dim or extremely literal quizmaster, who didn't
quite understand what the contestants were trying to say. It was a
considerable talent, as his friend Fred Allen was about to discover.

Of radio's greatest stars, Allen was one of the few unable to
make a successful transition to television. When he set out to host
an audience participation quiz show similar to "You Bet Your
Life," Groucho generously came forward to give Allen the benefit
of his considerably successful experience. His main recommendation was that filming of the new show was essential. Allen's
producers disagreed.

"As I told you last summer," Groucho wrote Allen in September
of 1953, shortly after the new show premiered. "The fact that you
are live will always be a handicap. It's a little like making a movie
without previewing, editing or cutting it, but apparently that is a
situation that you are going to have to face."

Groucho proved to be correct. "The quiz-game format seemed a
natural for Allen because he was one of that small minority of
comedians able to ad-lib," Steve Allen wrote in *The Funny Men*.
"Like Groucho and [Herb] Shriner, he was given the additional
benefit of interviews that were more or less written out in advance.
But Fred lacked a quality that Groucho and Shriner have. His mind
was rapier-quick, but he was not used to making small talk with
relative nonentities."

Despite his repeated comments to his dour-faced friend that
there wasn't enough Fred Allen on the show, Groucho couldn't
bring himself to tell his fellow comedian the main reason why he
thought Allen couldn't make it on television, as he told me almost
twenty-five years later. "Fred was a very funny man . . . one of the
funniest . . . but he didn't have the face for television. He was good
talking but he didn't look good."

As for "You Bet Your Life," its ratings were miles ahead of its
opposition on CBS, a situation comedy called "Life with Luigi."

353

Never was Groucho funnier than during this period, when matters in his personal life were at their most dismal. The many disturbed signals Miriam had been sending out over the years finally came to a head. Her alcoholism had become so severe that Groucho was advised to send her immediately to Menninger's. Her brother Arthur flew with her to the Kansas sanitarium which specializes in emotional illnesses.

Miriam's friend Sunny was married shortly thereafter, and she was perplexed when her childhood friend didn't even acknowledge her wedding invitation. She didn't discover the reason for Miriam's lack of response for some time.

That November, in a chatty letter to Goodman Ace, in which he described a visit to former President Harry S. Truman in Kansas City, Groucho parenthetically alluded to the visit he paid his older daughter on the same trip. "Miriam looks great," he wrote, "and is very happy, and I was glad I stopped off." If wishing would only make it so.

He returned to California to find himself embroiled in a controversy not of his making. The most charitable assessment of Groucho's behavior in its wake, however, is that his concern for Miriam may have clouded his moral judgment. He wasn't the only one to be caught up in the prevailing hysteria.

It had started in 1947, when hearings by the House UnAmerican Activities Committee resulted in the blacklisting of the Hollywood Ten, a group of Hollywood writers and filmmakers. Two years later, 151 people were linked in *Red Channels*, a pamphlet published by righteous Red-baiters, to Communist organizations. In the meantime, Senator Joseph McCarthy of Wisconsin had held up his headline-making list of Communists, none ever named, who had infiltrated the State Department.

Sniping since then had consistently been aimed at entertainers. Jerry Fielding, the band leader on "You Bet Your Life," around whom the tempest would soon revolve, feels he knows the reason why. "The entertainment industry was vulnerable because it was useable. It meant headlines. Those guys got a lot of press subpoenaing a Judy Holliday, much more than they got by picking some professor at a university or an organizer in Pittsburgh. You get a lot of press when you pick off the glamour names."

Earlier in 1953, the Committee held hearings in Hollywood,

drawing the zealous praise of several right-wing celebrities. Those who came forward to theorize about the creeping of Communist dogma in movie scripts—it was reported that Ginger Rogers had been required to say in one movie, "Share and share alike"—were flippantly accused of defending their swimming pools from the Communist menace.

Fielding, however, couldn't afford to be flippant, since he was being inexorably drawn into the fray. An item in Walter Winchell's column in which he was named as a Communist sympathizer, the band leader feels, was an unspoken invitation to present himself before the Committee and name other members of the ultra-liberal causes he had supported all his life. (Of the 240 organizations on the Attorney General's Un-American list, Fielding by his own count belonged to at least sixty.) Fielding ignored the Committee's tactics. When Gummo called the matter to his attention, Groucho said he would not sit still for a political firing.

"Assuming I was the most rabid security risk that you could dream of," Fielding said, "what could I do to really upset anything playing fanfares on the Groucho Marx show?"

He may have answered his own question when he said, "Quite frankly, I think they wanted me to name Groucho. What other service could I have been to them? Name a bunch of musicians? Had I gone in voluntarily to talk to them, I'm sure they would have brought his name up to me."

Fielding was further determined not to buckle under. "I had a lot to lose by taking the stand I took," he said. "My career was really soaring, and I knew that I was laying it all on the line. But there's no way I wanted it if it had to be on those terms. I have always been a terrible loudmouth about people who do things I think are wrong. And I still am."

Although Groucho might support left-wing causes, rarely had he publicly committed himself. Groucho had seen in the 1930s how ineffective the Algonquin Round Table had been in its quixotic crusades.

On a rare occasion, he lent his name to the Independent Citizens Committee of the Arts, Sciences and Professions. Under the group's aegis, he went to Seattle with Olivia de Havilland in June of 1946 to support some liberal candidates there.

"I was a naturalized citizen and was very nervous about joining any committee," Miss de Havilland recalled. "But James Roosevelt assured me this one was fine. Groucho and I attended this enormous rally. I saw some very odd things happen there. I sensed there were manipulations the larger body wasn't aware of. When the rally was over, I saw a lot of Communist leaflets scattered in the audience. I was furious. I resigned from the committee a few weeks later."

The Hollywood branch of the committee folded that September, and in the fall of 1947 it was placed on the Attorney General's list of subversive organizations, despite the fact it no longer existed.

Since that misadventure, Groucho was leery about lending his name to any cause. Appearing as a witness in a fraud case in April of 1966, he indirectly revealed what he learned from his past experience. A man was accused in a fraud case of using his name to raise funds for a testimonial dinner honoring Sándy Koufax, the pitcher for the Los Angeles Dodgers. Groucho denied he was so involved.

"Do you lend your name to any charitable organizations?" the defense attorney asked him.

"Rarely," Groucho replied. "I'm an extremely thrifty man."

In the current dispute revolving around Fielding, neither Groucho's thrift nor his discretion were the better part of valor.

He yielded to the pressure and permitted the firing of Fielding, to his continuing shame. "That I bowed to sponsors' demands is one of the greatest regrets of my life," he wrote in *The Secret Word Is Groucho*.

Fielding went on to become one of the most distinguished composers in films. Along the way, he led a band in Las Vegas and was recruited to perform on a radio program sponsored by the U. S. Treasury Department, touring top-secret military installations with his show. Yet, ironically, he was unable to work for any commercial sponsor because of the blacklisting.

He judged Groucho harshly, perhaps justifiably, and refused to speak to him for more than twenty years. In the rare instances when Groucho visited Las Vegas, he would make subtle overtures by sitting near the bandstand, hoping that Fielding would speak to him. It never happened.

Twenty years later, Fielding did unbend. Now a bearded, dis-

356

tinguished man—he had yet to reach his thirtieth birthday when the axe fell—he walked up to Groucho at an Orson Welles tribute sponsored by the American Film Institute.

"Do you remember me?" he asked.

Groucho looked him over. "You didn't have a beard when I knew you."

"I wasn't old either," Fielding laughed.

"You never should have left me," Groucho said.

"I didn't have much choice," Fielding replied. The two, finished with their pleasantries, went their separate ways.

When *The Secret Word Is Groucho* was published, a party was held at Groucho's house. Jerry Fielding, who was interviewed for the book, magnanimously accepted an invitation to attend.

For several days before the party, Groucho kept repeating how glad he was that Fielding was coming, and how ashamed he was of his behavior in the past.

In the book, Groucho wrote his *mea culpa* in some detail. And yet, when I took Jerry over to say hello to him, the seated Groucho was unable to speak the same words to Fielding's face. All he said was, "How are you?" Then he turned away, unable to say any more. The man he had wronged by his inaction might finally overlook an act that Groucho himself felt was an act of cowardice. In the final analysis, Groucho could not forgive himself.

Clichéd phrases come into existence because of their pandemic truths, and no one knew better than Groucho the enduring accuracy of the expression that it's lonely at the top. He was one of the few men who could be rueful and funny about his enviable predicament at the same time.

"Now the melancholy days have come," he wrote Fred Allen two days before Christmas in 1953. "The department stores call it Christmas. Other than for children and elderly shut-ins the thing has developed to such ridiculous proportions—well, I won't go into it. This is not an original nor novel observation and I am sure everyone in my position has similar emotions. Some of the recipients are so ungrateful. For example, yesterday I gave the man who cleans my swimming pool $5.00. This morning I found two dead fish floating in the drink. Last year I gave the mailman $5.00. I heard later he took the five bucks, bought two quarts of rotgut and went on a three-week bender. I didn't get any mail from December 24th to January 15th. I told my upstairs maid, who, by the way, bears a strong physical resemblance to Lena Horne, that I would buy her six pairs of nylons if she would let me try them on her. She said it was okay. Next year I am getting her panties. For Christmas I bought the cook a cookbook. She promptly fried it and we had it for dinner last night. It was the first decent meal we had in three weeks. From now on I am going to buy all my food at the bookstore.

"So you see, the life of a rich man isn't all beer and skittles (whatever the hell that means). We, too, have our troubles just the same as the lowly commoner and the shepherd in the hills."

Groucho's career was at its peak. He had bridled some years earlier, at the outset of "You Bet Your Life," when Bernie Smith suggested he be introduced on the show as the world's funniest man. Now others were paying him the same accolade.

Bob Hope had been asked by *Parade* magazine who he felt was the funniest. He replied, "Fellow comedians—myself included—are all openly and vociferously envious of Groucho Marx. I'll take Groucho because of his unfailing wit with what in the profession we call 'the word.' "

(When I brought up Hope's past observation, Groucho beamed. "Bob has the best delivery," he said. "He's the All-American boy.")

When, in March of 1954, *TV Guide* ran an article, "The Truth About Groucho's Ad Libs," its impact was minimal. The public might be pleased to find out that the quiz section of the show was scrupulously honest, but it didn't want to hear that the show was "the finest manufactured spontaneity television has yet known."

"You Bet Your Life" was consistently the Number Three show on television. The medium was eating up other comedians at an alarming rate, but Groucho flourished. If our conversations are any criterion, Groucho must have achieved a measure of security about himself. From that point on, he could talk about the funny lines others had said, and the way they topped him.

The first exchange I discerned involved the upstairs maid who looked like Lena Horne. "She was a beautiful colored woman,"

Groucho said, "with a light complexion. I once said to her, 'Sarah, you are a beautiful woman, and yet you never married.' She replied, 'No, but I was very well known in San Antonio.'"

He and Melinda were rattling around in the big house on Foothill, and despite Groucho's penchant for doing the family grocery shopping, supervising the servants, and tending his fruit trees, a woman of the house was desperately needed. Kay was still unable to pay a mother's attention to Melinda, and his daughter needed a woman's supervision. Yet, it was Groucho himself who was the lonelier of the two.

Dee Hartford, a well-known high fashion model, played a featured role in *A Girl in Every Port*. She brought her twenty-four-year-old sister, Eden, on the set to meet producer Irwin Allen, who in turn introduced the would-be model to Groucho. The last name of the two sisters—Mormons from Salt Lake City—had originally been Higgins. They later took the surname of their good friend Huntington Hartford. Eden's sister had recently married one of Hollywood's greatest directors, and the new Mrs. Howard Hawks thought Groucho would be a fine choice as Eden's husband.

Groucho was more than forty years older than Eden, and he was understandably hesitant about the commitment of marriage. And yet, there was no other girl he would rather be with.

Erin Fleming theorized that Groucho, in large part, married Kay because she had the sweetness of Olivia de Havilland and Eden because she suggested the sensuality of Ava Gardner. She was an erotic-looking girl, seeming to be specifically designed to revive Groucho's flagging sex drive. It was apparent to his friends that he was hooked. Yet he repeatedly sought their assurance that he wasn't making a serious mistake.

"Groucho was lonely," Dorris Johnson said. "He wanted to be married. Eden was an exciting girl—very beautiful—but he said he was afraid she was after his money.

"I said, 'Grouch, can you think of a way you could invest your money that would give you as much pleasure?' He made a defensive remark about her . . . not to me . . . mainly to himself, it seems. He told me he'd given her a piece of goods—some fabric—as a gift and something else that was equally trivial. It was an extraordinary statement coming from a man as rich as he was at the time. Who gives a girl he's in love with a piece of goods? I never asked Eden what she did with it. At that time it might have embarrassed her."

During a trip to New York, Groucho and Goddard Lieberson had lunch at Le Pavillon. "He was telling me about Eden," Lieberson said. "Knowing about his entanglements, I asked, 'You're not contemplating marriage, are you?'

" 'It's the last thing in the world,' Groucho said. 'Eden has these terrible parents. If I were married I'd have to put up with them.' "

Lieberson described Groucho as being more often moved by his heart than his brain. When Eden made a strategic retreat, going to Europe with her sister, Groucho proved his friend correct. Left with the fear of losing Eden completely, he capitulated.

When in the summer of 1954 Groucho went to Europe with Melinda to film some DeSoto commercials for the upcoming television season, Eden was invited along. The trip gave her and Melinda a chance to get acquainted.

As a prelude to marriage, Groucho specified Eden would have to sign the same prenuptial agreement that Kay had signed. This Eden agreed to with alacrity.

On July 17, 1954, the two were married in Sun Valley. Melinda arrived from Beverly Hills the day before the ceremony.

"Dear Aces," Groucho wrote his friends in New York after the wedding. "This is to notify you that I got married."

Ace wrote back, "Anybody you know?"

Norman Krasna had married Al Jolson's widow Erle a couple of years before. In a letter to Arthur and Gloria Sheekman, Groucho wrote, "The Krasnas are throwing a big affair for us . . . (personally I like my affairs in private) but they are both very rich in their own right and they insist on spending a substantial sum of money to show us off."

Harpo and Susan also honored the newly married couple. During the party, Groucho stood at the piano singing a mock love ballad to his young wife. Suddenly, he edged the accompanist off the piano bench, and started playing an old vaudeville tune, *"Ist das nicht ein Schnitzelbank?"*

His four brothers, sitting in different parts of the room, joined in.

"It was the number they used to sing in their vaudeville act when, under mother Minnie's guidance, they had trouped in their "boyhood through the hinterlands," Ben Hecht wrote in *A Child of the Century*.

It rose gaily again in voices as fresh as they had been thirty years before. The wedding vanished out of the room. The saga of gay talent and family love that was the Marx Brothers turned us from a wedding party into a happy audience. But happiest of all was Harpo. Looking at him as he stood singing in his corner, I understood my friend in a phrase. It was Harpo who was the bridegroom, here and everywhere else.

Yet, in affairs of the heart, it was Groucho who was the incurably optimistic romantic. "I don't know a thing about women," he once told me. "I'm a sucker for a pretty face. I married three pretty faces without brains, though Eden was a pretty good painter."

In moving into the Foothill house, Eden was succeeding Kay as Melinda's mother. It couldn't have been an easy adjustment.

Groucho's youngest had been pretty well winding her father around her finger for years. If he was manipulating her to go on to the show, she pretty well called the shots at home. Shortly after the latest wedding, Melinda was caught telling a lie, and was punished. Groucho showed me a note he had saved, in which his young daughter told him and Eden how sorry she was for her transgression, and added that she wouldn't blame them if they sent her to live with her mother.

When I asked Groucho how he reacted to the suggestion, he answered, "I wouldn't think of it. Melinda knew I couldn't do that."

Unfortunately, Melinda also developed an antipathy toward her natural mother. "A child is always intolerant of a parent's weakness," Dorris Johnson said. "I believe Melinda's hostility toward her mother may have grown out of the feeling that Kay had let her, the child, down. Maybe a child does have a legitimate position there. God knows parents do have this heavy responsibility toward the kids they create. I think Melinda was very intolerant of her mother, and that was one of the things that caused Groucho to get very rough on Melinda at times. He felt she was very insensitive toward Kay—at least he told me that—and he felt Melinda had no right to be."

361

Even as an emotional gap between Melinda and Kay was unavoidably developing, Groucho's son Arthur was risking a more deliberate alienation from his father. As a writer, he was the obvious choice to write a heartwarming book about one of television's foremost personalities. Both father and son may have been miscast. As Groucho once told a reporter, "I am not a lovable man." No one realized that more than Arthur.

"*Life with Groucho* was Arthur's first success," his ex-wife Irene said. "Up to then he had written for magazines. I typed the manuscript. I enjoyed that book."

Groucho, according to Arthur in *Son of Groucho,* a later book, cooperated fully during the book's writing.

That he succeeded in picturing his father as a warmhearted man was proven when the *Saturday Evening Post* bid $45,000 for the first serial rights on the book, provided that Groucho supply more impudent expressions and agree to plug the upcoming serialization on his quiz show.

When, after considerable prodding from his father, Arthur finally let Groucho read the manuscript, Groucho objected so strenuously to the way he had been portrayed that he threatened to sue his own son. Before long, attorneys for father and son were negotiating with each other.

An editor at the *Saturday Evening Post,* in the meantime, sent Arthur a letter telling him that galleys were on their way. The bristling author hit on a plan. As he described it in *Son of Groucho,* Arthur asked for two sets. When they arrived, he deleted material he felt objectionable to Groucho from one set, and sent it to his father for approval. He made his own revisions on the second set. Arthur, once Groucho had corrected the first set of galleys, dumped them in a trash can and returned his own corrected set to the publication.

It may have been an act of betrayal on Arthur's part, but it was also an act of independence. If Groucho felt Arthur's action was sharper than a serpent's tooth, he did not say so. When Fred Allen sent him New York reviews of the book after it was published in November of 1954, Groucho sent him a letter of thanks:

Even *The New Yorker* praised it. They astonished and delighted me. It seems to me I come off as quite a nut in this book and when I say, "a nut," I don't mean a deliberate one like Jack Rose or Coolidge ... I realize now I've been crazy all these years without being aware of it. Well, enough of me. I'm pretty sick of the subject and I hope this finds you the same.

David Astor of the *London Observer* later wrote Groucho, requesting that he name the three most interesting books of the past year. He replied by sending Astor a copy of *Life with Groucho.*

Something as intangible as her father's shadow had also proven on onerous burden to Miriam in the past, but it now appeared she might learn to cope with it. Reports from Menninger's were guardedly optimistic.

The cumulative effects of these developments in his older children's lives could not be said to make Groucho a happy man. Rather, he was less unhappy, and that was progress of a sort. Being married to a beautiful young wife also helped.

Arthur, in *Son of Groucho,* described his stepmother, as "extremely phlegmatic—almost torpid at times." Yet Eden was able to bring out the social Groucho to a much greater extent than had his first two wives. Perhaps, at almost sixty-five, he wanted to prove he could still kick up his heels. Suddenly he and his sultry-looking wife were being seen around town at charity benefits and movie premieres. And although Groucho over the years had regularly entertained in his home, guests were invited with much greater frequency after his third marriage.

"I think of all those happy times together," Dorris Johnson said, "those marvelous parties in his house, at our house, and at other friends' houses, where the greatest talent in the world got together. You couldn't have bought the talent that was on. Many of us used to say, 'There's five million dollars' worth of talent gathered in this room and it's all on from time to time.' They were the most exciting days, the most glorious experiences. If I started checking off the names it would be like calling a roll of the biggest motion picture, theatrical, and club entertainment of the last fifty years. I saw Groucho get up at these parties, and you couldn't be any better than he was. When you have the people around that stimulate you and feed you, the way that people that were always gathered did, you can't get any more stimulation. I can't remember the jokes, the anecdotes, the comedy routines they did, because one segued into another so fast. It went on for a long time, and it was top stuff. I don't think one person could write, nor could you set out to buy, that kind of entertainment. That's something that happens with the chemistry of the people and the moment and degree of stimulation."

The positive aspects that came from being tabbed a winner naturally spread over to Groucho's everyday life. Now, toward the end of the fifth year on television and the eighth year on radio, "You Bet Your Life" was still in the Top Ten on both media. The American Research Bureau listed the show as the most-watched, as well as the most frequently reviewed, while the Nielsen ratings consistently pegged it second behind "I Love Lucy." Columnist Jack O'Brian, in an article extensively reprinted in the nation's newspapers, termed Groucho's formularized, visually static quiz show the best on television. (The recent advent of big money quiz shows was creating a separate audience which cut into the ratings of other types of programs, but "You Bet Your Life" had as yet not been affected by them.)

Rain, after such an extended period of fair weather, had to fall in Groucho's life, and it was again Miriam who was rebelliously hurling thunderbolts. Her improvement at Menninger's had been so marked that she was permitted to take a job as a writer for a Topeka television station, virtually functioning as an out-patient. With the freedom she'd earned, she eloped in April of 1955 to Santa Fe, New Mexico, with another Menninger's patient, the scion of a wealthy New England family, who had also been permitted to take an outside job as an automobile salesman in Topeka.

Hospital policy forbade patients to marry, and because of their defiance of this stringently enforced regulation, Miriam and her new husband were asked to leave the institution. The seriousness of the matter was impressed on Groucho, for Miriam simply didn't have the stability to enter into such a union, particularly not with a young man whose own history was equally turbulent. Marriage in their case not only smacked of resistance to authority; it was a deliberate self-destructive act which could only lead to disaster.

The newlyweds went to California on their honeymoon. Groucho could not disguise his displeasure at the situation and his dislike of the young man. Within a short period, the couple moved back to

Connecticut where they would embark on a charade of married life.

Groucho at the moment was having greater success with the institution of marriage than his daughter. Because Eden felt uncomfortable in Groucho's rambling Spanish house on Foothill, the couple agreed to build a contemporary house in a new development called Trousdale Estates. Wallace Neff, a distinguished Southern California architect, was commissioned to design the $300,000 house. Groucho specified a study for himself, while Eden wanted a round bedroom, its adjoining bath to have a sunken tub.

While waiting for the construction to be completed—it proved to be a nearly interminable process—Groucho had plenty of time that summer to mix with his cronies at Hillcrest Country Club and to catch up on personal correspondence. He deliberated about a gentle way to state his opinion that he didn't think television was up Fred Allen's alley. "At one point in the proceedings last Sunday," he wrote his friend in July, "you wore glasses. I wish you would always wear them. They make you look years younger and give your face the same kind of softness that General Grant had at Appomattox." He didn't presume to venture more.

Norman Krasna heard of Groucho's plan to build a new house. Consequently, he wrote, "For ten minutes we toyed with the idea of writing you a letter during which I would casually mention an acquaintance of mine who got rooked by some architect named Neff, but we decided the joke was a little too terrifying."

Arthur Sheekman, in London at the time, wrote Groucho, "How is your insomnia? In Paris I came across a new kind of soporific. It isn't a pill; it's a suppository. The other day I stepped on one and my foot fell asleep."

In his answer, Groucho told of the visit Eden's sister, Dee Hawks, was currently paying. He snarled as expected, but his bite wasn't totally convincing:

At the moment I have a house full of people. There's Mrs. Howard Hawks; the nurse, and a year-old squawker, and the joint is teeming with wet diapers, mildewed milk bottles and running water . . . When I casually invited Eden's sister to spend a week or two, I had no idea it would lengthen into six.

And the way she eats, one would think that the baby is still inside of her instead of fouling up my house with baby toilet seats, wet bed sheets and flying rattles. Her nurse is very eager to appear on my show as a contestant, and nails me every time I come out of my bedroom. My bedroom exits are becoming more infrequent all the time. Beginning Monday, I am holing up in my boudoir until the taxi (with Mrs. Hawks) leaves for International Airport.

As a matter of fact, Dee is a charming girl—both pretty and bright—and if she were here alone, without the nurse, the baby and Eden, I'd have a hell of a time.

(Groucho didn't have the same regard for Howard Hawks, his wife's brother-in-law. "I could never get close to him," Groucho told me. He added with great sarcasm, "Hawks was a great liberal. We were talking about sports one day and he told me, 'Imagine allowing Negroes to play football.'" Such a sentiment might be understandable, if not excusable, coming from a man from the South, but Hawks was born in Indiana.)

As the show embarked on a new season, a column by television critic John Crosby explained why "You Bet Your Life" continued in popularity despite the minuscule prize money being offered on the show:

Well, there's going to be a $100,000 quiz to offset the $64,000 one. I suppose there'll ultimately be a $1,000,000 one to offset the $100,000. After all, if they can pay Jackie Gleason $11,000,000, they can well afford to pay a million bucks to some poor needy old lady who knows baseball averages. Or how are the poor, needy old ladies to manage?

... Me, I'm educated in the old-fashioned well-rounded way, and I'd be no good at all on that kind of quiz which requires specialization. For relaxation, we unspecialized ignoramuses infinitely prefer Groucho Marx. You won't learn half as much about the Bible, but you'll get a lot more laughs ... What I like about Groucho's wit is a certain salty flavor as if he distrusted the motives of practically everybody.

... Many of his quips are a lot more than just wisecracks;

they are simple truths. I rather like the time Groucho was talking to Rear Adm. R. W. Barry, director of civil defense for Los Angeles. Barry said that the most important aspect of his own job was to make every man, woman and child in Los Angeles conscious of civil defense.

"That's a very big job," observed Groucho. "It's tough enough just to see to it that every one in Los Angeles is conscious."

In its new season, the show's payoff for saying the secret word was decreased from one hundred and one to ninety-nine dollars. The economy wasn't instituted because its owners, Groucho and Guedel, needed every dollar they could scrape up to defend themselves from a recently filed tax suit. It was meant instead as a dig at the escalating prize money represented by "The $64,000 Question," which had shot up to second in the Trendex ratings, just behind the Ed Sullivan show. "You Bet Your Life" was seventh.

The federal suit against the two men, filed in October of 1955, claimed they owed a combined total of nearly $100,000 in back taxes for the years from 1950 to 1951, for moneys derived from the sale of the television show to NBC. Both claimed the income, of which Groucho received seventy-five percent and Guedel the rest, was a capital gain and thus taxable at twenty-five percent. The government contended that only one-quarter of each man's share could be considered a capital gain and the remainder should be taxed at regular income rates. At issue was the question of whether proceeds from sale of a partnership qualified under the capital gains guidelines of the Internal Revenue Service. The case was held over.

By the end of the television season, "You Bet Your Life" was still in the Top Ten, hovering between seventh and eighth in the ratings, while a "$64,000 Question" sequel—"The $64,000 Challenge"—and two panel shows, "What's My Line?" and "I've Got a Secret," had pushed the "Perry Como Show," "I Love Lucy," and two situation comedies out of the Top Ten. This might be a new era in television, but Groucho's show would still be very much a part of it.

When filming ended for the season and summer reruns started, Groucho checked into a hospital. He was exhausted. The grind of the quiz show and his ongoing guest appearances on virtually every variety series on television was beginning to take its toll.

A comedian and his wife, who had a house in Palm Springs, sent him a get-well wire. (One of Groucho's most quoted lines at Hillcrest involved the comedian's wife, who drove off the highway to Palm Springs and hit a hay stack. Groucho observed, "That's the first time she's been in the hay in twenty years.")

In answering the telegram, Groucho wrote:

I am coming down to Palm Springs for Easter week, and if you will send me your phone number I will call you when I'm there. You could call me but I'll be living in a shabby dump that not only has no phone—but also is sans furniture. It is run by one of Gummo's relatives. Fortunately, I am still young enough to withstand the rigors of those Palm Springs nights, and won't mind sleeping on the sand with nothing over me but a tumbleweed. If the Jews in Israel can sleep in the sand surrounded by hostile Arabs, I'm sure I can slumber peacefully in the sands of Palm Springs—surrounded by nothing but gentile golf clubs.

Despite the rampant anti-Semitism in some Palm Springs quarters, several of the Marxes preferred the leisure life there. Harpo had decided to retire to Palm Springs, he and Susan having built a house on the edge of Tamarisk Country Club, which has a predominantly Jewish membership. Zeppo and Gummo lived nearby. Eden talked Groucho into buying an unpretentious condominium in the same area as his brothers, this being the shabby dump he referred to in his letter. It was here that he recuperated after his hospital stay. There was one Marx who spent little time there. Chico, whose failing health could have been immeasurably improved by the clear sunshine, had been forced to keep working in smoke-filled nightclubs and drafty theaters to pay off his gambling debts. He was currently touring in a play, *The Fifth Season.*

Groucho wrote again to Fred Allen while he was still in the hospital:

This year I surmise that overexposure will be the death of many a half-hour show. I'm surprised I've lasted this long and I attribute this to the fact that nobody sees my show. By comparison, what a leisurely business vaudeville was. TV is the rat race of the century. The sponsor on my show now has a commercial which shows De Sotos flying in the air. Why this should make it a satisfactory vehicle in which to drive to the supermarket, is beyond me, but I have a remote control on my set and I just don't listen to anything.

Groucho may have been trying to spare his friend's feelings by stating that nobody saw his own show. The truth was quite the opposite. NBC had recently run a trade ad, the results of its marketing department's cumulative research. Next to a silhouette of Groucho's head was the inscription, "One man on a chair has drawn more viewers over the last six years than any other attraction on television."

In the show's first nine seasons of 341 shows, before a collective studio audience of 119,350 people, contestants had won a total of $463,514. The giveaway question had been answered 156 times, and the secret word guessed 256 times. Groucho had smoked twelve dozen cigars, had worn out three jackets and seven bow ties. The show had used 1,938 miles of negative film and 685 miles of recording tape. Such conspicuous consumption accounted for a large part of the show's 1955 weekly budget of $47,500, which was higher than that of any of the big money quiz shows.

A more significant statistic, a tribute to Groucho's ultra-professionalism, was the extremely low turnover among the show's personnel over its fourteen-year life. Only three members of the staff dropped out along the way. One defected to CBS early in 1955, taking the expertise acquired from "You Bet Your Life" and lending it to Edgar Bergen's show, "Do You Trust Your Wife?" Among the refinements the CBS show copied was the use of multiple cameras. Yet the Bergen show lasted only two seasons. The essential ingredient apparently was Groucho.

Though he rarely expressed it, Groucho was grateful for the loyalty of his associates. As I got to know them, I was struck by the uncommon decency of them all. Fifteen years after the fact, they continued to be loyal to Groucho. His former associates could not recall a single act of cruelty on Groucho's part. They submerged their egos to the greater cause, Groucho himself. In later years, several comedy writers on other shows became performers in their own right, but if any of his writers ever had that ambition, none of them acted on it.

He never minimized the value of their contributions. Although he freely aimed many barbs at them, he wouldn't allow others to say anything against them, even in jest. When we were collaborating on *The Secret Word Is Groucho*, I had the temerity to insert a line about the crew: "They were rank amateurs . . . bathing wasn't their strong suit." It was one of the rare times when Groucho snapped at me. Mine was a multiple offense. First, I'd disparaged some men by implying their personal habits were slovenly. Second, it was the kind of line Groucho would never use, for he considered it a breach of taste. Third, it simply didn't play. Groucho patiently told me, not unkindly, "You shouldn't write funny."

On another front, Max Gordon optioned a play by Arthur Marx and Mannie Manheim, which he planned to open in New York in mid-December, 1956.

Everybody Loves Me was not destined to match the contemporary sparkle of Neil Simon's comedies, but it marked a more personal milestone in Groucho's relationship with his son. If *Life with Groucho* could be said to represent a loving view of his father, Arthur's current collaboration might show the opposite end of the spectrum.

Arthur, in declaring his individuality, perhaps accomplished it by capitalizing on the relationship from which he was trying to break free. There were disturbing parallels in the comedy with Groucho's own life. Arthur also revealed his unfulfilled desire to become a star in his own right, an ambition thwarted by his realization at the age of fifteen that he lacked both the talent and the presence to be an entertainer. Arthur left himself open to the charge that he was indulging his private fantasy at his father's expense, no matter how adamant his disclaimers to the contrary.

In an interview with the *Philadelphia Daily News*, Arthur described the character of "Gordy" Williams, an aging television star, as being "a composite of a lot of different types we had the misfortune to run into during our travels around Broadway and Hollywood."

Arthur's wife Irene—the daughter of the great Gus Kahn—collaborated on a song with Martha Manheim. Its sole purpose was to give the Gordy character an opportunity to say, "That's the worst thing I ever heard."

Groucho might have had an inkling of the tone of the play. Asked if he would attend the Broadway opening, he told a *Variety* columnist, "It's the worst thing for pop or mom to be up in the stands watching a would-be champ play tennis."

The production's out-of-town opening was at the McCarter Theatre in Princeton, New Jersey. *Variety*'s review of November 8 found it "a fast, hard-hitting insidey comedy about an egomaniacal TV entertainer who gets his comeuppance the hard way and all at once. Played by Jack Carson, the protagonist emerges as mean, ambitious and somehow pathetic as his son breaks away from his control, his fiancée leaves him and his sponsor threatens to give him the gate ... Although there are obvious parallels between the stage character and various entertainers, the authors carefully state that the characters are fictitious. Perhaps so, but they're alive enough to demand attention, if not respect."

The show grossed a dismal $5,700 for its four-show stay in Princeton. From there it moved on to the National Theatre in Washington, D.C., for a week's run, a house with a capacity for a $40,000 weekly gross, where it brought in an even poorer $7,900.

Everybody Loves Me next moved to Philadelphia for a two-week run at the Locust Theatre before going on to its scheduled New York opening at the Belasco Theatre.

"Gordy has quirks," Henry T. Murdock wrote in his November 20, 1956, review in the *Philadelphia Inquirer*. "His stinginess becomes a running gag during the play—and a good one. While he loves the blonde ex-cover girl who shares his Park Avenue apartment almost as much as he loves himself, before he marries her he demands a prenuptial contract. He has had experiences with three other wives and community property laws.

"His real crisis occurs when his son becomes a TV celebrity in his own right and is approached to be his dad's summer replacement. With youth treading on his heels Gordy goes to great lengths to fight off this menace to his ego. This being a comedy, of course he never has a chance to win."

Jerry Gaghan of the *Philadelphia Daily News* found the play starting ". . . with the speed of a TV comedy segment. Throughout the first act, the gags fall thick and fast. Everybody in view has good lines to toss about and some of them are hilarious.

"Unfortunately, the writers are not able to sustain this high laugh quotient during the remaining two acts. Jack Carson is wonderfully cast as the aging network star, who can't bring himself to face competition from his own son."

Rex P. Sensenderfer of the *Philadelphia Evening Bulletin* described the Williams character as "a mean, arrogant, penny-pinching egocentric, and it is to Mr. Carson's credit that he manages to squeeze just a little pathos out of the role, but it's hardly enough to get much sympathy from the audience."

Perhaps the public didn't cotton to a villainous protagonist, or sensed there was something distasteful in Arthur's use of the play as an emotional catharsis, because it put the seal on the critics' assessments by staying away in droves. The production folded in Philadelphia after the first week, never to reach Broadway. Despite a block booking by the First-Night Club on opening night, the show grossed only $8,600 in a $30,000 house. It left producer Gordon and his backers with a $75,000 loss.

I never broached the subject of the play with Groucho. If he felt any personal pain over it, he never mentioned it to me . . . and he freely talked about aspects of his relationship with his children which were cause for greater sadness. Perhaps he felt this was an instance where a discreetly deaf ear was to be preferred. Yet, if Arthur and Manheim had in actuality written a damning indictment of Groucho, the ears of the public were even deafer.

The television show, along with those of Jack Benny and Burns and Allen, constituted the medium's "class" acts as well as its standout survivors. Comedians were discovering that twenty years on radio were being condensed to five years on television. By 1957, the television careers of Milton Berle, Jackie Gleason, Sid Caesar, Jonathan Winters, Red Buttons, and Edgar Bergen were virtually over.

"The valuable commodity in 'You Bet Your Life' is Groucho alone," Jack O'Brian wrote in the *New York Evening Journal*.

His virtuoso impudence remains at the top of the TV heap, where it was when the-quick-and-the-dead imitations of comedians first arrived on television, and it hasn't changed much through the seasons, in point of view or the ratings. His ad libs are priceless, even those whose price is paid to gag writers, for it is no secret Groucho prepares a great many of his impromptu insults and insanities. His fund of stooges will remain constant, for the lay citizenry fight to get on his show. It has a wonderfully lively level of lunacy and a built in "style" the public knows and loves. Its habit pattern is Groucho; its always changing elements are the contestants; together they provide the consistently best comedy in television.

Groucho offered his own analysis in a later *Newsweek* interview. "I'm not overexposed," he said. "I focus on the guests. I let them talk until they get confused. Then I move in ... When some contestant puts his foot in his mouth, I just push it in a little further. That small box is no place for frenetic comedy. Casual shows like ours are the ones which last. I'm relieved when people say they've missed my show. I don't want them to see me every week."

While other comedians were fighting to keep their careers afloat, Groucho was parceling out portions of himself with an abandon that belied his approaching sixty-seventh birthday. He appeared as a surprise guest in the film version of *Will Success Spoil Rock Hunter?* He played Peter Minuit, and Eden and his close friend Harry Ruby portrayed Indians in Irwin Allen's production of *The Story of Mankind.* The film, based on the Henrik Van Loon book, cast, among others, Hedy Lamarr as Joan of Arc and Edward Everett Horton as Sir Walter Raleigh. Groucho's two brothers also appeared in the picture, Harpo enacting Sir Isaac Newton and Chico being cast against type as a monk. The appearance of the three Marx Brothers in the same film wasn't a reunion since they had no scenes together in the all-star production, which was packaged on the heels of the enormous success of *Around the World in Eighty Days*.

Groucho held in abeyance a decision to write his autobiography for Little, Brown and Company, while he prepared to star on the New England summer stock circuit in his and Norman Krasna's play, *Time for Elizabeth*. Eden would be making her stage debut in the play.

Miriam met her father and Eden when they arrived at Idlewild Airport, two weeks prior to the August 19 opening of the play at the Grist Mill Playhouse in Andover, New Jersey. Her three-year marriage was virtually ended, Miriam having been intermittently institutionalized, and she had begun making plans to return to California. Arthur and his family, along with Melinda, joined Groucho and Eden at Andover. They all stayed at a farmhouse nearby. Groucho, who always complained about his insomnia, raved about the country air, saying he had had the greatest night's sleep of his life.

By the time the production moved to Matanuck, Rhode Island, his ebullient mood evaporated. At Groucho's request, Goodman Ace had come to catch the play and offer his opinion and advice. But Groucho was so disturbed about the play's as yet unsmoothed rough spots that he didn't remember Ace's being there.

Reviews weren't encouraging. Ted Holmberg in the *Providence Journal* found the play "lacking in sharpness and satirical bark." He found that the star "seems rather uncomfortable during most of the play. His speaking TV personality is often crushed by dialogue which is mundane and obvious."

When the tour ended, Ace arranged for the elder Marxes to stay at an apartment in his building in New York. Groucho told Ace that the only exchange he and Eden had had during the long automobile trip came as their driver stopped at their destination. "There's the Ritz Tower," Eden said. Groucho merely grunted.

Yet with Bob Dwan, his television director, supervising the

staging, Groucho over the next three summers played *Time for Elizabeth* to increasing success all over the country. As Groucho loosened up, the play began taking on more of an ad-lib quality.

The ad libs soon found their way into the actual performance. Soon, he was giving a twenty-minute talk after the curtain went down, and it was getting bigger laughs than the play itself.

He wrote Norman Krasna, telling him that the play was selling out. Krasna in turn wrote Gummo, asking, "How can it be such a success when it was such a failure at the Lyceum Theatre?"

"It turned out that if you're in summer stock," Krasna later said, "and you have the name of Groucho on the marquee you can sell out *Cyrano* or *Little Women*.

"Yet, Groucho was more vain as an author than as an actor. He used to say, 'Our play is selling out.' He didn't say, 'Groucho is selling out,' which was the actual truth. Soon he was inventing things I'd never heard of before. He once wrote me, 'The rabbit scene is the best thing in the play.' There wasn't a rabbit scene in the play."

After Groucho's death, Bob Dwan reminisced in an article he wrote for the *Los Angeles Times:*

Groucho's audiences expected to be amused. They arrived prepared to laugh. Usually, he rode a rising tide. Tension grew and finally exploded into applause. When the spell was working, he could do no wrong. The audience knew what he was going to say next and were delighted when he did not say it.

But I saw him work the magic once in a small town in Germany where no one had ever heard of him. [The group had extended its *Time for Elizabeth* tour into a European junket.]

The place was Dornum. Minnie, his mother, had been born there . . . Groucho wanted his daughter, Melinda, to see it. We drove from Amsterdam, behind the dikes of the lowlands, over the great causeway that crosses the Zuider Zee, into Hanover in northwest Germany.

Dornum is in the flatland between Essen and

Wilhelmshaven, larger than I had expected, six or eight blocks of brick and stone houses. A church was on a low hill at one end, and what looked like a small castle at the other. The streets were narrow and cobblestoned, so we left the car and walked. The one-story houses backed blank walls against the street. There were no cars, no bicycles and no people. Two children scampered out of sight around a corner.

We found an inn. Groucho spoke with confidence and fluency in what he called Plattdeutsch. The proprietor was delighted. His wife, as large and friendly as himself, brought a most wonderful chicken soup, summer sausage, Meunster cheese, black bread and beer. As his command of the language grew more flexible, Groucho had them laughing.

"I wonder if he knows who you are?" Melinda asked. But, "nein," they had never heard of the Marx Bros., never seen the movies. Groucho tried to explain. One had a mop of hair and played the harp, another was a short Italian fellow who played the piano—with an orange. "Nein." Then Groucho did himself. He put his cigar in his mouth, glided around the room in his lope. They laughed. He wriggled his eyebrows. They laughed again, but they did not recognize.

The food had been excellent, the proprietor and his wife had been friendly and perhaps there was a small measure of relief in not having a reputation to uphold.

. . . Two young women with babies had come out of their houses. A few sentences had them laughing and blushing. They went with us to point the way to the church.

We stayed a long time in the churchyard, looking at the headstones, and then a long time inside the church with the pastor. We found nothing. There was nothing of Minnie; nothing of her family; nothing of her life before she left Dornum; no record of any kind of the family that remained behind.

As the group left the village, Groucho was surrounded by townspeople who were laughing at his every gesture.

In late summer of 1957, Groucho and Eden were finally getting settled in their new house. Melinda, an impressionable eleven, was dreading her upcoming appearance on the television show. The nation might find her an adorable sprite, but her classmates were less admiring.

Miriam, back in California, her marriage over, had recently committed herself as a patient at Mt. Sinai Hospital. On the same floor was her father's friend, Oscar Levant.

Sunny, her childhood friend, had been married in 1953 and was now living in an apartment complex in the mid-Wilshire area of Los Angeles.

"They would let her come out and visit me at Park La Brea," Sunny said. "She would take a cab to see me. Miriam would have to call when she was going back. She came to see me three times, and each time she didn't get back on time. On her last visit, she was in the bathroom for forty-five minutes. After she left, the hospital called and asked what she had taken at my house. She had no sooner returned there than she passed out. I figured the only thing she could have taken was sleeping pills. They wouldn't let her come anymore."

When Sunny went to visit her at the hospital, Miriam requested that her friend bring her a bottle of salad dressing. This Sunny did, only to discover later that Miriam was using the bottle to hide the vodka that was being sneaked into the hospital for her by others.

Miriam sought oblivion primarily with alcohol, but occasionally with drugs. When, a few years ago, Sunny asked Miriam if she had ever tried marijuana, Groucho's daughter answered, "I'm an addictive personality, and I don't need something else to become addicted to."

Miriam also spent some time at a state-operated institution after Groucho had issued an ultimatum that either she commit herself to the state mental hospital or he would have nothing more to do with her. In a bitter letter, she accused him of not loving her. Groucho caustically answered that if this were true, he wouldn't have spent over $100,000 on psychiatrists for her care. Yet here Miriam had the last word. When she answered her father's letter, she corrected his grammar. She too could strike at vulnerable points.

During this period, another member of his family was also in sad straits. The September 7, 1957, issue of *TV Guide* reported:

377

Groucho, Chico and Harpo Marx will reunite on TV in a humorous history of Manhattan—a single show, to be their last ever as a team. Two of them don't want to do this one, but the third needs money very badly.

Chico's financial picture was so dismal that he was reduced to accepting a one-thousand-dollar fee for an appearance on "Playhouse 90."

In October, Groucho and John Guedel won their tax case. They were allowed to take all of the proceeds from their sale of the television show as capital gains, as they had originally done. Chico was also about to make peace with the government to which he owed $77,564 in back taxes. His brothers put up the $25,000 which the government accepted in partial settlement. He would also be required to turn over all his earnings in excess of $7,000 yearly for the next five years. Drew Pearson wrote a column about Chico's dilemma, describing the heart condition which had forced him to withdraw from the summer stock circuit the previous year. Pearson called for new tax laws which would permit actors to depreciate their reservoirs of talent just as oil men were allowed a depletion allowance.

Periodically, in order to raise quick money, Chico would be forced to sell his membership to Hillcrest, but his brothers kept buying it back for him.

Groucho himself was better fixed than ever, thanks in good part to the acumen of his stockbroker, Salwyn Shufro. "In spite of his insecurity," Shufro recalled, "Groucho was not averse to taking good risks. He didn't take his earnings after taxes and put them in a sock. He was willing to take any reasonable chance. I think he would have been a very fine businessman. His thinking from the standpoint of business dealings and economics was also along good lines. In discussions with Groucho, he would talk about companies in which he had an interest.

"He never let any of his political beliefs influence his investments," Shufro said in answer to my question. I was curious to determine if, for example, Groucho, because of his political beliefs, refused to invest in the war machine. "I think his economic position may have helped influence his politics. While Groucho may have espoused causes that were not right from an economic point of view, if it came to a point where it jeopardized his economic position he would try to protect it. In financial matters, if not in his approach to romance, he didn't permit his heart to rule his head."

His current sponsors, much as they liked Groucho, were being forced to take a hard-headed look at "You Bet Your Life" after an eight-year association. The five-thousand-dollar DeSoto was a moderately expensive product for the time, beyond the financial reach of most of the mass audience which consistently put the show in the Top Ten. And the car was not selling well.

So the show's producers and Chrysler reached an agreement by which Chrysler would abandon sponsorship. Waiting in the wings was Lever Brothers whose Toni Home Permanents division was eager to sponsor "You Bet Your Life." Western shows had begun to dominate television. By 1959, there were thirty-two such shows on the three networks, all produced on considerably higher budgets than Groucho's show and geared to a predominantly male audience, which didn't buy home permanents. Lever Brothers signed on as sponsor for the program's upcoming ninth season.

Groucho's services were still much in demand. He was offered $100,000 for a two-week appearance in Las Vegas. He turned it down, saying, "I don't want to work for hoodlums and gangsters." Rudolf Bing from the Metropolitan Opera Company asked him to appear as Frosch, the drunken jailer, in *Die Fledermaus*, offering Groucho $1,000 for each of four performances over four months. Groucho felt he would be losing money on the deal, so the four nights at the opera were also turned down.

He was happier staying at home to entertain Goodman Ace, who was in Southern California on a screenwriting assignment. When he learned that Ace was coming to California, Groucho told him their friendship would end if Ace didn't accept his invitation to stay at his house.

The morning he arrived, Ace found Groucho seated at breakfast. An attendant came through the room, carrying Ace's suitcase, a small briefcase, and a portable typewriter.

379

"Well," Groucho observed, "three bags. How long are you staying?"

At that point the maid offered Ace some orange juice. After he drank it, she asked if he wanted more. Ace declined with thanks.

"I'm glad," Groucho said. "Oranges don't grow on trees, you know," With that, Groucho handed Ace a key to the back door. "We don't like writers coming in the front," Groucho told him. And Ace was a *welcome* guest.

Miriam was out of the hospital during Ace's visit, and the two spent some time together. Noticing her careless dress, Ace asked Groucho why he didn't buy his daughter some clothes. To his friend's surprise, Groucho seemed indifferent to Miriam's shabby appearance. Ace took her to downtown Beverly Hills and bought her a new outfit.

In the future, Miriam would in large part have to cope on her own with her many demons. Groucho set up a small trust fund for her, and his daughter lived off its income. When she wasn't institutionalized for her ongoing alcoholism, she lived in a small house in Culver City, occasionally with a female companion.

Groucho of the liberal bent could profess a vast love for all mankind. He was proud that he actually never insulted contestants on the quiz show. Yet he was unable to show similar consideration in his vastly more important personal relationships, and Miriam had proven to be the most tragic victim of his insensitivity.

He was not a loving man. Nor, as he was well aware, did he inspire the blind devotion that Chico and Harpo did. Gravely ill and close to bankruptcy, Chico in August, 1958, married actress Mary Dee after a sixteen-year courtship. His new wife had waited that long to marry him. Harpo's son Bill also noted that Groucho seemed jealous of his parents' happy marriage.

He functioned much more effectively before the public, and this realization must have been the stimulus that sent him out on tour in *Time for Elizabeth* year after year.

"I'm sorry you didn't get a chance to see the show," he wrote Abel Green of *Variety* that summer. "In the last two years I played seven weeks of straw hat and broke the house record in each theatre. The money I give to the government, but the laughter I get still rings in my ears. That's one thing Uncle Sam can't take away from me."

The camaraderie of the troupe recalled his old touring days in vaudeville, and Groucho enjoyed the climate of solidarity. Still, it was an arduous grind and his energies often flagged. "After the show the whole group would get together at a delicatessen or a night spot to have dinner," Robert Allen recalled. "The only time I saw Groucho being mean—which wasn't really mean—was on one of those occasions. We were at some club after the show. This group of World War II veterans—fourteen or sixteen guys with their wives—were there. One of the veterans came up to Groucho and asked if he'd come to their table and say a few words. Groucho was very tired and begged off. Later when we were leaving, these veterans stood up and booed us. Groucho lifted up his coat tails and bent over and poked his ass at them, as if to say, 'Kiss my ass!' But he didn't say it. He made the gesture and left. But that was the only time in the many weeks we were together that I ever saw him do anything ungracious. He was not a mean person. Everything he said was in fun. A lot of other comedians can get humor out of making someone feel bad, but that wasn't Groucho's style."

Groucho was both tired and depressed as he returned for a new television season with a different sponsor. He was beginning to have serious doubts about the show's staying power. His apprehensions were later proven right, for the decline of the show started in this, its ninth season. "I've given up trying to understand the peculiar thinking that TV is infested with," Groucho wrote Dr. Bergen Evans. "It makes me laugh when I read Jack Gould, John Crosby and all the other earnest 'uplifters.' No one gives a damn what they write. The air is now completely filled with inanity. The country is full of jerks, and they're now getting exactly what they deserve."

Evans wrote in reply, "I would join you in damning the jerks were it not for the healthy rating and vigorous continuance of *You Bet Your Life.* Someone, somewhere, still knows a good thing."

(The viewers would briefly return to Groucho and his show in greater numbers. Revelations late in 1958 that the big money quiz shows had fraudulently supplied answers to some contestants virtually finished them off.)

Because he was basically a malcontent, Groucho would find fault wherever he looked, and since the bulk of his time was spent with Eden, she bore the brunt of his frustrations. Yet she couldn't have been the reason for his recurring churlishness. "The wife was so lovely," Robert Allen recalled. "He had opportunities when we were on tour, but Groucho never played around. Eden was a beauty and he was very much in love."

Groucho simply refused to admit the possibility that he was growing old. Having a much younger wife may have precluded that. He was dissipating his energies in stage appearances, the television show, guest shots, and the finishing of his autobiography.

Writing without Arthur Sheekman's collaboration proved to be considerably more enervating than he had anticipated. He had taken great pride that *Groucho and Me* was unghosted, a claim he couldn't make for his previous books. The experience left him with even greater respect for writers. In answer to a letter from Leo Rosten, he wrote:

> In your note you said it [writing] was a tough struggle and, as a budding author who has just said his farewell to literature, I know exactly how you feel. It's like giving birth to triplets with no one around to help except the midwife's husband, who is a carpenter by trade.

In the spring of 1959, the three Marx Brothers were reunited for their umpteenth farewell performance, a half-hour comedy on television's "General Electric Theatre," called "The Incredible Jewel Robbery." Because the show was telecast on CBS and Groucho was under contract to NBC his cameo appearance couldn't be advertised.

The comedy, performed in pantomime, was a dismal exercise, the joint career of the brothers ending with hardly a laugh. "As the film progressed," Harriet Van Horne wrote in the *New York World Telegram*, "the absence of dialog grew more irksome. A few bits of business were original and witty, but the mocking hilarity of the old days was missing.

"Also missing was the mad, glad, bad brother, Groucho. True, he made a sudden, surprise appearance in the very last scene. But he was late by some 27 minutes."

In that same month of March, Groucho's autobiography was published. It hit the best seller lists for a few weeks, although few reviewers found its prosaic prose to be great literature. *Groucho and Me* was a chatty book, sparing with the one-liners and occasionally straying from the facts. Although he had begun writing the book for Little, Brown and Company, *Groucho and Me* was ultimately published by a new house, Bernard Geis Associates, of which Groucho was a five-percent owner.

The upcoming summer tour in *Time for Elizabeth* would be Groucho's last. Before embarking on it, he wrote a farewell letter of sorts to Edward R. Murrow, who was taking a one-year sabbatical from his duties at CBS. The two men first met by electronic means in the early 1950s, when Groucho and Melinda appeared on "Person to Person," Murrow's interview show. Groucho's penchant for writing letters to people he admired, even though he may not have met them as yet, invariably led to an actual person-to-person meeting. He continued a friendly correspondence with Murrow, Groucho typically making handwritten amendments and corrections on the letters his secretary Dorothy typed for him.

"You say you are glad you're going to be away for a year," Groucho wrote Murrow. "Well, I've got news for you (as Leo Durocher so ineptly starts every statement), no one else is!

"You may or may not know what a severe loss your voice will be to liberty, democracy, the American flag and prostitution on radio. Anybody that's worth a damn is going to miss you. Don't stay away too long. We can ill afford to lose you.

"I can't send you my love because I understand you're not a female. However, if you should happen to journey through Denmark on your travels, and get fixed, we would certainly have a common meeting ground."

The summer tour was not a particularly happy one. Nunnally Johnson had moved with his family to Italy for a film assignment, and Groucho wrote him about the misadventure:

I just returned from a triumphant tour of midwestern slums. In Chicago I played a tent. This tent had more holes in it than the play. It rained fairly often. One night the rain was so loud and steady, accompanied by thunder and lightning and the cursing of the audience (who were getting a good rooking not only at the box office but also from the holes in the roof) that we were obliged to move the show over to an adjoining ballroom in the Edgewater Beach Hotel.

In the same letter, Groucho told Johnson that Norman Krasna also was on the move: "Krasna is selling his house, a few of his children and most of his possessions and is moving to Switzerland ... I give him two years." The prediction was incorrect. Krasna to this day resides in Switzerland. Johnson remained in Europe for nine years, in which time he made several more films.

At the same time that Johnson and Krasna were settling in Europe, Chico was also there on tour. He was scheduled for a vaudeville stand of England, as well as for appearances on BBC radio and television shows.

A London-datelined story in the *New York World Telegram* quoted him as saying, "I guess I have lost around two million dollars gambling. I had money. I lost it—Las Vegas, the races, women.

"The first crap game I played I lost $17,000 in one night. But I learned as I went along. In time I was able to lose more than that.

"Now Groucho is rich. He never went to Las Vegas. But he spends cash other ways. His present wife is the third."

Within hours, Chico was forced to cancel his appearances because of attacks of nausea. He had not mentioned during the interview that he had been suffering from a stomach disorder since his arrival in England six days previously. The tour was abandoned and Chico and his wife Mary returned to Los Angeles, so that he could recuperate at home.

On a larger front, television too needed a recuperating period. The quiz show scandals had left such a blot on the industry that even a scrupulously honest show like "You Bet Your Life" got a going-over from government investigators. The only area where chicanery might be possible was in the dual responsibilities of Marion Pollock, who, in addition to compiling the quizzes, also

Groucho, photographed at the radio studio where "The Circle" originated. The show was a full-hour variety series on the NBC Red Network in the late 1930's. (Paul Wesolowski Collection)

The brothers surround their secretary, Rachel Linden, whom they stole from producer-screenwriter Herman Mankiewicz. (Paul Wesolowski Collection)

A scene from *At the Circus*. (John Tefteller Collection)

With Diana Lewis, William Powell's actress wife, in a scene from *Go West*. (John Tefteller Collection)

Harpo, director Charles Reisner, and Groucho on the set of *The Big Store*. (John Tefteller Collection)

Groucho with his second wife Kay, who had a bit part in *Copacabana.* (Henry Golas Collection)

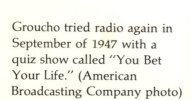

Groucho tried radio again in September of 1947 with a quiz show called "You Bet Your Life." (American Broadcasting Company photo)

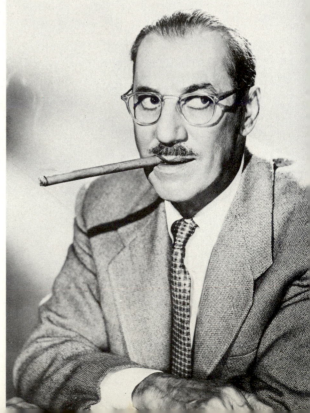

Groucho guest-starred in January, 1949 on "Kraft Music Hall" with Al Jolson and Oscar Levant. (Paul Wesolowski Collection)

Announcer George Fenneman was described by Groucho as one of the great straight men in the business. (National Broadcasting Company photo)

Groucho with his third wife Eden and daughter Melinda. (John Tefteller Collection)

Phil Silvers and Groucho meet with George Grant Burnside, curator of Grant's Tomb. (National Broadcasting Company photo)

The so-called Laughing Cavalier. (Bernie Smith Collection)

Melinda appeared on the quiz show a dozen times during its fourteen-year run. Here she dances with Gene Nelson. (National Broadcasting Company photo)

General Omar Bradley, Groucho, and producer Bernie Smith after the General appeared as a contestant on the quiz show. (Bernie Smith Collection)

Groucho served as interim host on "The Tonight Show" after the departure of Jack Paar during the summer of 1962. The five brothers appeared on one of the shows. (Paul Wesolowski Collection)

Groucho with contestant Sarita Pelkey. (John Tefteller Collection)

The new host of "The Tonight Show," Johnny Carson, was introduced by Groucho.

With Eden in the Bob Hope
Chrysler Theatre production
of *Time for Elizabeth*, a play
Groucho wrote with Norman
Krasna.

Melinda and Harpo's son Bill, a
pianist-composer, were both
signed to recording contracts by
the same company in 1965. (Bill
Marx Collection)

Erin Fleming and Groucho.
(Photo by Frank Diernhammer)

On his eighty-fifth birthday.
(Photo by Frank Diernhammer)

—still thumbing his nose at
convention. (Photo by George
Fenneman)

The voracious reader—(Photo by Richard Berman)

One of Groucho's last public appearances, the book publishing party honoring Hollywood columnist James Bacon. He is seen with Cindy Williams, Bacon, and Henry Winkler. (John Tefteller Collection)

Nat Perrin, Groucho's long-time friend who was named temporary conservator during the much-publicized court fight during Groucho's final illness, is kissed by Lois Marx as her husband Arthur looks on. (Copyright 1977, *The Santa Monica Evening Outlook*, Reprinted with Permission)

(Photo by George Fenneman)

interviewed prospective contestants. Her interviewing duties were reassigned to other members of the program staff, with Miss Pollock continuing to phrase the questions. Guidelines later published by the Federal Communications Commission forbade those who framed questions to have any dealings with the contestants.

In a letter to Norman Krasna in December of 1959, Groucho wrote:

I remember two distinct times when you were terribly angry with me. This was when we had two Congressional Medal of Honor winners on our show and neither of them won as much as a Swiss franc. It's a good thing I didn't yield to your blandishments or I would now be in some Federal Court, perjuring myself under oath. I don't quite know why I remained honest, for I spring from a long line of thieves. I guess I was just plain lucky.

Curiously enough, the disappearance of all the big money quiz shows has boosted my stock considerably. The last Nielsen rating had me top man on the totem pole which included "Playhouse 90," Goody Ace's "Big Party" and "The Untouchables."

Any feelings of lassitude evaporated. A revived Groucho was ready to take on other challenges. He gave little more than passing notice to the precipitous drop the show suffered shortly thereafter in the ratings.

Early in 1960, he wrote Nunnally Johnson, now living in London:

I have been engaged by the Bell Telephone Company (whose rates, incidentally, have gone up three times in the past two years) to portray Ko-Ko in *The Mikado*. They call it "institutional advertising." Translated, this means that a few of the executives will get a chance to screw one or more of the Three Little Maids from School.

Incidentally, Melinda is going to be one of the three little maids, and I plan on keeping a sharp eye on her. There'll be no "Lolita" stuff if I can help it.

At the conclusion of this 54-minute rape of Gilbert and

385

Sullivan, I predict that thousands of people will not only have their telephones disconnected permanently, but will also have their TV sets removed.

This is a foolish enterprise that I have consented to embark upon, but they're giving me so much money I didn't have the heart to turn it down. I won't get to keep much of it, but I can look at the check as it passes swiftly by me.

Actually, according to Goddard Lieberson, Groucho was delighted that he would be finally interpreting his revered Gilbert and Sullivan before a mass audience. He was pleased as well that Lieberson decided to record the performance for Columbia Records.

"Helen Traubel could have taken the place of Margaret Dumont," he said of the operatic soprano who sang the lovelorn Katisha. "She loved to laugh. Traubel's was a Wagnerian laugher. Her tones were shattering. While recording, we were all laughing."

Lieberson was in London on a business trip when the abridged version of *The Mikado* aired on April 29, 1960, and consequently was unable to see the impressive performance director Martyn Green extracted from Groucho. His Ko-Ko was faithful to the spirit of the masters, yet the Groucho mannerisms were suggested—if somewhat economically—so that the public would know who the funny man was beneath the bald pate and layers of makeup.

Reviews were nevertheless mixed. Some accused Groucho of turning arty, unaware of his lifelong passion for Gilbert and Sullivan. As Harpo's son Bill put it, "I used to love to watch his face when he would do Gilbert and Sullivan. It was his own special heaven." Groucho was consequently unperturbed by the critics' conclusions, for there were two important groups which apparently found his performance more than adequate. "The sponsors were delirious with joy," he wrote Lieberson, "and the rating was the highest they had all season. The gratifying part of it was that we had a bigger rating the second half than we had the first. So apparently the audience stuck with it all the way." The Bell Telephone Company, in confirmation of the enthusiasm Groucho's performance generated, asked if he would consider performing

The Pirates of Penzance the following season. The offer was taken under advisement.

On the same day that *The Mikado* was telecast, the *New York Times* reported that NBC was renewing the quiz show, even though Lever Brothers was dropping out as its sponsor at the end of the summer rerun season. Though another sponsor was quickly signed, Groucho took Lever's defection as his cue. Over the summer, he decided that the upcoming season would be his final one with the show.

He spent much of the summer alone, cancelling a trip to New York he had planned with his wife, because—as he wrote Goddard, "Eden has signed on with some moth-eaten group of hams to appear nightly as Columbine with some seedy and half-assed Pierrot."

They were now in their sixth year of marriage, and Groucho had reverted to the same baiting that had so decimated his previous wives. Eden proved to be adaptable and unruffled. "I thought she was dopey for a long time," Harpo's son Bill said. "After a while I may have still thought she was dopey, but she was dopey smart. She always did what she wanted to do. She took up painting and crafts. Mother became very fond of her. They went to the Orient together. Eden did a damn good job of raising Melinda. She's not a malicious human being. In fact, she's a very honorable lady, and I like her.

"When Groucho would say something relative to her stupidity— 'Be quiet. You don't know anything anyway'—I used to want to crawl under the table. I never could understand why he didn't have a literary person as his wife. I saw him insulting her at her most vulnerable point. Yet I saw how she was able to completely extricate herself, to continue doing what she wanted to do."

The nominating conventions of 1960 were both the high and the low spots of Groucho's summer. He followed them avidly. "I'm goggle-eyed," he wrote Goodman Ace. "Until TV nobody knew the calibre of the clowns that govern the country. It's impossible to observe these chowder heads in action with their funny hats and balloons without feeling sure we're destined to go the way of Rome, Greece and big time vaudeville . . .

"I read a very interesting quote by Senator Kerr of Oklahoma. In summing up Ike he said, 'Eisenhower is the only living unknown soldier.' Even this is giving him all the best of it.

"Personally I hope both parties lose the election. If I vote at all, my vote will go to Casey Stengel for President. Incidentally, it looks like those dirty bastards at the stadium are going to win the pennant again and this is the real reason why I'm not coming to New York until the World Series is over.

"Melinda is at summer camp and our house is now as quiet as the balcony of the Fulton Theatre when *Time for Elizabeth* was playing there.

When he resumed filming the quiz show in the fall, NBC changed the show's name to "The Groucho Show." Despite the gesture, Groucho was determined this would be its last season. He overcame his aversion to the Palm Springs house, joining Eden there more often than in the past. He was seventy years old and needed the rest.

"I have a small hovel in Palm Springs," he wrote Nunnally Johnson, "and, to get away from it all, I frequently go down there, and whack a golf ball. We also have two poodles, Dreamboat and Soto. Dreamboat is housebroken. Soto has to be taken for a walk. When I'm in town, I take him in the car, run him up the hill and sit there until he does something. If I don't take him up the hill he will only discharge himself (from both ends) in front of the refrigerator in the kitchen. Last week, while we were in the Springs, Sarah (our maid) called to inform us that the stench in the kitchen was becoming unbearable. She added, 'I am getting too old to walk Soto up the hill.' The rest of her statement was an ultimatum. As you can see, it was quite a problem. However Eden (that's my wife) solved it neatly and quickly. At a certain time each afternoon a Yellow Cab appeared at the front door, the driver picked up Soto, drove him up the hill and waited until he'd done his stuff. This worked out fine. Eden's taxi bill for the week we were in the Springs (for the dog in Beverly Hills) came to fifty-one dollars ... This means that instead of her getting a brand new hundred-dollar bill for Christmas, she gets only $49.00. I don't like

388

to say we're going Hollywood, for that is such a tired and weary expression—but I doubt if there's a poodle anywhere in the U.S. or Europe who is picked up in a Yellow Cab each afternoon just so he can discharge his obligations. I hope this never happens to you—or your dog.

"Actually, Soto has two problems. On his way up the hill to answer nature, he has to pass a house where there is a female poodle in heat. This confuses him quite a bit for I've been told by medical authorities that it is virtually impossible to have a bowel movement while you are crazed with lust."

That December, a film project was suggested to the three brothers, and it was so intriguing that it looked as if they would be reuniting for yet another picture. Director Billy Wilder had been shooting *The Apartment* on location in New York at a time when the world's eyes were focused on Russian Premier Nikita Khrushchev's shoe-pounding demonstrations at the United Nations. During discussions with his collaborator, screenwriter I.A.L. Diamond, Wilder suggested the possibility of a picture starring the Marx Brothers. While the city's police were guarding the UN, the Marx Brothers would pull a robbery at Tiffany's. The two men prepared a forty-page treatment and showed it to the brothers when they returned to California.

All three were enthusiastic about the proposed film, to be called *A Day at the United Nations*. For one thing, in Wilder they would have a top-notch director. Groucho didn't think they'd had a good one since Leo McCarey supervised the filming of *Duck Soup*. The long preproduction phase began.

Harpo, who had made numerous appearances with Chico so that his older brother could continue to command an income, was currently working alone. His autobiography, *Harpo Speaks!*, had just been published, and he was extensively promoting it on television shows . . . including Groucho's. He had also appeared in a dramatic role on a television series, in which his son Bill made his acting debut.

As "You Bet Your Life" wound down in late spring of 1961, plans were announced for a new television show starring Groucho, to be called "What Do You Want?" Groucho didn't regard the project with much enthusiasm, although it reassured him to know that he was still in demand.

"Wednesday night, the 17th of May," he wrote Norman Krasna, "I will wind up a 14-year career as the world's most prominent quiz master. No tears will be shed by yours truly. It's done wonders for me, psychologically and financially. Physically and mentally the show has always been a romp. It's rather odd not having anything facing me after this last show. I've had a number of offers to do different TV shows and also received a play from George Axelrod which I immediately returned. I am too old to be holed up in a second-rate hotel in New Haven, and at three in the morning, loaded with Seconal and Dexamil, to be contributing my feeble best to rewriting the second act curtain and the entire third act."

CHAPTER THIRTEEN

For solitude sometimes is best society,
And short retirement urges sweet return.

John Milton, Paradise Lost

The next few years would prove to be anticlimactic. Groucho's ambivalence toward performing was never more evident. On the one hand, he professed to want more leisure time. On the other, his ego required that he still be in demand, and the most tangible proof of his desirability was the money offers that continued to flood in. He needed to know he was still able to make a living, despite holdings reputed to be in excess of $12,000,000.

The ham in him won out. He would continue recycling his act, while allowing it little fresh input. Any efforts he made to show his versatility were merely token. If within every comedian there lurks a dramatic actor, the desire in Groucho was deeply submerged.

The proposed heist film with Billy Wilder was a case in point. As the screenplay developed, Groucho would play the brains behind the mob of thieves. Chico would be the strong arm of the gang, and Harpo would play a safecracker. They would dynamite their way into Tiffany's and abscond with four suitcases filled with diamonds. Then they would make their getaway on a tramp steamer headed for Brazil.

But the police would interrupt their flight and, mistaking the brothers for the Latvian delegation, would escort them to the UN, where Harpo would address the delegates in pantomime, while four simultaneous translators offered differing interpretations of his horn-tooting and blonde-chasing.

The parallels with *A Night at the Opera*, as well as with other Marx Brothers pictures, were obvious. Yet, if any director could bring the proper fresh view to the enterprise, it was Billy Wilder. His outrageous humor had most recently evinced itself in two major successes, *Some Like It Hot* and *The Apartment*.

In the recent past, Harpo had jeopardized his own health to appear with Chico, who desperately needed the money. Groucho, too, made appearances as part of the team as a favor to Chico.

Now that Harpo and Groucho needed Chico for a project *they* wanted to do, Chico was unable to return the favor. Four days after "You Bet Your Life" aired for the last time, Chico was rushed to the hospital. His ailment was not publicly disclosed. Statements to the press termed it "chest congestion." Because of his past history of heart trouble, it was feared that he had had a heart attack. While spokesmen tried to minimize the seriousness of his illness, Chico was actually indeed gravely ill, having suffered from the arteriosclerosis he had suffered from for the past five years now further complicated by edema.

Wilder and his associates had ample reason for wanting to quash talk of a heart attack. The illness would make Chico uninsurable, and no studio would start a $4,000,000 picture with one of its main stars so sorely afflicted.

Chico was as disappointed as his brothers when it was decided they could not appear in the Wilder film. Yet it may have been for the best, for it is doubtful that either Harpo or Groucho still had the stamina to perform in so physically demanding a picture. Wilder was equally unhappy, for he could not see any other comedians in the roles, and the project was scrapped.

If Groucho was not going to return to films, it looked as if he wasn't going back to television either. For the first time in twelve years, Groucho's name was not on NBC's fall roster. Rumors—unfounded as usual—had it that he might return to ABC in a reincarnation of "You Bet Your Life," whatever its name. They would be proven wrong.

A rumor which had a more direct bearing on his everyday life, however, was substantiated. Groucho's son Arthur would be divorcing his wife to marry his brother-in-law's wife, Lois Kahn. The two had been conducting an off-and-on romance for several years.

The two Kahn children had married at about the same time, early in 1943. Donald's bride was Lois Goldberg, a beautiful girl whose father worked for a local brokerage firm.

In *Son of Groucho*, Arthur noted Groucho's initial acceptance of the affair. This turned to opposition when the two decided to divorce their respective mates to marry each other. Groucho's son thought his mother-in-law, Grace Kahn, may have been the person who talked his father into changing his mind. "I don't remember that Groucho and I ever talked about it," Mrs. Kahn said.

Her daughter Irene similarly didn't recall discussing the situation with Groucho. "He never talked to me about the divorce," she said. "It was a slight embarrassment between us. Neither of us knew *what* to say. Groucho continued to invite me over to his house with the children."

It is not unlikely that Groucho came to oppose their marriage on his own. He may have seen himself in competition with his son and in peril of losing in the greatest game of all. It's possible that he resented and envied Lois's devotion to Arthur and her ferocity of purpose. Certainly, no woman in his life had risked as much for him as his prospective daughter-in-law was risking for his son.

Groucho could not justifiably point to the psychological damage this remarriage might cause Arthur's two sons and Lois's daughter. He had created enough with *his* children.

Had Lois been a much younger starlet about town, Groucho could have better understood his son's infatuation. He might have resigned himself to their eventual marriage. But Lois was a woman of Arthur's social class, and several years older than her future husband to boot. Groucho might understand their infatuation, but he could not admit their love. It was too awkward to deal with, and

Groucho had never borne discomfort with any great patience. Groucho removed himself from the matter when he flew to New York in early June of 1961 to attend the funeral of George S. Kaufman.

The playwright had died on a Friday, and that same night, Dick Cavett, then a writer for television's "Tonight Show" was sent to the Blue Angel to scout a young comedian named Woody Allen. The two young men—with a wealth of show business knowledge and a love of comedy in common—became immediate friends. They discussed Kaufman's death that day. Although neither had known him personally, they felt compelled to pay their respects at the funeral. Allen, however, had a previous engagement, so Cavett went alone. Later, he described the experience in *Cavett*, the book on which he collaborated with Christopher Porterfield:

> About halfway through the eulogy I happened to notice that the man across from me was holding an unlit cigar, and at the other end of the arm holding the cigar was Groucho Marx. I sat there numbly staring at him. He suddenly did a characteristic lip-moistening mannerism that I'd seen a million times on "You Bet Your Life," and I had that thrill you get when there is nothing but air between you and, yes, an idol.
>
> Later, on the sidewalk, I stood near him, and heard a woman say, "Hello, Groucho, I'm Edna Ferber." I could hear the famous voice respond, but missed the words ... Groucho was joined on the sidewalk at Eighty-first and Madison by Brooks Atkinson and Abe Burrows. I watched them stroll toward Fifth Avenue, wishing I was someone in show business so I could join them. Then I decided, "To hell with it. I will anyway. I write for the *Tonight Show*, don't I?" As I neared the corner, with too-contrived timing Atkinson and Burrows both left Groucho alone. I approached and said, "Hello, Groucho. I'm a big fan of yours." Groucho said, "If it gets any hotter I could *use* a big fan," and we were off.

As they walked toward the Plaza Hotel, where Groucho was staying, the two men got acquainted. To Cavett's surprise, Groucho invited him to lunch.

In the Oak Room, Groucho asked a waiter, "Do you have any fruit? I mean *besides* the head waiter."

Cavett said he liked an epigram Groucho had chosen for his latest book. He quoted the La Rochefoucauld maxim in the original French. "You speak very good French," Groucho observed. "In fact, it's so good you could only have learned it in a whorehouse."

The two quickly became friends. Groucho, who came to New York to lay to rest one friend, returned to California having made another.

Within two weeks, Arthur and Lois had their quickie Mexican divorces and were married. Irene was remarried at the same time to Lenny Atkins, a violinist. His former daughter-in-law continued to be welcome in Groucho's home. Lois was not as enthusiastically accepted, and she wondered if trying to win over Groucho was worth the effort.

Groucho's attentions were now focused on future professional plans. He had recently turned down offers to appear in two upcoming stage productions, *A Funny Thing Happened on the Way to the Forum* and *Young Enough to Know Better*. "If I were ten years younger I might have tackled one of these assignments, but I am old enough to know better," he wrote Norman Krasna. "If it's a hit, you're trapped in what is probably one of the world's worst climates. If it flops, suicide seems like a very pleasant solution."

He had been out of the television-viewing public's eye for all of two months when the ninth and final season of summer reruns began in mid-July. As "The Best of Groucho" ended its rerun season, daily syndication of the show started. For the next five years, starting in late September of 1961, there wouldn't be a minute of the broadcast day where his show wasn't being seen somewhere in the country. At this juncture, Groucho was also filming a "General Electric Theatre" production, "The Holdout," on CBS. He wrote Nunnally Johnson:

> This is a far cry from the man who fractured audiences in *Cocoanuts* and *Animal Crackers*. In this little playlet I appear as the father of a young girl, 17, who insists on marrying a boy, 19, who is also out of work. I tried to play the part in the tradition of Lewis Stone and C. Aubrey Smith, who are both dead, and this may do for me what it did for them.

G.E. has some peculiar rules they lay down to the actors. As you know, they manufacture dynamos, turbines, toasters, radios and TV sets, and it's only been a few months since some of their head men were indicted by the federal government for fixing prices. In high government circles, this is called "collusion." If it's done by a man who operates a delicatessen, it's just called crookedness. At any rate, one of their dictums is that nobody on their show can smoke a cigar. I tried to question them about this restriction, but they refused to disclose anything that might give me a clue. Maybe they are trying to cripple Castro and the Cuban cigar industry, or maybe they assume that the officers of their company who were indicted were cigar smokers and the mere sight of me smoking a stogie might remind the American public what kind of an outfit has been swindling them all these years.

The CBS appearance preceded his commitment to move his new television show, "Tell It to Groucho," to the network sometime the following year. There would be no turning back, no teaming up again with his brothers. From this point on, the performing Marxes were to be no more. On October 11, 1961, Chico's heart gave out. He was seventy-four.

The *New York Times*, in an editorial, "An Echo of Lost Laughter," expressed the sentiments of millions:

When the news of Chico Marx' death was published millions of Americans had to accept another disturbing fact. The Marx Brothers as a band of slapstick clowns will never play again. Excepting expert comic pantomime on television two years ago, called "The Incredible Jewel Robbery," and grossly unappreciated, they have been going their separate ways for years. Chico amused himself by leading a dance band orchestra.

But while Groucho, Harpo and Chico were all available, there was always an outside chance that they might vandalize the land of cuckoo once more. To theatregoers and moviegoers it seemed simple enough. All Groucho had to do was to paint on that mustache, clamp a cigar in his mouth, and walk with a stoop. All Harpo had to do was slap on the wig, toot the rubber horn and leer at girls. Chico had only to put on the pointed hat and short jacket and shoot the piano keys. Nothing looked simpler.

It can never be. The funniest team of twentieth century mountebanks is broken, beyond repair ... No more. Alas, poor Chico. Alas, ourselves.

On a sweltering October day, the Marxes gathered at the house where Chico and his wife Mary Dee had lived and awaited the limousines which would take them to the services at Forest Lawn Memorial Park. Miriam joined Groucho, Gummo, and her cousin Maxine in one of the funeral cars, much to her father's annoyance. The drive to the services was awkward for them all.

The cortege arrived at Wee Kirk of the Heather Chapel, outside of which a cluster of fans had gathered. In the crowd, incongruously dressed in a full-length mink coat, stood a bloated figure, Groucho's first wife, Ruth. He quietly acknowledged her boozy greeting, then walked on.

That night, Groucho took his son Arthur and his daughter-in-law Lois to dinner at Chasen's. He ordinarily had one drink at most before dinner, but on that occasion, he downed four straight whiskies. Groucho got very drunk. So much of his past had caught up with him that day, not least the memory of the favored oldest brother who had taken a huge bite out of life with such relish and dash while he had settled for crumbs.

Even in death, Chico's recklessness could instill feelings of envy in Groucho. Years later when I asked him about Chico's death and his reaction to it, Groucho inhaled deeply. Because of his respiratory problems, it sounded like a dry, broken whimper.

"Chico used to tell a story," he began. "There's a man in the woods. He hasn't seen a woman in two months. He comes across a log cabin. There's a knot hole in the wall. He sticks his pecker in it. From inside comes a voice: 'Would you mind coming in and fucking out?' "

By mid-November, after a test film for his new television program had been shot, a definite January airing date for "Tell It to

Groucho" was set. An attempt had been made to give the show a new look, the first casualty being George Fenneman. In his place two teenagers, a polite young man and a pretty girl, alternated as the show's announcers.

"I am doing a new show," Groucho wrote Goodman Ace, "which is precisely the same as the old show except that we have traded Mr. Fenneman for a spritely young doll with oversized knockers who leaps around the stage with all the abandon of a young doe being pursued by an elderly banker."

The new format called for an interview-variety show, with guests narrating their stories or problems, then playing the quiz. In essence, it was not much different from "You Bet Your Life."

It was first telecast on January 12, 1962, two days before "The Holdout" was aired by the same network. Harriet Van Horne of the *New York World Telegram* wrote a positive review.

Groucho, in his letter of thanks, wrote without much conviction:

> I think the show has a good chance, although the opposition is about as strong as one can get. I had three years of "The Untouchables" and now CBS has thrown me into a raging sea surrounded by "Dr. Kildare" and "My Three Sons." (I occasionally need a doctor, but not Thursday nights at nine.)

"Tell It to Groucho" lasted for only twenty weeks before it was dropped because of low ratings. Groucho had briefly been considered as the successor to Jack Paar on the "Tonight Show," but he thought it would be too arduous a task for a man his age. He now wondered if he shouldn't have made a greater effort to get the assignment when the possibility had first been raised.

While Melinda, now fifteen, was making her film debut, supporting Ann-Margret in *Bye Bye Birdie*, Groucho went East to test the talk show waters. For the week of August 20, he acted as guest host, one of a series of entertainers to do so until a permanent host for the "Tonight Show" was found. Johnny Carson would ultimately be tapped. Groucho maintained a high level of witty and spontaneous conversation during the week in New York, helped by the appearances of such friends and associates as Harry Ruby,

Lillian Roth, Martyn Green, Betty Comden, and Adolph Green. He was also aided by an appearance by the talented Barbra Streisand.

Each day he had lunch at the Friars Club with Goodman Ace, or with other old friends. In addition, he and Dick Cavett tried to arrange a meeting with Woody Allen, but it didn't work out.

That whole week, as comedians put it, he was on a roll, zingers and *bons mots* tripping easily off his tongue. NBC asked him to extend his hosting duties for an additional week, but he could not accept because of a prior commitment.

When he returned to California, he wrote to the network's Perry Cross, and his hint couldn't have been broader:

> All my friends seemed to like the week I was on very much. Of course, I told them before I left here that I would be magnificent but, as you know, it's very difficult to convince your friends of anything—unless you're terrible.
>
> Now that I've tackled this opus once I believe I could do it again without being apprehensive about it. It's not nearly as tough as I visualized, and your assistance and encouragement went far beyond the call of duty.
>
> . . . At some future date, if feasible and there is no conflict with anything else I may be doing, I could very easily be persuaded to do the show one week a month.

Director George Cukor had approached him about making a guest appearance in *Something's Got to Give*, Marilyn Monroe's aborted last picture. Nunnally Johnson had written one of the scripts, and Groucho sent him his opinion:

> I enjoyed it a lot. Good job, my lad, and I'm sure it will eventually be done. The reason I read the script is because Cukor wanted me to play the hotel clerk. He said it was just a little cameo. (That's the euphemism they now employ when referring to a bit.) Then, as you know, Monroe refused to show up and the whole thing is now back in the bull pen.
>
> I was then offered a part in Stanley Kramer's *Mad, Mad, Mad, Mad World*. Two weeks later I received word they were

replacing me with Ethel Merman. I know show business is a strange profession but ... However, I later saw Merman one night and realized she would be ideal for the part. She has enough balls to get to first base without a hit.

Groucho went on to offer other pleasantries, closing with, "If you hear of any cameo jobs in Europe that would fit Ethel Merman, let me hear from you as soon as possible."

In the meantime, Groucho was on his way to New York where, on October 1, Johnny Carson made his debut as the permanent host of the "Tonight Show." Groucho, in an unbilled appearance, introduced him to late-night audiences.

He wasn't present, however, at an equally momentous occasion the following January at the Pasadena Civic Center. Over the past few years, Harpo had been performing money-raising concerts for various symphony orchestras, wearing his usual khaki pants, white sneakers, tails, and a battered top hat.

Now Harpo had informed fellow performer Allan Sherman— "My Son, The Folksinger"—that this would be his final appearance before the public. After Harpo performed, Sherman took the microphone.

"Ladies and gentlemen," he said. "Harpo Marx has been delighting the world for fifty-six years. What you have just seen—these beautiful minutes we have just spent with Harpo—this was the last—it was Harpo's final—" Sherman, in tears, couldn't continue.

"Three thousand people sat there ... watching a short fat man with glasses crying like a baby," he later wrote about that night. "I couldn't pull myself together and I couldn't leave the stage either. The audience began to mumble. They didn't know what was going on."

Then Harpo came out from the wings. The audience began to applaud. He waved his hands to stop them, and in the soft and gentle voice he had been saving for years, he turned to Sherman and said, "Allan, you're too emotional." Then he turned to those assembled: "Now, as I was about to say in 1907—"

The audience roared. "Say"—Harpo brightened—"I like this talking business. I think I'll start a whole new career." After the laughter and applause died down, Harpo shook his head. No, that wasn't to be. This was, as Sherman was now able to explain, Harpo's final performance.

From the audience came calls of protest: "No ... no!" Harpo shrugged. Then, with Sherman in tow, he walked off the stage.

Throughout 1963, in the absence of any appealing professional offers, Groucho worked on a second book for Bernard Geis, *Memoirs of a Mangy Lover.* Several of the essays on romance had previously been published in humor magazines. Others, which were written in collaboration with Arthur Sheekman, were passed off as Groucho's own.

When the book was published late in the year, Daniel Talbot's review in the *New York Times* may have had the "author" wanting to place the blame on anyone other than himself:

> Sad to report, the book is an atrocity. It consists of several hundred paragraphs strung together, each paragraph a feeble gag about some lecherous horse-play or social *faux-pas.* The punch lines and the structure of the book are a throw-back to his old movies. But it is all so painfully silly that I refuse to believe Groucho had anything to do with it—except to sign the contract.
>
> Who on earth reads books like this? Newts? Or real people? As to the publisher, one can only repeat what Groucho once said of a character played by Margaret Dumont—while bombs whizzed through the windows of the bungalow on the battlefield of "Duck Soup": "At least we're fighting for her honor—which is more than she ever did!"

Geis, in a letter of reply, defended Groucho by saying that he never used a ghostwriter. That the book was, nevertheless, moderately successful is a tribute to the Groucho name and its still considerable appeal.

Groucho was understandably eager to return to performing, and the most intriguing opportunity was provided by the television version of *Time for Elizabeth* on the Bob Hope Chrysler Theatre.

"I was against his doing it on TV," Norman Krasna said. "He committed me to it and I was far away. Jack Benny wanted to do it. There was a time when Groucho as an author should have been happy to have another actor do it. Groucho used it up himself. It was no great tragedy."

"I never worked so hard in my life," Groucho wrote Krasna of the 46-minute production. "We shot 62 pages in five-and-a-half days. I remember the lush days at MGM and Paramount when we all considered the day a triumph if we had one shot in the can by noon. Revue (where the show was shot) operates a good deal like a department store on 14th Street."

His appearance, mercifully, was not extensively reviewed. Kay Gardella of the *New York Daily News* wrote:

Unfortunately, the frothy plot about a high-pressure business-man who escapes the harassment of his pompous boss by retiring to a leisurely life in Florida, is hackneyed, at best. But a few amusing comedy lines, delivered in the biting Marx style, kept the hour from being a total loss ... Also in the cast was Groucho's wife, in real life, that is. She's a tall jungle-type brunette, who carried off her small acting assignment adequately.

Figuring that as a moving target, he couldn't be hit, Groucho was already in England discussing plans for a panel game show, to be called, "The Celebrity Game," when *Time for Elizabeth* aired. Eden would be one of the members of the panel, along with actress Susan Hampshire, writer Kingsley Amis, and Beatles manager Brian Epstein.

The British press descended en masse at a press conference to hear and quote Groucho's celebrated asides. In explaining that he made the trip and the show to see the setup of British television, he added, "... much to the surprise of my wife, who complains that we never go anywhere in June."

Asked his opinion of humor, Groucho replied, "Women don't understand crazy humor such as that of Perelman or Benchley or even the early Marx Brothers. I think our earlier films were funnier than the later ones, but they didn't gross as much as those in which we dragged in a story and a love interest or 'messages.' We just set out to try and be funny. It seems we succeeded in being funny and making a little money . . . though one critic asserted that I was the symbolic embodiment of all persecuted Jews for 2,000 years. What sort of goddamned review is that?"

Only one show was produced, and no new ones were ordered. Of the trip, Groucho recalled two bright spots. The first was dinner with T.S. Eliot and his wife. The two men had been carrying on a correspondence over the last few years, and this would be Groucho's only meeting with the gravely ill American-born poet. The second bright spot involved a London taxi driver. In the course of the small talk which seems to be a part of the occupation, the cabby asked Groucho, "Are you going to Wembley?"

"What's at Wembley?" he asked in return.

"There's a big soccer match."

"I don't understand soccer," Groucho said, beginning to get testy. "I'm a baseball fan."

"The Queen will be there," the cab driver persisted.

At this, Groucho exploded, "Fuck the Queen!"

"Why, sir," the cabby said, "you can't hardly approach her!"

Groucho was doubled over in laughter the rest of the way to his hotel.

On his way back to California, he stopped off in New York to serve as a guest host for one week on the "Tonight Show." His young friend Dick Cavett was still on the writing staff, having been kept on by the Carson forces after Paar's departure. A meeting with Woody Allen was finally arranged.

"Groucho was completely aware of Woody," Cavett recalled. "He was a fan. . . . Groucho would talk seriously and then comically. We all became good friends. Groucho didn't care for old people. He said he couldn't stand any conversation that begins with, 'There's only a few of us left, Groucho.' I always felt he was my age whenever I was with him. He was utterly hip and current. He knew everything that was going on. There were no references that were out of his ken or beyond him. I remember a bizarre lewd monologue he once improvised in the men's room of the Rainbow Grill. It was about a man who went into the men's room and didn't realize Sophia Loren was in the next booth. I can't remember any of it, but it was so bizarre and so funny . . . hilarious, lewd, bizarre, and surreal."

Cavett doesn't recall if the three were ever again together, although both he and Allen saw Groucho separately many times.

"After that," Allen said, "we corresponded and saw one another whenever he was in New York or I was in L.A. I had dinner at his home a few times. Generally our conversations revolved around me asking questions about people he knew . . . about T.S. Eliot . . . and about his early work. The most interesting thing to me, and the most telling, was how surprised he was that the Marx Brothers movies had been taken up over the years by so many intellectuals. He felt the brothers were just a group of vaudevillians who were trying to be funny, to make jokes that worked and didn't have the vaguest relation to any kind of intellectual content.

"Groucho and I never worked together, or traded lines when we were together. I was always real deferential toward him, always drawing him out on stories and anecdotes, and what he had to say about his early films.

"He was very generous with me all the time. I knew he liked me. I immediately related to him on a personal level because he treated me as a member of my own family. The first time I met him at Lindy's, he reminded me of an acerbic Jewish uncle, who you would meet at family gatherings, who makes biting and amusing remarks. But Groucho's remarks were extraordinary."

Groucho returned to California to be the guest host on "The Hollywood Palace." Eden and Melinda stayed on in the East for a few days. During this brief separation from his wife and child, a rumor spread that the anarchic Groucho deliberately set fire to the dining room of director George Cukor, Hollywood's most distinguished host. The truth of the matter was sufficiently amusing without its subsequent embroidery.

Olivia de Havilland had arrived from Paris to star with Bette Davis in *Hush, Hush Sweet Charlotte.* Groucho called and asked if she would like to go to a movie. Miss de Havilland gladly accepted.

In the meantime, Cukor was putting together his guest list for a dinner party honoring Igor Stravinsky. Katharine Hepburn and Miss Davis had already accepted when he called to invite Miss de Havilland.

"I'd love to come," she told Cukor, "but I have a date."

"A beau?" Cukor asked. "Who is he?"

"Well," she hesitantly replied, "it's Groucho Marx."

"Groucho Marx?" Cukor was incredulous. Once he recovered from the surprise, he asked her to bring him.

Miss de Havilland couldn't believe that Groucho had never been invited to Cukor's, since the most noted people in the world had been entertained in the director's showplace home.

After dinner, Cukor recalled, most of the guests retired to the drawing room while Groucho stayed behind to talk with a pretty young girl. When I asked Cukor who she was, he flippantly replied, "Say it was Greta Garbo or Evelyn Nesbit Thaw." (Garbo is a frequent guest at Cukor's when she is in California.)

As Groucho and the girl rose a bit later, he tossed his napkin on the table. Cukor's housekeeper had set out unshaved candles at each place, to be used for lighting cigarettes. The napkin fell on one of the candles. Groucho and his new girlfriend went on to the drawing room where, as Cukor describes it, "We were all being very witty. Oh, yes. Add that Stravinsky was playing *The Firebird.*"

A few minutes later, the butler came in. "He was rather pale," Cukor said. "He whispered to me, 'There's been a fire.'"

"Fortunately, there was a very heavy pad," Cukor said, "and the table was not marred. Groucho never knew he'd ignited the fire. There wasn't any need to tell him."

When Miss de Havilland called to thank her host the following day, Cukor told her about the fire, which was set "by a man who smokes cigars." Cukor, however, bore no grudges. "I truly don't think Groucho's a firebug," he cracked. "Tell him he's invited back any time. I've had the dining room redone in asbestos."

Four days after his "Hollywood Palace" stint, Groucho returned to England to film a commercial for Players Cigarettes. In addition, he signed a thirteen-week contract for a British quiz show, which was to air the following April. He would be getting $40,000 for the stint, and there was a thirty-nine week option on his services at the same proportional salary, should the show be a success.

He had perhaps earned the right to get by on his name by this time. This he was very much doing, for the quality of his performances was uneven at best. But Groucho had to remain in the public eye, even if it meant accepting a considerably lower salary than he'd received on "You Bet Your Life." An element of desperation was creeping into his work. Not wanting to vegetate until his British commitment the following spring, Groucho began discussions in the fall of 1964 with his friend Sidney Sheldon, the producer of a highly successful series, "I Dream of Jeanie," about a situation comedy of his own. His desire to remain a performer, no matter what the cost to his health and image, was beginning to reach manic proportions.

Harpo's reputation had remained intact. He had retired as a beloved man. Yet even he may have retired too late, since his health had begun deteriorating long before his harp was publicly stilled. Now his condition was serious.

Gummo suggested a heart bypass operation, which might solve Harpo's circulatory problems. Susan was opposed to it, but her husband decided to take the chance.

Groucho, as always with those he loved, could not openly express his devotion to his brother in his illness. Yet it came out obliquely in a letter he wrote Harpo shortly before the operation. Groucho's ostensible purpose in writing his brother was to warn him against making a $100,000 investment in a savings and loan association.

Almost as a postscript, he ended the letter, "I'm glad you are in almost perfect physical condition and not tossing the 100 grand into the crumbling sands somewhere east of India will surely help to keep you that way." Groucho's apprehension was skillfully masked.

On September 28, 1964, two days after entering Mt. Sunair Hospital in Los Angeles for the corrective operation, Harpo died, his wife Susan and two of his sons at his bedside. Groucho was inconsolable. Arthur recalls it as the only time he ever saw his father cry.

There was so much Groucho admired in Harpo. He was moved by his brother's gentle ways, his complete lack of malice, the devotion of his wife and adopted children. Groucho might envy Chico's way with his wives and daughter, since he felt Chico was so transparently unworthy of their love, but he could never

406

begrudge Harpo receiving his just due. If Groucho never said the loving words, Harpo the mime hadn't either. Words hadn't been necessary between them in the past. They weren't possible now.

Life, as well as the show, must go on. Harpo's daughter Minnie was persuaded not to cancel her wedding, scheduled for two months after her father's death. Groucho performed the happy-melancholy task of giving the bride away.

In New York, Dick Cavett was making his debut as an entertainer with an appearance at Bitter End West. Soon his articulation and urbanity would mold him into one of television's most promising lights. His strongest champion was Groucho.

"When he really liked something, he became a tout for it," Nat Perrin said. "Like with Dick Cavett. He could never stop talking about this young guy, and he insisted that you see him. I remember vividly the first time I saw Cavett was on a show at noontime. I got a call from Groucho, saying, 'The guy is on now. Tune him in. You'll see.' He was always generous like that with people he liked, and he helped their careers."

Jack Lemmon agreed. "I was always struck by Groucho's appreciation of other people's work. He did not seem as self-absorbed as many performers can be. Whether he was aware of it or not, it was damn nice of him. It was a great lift to young performers who had a chance to meet him, coming from someone who is so high up there."

Lemmon was one of the recipients of Groucho's magnanimity. He became a star in 1953 in his first film, *It Should Happen to You.* Groucho saw the movie at a studio screening and made a point of seeking Lemmon out to tell him what a polished comic actor he was.

"I didn't become a close pal or anything, but I would bump into him from time to time. Then I noticed that at certain times over the years Groucho would suddenly show up at a screening of a film I was in. I slowly got to know him better. I would get a chance to chat with him but never for great lengths of time. But, hell, five minutes of Groucho was like two hours of somebody else, you know, for what you'll get out of it. Although my wife and I never

407

saw him continually, we always considered him a very rare person ... someone we loved to be with."

In the last few years of Groucho's life, when honor was being piled upon honor, Lemmon could always be counted upon to lend his stellar name to the enterprise, whether presenting Groucho with his honorary Oscar or reading from Groucho's writings at charity functions. The older man's expressed admiration in the past came back to him tenfold.

Within his own family, however, Groucho's encouragement wasn't particularly welcome. Since Melinda had started her career on "You Bet Your Life" at the age of five, singing a duet with her father, Groucho had continually pushed her into show business. She was part of the package in several guest appearances he made on variety shows. Melinda was almost nineteen in February, 1965, when she gave an interview to Bob Thomas of the Associated Press. Her Penthouse recording of "The East Side of Town"— strongly reminiscent of Petula Clark's "Downtown"—was getting good air play. Melinda told Thomas that Groucho had maintained a hands-off policy on matters concerning her career. "He's pretty sneaky," she said. "He has always said he thought I had talent and it would be a waste if I didn't do something with it. But he has never wanted to put himself in the position of pushing me into show business."

Not much, since Groucho had already booked his daughter to sing her semi-hit when next he hosted "The Hollywood Palace." Not only was he nurturing her professional career, he also was hovering over Melinda—to her great discomfort—at home.

She was a product of the liberated Aquarian age, and Groucho's thinking was still Victorian. "Those were almost opposite poles of conditioning," Dorris Johnson said. "She was intolerant of her father's attitudes. She thought he was rigid ... and wrong. I must say I agree to a large extent with Melinda. I had children close to her age, and the way I felt about political conditions and the impact of the political scene—the Vietnam thing—certainly altered my attitudes. I was conditioned to the social order that meant sexual experiences usually meant promiscuity. It was the cardinal sin. Well, I changed my opinion, as did most young people. You begin to see evils that are far greater. Melinda felt that. I remember her saying, in defense of premarital sex, 'The arch evil is inflicting pain, not in sharing joy.' "

Unregenerate Groucho derived no such joy from Melinda's attitude. The paternal attention of which he was capable was paid to her, to the exclusion of his two older children and Arthur's two sons. Now, she was drawing away. Her own sense of values was being defined, and in a roundabout way they would be more conventionally oriented toward the home and hearth than Groucho's had ever been. In many ways, Melinda's natural parents declined to be responsible for her rearing. Kay was unable to take responsibility for her upbringing, and Groucho was unwilling to involve himself in the more mundane aspects of raising a child. It was left to Eden to drive Melinda to ballet class and to have conferences with her teachers.

It was hardly a healthy example for Melinda to have to hear her father's denouncement of Eden: "You made a goddamn fool of yourself last night in conversation and you embarrassed me and you didn't know what the hell you were talking about on subjects you have no familiarity with and I attribute this to the fact you were loaded and I always said to you when we sit down at the table don't drink wine after you've had martinis so quit!"

Neither was it a tribute to his love of family that, for nearly thirty years, he spent every Thanksgiving and Christmas with Bert and Charlotte Granet. Nor did it reflect well on him when, lunching one day at Hillcrest with Granet, a boy came up to him and said, "Hello, Groucho."

"Who are you?" he asked.

"I'm your grandson—Andy."

But once reminded, he didn't forget his grandson's face. A few weeks later, while having lunch with Harry Ruby at a delicatessen in Beverly Hills, Andy approached him again.

"I'm ashamed to see you here," his grandfather said.

"How do you think *I* feel?" Andy replied.

It set Groucho to laughing.

A short time later, he went on the Steve Allen show with his two grandsons, who played an original song they had composed. Steve

409

played the banjo and Andy the ukulele. Then Allen talked to the two boys. To his every question Andy answered, "Uh-huh." Groucho was moved to observe, "He's a great conversationalist."

Groucho's grandsons could have been much closer to him, had he made some effort. Arthur hadn't infected them with his attitude toward his father, since Steve and Andy were permanently in Irene's custody. They also didn't have to surmount the obstacle of being related to a legend.

"When I was growing up," Andy recalled, "Groucho was not the superstar he later became. He was a TV star, but a lot of friends had relatives who were TV stars. He didn't become a legend until I was about twenty."

When he returned from his thirteen-week British engagement—the show wasn't renewed—Groucho began putting together his collection of letters which the Library of Congress had requested he donate. Many of them were later published in *The Groucho Letters*.

In the fall of 1965, Arthur scored a tremendous hit on Broadway with his collaboration, *The Impossible Years*. No longer could he remotely be accused of capitalizing on his relationship to Groucho. The play was based on the rebellious exploits of his stepdaughter (née niece), Linda.

Life had finally begun to imitate art. In Arthur's previous play, *Everybody Loves Me*, the plot had revolved about a father whose entertainment career was on the descendant, while his son's was on the rise.

Throughout 1966, this would be true of Groucho and Arthur. A chronic bladder condition hampered Groucho considerably, the first in a series of disabling ailments. His career of necessity slowed down, poor health succeeding in doing what poor notices hadn't.

He did travel to New York late in the year to promote *The Groucho Letters*. Goodman Ace, a columnist for the *Saturday Review of Literature*, wasn't impressed by his literary efforts.

"If you think," Ace told him over the telephone, "that publishing a book of letters that people have written to you makes you a man of letters, you're mistaken."

Groucho hung up. Ace wouldn't let the matter rest when he talked to him a few days later. "And another thing, Groucho. I read

410

your book, *Groucho and Me,* and I thought the writing in it was pedestrian."

"What does that mean?" Groucho asked.

"It means the author should have been hit by a truck."

As much as he liked his friend, Ace had a healthy ego of his own, and he refused to fawn over Groucho. Once, after years of lunching together at the Friars Club, Groucho suggested a change of scene and cuisine. The pair went to an exclusive French restaurant down the street from the Ritz Tower, where the tie-less Groucho was barred from entering. He stood in the foyer, staring daggers at the *maitre d'hôtel.* Finally Groucho said to the man, "I'll never come here again," and he and Ace left. "This is the great Groucho," Ace later observed, "who's never at a loss for words?" Groucho replied, "I couldn't help it. I was too mad to say anything."

Despite Ace's refusal to place Groucho's name among the literati, he was nevertheless admitted to the circle. Perhaps the imprimatur of the Library of Congress was his ticket. Library officials, in explaining why they had requested the letters, told the *New York Times* that "Mr. Marx is part of the American scene and we are not without appreciation of Mr. Marx's humor."

His letters revealed another aspect of his humor. Outrageous as his lines were during public performances, they were safely within boundaries calculated not to offend public opinion. In his correspondence, he could snipe at sponsors, television, and the governemnt, with impunity as well as wit. The more personal references, which have not seen print until now, revealed his ribaldry to be Rabelais turned inward, friends being informed of his latest catastrophe in the bedroom, for which he invariably took responsibility.

In his everday conversation, he had his own bounds of taste. "I never tell dirty stories," he once said, "unless there are ladies present." In fact, Groucho—like his brothers—was a bit of a prude. It took him many years to change his opinion that any woman who used the word "fuck" was not a lady. To his generation, the word still had shock value.

Indeed, in his later years he may have taken greater relish in using the proscribed word, since it was the ultimate forbidden one.

The brothers had come up through vaudeville where performers using the words "hell" or "damn" on the stage were automatically fired. The movie code created similar restrictions. Four-letter words would have introduced a jarring note of reality in their make-believe world. That they still weren't needed was evidenced by the record crowds that attended the Manhattan Gallery of Modern Art's tribute to the Marx Brothers from the spring until early summer of 1967.

A hard core of Marx Brothers fans, among them a number of the world's intellectuals, had kept their films alive. With this retrospective, the revival of the brothers' art before a far wider group could be said to have begun. It was a happy development, yet few of the Marxes—Groucho in particular—anticipated the exuberance their films would incite on college campuses and in movie houses throughout the world.

Groucho and Zeppo, along with their wives, attended the opening reception on April 18. They had traveled from California with Harry Ruby, and were joined by Chico's daughter Maxine, who had agreed to appear at all screenings of the recently resuscitated *Animal Crackers*. Because of legal complications, the picture hadn't been publicly seen since its original release in 1930, although pirated prints were being privately shown.

Groucho received a standing ovation at the screening. He introduced his baseball-playing composer friend by saying, "And now I want you to meet one of the biggest jerks in the world."

Harry Ruby walked on and sat at the piano. Before he played eight bars, Groucho stopped him and said, "Fine piano player. The least you can do is give me some support. I don't know where you learned to play the piano—maybe when you were sliding into second."

"Ladies and gentlemen," Ruby responded. "I want to tell you something. Forty years ago when I first played for Groucho he insulted me. Success hasn't changed him a bit."

At the cocktail party following the screening, Groucho invited Ruby to join him for dinner at Dinty Moore's. None of the Marxes showed up.

The next day, when he saw Ruby, Groucho asked, "Where were you?"

"Groucho," Ruby replied. "I could kill you."

"Well," Groucho hedged. "I was there ... maybe a minute, or a minute and a half."

Ruby knew this wasn't true, having been taken in for the umpteenth time by an ongoing practical joke that went back thirty-five years. The brothers had asked Ruby and his partner Bert Kalmar to meet them at the studio one morning. The composers showed up at Paramount. The brothers had neglected to say they would be at RKO.

A man of Harry Ruby's accomplishments could never be considered the world's biggest jerk, as Groucho characterized him at the retrospective. Yet, around his comedian friend, Ruby was the biggest patsy.

"I got the feeling Harry could be hurt by Groucho," George Fenneman said. "He would get that look: 'Why would he say that to me?'"

If he was again hurt by Groucho at being stood up in New York, his forgiving nature soon won out. Upon their return to California, the two men resumed their collaboration as composers, their songs tending to sound as if they had been written circa 1900.

Ruby was a wonderful comic foil as well as marvelous company for Groucho. He would soon be serving as a distraction during one of Groucho's most troubled periods.

In the summer of 1967, Melinda—having won an African safari on television's "Dating Game"—talked Groucho into letting her stay on in Europe.

His letters to friends over the next few weeks charted her travels and his travails. Groucho wrote Nunnally Johnson that July."

Melinda is in some place in Israel in a kibbutz picking apples or pears—or maybe picking out fellows, I don't know what she's doing except that I paid her fare and that's the last I heard of her ... I would like to tell you about Melinda. Melinda seems to be running out of countries. She's been in New York, Israel, Grecian Islands, Paris, Africa, London, and I'm predicting in two weeks she'll be in Viet Nam—in the northern section.

Two weeks later, however, Groucho had no idea where she was, and was consumed with worry. Gregory Peck's French-born wife Veronique helped Groucho hire detectives in Europe to find his missing daughter. Melinda was finally located in the company of a French government worker, whom she had met at the kibbutz. An engagement was hurriedly announced. The wedding was scheduled for her twenty-first birthday.

While wishing her happiness, Groucho, in a statement to the *New York Post*, added about the prospective bridegroom, "The main thing I want to know is can he support her? I've been doing it for 21 years and that's long enough.

"It seems to me there is a great resemblance between a funeral and a wedding. There is no gaiety in either affair. Nobody smiles at a wedding—maybe that's a harbinger of what's to come."

The wedding that was originally set for August 14 was quietly pushed back until September 15. When his editor at Simon & Schuster, Robert Gottlieb, wrote to discuss promotional matters for *The Groucho Letters*, he parenthetically said he rather liked the idea of Melinda's marrying someone from a different world.

Groucho replied:

Everyone marries someone from a different world. Even if it is the girl next door. I always thought it would be a wonderful idea to live next door to a whore house. Then you could not only be in love with the girl next door, but all of the rest of the girls next door including the madam.

About Melinda—I can't tell you anything about her because I don't know anything about her. She wrote me a letter from France, but France, despite De Gaulle, is a very large country. I sent her a cablegram wishing her whatever a puzzled father can with an uncertain daughter, marriage and birthday congratulations. I think if you read *Time* magazine next Tuesday they can probably tell you more about her than I can. She may have gone back to Israel. I may have a form letter written, explaining what I have just told you. I have a hunch that one day when her money runs short, she will get in touch with me. I wish her well wherever she is. I know she is alive—that is all I am concerned about.

I hope you and your belly dancer are well and enjoying what is left of New York and that sometime in the fall we can go to Horn & Hardart and match for the check. The last time I had lunch there I took Melinda. She was then around 12. I gave her a lot of nickels for she wanted a roast beef sandwich which was 50¢. After she had dropped into the slot what she claimed were 10 nickels, a buxom woman, who was hiding in the back of these slots came rushing out and claimed Melinda had only put in 9 nickels. A hell of an argument ensued. I was the center of attraction. Melinda walked out of the restaurant and left me there to argue with this ogre who demanded another nickel before she would relinquish the roast beef sandwich. This was when I first began to realize that Melinda wasn't as reliable as I thought she might be.

When, a few days later, a French newspaper called to ask him what had happened to the romance, Groucho said, "It's none of your business. If you want to worry about something, why don't you go after De Gaulle? He spent three days in Canada and tried to cut the country in two."

The wedding never took place—to Groucho's relief. Melinda broke the engagement after accusing the young man of wanting to marry her for her father's money. She decided to stay on in London for a while, and Groucho gave her permission to do so, since she would stay there without it anyway.

With some trepidation, he could return to everyday concerns and even try to introduce some humor in his letters to regular correspondents. He wrote Norman Krasna:

I have nothing to tell you. Things at Hillcrest are about the same as always, except they raised the price of their food and to hear those rich Jews moaning that white fish is now $3.50 a throw would make your heart melt. There is hardly anyone left young enough to play golf, so it's white fish (anti-cholesterol, by the way) and then off to the card room, each one with his own deck of cards.

[George] Burns has invited me to go to Vegas next Friday to see the opening of Ann-Margret and I asked him if he couldn't possibly rephrase that statement because this letter, such as it is, does have to go through the mails. He said he would try, but that he was accustomed to saying it that way. If it's true, it will be a hell of an opening.

Later that summer, Groucho wrote Krasna that he was seriously thinking of finally retiring. First, however, he had a commitment in late October to star in a "Kraft Comedy Hour." "When I get through with them, I'd be willing to bet they'll change the name of the show to something like 'An Hour With Utter-McKinley,'" Groucho cracked. (Utter-McKinley is a Southern California funeral parlor.)

Before that appearance, however, Groucho was drawn into a controversy involving his former publisher, Bernard Geis. In 1959, Art Linkletter had been the moving spirit behind the formation of the new publishing venture. John Guedel and Groucho had been brought in, along with others, including television producer Mark Goodson and Alfred Bloomingdale, founder of the Diners Club. Geis's most prestigious book to date had been *Mister Citizen*, Harry S Truman's autobiography.

Now, Geis planned to publish a thinly disguised novel, to be called *The Exhibitionist*, which purported to tell of the sexual adventures of a famous actor and his equally famous actress daughter. Random House, which had distributed the company's books up to now, refused to handle the new one. Also upcoming on the Geis list was another piece of fiction, *The King*, reputedly based on Frank Sinatra, and *Valley of the Dolls* by Jacqueline Susann.

Six of the company's twelve limited partners now surrendered their interests in the company, in protest against Geis's new *roman à clef* editorial policy. They included Esquire, Inc.; Cowles Communications, Inc.; Linkletter; and Groucho Marx.

Groucho was a public figure and could easily be depicted in future novels . . . as he soon would be. But he had a contempt for such dealings. It simply wasn't right to supply public figures with fictitious sexual lives. Let the public find its vicarious thrills elsewhere. His conviction was strengthened in the wake of Melinda's recent escapade. What if some author chose to improvise on it to produce a novel? His daughter may have been willful, but she was not wicked, and she didn't deserve such treatment.

In the meantime, Melinda was back at home, starring in an exploitation film, *The Violent Ones*, which Fernando Lamas was directing.

After his appearance on "Kraft Music Hall," in which the now celebrated Dick Cavett was one of the guest stars, Groucho was left pretty much to his own devices, Eden having gone off to tour the Orient with Harpo's widow Susan, and Melinda being otherwise occupied. As the year ended, he mulled over a few offers. None of them involved big money. One was a series of interviews for Public Broadcast Library; another a nightly news commentary in tandem with Goodman Ace; a third a syndicated series of five-minute television tapes with Groucho commenting on the contemporary scene. He had already declined an offer from Federico Fellini to appear in *Satyricon*, the great Italian director's planned satire on fascism.

Groucho had turned down the offer, he told United Press correspondent Vernon Scott, "because it meant spending three months in Rome during the winter. I couldn't take it. I don't want to work that hard."

Groucho's New Year's resolution for 1968 was to retire once and for all, although he set strings on his resolve when he went to New York and was interviewed by columnist Earl Wilson. "I'm not interested in shows where I can make a lot of money," he said, "and I'm not doing this because I can't get other jobs." Instead, he would only appear on television and radio programs that would help America, "because my conscience tells me I owe something to my country."

Among his first altruistic acts was to rise in a half-filled theater after a performance of Carl Reiner's play, *Something Different*, to chastise the critics and the public for not flocking to see a very funny comedy.

When *Variety* called him at his hotel for comment on his extraordinary action, Groucho said:

It's a sad commentary on New York and on Broadway that a show like this doesn't do great business. Apparently the only

417

thing audiences will go to see any more is complicated, obscure, non sequitur plays that make no sense. I think the reviewing is in the wrong hands in New York, and most other places.

. . . What's wrong with having a play at which the audience screams with laughter? I laughed like hell and so did the other people. Somebody ought to do something about this situation. It's a shame.

In conclusion, he aimed a barb at New York City: "Of course, you can't get a cab. The only thing you can catch . . . is leprosy."

Over the past five years, Groucho had discussed with a number of people the possibility of mounting a Broadway musical based on the brothers' lives. At one time, Lester Osterman and Jule Styne were interested in the project. So, at another time, was Fred Coe. None of the plans went beyond the discussion stage.

Arthur Whitelaw, a young producer whose previous experience included the *Best Foot Forward* revival which introduced Liza Minnelli to the Broadway stage, had never discussed the matter with Groucho. Nevertheless, while having lunch at Sardi's with Richard Friedberg, who was then the head of Premier Talent, he commented on the Marxian antics of the Beatles and the Monkees. As their conversation progressed, Whitelaw said he thought a musical based on the Marx Brothers would be a good idea.

Friedberg was married at the time to Stevie Phillips, an agent with Creative Management Associates. The next day she called Whitelaw and said, "I understand you're doing a musical about the Marx Brothers."

"Well," Whitelaw responded, "I just had the idea at lunch."

"It's a stupendous idea," Miss Phillips said.

Whitelaw proceeded with his plans to go to England for the opening of the London company's *You're a Good Man, Charlie Brown*, which he was producing. While in London, his father suffered a heart attack, and Whitelaw flew back to New York to be with him. He was in the hospital awaiting the doctor's report when Stevie Phillips called him.

"I know this is probably not the most opportune time to discuss this," she began.

"Oddly enough," Whitelaw responded, "it probably is a very good time to discuss this."

"Well," she said, "I've talked to Groucho Marx and he would like to meet you. Could you fly out to California immediately?"

"No, I can't, because my father is very ill. The minute I know he's all right I have to go back to London for *Charlie Brown*. We're in rehearsal right now. What I *will* do, if everything works out well here, is go back to London and then fly to California."

This was agreeable to all concerned. As soon as the London show opened, in February of 1968, Whitelaw flew to California to meet Groucho, who himself had just returned from New York.

Since a Los Angeles production of *Charlie Brown* was scheduled to open, Whitelaw had a dual reason for going to California. During the week he spent with Groucho they came to an agreement on the concept.

"I thought it should show the Marx Brothers growing up," Whitelaw said. "I didn't think you should imitate them on the stage. It would be better to let the audience find out bit by bit during the course of the evening who was who. Groucho loved the idea. We got to be very, very close during that time."

Whitelaw returned to New York. Groucho, who was to be one of the presenters at the annual Tony Awards arrived shortly thereafter. Whitelaw wanted the story to be in the form of a vaudeville show, with each act portraying a different stage of the brothers' lives. Groucho was enthusiastic about the idea. When Whitelaw suggested someone young and contemporary to write the book, Groucho was intrigued.

"Who?"

"David Steinberg," Whitelaw offered.

Groucho respected Steinberg as a comedian, but was unaware that he was also a writer. Steinberg soon came up with an outline, which Groucho hated.

"Having done research on the Marx Brothers," Whitelaw said, "I knew he'd done that with every writer he'd ever worked with before. So I pursued it a little bit more, and David pursued it a little bit more."

Groucho was adamant. Steinberg still wouldn't do. At lunch one day, he asked Whitelaw, "How about using Arthur?"

"I thought you didn't believe in nepotism in the theater," his young friend replied. Groucho had previously rejected Whitelaw's suggestion that Arthur write the book.

"Well," Groucho went on, "he's done a couple of shows, and one of them was fairly good. Maybe he can do it." When Whitelaw approached Groucho's son, he jumped at the chance. Arthur and Robert Fisher, his collaborator, began to work.

Groucho, during his New York stay, had dropped all talk about retirement and good works. Not only was the musical closer to fruition than it had ever been, he was due back in California to start work on a new film.

Otto Preminger offered Groucho $25,000 for five days of work in *Skidoo,* a comedy he was producing and directing at Paramount. Groucho would be cast as God, the head of a crime syndicate. Playing his improbably tall mistress was Donyale Luna, the exotic black fashion model.

Groucho, his toupee and mustache dyed a coal black, looked not so much made up as embalmed. Even he couldn't ignore the incongruity of his appearance and his wardrobe. In one scene he was forced to wear a floor-length parchment-colored meditation robe and a long strand of hippie beads. There was something unseemly about Groucho's attempt to be *au courant.* Groucho's judgment had been faulty and Preminger had performed him no service.

"I was lousy," he told interviewer Roger Ebert. "I played God. Jesus, I hope God doesn't look like that.

"I think Preminger wanted to make a movie about the hippie movement. . . . You know, they wanted me to testify in Chicago at the conspiracy trial. They wanted to bring me in as an expert on humor. I turned them down flat. I'm not too familiar with the case; I was afraid I might be held in contempt of court. . . . I told them, why don't you get Steve Allen or Paul Newman, one of those guys always trumpeting about freedom of speech. . . . A week in the cooler, that's what I'd get."

Had *Skiddo* been a success, Groucho probably could have handled an ensuing irritation with equanimity.

Arthur, in *Son of Groucho*, quoted his father as saying about Eden, "Look, let her have a good time. She's a young girl. If she wants to have an affair with someone else, let her. As long as I don't know about it, I don't care."

Yet, when in the summer of 1968, another of those ubiquitous *roman à clef* novels surfaced, Groucho didn't exhibit such tolerance toward his wife. Groucho felt betrayed by what he felt was her lack of discretion. He forced a confrontation. Had he read the book more carefully, he would have discerned that the vicious narrative was aimed primarily at him, while Eden was used as a convenient plot device to extract revenge.

Entertainer Keefe Brasselle wrote in the book, *The Cannibals*, about a senile, impotent, "ad-lib artist," married to a beautiful wife, who takes in the protagonist's Las Vegas show. The old man talks to people at his table throughout the performance. When the entertainer makes the obligatory introduction at the end of his performance, Mr. Ad Lib stands and takes a bow without even acknowledging the star of the show. The slight is evened when the hero purposely seduces the old man's wife.

Eden denied that any such event had taken place, and after much commiserating, Groucho showed he believed her by throwing a copy of the offending book in the living room fireplace.

His third wife had indeed been dutiful. She had raised Melinda, and Groucho could not criticize the job she had done. She tried to bring Groucho and Miriam closer together, an impossible task since her husband felt uncomfortable around his elder daughter, his guilt being too enormous to face. Eden nevertheless helped Miriam try to make a separate life for herself. Arthur and Lois were harder to reach, had Eden been expansive enough to try, because Groucho still couldn't emotionally accept Arthur's second wife, and Lois in turn didn't feel she had anything to prove to Groucho. She was the product of a respectable background and the wife of a successful playwright. (*The Impossible Years* had recently been made into a film starring David Niven. Although reviews were mixed, the picture was a moderate success.)

Harpo's widow had long given her seal of approval to Eden, and Groucho greatly respected Susan's opinion. Although Nunnally and Dorris Johnson didn't know Eden as well as Kay, having lived in

Europe during nine years of the marriage, they, too, liked Groucho's third wife.

"I think Eden is a kind person," Dorris Johnson said. "I also think she had lots of problems that were becoming more and more assertive as time went on and that marriage began to show a fracture that widened. How easy that is for a child to deal with—especially since Melinda would have been in her teen years at the time—I don't know. The teen years are difficult no matter what the circumstances are. But I suspect that Eden was probably more tolerant than most people would have been, because I think she has a basic kindness in her makeup."

Many of Eden's problems, of course, involved the super-critical Groucho. As he chipped away at her self-confidence, she was beginning to turn to alcohol ... as his two previous wives had done. Only later did Groucho concede there was a pattern to Eden's drinking. She drank whenever they had guests or whenever they went out among Groucho's intellectual writer friends. On quiet evenings at home she didn't drink at all.

Certainly Eden wanted to be a credit to Groucho. She embarked on a curriculum of study, seeking to develop her own creativity. But Groucho invariably had a devastating comment about her every new interest.

When she took up French, Groucho volunteered that she certainly didn't speak like De Gaulle. When she began studying the piano, Groucho thought her teacher was on the make. "He kept feeling her leg," he said. "Luckily he died, so there was no more crisis."

Eden had also taken up acting, although it, too, was to be a brief interlude. After one production, she had invited members of the cast back to the Marx house for a nightcap. Groucho was infuriated that the actors, only a step above amateurs, had come into *his* house and drunk *his* liquor. He delivered an ultimatum. "You have to decide whether you want to be married or be an actress," he told Eden.

So Eden went back to studying sculpture and painting, for which she had a natural aptitude. Groucho, in fact, had offered to pay her expenses to New York to show her paintings at the Hammer Gallery. Eden didn't think she was ready. George and Peg Fenneman also painted, and on many social evenings at Groucho's, they would sit with Eden in a corner discussing media and techniques while the other guests traded high-level insults.

Actually, Eden had never really crawled out of her shell during their thirteen years of marriage. Groucho had been largely responsible for further enclosing her in it.

The same behavior pattern that had totally defeated his two previous wives was again being repeated. If something in the house needed repair, Eden was overruled by Groucho, who complained it would cost too much money. He continued supervising the menus in the house. It was almost as if he expected that she would become, as Groucho described her, a "semi-alcoholic."

Susan Marx was among those quoted in *The Marx Brothers Scrapbook,* a collaboration of Groucho's with Richard Anobile. Although Groucho would later bring suit over the 1973 book, claiming a breach of trust over statements attributed to him, Harpo's widow stood by her comments in the book. About Groucho, she said:

> He destroys people's ego. Groucho has driven three wives to drink, including his children *(sic).* The only one who has survived the relationship is the one he really adores, and that's Melinda. And she doesn't want any part of him.
>
> Eden, his third wife, came out all right. Her sister sat down with her and told her she'd be in as much trouble as the others who'd been close to Groucho. . . . I think one year with Groucho could destroy anybody. Eden finally took a good look at the situation, quit the drinking and started to realize she just couldn't stand Groucho's attitude toward her. They were just fine when they were alone. She enjoyed him enormously. She was really in love with him, strangely enough. But he would needle her and do mean things when friends were around. She didn't know how to handle that. He destroyed her in front of people. . . .

The time would come when Eden didn't feel comfortable even when she and Groucho were alone. When they decided to remain at home for an evening, she would stay in her room, working on crossword puzzles or watching television. Fearing he might say something derogatory to her at dinner, she would even have the cook bring a tray to her room.

There matters stood in late 1968, when Melinda and producer Mack Gilbert decided to marry. Melinda had just spent three months starring in Gilbert's independent film, *No Deposit, No Return.* Groucho couldn't have been more delighted with his daughter's choice.

"Mack was a moneyed guy," Bill Marx, who later worked with Gilbert, said. "His father owned the largest shoe store in Columbus, Ohio. He loved Gilbert and Sullivan too. He filled all of Groucho's expectations. Mack was a cute guy—in some ways the most eccentric guy I ever met—but honest. With Melinda it was the classic tale of marry me and I'll make you a star."

The wedding was set for December 8, 1968. Groucho was well satisfied with Melinda's plans, if not some of her actions. "He wanted her to have more family feeling about her mother," Dorris Johnson said. "He thought Kay should share Melinda's life when she was approaching her marriage and there were parties being given. I think this was very hard for Melinda to do. That's where I think Groucho got tough on Melinda."

Only days after the wedding, Melinda ran off with her leading man in the film, Sanh Berti. "The marriage was so short," George Jessel cracked, "the bride got custody of the wedding cake."

Melinda's cousin Bill, although he never knew her well, was of her generation and could understand her actions. "I believe Melinda resented her father's always making her a puppet. She probably felt it was better all these years not to test herself. All of a sudden she freaked. She decided to be herself. There was no turning back."

Groucho was left to cope with yet another humiliation brought on by his daughter. He didn't take it well. To compound the situation, Eden had decided that she, too, should move on.

A month after Melinda left home, Eden walked out of the house. Groucho was still in shock when Irving Brecher, unaware of Eden's departure, called him to say hello.

"Eden has left me," Groucho said, "and what's more, I have a cold."

"I felt very moved by his unhappiness," Brecher recalled, "and I must say Groucho didn't often move people. He rarely exhibited too much in the way of a sense of loss. But he seemed a little pitiful. I had the honor of cooking bacon and eggs and serving them to him in bed."

In the divorce suit filed on January 8, the day after she walked out of the house, Eden charged that Groucho had an uncontrollable temper and had threatened to kill her. She asked for division of community property in excess of $3,000,000, and $5,500 monthly alimony. In addition, she sought possession of the Trousdale house, valued at $350,000.

Groucho accused Eden's sister of convincing Eden to file for divorce, and he never forgave her for the alleged intercession. Long after Erin Fleming had come into his life, he was still railing bitterly at Dee. He had been fond of his sister-in-law and he felt somewhat betrayed.

More poignant was Eden's heartfelt cry to Charlotte Granet. She would have stayed with Groucho, taking care of his many needs during his now very evident old age, "If only once he'd told me he loved me."

In March of 1969, while Groucho was still brooding about his impending court appearance, Melinda got a quickie divorce of her own in the same Juarez, Mexico, court where Arthur had divorced Irene. Shortly thereafter she married Berti in the same month *Skidoo* was released nationally. Groucho said he didn't know which would be the bigger disaster.

He was called to the offices of Eden's attorney two months later to give a deposition. He complained that Eden drank too much at parties, and that he had remonstrated with her about it. He said it fell to him to plan the meals because Eden didn't get up until eleven or twelve o'clock.

"She had no enthusiasm for running the house," he stated. "She left that to me. If there was something broken in the kitchen, I would get the responsibility from the cook."

He recalled that during their courtship he would give Eden money after each date. "Since I'm a very bad lay," he explained, "she was entitled to this."

Groucho was also critical of Eden for changing her perfectly respectable name of Edna Higgins to the sleeker Eden Hartford. He told of the securities he bought for her as birthday presents, and of the four-hundred-dollar monthly living allowance he gave her, as well as the one hundred dollars he sent monthly to her mother.

"Her dog bill was two hundred dollars a month," he continued in his deposition. "She had four animals in the house and she rushed one over every day to the dog doctor. Her medical bills for the dogs and cats were more than for my medical bills."

And yet, despite all his complaints, Groucho pointed out, "I hope I'm not painting Eden as the most terrible, horrible monster in the world, because she wasn't." He added that Eden, not he, wanted the divorce. "This is the biggest surprise in my life," he said in reference to her action.

When the questioning by Marvin Mitchelson, Eden's attorney, ended, Groucho said to him, "Thank you. You're a very nice man. I hope you lose your case and get as little money as possible. But I've enjoyed meeting you and I think you're a good guy, and I think you've got a lousy case and that it may be decided in a courtroom. That I can't help. But I have a clear conscience. I haven't fucked anybody."

His ace in the hole, he felt, was the prenuptial agreement Eden had signed. His estranged wife, however, claimed the agreement was to have been disregarded if the marriage worked out after two or three years, and they had been married for fourteen.

There matters rested for nearly a year. In the meantime, a very frail Groucho, increasingly afflicted by a chronic bladder condition, turned his attentions to the proposed musical. Whitelaw, in his discussions with Arthur, was beginning to have reservations.

"Arthur was too close to the material," he said, "and his thinking was very old-fashioned. He turned out an old-fashioned book."

A friend had smuggled a copy of the script to Maxine Marx. "I called the play *Groucho's Fantasy*," she said, "for that's what it seemed to me that it was. It was how he envisioned their start, not the way it really happened. I was quoted as saying, 'If they open this show, I'm picketing opening night.' "

Financing was still a problem, for Whitelaw was attempting to stage two shows at the same time, the second being *Butterflies Are Free*. "I was treating this as my B production," Whitelaw recalled, "and *Minnie's Boys* was going to be my big, big musical. At that point it was budgeted at $550,000. *Butterflies* opened and was a big success. All of a sudden the Shuberts said I could have the Imperial Theatre for *Minnie's Boys*. The doors started to open."

One of the main areas of disagreement with Groucho, who was billed as the consultant on the show, was the choice of an actress to play Minnie. Whitelaw wanted comedienne Totie Fields, but Groucho thought Shelley Winters looked a lot more like Minnie. Fields also was raucous, whereas Minnie had been soft-spoken and flirtatious. Shelley Winters auditioned, and the producers thought she would be passable. At that point she was signed to a run-of-the-play contract paying her $5,000 a week against ten percent of the gross.

During rehearsals, Whitelaw wanted to fire his star. A meeting was called. Because the rest of the cast was on the stage rehearsing, the largest space they could find for the meeting was the men's room of the Imperial Theatre. Room was needed, because Miss Winters brought an entourage, including her lawyer, maid, chauffeur, daughter, and agent. Whitelaw's lawyer, agent, and manager were there with their client, as were composer Larry Grossman, lyricist Hal Hackady and *their* agent. All were present to see Miss Winters give the performance of her life.

"I want to do this show," Miss Winters said. "I promise I'll be good. I will learn my lines. I will not stutter. I will take direction."

"All of which she had not done," Whitelaw recalled. "We had to literally fire the director because he could not cope with her. She couldn't remember her lines, so she'd stutter. She said that was the Shelley Winters style. We told her we didn't want that, because Minnie Marx to my knowledge didn't stutter. I had Totie Fields ready to go into the show, and she desperately wanted to do it. She would have been a very good Minnie. She sang well. Certainly she was funny."

Again Groucho vetoed Totie's being cast. Although he couldn't take the rights back from Whitelaw, the producer didn't want to jeopardize their relationship. Consequently he yielded.

Late in 1969, with substantial advance ticket sales booked, previews started. The show still didn't satisfy Whitelaw.

"There were problems," he said. "The book was too old-fashioned. It didn't really have a beginning, middle or an end. The show was very identifiable to the audience because they could feel for those people. What they wanted to see, which is what I wanted to give them, was the kids becoming the Marx Brothers."

A script doctor was brought in. If it was going to be an old-fashioned musical, Whitelaw wanted it to be the best.

"We were out of town but actually in New York City," Whitelaw said, "doing our dirty laundry on Forty-fifth Street."

There was no dirty laundry aired when Eden's divorce petition was finally called up. Her attorney wanted the hearing to be scheduled before January 1, 1970, when a new California law would go into effect which would make it no longer necessary to prove either marriage partner was at fault in order to obtain a divorce.

Groucho capitulated and met the bulk of Eden's demands. The property settlement provided for $210,000 in alimony over a seven-year period, $337,000 from Groucho's television contract, and half of the proceeds from the sale of the Trousdale Estates house. Eden also received stocks and bonds, bringing her total settlement to nearly one million dollars.

Within weeks after the divorce, Groucho was dating a young divorcée named Eden Marx. "I want to be near my money," he explained to Bert and Charlotte Granet when he took his ex-wife to a dinner party at their house.

"I think Groucho liked all his wives despite the divorces," Nat Perrin said. "The marriages just got impossible. I know he was terribly fond of Eden."

Groucho returned to New York a month before the official March, 1970, opening of *Minnie's Boys* to lend his expertise. He had already worn his son Arthur's patience to a frazzle. "Groucho got to be impossible," Whitelaw recalled. "He was making suggestions I then realized were no good and not valid. I had a secretary named Susan Bell, and I said, 'Just take care of him and get his mind on you and off the show, so he'll leave us alone and let us work.' Which she did. Groucho wanted to marry her."

Eden, however, was his date for the opening. "He was in terrible shape," Whitelaw recalled. "He was depressed. Being with him was

428

usually an up for me, and I loved being around him. This wasn't so in New York."

Groucho nonetheless loved the show. "Except for Shelley, the reviews were good," Whitelaw said. "She didn't know her lines, and she couldn't sing. She doesn't have a winning personality on the stage. I didn't fire Shelley. She wasn't willing to make a settlement because she wanted to be in the show. Actors Equity has a ruling which states that if an actor is fired you have to pay the new actor the same contract. That meant I would be paying $10,000 a week against twenty percent of the gross.

"In retrospect, with a star of any magnitude in the part, it throws the focus off, which should have been on the boys instead of the mother. She was a very important character in their lives, except she was not the reason we wanted to do the show. We wanted a show about the Marx Brothers, with the mother and father as a subplot. If we did that today, that's what I'd do. It's a shame. I loved the show. It's got a wonderful score, but it just never reached its potential. By placating Groucho, I was hurting the show. I should have followed through with what I wanted."

Minnie's Boys closed on May 30, after eighty performances, with a loss of over $500,000.

Back in California, Groucho was attempting to adjust to a life alone. The unhappy experience of *Minnie's Boys* had certainly not reconciled father and son. Miriam had long since surrendered to her demons. Melinda was occupied in her new marriage. Despite his occasional dates with Eden, they both realized they would have to make new lives for themselves. Eden decided to go into real estate.

As for Groucho's newest preoccupation, it was charter membership in the Geezer Club, which also consisted of Harry Ruby, Arthur Sheekman, Nunnally Johnson, and other expatriates from Hillcrest Country Club. The group met every Friday for lunch at Nate 'n' Al's Delicatessen. Its motto was "Geezer Power." Each week, Groucho would call the Johnson household and ask, "Is the old geezer going to meet us for lunch?"

"Oh, yes," Dorris Johnson would reply. "He's getting ready. What's on the agenda today?"

429

Groucho might answer, "Girls and geezers," or "Waitresses and operations."

Lunch over, his friends would return home to their wives. Because of his precarious health, Groucho had to spend the majority of his evenings at home. He would retire at night, locking his bedroom door for protection. His career had reached the stratosphere, but he was still not far removed from the tormented vaudevillian of sixty years past who shoved bureaus in front of hotel room doors.

During this lonely period his cook, Martha Brooks, became his close confidante. He would come into the kitchen after dinner while she was cleaning up. Seated at the chrome and formica table, he would tell her of the happenings of the day and ask her advice.

His driver's license was due for renewal at about this time, and Martha coached him so that he could answer the questions on the test. She went with him to the Department of Motor Vehicles. Groucho, with Martha's surreptitious help, passed the written test. Unfortunately, the examiner insisted that Groucho take the wheel for the driver's test. He returned to her, totally dejected.

"Martha, I don't understand it," he said. "I gave him an autographed picture and an autographed book. I gave him a good cigar, not one of the cheap ones I usually give away. And he still failed me."

From that point on, Groucho realized that he was truly old. He had the state of California confirmation of the fact. He would need someone else to drive him around.

Sometimes, after meeting for lunch, a friend might take him home. Groucho would sit for hours while the friend tried to figure out a way to hint graciously that the family's evening plans didn't include the country's emerging living legend.

In the months that followed, Groucho seemed to have lost the will to live. His health continued to bother him. He was now afflicted with arteriosclerosis. And he was alone.

Sometime in 1971, he suffered a stroke, and thereafter his keen mind was impaired. His words came slowly. Eden volunteered to come back to take care of him. Groucho, too proud to accept this act of charity, declined the offer.

One day, he was ambling down Beverly Drive when a pretty

blonde girl stopped him and introduced herself. She was Roxie Johnson, Nunnally's daughter, whom he hadn't seen since she was a little girl playing dolls with Melinda. "We'll have to get together sometime," Groucho told her at the end of their brief conversation.

A few days later he called her and asked her to lunch. She agreed to pick him up, and they went to the Beverly Wilshire Hotel. "It was all very nice," Roxie said, "and I guess that out of that kind of uninspired meeting, I was asked again. It was easy for him to ask me. I was a single girl who knew his background. He liked having girls around. I was a good date for him. He adored my dad and he liked me. I drove. I could come and pick him up and take him wherever he wanted to go. I would see him about once a week. He treated me fatherly, and when he didn't I was very uncomfortable. He talked a number of times about marrying me. I told Dad, but he never took it seriously.

"Groucho was very nice, very civil, very kind. He was very straight with me. He just wanted to cuddle a little and, although it made me feel a little uncomfortable, I understood and didn't feel that he was overstepping."

He wasn't the most constant of suitors, however, since he was also seeing a young department store heiress. It was during this period that I first met Groucho. He was a fellow guest at a big party celebrating the fact that "The Odd Couple" television series would be filmed before a live audience, starting with the 1971 season. Groucho sat in the front row during the taping of the program which preceded the cocktail buffet, and he insinuated himself into all the proceedings. When we were introduced by a mutual friend, I found him friendly enough, but subdued. He left the party soon after.

In mid-August he received a call from television producer Jerry Davis. A friend from New York had brought a girl to California with him for a holiday, but had been called back home unexpectedly. Would Groucho like to meet her? Her name was Erin Fleming.

CHAPTER FOURTEEN

Hitch your wagon to a star.
   Ralph Waldo Emerson, Society and Solitude: Civilization

She was an attractive young woman—how young or how old was never established to the satisfaction of the curious—and, when she wanted, she had a winning way about her.

Groucho was not the first member of the Marx family to know her. Maxine, who after her divorce went on to carve out a career as one of New York's top casting directors, had auditioned the Canadian-born Erin for television commercials. She had found Erin to be pleasant and agreeable.

Groucho was rattling around in the house on the hill, the same one he had paid for one-and-a-half times by giving Eden fifty percent of its worth in the divorce settlement. Paranoia was again rearing its head. The bedroom door was kept locked at night for good reason.

Earlier in 1971, Groucho had given an interview to an underground newspaper published in the San Francisco Bay Area. He discussed in detail his career in films and his attitudes toward women.

"As a rule a young fellow marries a girl to go to bed with her," he said. "This is normal procedure. I did that three times with very beautiful girls. When the beauty started fading, there wasn't any reason to stay married. The sex stimulant was gone."

As for companionship:

For that you need a different kind of girl. You don't necessarily need a girl with big tits. You need a girl who normally you wouldn't marry, or you wouldn't try to lay. But if a fellow gets both, he's a very fortunate man. If he gets a woman he enjoys sitting with and talking to and she understands what he's saying, he's a lucky fellow. You see, I don't believe there's such a thing as love. I believe two people can like each other, and I think that's more important than love. Love just means going to bed and fucking. You can get that anywhere, if you're young and partially attractive.

It wasn't his reflections on male-female relationships, however, that worried him these days. During the interview, in which he expressed a highly negative view of politicians in general, Democrats included, he said, "I think the only hope this country has is Nixon's assassination."

The article was picked up by an underground newspaper in London, and the statement about the President was run in turn by the *Berkeley Barb*, yet another Bay Area underground newspaper.

When it was picked up by the wire services, Groucho disowned the statement. "I deny everything, because I never tell the truth," he said. "I lie about everything I do or say—about men, women or any other sex." Yet, his disclaimer was not accepted by the Nixon administration, and in a file numbered CO 1297009205, Groucho Marx was listed as a potential threat to the life of the President. He later suspected that his phone had been tapped.

The Groucho Erin first got to know was afraid and lonely. Melinda saw him infrequently, and he didn't seek out the company of his other daughter, since he either couldn't or wouldn't cope with Miriam's problems. He began making overtures to Arthur *and*

434

Lois. Yet, his efforts were only partially successful. Arthur was cordial enough, but he had his own life to lead. What's more, a solicitous and caring Groucho at this late a date didn't quite ring true.

"In the last few years, I had the impression that Groucho wasn't too interested in Arthur," Irving Brecher said, "and I never heard too much about Miriam except when he talked about the expense he was undergoing in keeping her in a climate where she could be cared for. He seemed fond of Melinda, but up to a point. You know, as people get older and sicker they don't have as much energy to be that concerned anymore. And if they feel as Groucho did, that the children are a financial drain, then some parents react more than others to the business of putting out the money, even if they have it. They feel that somehow the children are exploiting them."

It was this conflict of love versus resentment toward his children that Erin found in him when she came into his life. She agreed to supervise the answering of thousand of pieces of fan mail that had accumulated in Eden's former painting studio over the last few years. Their relationship at first was primarily that of employer and employee. Groucho, in December of 1971—four months after Erin began working for him—was still going out occasionally with Eden, who admitted she hadn't met any new men as interesting as her former husband. Groucho did not give great credence to this. About his last marriage, he told Michele Willens of the *Los Angeles Times,* "I was married fifteen years and I think as my sexual powers decreased, her love for me waned. You shouldn't marry a young girl when you're sixty-five."

Soon, Erin succeeded in showing him how well loved he was elsewhere, showing Groucho reverential letters from fans. She instilled the thought—as no one else had succeeded in doing—that Groucho Marx was a giant. He was the center of a Marx Brothers revival that spanned the globe, but was less aware of it than the average college freshman.

Offers were being tendered, and Erin would be there to encourage and advise him every step of the way.

"Erin was the girl who appeared at the right time in his life," Dorris Johnson said. "She came on the scene, I think, with great expectancy of finding, with Groucho's help, a foothold in the picture business. She might be able to become either a star or a distinguished actress on her own."

How she expected to accomplish this, using as her mentor a man so notoriously contemptuous of the institutions whose walls she wanted to scale, is a puzzle. Hers wasn't a brilliant acting talent, and her achievements as an actress were, thus far, quite modest. She didn't radiate the sexiness of a starlet. Yet that is precisely what Groucho cast her as, and what she tried to play. Suddenly she was pictured with Groucho on the covers of *Esquire* and the *National Enquirer.* Erin had willingly become the sexual innuendo.

A few years later, after she had established a place in the public consciousness, she said to me, "People don't think Groucho and I actually have sex, do they? I never would have gone along with it if people actually believed it." The public knew this. Groucho, in his many interviews of recent years, had not hesitated to say his sex life was a thing of the past. The old man and the much younger woman performed a merry charade, Erin engendering what-a-way-to-go snickers. It was calculated to amuse everyone but Groucho's own children. Any observer of the Hollywood scene could have told Erin that hers was no route to success. Yet none of Groucho's advisers—public relations men and attorneys included—did. Groucho could have told her, but it was in his selfish best interest not to.

Thus, Erin embarked on a Hollywood "career." She would put Groucho's life in order, and just incidentally set her acting ambition on the right track.

Martha, Groucho's cook and confidante, liked Erin at first. Her opinion was to change as she—like others around Groucho—was exposed to Erin's tempestuousness. Erin was quick to anger, and slow to forgive or forget.

At the outset of their relationship, Erin refused to take any money for helping Groucho. It was a gesture the frugal Groucho could appreciate. He in turn talked to his friends, and Woody Allen cast Erin in a featured role in his next picture. (Groucho said in a later *Esquire* interview, "She does things in it I've never been able to persuade her to do in the privacy of my own home.")

During the filming of *Everything You Wanted to Know About Sex But*

436

Were Afraid to Ask, Irving Brecher and his wife gave a party to which Groucho and Erin were invited.

"I was, from the day I first saw him, a Woody Allen admirer," Brecher said. "In fact, I told people at Hillcrest in the business about this fellow I had seen that they had never heard of. That night, Erin was holding court in an arm chair, with a lot of people around, sounding forth on her role in the picture. She said to me, 'What do you think of Woody Allen?' "

"I said, 'Well, I'm a big fan of his, but in his last picture, I think he's beginning to sound a little less original and is beginning to do a little bit of Harpo.'

"And she said, 'What the fuck do you know about comedy?' Well, I couldn't answer her because it was my home." A man with *Meet Me in St. Louis* and "The Life of Riley" among his credits, of course, shouldn't need to prove his expertise.

"Everybody around thought it was fairly amusing in an unpleasant way. What bothered me was not the fact that she took that position, but that Groucho didn't say anything. He was possibly as great a champion as I've ever had in the profession. He'd gone around here and in England saying marvelous things about me. He seemed to be so much under her domination that he didn't do what he normally would have done. He would have said, 'What in the hell are you talking about?'

"I wasn't hurt because she didn't think I knew anything about comedy. I felt something was changing in Groucho. There was a coolness after that. In fact, I don't think we got together again for over a year."

Despite his protestations of the recent past that he didn't believe in love, it was apparent Groucho was very much in love with Erin. The fact he didn't have to prove anything sexually to Erin—as indeed he couldn't—tied them closer together. Many times, I heard him say to Erin, about a current boyfriend, "I can't do for you what he can, but no one could love you more." He was liberated by this, and could learn to admire something he had never taken much stock in, a woman's mind.

"She had a driving ambition," Dorris Johnson said. "She caught Groucho's support and interest and restimulated him into the performing career that nobody else could have directed him toward. She gave him a new confidence in himself when she started the whole thing of the concert tours. . . . It was what she needed, a commodity that was pre-sold, that had an established legend. She couldn't go wrong. . . . I don't minimize in any way what Erin did for Groucho. . . . It happened to be self-serving too, so it was the right combination.

"As events went along, I think I saw evidence of her disappointment and, possibly, bitterness. But Erin had the ability and the drive and the *need* to rechannel that ambition, and she had the right property for it. I don't believe anyone could have done all of the things for Groucho that she did. She brought him back to public attention, awareness, and performance, when he had pretty much subsided and was quite lonely . . . and frustrated because he wasn't working more. I also don't think he was as much aware of the legend he had become among the young as maybe the greatest of the anti-Establishment people. Because he was the last of the performing Marx Brothers to still have any ability to function professionally, I think it worked out very favorably for Erin *and* Groucho."

As Erin was becoming entrenched in Groucho's household, his first wife Ruth quietly died. Groucho, caught up in the renewed excitement, seemed to pay scant notice to her death.

The first important engagement under the Erin regime was a concert at Carnegie Hall. An engagement at Iowa State University was scheduled to serve as a dress rehearsal to the New York appearance. It was coordinated by a nineteen-year-old student, Tom Wilhite, who both Groucho and Erin became so fond of that they recruited him to come to California to work as their public relations man after his college graduation.

Erin had asked Harpo's son Bill, an accomplished pianist-composer, if he wanted to accompany Groucho on the concert tour. There was no follow-up offer, and Bill probably couldn't have gone, since he was scoring Mack Gilbert's picture—the one Melinda had starred in—and had another film assignment waiting. Erin was then dating Marvin Hamlisch, who also had impressive credits composing musical scores for films. With this tour, Hamlisch would become a celebrity in his own right.

Just prior to their departure, Groucho and Erin attended a party at the Walter Matthaus' honoring Charlie Chaplin, who was in California to accept an honorary Academy Award. The two legends hadn't seen each other for nearly thirty-five years, but they took up where they'd left off. As Groucho was leaving, Chaplin—his elder by a year—advised him, "Keep warm."

The Iowa concert proved that Groucho could still hold an audience. Just the magic of his name captivated them. It was on to New York.

At a jam-packed press conference prior to the Carnegie Hall concert, Groucho arrived wearing bell-bottom blue jeans, a blue blazer, a red sweater-vest, a work shirt, and a beret.

When he was asked why he wasn't smoking his traditional cigar, Groucho replied, "I'll smoke it if it'll amuse you. I didn't know I was going to have to put on a show for you boys. You see, I just got out of the shower and I generally don't smoke while I'm under water."

Asked what he would do with the ten thousand dollars he was receiving for the sold-out appearance, Groucho replied, "I'll spend it on my secretary ... which is a euphemism for this girl over here."

In a separate interview with Israel Shenker of the *New York Times*, Groucho acknowledged in a reverse way that his relationship with his son Arthur had improved. "Children are rough going," he said. "They have no respect for their elders. All daughters do is get married, and then get divorced. Either that or they drink. I think it's easier to raise the male than the female. Things happen to women at different times." That he was referring directly to his daughters, Miriam and Melinda, was apparent.

Such notables as New York Mayor John Lindsay and his wife, Senator and Mrs. Jacob Javits, Mike Nichols, Elliott Gould, Woody Allen, Diane Keaton, Art Garfunkel, and Neil Simon were in the audience at Carnegie Hall. Many others were long-haired and dressed in blue jeans; some came as their favorite anti-Establishmentarian.

Dick Cavett had agreed to introduce Groucho.

"He seemed terribly frail and out of it that night," Cavett recalled, "and I pictured disaster. He seemed terribly quiet and without any energy at all ... [coming] through the thronging, surging mob of adulators, many of whom were made up as Groucho and Harpo. I said, 'Oh, my God. It's going to be something out of *The Blue Angel*. Who'd be the Lola Lola figure? I can't work that out quickly enough.' Anyway, I introduced him and took a seat in the audience next to Woody and Diane Keaton. He read off cards and they loved every minute of it. They saw nothing wrong with it. But I knew he was on the brink. Maybe he'd taken a pill or not taken one or something.

"At intermission I suggested they cut the number with Erin ... 'Heaven's Above.' You can imagine how *that* went over. The film failed. They were supposed to show the stateroom scene and the projector didn't work, in a Robert Benchley classic fuckup. They never got it on the screen. Groucho, not knowing he was on mike, made some disgusted remarks which got huge laughs. He got through the concert, to a huge ovation. Later, during some picture taking, he was in quite a good mood. He seemed fine and clowned a bit. I had gotten tired of thinking this was the last time I was going to see him, because luckily I had been proven wrong."

Next, Groucho and Erin were off to the Cannes Film Festival, where he was due to receive the French *Commandeur des Arts et Lettres* medallion. Charlie Chaplin had been the first non-Frenchman so honored.

They returned to California for the next concert date in San Francisco. All involved agreed this was the best of all of Groucho's performances. He received four standing ovations.

During their stay in Europe, an article written by Erin appeared in *Vogue* magazine, purporting to be an intimate conversation on the subject of women between Groucho and "his very private secretary."

Groucho said the most important thing about a woman, "and it took me a long time to learn this—is intelligence. If a woman is smart, she knows how to look good. I like a woman to be an interesting conversationalist and a good listener ... that's because I never stop talking."

Erin quoted Groucho as saying to her, "If a woman cares about a man, if she has a genuine concern for him, affection, like I sometimes think you have for me, well, then she can get away with murder in other areas."

Within two weeks after his San Francisco concert, an exhausted

Groucho was hospitalized with a stroke. A scheduled Los Angeles concert had to be postponed until his recovery. The press reported that he was hospitalized for severe depression over the killings of the Israeli athletes at the Munich Olympics.

Upon his release, he formalized his business relationship with Erin when, on October 12, he signed a written agreement employing her as his executive producer, associate producer, coordinator, and secretary. The terms of the employment consisted of a salary of one hundred dollars per week, ten percent of his gross income from all personal appearances, five thousand dollars of the $17,500 he was getting for a Teachers Scotch endorsement, and fifty percent of the net income received for the A&M record album of his concert tour. The press later reported that Erin grossed $100,000 from the album alone.

Three weeks later, another document was signed, in which Erin was hired as Groucho's personal manager, to be paid twenty-five percent of all his earnings after agent commissions were deducted.

His children were not happy at this development. Arthur had already served notice of his displeasure in his just published book, *Son of Groucho,* which he had finished months before the agreements with Erin were signed. Discussing cash gifts his father had given him, he said that over the years their size depended on: "(1) whether he's steadily employed, (2) the current state of the stock market, (3) how much alimony he's paying his last wife, and (4) what his girlfriend of the moment is euchring him out of in exchange for posing as his secretary."

Erin blithely went ahead with her plans for Groucho. Her devotion was more immediate than his son's written words. Groucho felt a security with her he had never felt before with any other woman, including his mother and his wives. Even his insomnia was, miraculously, largely a thing of the past.

Arthur's ambivalence toward his father was much in evidence in his book. It took the son of another famous comedian, writer John Lahr—the son of Bert—to put the matter in perspective in a devastating review that appeared in the *Washington Post Book World:*

Struggling to love the viciousness that millions find endearing, the sons of famous clowns cannot face the fact that comedians are killers and laughter is their revenge. No comic is more adroit at 'knocking 'em dead' or reveling in his vindictive triumph than Groucho. As any psychopath might, Groucho deploys his wit ruthlessly and without a tinge of guilt. No person is safe, no institution is sacrosanct . . .

What we love in Groucho is his rampant megalomania. We have invested our dreams of anarchy and retribution in him; and his antics are our reward . . . Groucho's humor is belly. Sex, money, food—whatever is basic to the Good Life—is the comic vein he's mining. Like any old-timer, laughter for Groucho is not a way of scourging society, but winning a place in it. Groucho has never, sadly, been much of a social critic, although occasionally some of his roundhouse verbal punches can betray cultural hypocrisy . . .

The envy and frustration which *Son of Groucho* documents in a benign and banal way has only to do with success in terms of material well-being, social prestige and personal recognition. But in the relentless coming-to-grips of son with famous father, there is an anger much deeper and more confusing: the child, although younger, is never more resilient than father. No matter how old and febrile Groucho gets as he moves into his eighties, he is preserved forever in his prime in movies and in our minds . . .

There are moments in *Son of Groucho* that make the reader furious with the oafish public which will not allow the hard-won effort of Groucho's son to stand by itself. . . . The public wants its stars to succeed almost as much as it expects, even yearns, for their offspring to fail. The tales of the stars and the decline of their dynasties are America's tinsel-town epics.

But *Son of Groucho* finally evokes no sympathy because it is so sloppily and insensitively written. To be born the son of a great man is an opportunity as well as an oppression, to live among the famous and talented, to experience the limitations and allure of America's golden payoff is something that should yield insight. But Arthur Marx, posing as an auto-biographer, is really only interested in spinning some good stories about Pop. He never inquires with any depth into his father's art. He never sees the neurosis behind Groucho's insomnia and the maliciousness of his humor. He skirts the pain of the paternal bond and settles for puffery.

Groucho's humor never suffers fools gladly ... Groucho's gibes have an essential honesty. When he read Arthur's first literary effort, Groucho threw it aside, exclaiming, "Amateur Night." Thirty years later, Dad's verdict would be apt for *Son of Groucho*.

The great man himself never voiced such complaints. He found Arthur's book a worthy effort, and in his conversations to me, paid his son the highest accolade: "Arthur is a good writer."

If only Groucho, now eighty-two, were as good a performer. The postponed Los Angeles concert was finally held on December 13. (The press had reported that he had given up smoking cigars until after the concert. He would in fact give them up completely.)

"I thought it was an acute embarrassment," Dorris Johnson said of the program. "That's pretty blunt and pretty harsh, but that's the way I judged it.

"I felt embarrassed for both. It was sad for me to see Groucho exposed in that way. He was not capable of entertaining an audience. I will say this. The way the show was put together, the mixed media form, with clips from the old pictures, there was so much amusing stuff going on that I don't believe the audiences were disappointed ... the majority of them anyway.

"Every step of Groucho's had to be a shuffle, because the joints didn't move easily anymore and there was always the uncertainty of falling. And the eyes didn't read clearly. The tension of the moment removed him from what used to be his forte, which was improvising. Having seen him through so many years of just being the top one, it brought tears to my eyes. Erin's skill was not stand-up entertainment. She went out to try to support, but Erin was out of her métier there. There were females that *could* have gone on and helped him. If you had an entertainer like Edie Adams or somebody who knew how to handle a live audience, somebody with comedy skill, somebody that could romp through a routine without using him as anything but stage center, the target to work around, it could have been amusing. But that takes a very special experience and skill, and Erin didn't have that. She should never have exposed herself and him in such a way. Her justification for it would be to say, 'We sold out! We had standees! We made X number of dollars!' That to me is not justification. That's blind ambition. You don't take a great star and performer and legend and memory like Groucho, and expose him to a live audience that he is not capable of entertaining at the level he is remembered as having."

No more concerts were scheduled.

Groucho told me, "Whenever a comedy team breaks up, it's the women behind them that are responsible." He could have added the same thing about the estrangement of father and son. I have no doubts that the two would eventually have become much closer had Erin and Lois not thoroughly detested each other.

Erin, by virtue of her easy access to Groucho, was in a good position to convey her dislike of Lois, who had never achieved the same friendly relationship with him that Irene, Arthur's first wife, had. Erin's actions could not be proven to be intentional, yet they succeeded in driving Arthur and Lois totally away.

Both Grace Kahn and her daughter Irene were aware that Erin invited them to social gatherings at Groucho's as an affront to Lois. They continued accepting invitations, as they had accepted invitations from Groucho before the advent of Erin and after Irene's divorce from Arthur. Both women tendered invitations in return, because they had been close to Groucho a long time and he was always genuinely happy to see them.

Lois, a talented interior designer, had begun work on Groucho's house, trying to inject style into the tastelessly furnished home. On short notice, she was dismissed in favor of the noted decorator Peter Shore. He had designed the interiors of Erin's little jewel of a house—in which Dorothy Parker had reputedly once lived—and now he was asked to attack the white mausoleum on Hillcrest Road.

"Arthur's wife Lois had started the house," Shore said. "She fluffed it up, as they say in the parlance of the decorator. Just the living room had been started. The rest was a shambles. The furniture was unkempt.

"Erin took me to meet Groucho. He said he wanted to redecorate the house, but I kept putting him off. I thought maybe it was the fact that Erin wanted it done.

"Finally, when I couldn't put him off any longer, I took Groucho up the street to show him the house of Irving Levin. He owns the Boston Celtics. There was a long step down from the entry hall into the living room. 'Watch the step,' I told Groucho. He stood there for a moment. He asked, 'What's it going to do?' He loved the Levin house, and said he wanted me to work on his."

Shore describes his look as "comfortable, informal, understated country, top quality, *expensive.*" His client list is the most enviable in Southern California, including Paul Newman, Steve McQueen, Henry Fonda, Rock Hudson, Neil Diamond, and James Stewart. Shore met with Erin and Groucho to try to determine his new client's needs.

The first two rooms to be redone were Melinda's, which was papered in a *Cocoanuts* motif and Eden's, which was converted into Erin's office. "It had pretentious cheap white and gold furniture," Shore said.

Shore tried to find motifs that symbolized Groucho's career. One of the living room sofas was upholstered in a red *Animal Crackers* print. The wallpaper in the guest bath showed monkeys in endless repetition. Ornaments in the form of silver, ceramic, and wooden ducks were placed throughout the living room.

Shore had found the doors from an old circus wagon in Laguna Beach, and he had them converted into a headboard for Groucho's bed. The doors, of course, symbolized the tours of Opie and Omie a century before.

Before the piece could be installed, it had to be stripped and bleached. Groucho would call Shore at seven every morning until the headboard was delivered. "Where's my headboard?" he would ask. When it was delivered, Groucho was delighted to see that Shore had had the name of Lydia painted on the center of the piece, in honor of the tattooed lady from *At the Circus.* When a friend visited him, Groucho proudly said, "I want to show you my headpiece. It's the only piece I get these days."

The major part of the decoration was completed by Groucho's eighty-fifth birthday. "The most lovable part of him," Shore recalled, "was that he always called me a genius. Everybody has got to like to hear that. What I did was top quality. I went to Portugal to get needlepoint rugs for the dining room, for example.

Yet, I don't think there was a great deal of money spent. There were already pieces there to work with, mainly upholstered pieces. I didn't put in many wood pieces. The coffee tables that were there to begin with, which I think are terrible, are still there. I think it totaled a little over $60,000. My average installation is $150,000."

Shore, the better-established interior designer, may have felt the budget he was given to work with was not a large one, but Lois had not been given one remotely approaching that figure when she started working on the house.

Shore, a staunch defender of Erin, said, "I never saw anything but the most loving relationship between her and Groucho. She'd walk into the room, and he would light up."

As for her temper, he found it mainly directed at those who did their work poorly. "One thing Erin hated was people who were incompetent, who didn't do their job."

Neither did he feel that Erin in any way used him to further her social ambitions. Shore's social life is much caught up with his superstar clients, and not once did she ask to be included when he mixed with them.

"People were amazed that she would devote her time to Groucho," Shore said. "They couldn't understand why. They said she really must love him. I thought she was truly devoted to him, and I could see he truly loved her. It was a relationship I didn't understand.

"I don't believe she alienated Groucho's friends for a minute. She would invite anyone to the house that Groucho wanted to see. If there was someone on television that he liked, she would call and invite him for lunch or dinner or whatever.

"I think Erin made Groucho very happy. If she had taken diamonds and fur coats there wouldn't have been any problems later."

Groucho's tie to Erin became total after a confrontation at Matteo's Restaurant in West Los Angeles. She had gone there with a male friend from New York to have dinner, and the couple ran into Arthur and Lois. Words were exchanged, and the volatile Lois threw a drink at Erin. Both Groucho's son and daughter-in-law felt that Erin's seeing another man was inexcusable.

I don't know Groucho's feeling at the time. About the incident,

446

he would only say, "Arthur's wife threw a drink at Erin. We don't see them anymore." He did not, however, object to Erin's dating during the time when I was spending many hours with him. Erin, in talking about the incident with Lois was unperturbed. "She missed me and hit somebody else," she laughed.

For the first time in his life, Groucho was spending money lavishly. Not only was he decorating his house, he was buying six-hundred-dollar suits. The entertainments he hosted, which were often catered, accelerated. Bill Marx was often included at these social gatherings. "I found the formula the same," he said. "There was a certain expectancy, a prescribed behavior. It was as if Hillcrest Road was the road people took, walking up it with their camels, to pay homage. Groucho didn't know who some of the people were. The homage they paid went to a ridiculous degree. They might as well have been paying their respects to an eight-by-ten glossy from *Horse Feathers.* That was the real Groucho to them. At the house on Hillcrest, life wasn't even standing still. It was regressing to a past that never existed."

As part of this celebration of the past, Groucho had recently started work with Richard Anobile on a book which was to become the controversial *Marx Brothers Scrapbook.* Three years previously, in an "Arts and Leisure" interview for the *Sunday Times,* Groucho had observed about the proliferating books extolling comedians of the past: "A lot of these books, I've looked at them. They're crap. They do a new kind of writing. They rent our movies, tape-record them, and write down all the good jokes in their books. Quite a writing feat!"

Anobile had recently pasted together *Why a Duck?,* taking frame blowups from many of the Marx Brothers movies and matching them with the appropriate dialogue. The inconsistent Groucho wrote the introduction.

Groucho taped reminiscences throughout 1973, offering unsuitable and presumably unprintable observations about the sexual activities of his collaborator, the less than honorable beginnings of a now prominent banker, and the sexual aberrations of other celebrities. It was a shabby exercise. Though Anobile later claimed that Groucho had approved the manuscript and that the book was of historical value, the manuscript would never have been approved by Groucho's lawyers had they seen it, since it left Groucho open to legal action. As for its historical import, Anobile brought so little preparation to his work that some of the names were spelled phonetically. The Gus Sun Circuit came out Gerson, Jack Root was identified as Jack Ruth, Hattie Darling was identified as Patty Darling, Salpeter, the real surname of Max Gordon, was spelled "Saul Peter."

Several friends said that age had impaired his judgment. Still, it is hard to believe that Groucho had totally abandoned his code of ethics only several years after his withdrawal as a partner at Bernard Geis in protest against the publisher's turn to smut-filled fiction. Whatever the case, it was under Groucho's name that the sexual habits of his contemporaries were being revealed, in a book that purported to be factual. Its publication drove Groucho into a brooding depression.

In the months of August and September, Groucho was hospitalized twice. His physician said he was "suffering from probable pneumonitus, acute anteroseptal myocardial infarction, arteriosclerotic cerebrovascular disease and chronic urinary tract infection secondary to bladder retention." All such ailments commonly afflict elderly persons.

A month after being released from his second hospital stay, Groucho filed a fifteen-million-dollar lawsuit against Darien House Inc., the publishers of the *Scrapbook*; W.W. Norton & Co., the distributors; and Penthouse Publications Ltd., and Penthouse International Ltd., which was excerpting portions of the book in the December issue of *Penthouse* magazine. In addition to damages, he asked that distribution of the book be halted. In his complaint, he maintained that the book contained "defamatory, scandalous, obscene and inflammatory matter."

Darien president Jack Rennert, in defense of the book's publication, stated that it was based on thirty hours of tapes. He surmised that Groucho's family was behind the suit. Anobile, reacting to Wilfrid Sheed's *New York Times* dismissal of the book's contents as "sleazy breaches of trust," said later that Groucho had approved the contents of the book and had even agreed to go on talk shows to promote it.

The New York judge lifted his injunction against *Penthouse* three days after the suit was filed, but let that of the other defendants stand. A few days later, the injunction was lifted against them too, the judge stating that Groucho had signed the contracts that allowed the distribution of the book in whatever form the publisher chose.

The last year had not been a productive one for Groucho. His Los Angeles concert had started the downturn. Throughout 1973, his health grew steadily worse.

The only promising note was the pending re-syndication of "You Bet Your Life. In August, NBC had informed Guedel that it was going to destroy the film of the show in order to clear some space in its New Jersey warehouse. Studio executives maintained that the show was too slow and old-fashioned to justify re-syndication. But Groucho and John Guedel worked out a royalty deal with NBC. Groucho's grandson, Andy, a recent graduate of UCLA, was hired to put the programs in some semblance of order. Locally, KTLA—Channel 5 in Los Angeles—agreed to take a thirteen-week chance on "The Best of Groucho."

His life in the new year was taking a turn for the better. Early in February of 1974, the Academy of Motion Picture Arts and Sciences announced Groucho would get a special Oscar for the "brilliant creativity and unequaled achievement of the Marx Brothers in the art of motion picture comedy." Erin had discussed the possibility of such an award with Nunnally Johnson, and Groucho's old friend wrote a letter to the Board of Governors urging that Groucho be so honored. The Board happily agreed to the suggestion.

At the same time, a campaign to re-release *Animal Crackers*, the forty-four-year-old film, was under way. Steve Stoliar, a history major at the University of California at Los Angeles, spearheaded the campaign. He had driven to Anaheim to see a bootleg print of the picture in December.

"I had no way of knowing if Groucho had a print," he said. "Coming back I wanted to let him know that it was playing there." Stoliar knew that Harry Ruby's number was in the telephone book. He called and said he wanted to tell Groucho about the picture. Ruby promised to pass on his name and telephone number.

On New Year's Day of 1974, Erin called Stoliar. Instead of

449

thanking him for letting Groucho know where the movie was playing, she expressed her anger at Universal Pictures—which now owned the rights—for not re-releasing the picture. The studio felt there wasn't a big enough market to warrant striking fresh prints.

A few days later, Stoliar and some friends formed the "Committee for the Re-Release of *Animal Crackers.*"

The petitions totalling several thousand signatures—the figure was inflated to 18,000—were never submitted to Universal. The studio bowed to public demand after Groucho and Erin appeared before the press and television cameras at UCLA to talk about the corporate ogre trying to keep a great film from the public. The studio agreed to test market the picture in Westwood that May.

Two weeks after Groucho's trip to UCLA, his friend Harry Ruby died of a heart ailment at the age of seventy-nine. His death left Groucho disconsolate. Ruby was the first of the Geezers Club to die.

Groucho, along with most of his friends, found funerals barbaric. He felt uncomfortable with sanctimonious postures, and disliked the hypocrisy of venerating people who had not been that well regarded in life. But Ruby was a lovable man, and worthy of encomiums. "I went to the synagogue for Harry," Groucho told me. "When he died, a part of me died too."

On the night of April 2, Groucho and Erin were being driven to the Academy Awards ceremonies at the Music Center in downtown Los Angeles, in an $87,000 Stutz Blackhawk, when the car broke down. They had to hitch a ride the rest of the way.

"There are two very memorable moments for me about the Oscars," Jack Lemmon said. "It's not the receiving of two of them. But being able to present the Academy Award to Charlie Chaplin and to Groucho! Why I got lucky enough to get picked, I don't know, but I couldn't have been more proud than to be picked to present the Oscars to these two. About Groucho, he wasn't just a great performer. He was a marvelous writer too. Whatever the ingredients that made up his talents, he is unique. You can be a great actor, you can be this or that, but some people are not just better than other people doing the same thing. They are totally unique. He didn't just interpret it. He created it and then did it. He was off for the moon when everybody else was down here somewhere. It comes down to one truism, at least as far as I'm concerned. There has never been somebody really on the top level that wasn't very bright. The talent and various abilities seem to go hand-in-hand with two things: sensitivity and intelligence. Now you can have the most usurping wit in the world, caustic too, but you still have to be ultra-sensitive or you would not be able to even see things in a caustic way. The majority of the great creative people have always been unusual ... very unhappy, I think, because of the ultra-sensitivity. They're just more aware of human problems, human suffering, human foibles, or the things that are ill in the world and in society. They seem to be touched more deeply by it. They might be able to laugh louder and longer and enjoy things more but they also have the greater capacity for sadness."

As Lemmon presented the award, Groucho was greeted by a prolonged standing ovation. In his acceptance, he said, "I only wish Harpo and Chico could have been here—and Margaret Dumont, who never understood any of our jokes. She used to say, 'Julie, what are they laughing at?' But she was a great straight woman and I loved her. And then, I'd like to thank my mother, without whom we would have been a failure. And last, I'd like to thank Erin Fleming, who makes my life worth living and who understands all my jokes."

A few weeks later, Bill Cosby, Jack Nicholson, and Marvin Hamlisch acted as co-hosts for hundred guests at Hillcrest Country Club to honor Groucho for the award. The guest of honor picked up the $10,000 tab.

He didn't recover any of the party expenses when *Animal Crackers* was re-released at the UA Westwood Theatre, since neither he nor his brothers had any financial interest in the picture. Universal got the word on potential acceptance when the film broke the house record set by *The French Connection*. It then decided to re-release the picture nationally.

Groucho, at Erin's urging, agreed to go to New York for the opening in late June. The mobs around the Sutton Theatre were so enthusiastic that mounted police had to be called to keep order.

That such public appearances were a physical strain on Groucho is evident. Yet he also had a great need to remain before the public eye.

The revival, for which Erin was largely responsible, had brought forth a flood of fan mail. Since her attentions were now devoted to grander projects, Stoliar was hired to handle the correspondence, and to put Groucho's memorabilia in order, prior to its eventual donation to the Smithsonian Institution.

In mid-year, Groucho made out a new will. Among its provisions was the bequest of the Hillcrest Road house to Erin. Arthur, when he heard of Groucho's intentions, strongly objected to this provision.

Groucho was again hospitalized late in the summer, the victim of another stroke. His ailments were coming with greater frequency, incapacitating him even further. He had already suffered several strokes, in addition to his other major illnesses. He was now experiencing difficulty with his speech. He occasionally had difficulty standing. His comprehension was affected. But his powers of recuperation were strong.

When "The Best of Groucho" premiered in New York and Philadelphia that September, the next phase in the re-syndication of the show began. Within months, it would be airing in nine of the ten major markets, being telecast in a total of forty-five. The durability of his appeal, both as a member of an immortal comedy team and as an individual, was again proven.

That same month, a new will was drawn up, providing for the sale of the Hillcrest house after his death, the proceeds to go into the estate of which his children were the principal heirs. A truce of sorts between Groucho, Erin, and his children had been temporarily effected. Nevertheless, another schism was in the making.

Arthur Sheekman was ill with arteriosclerosis and fully incapacitated. His wife Gloria, after discussing the matter with their daughter, as well as with Nunnally and Dorris Johnson, decided that he could get the best care in a nursing home. Groucho, for over a year, would periodically visit Sheekman there, taking whiskey and cookies to his friend.

"He was the only one I let see my husband," Gloria Sheekman

452

said. "Groucho was very fragile. He'd come to my house for lunch, then go see Arthur."

One wonders what Groucho said to his invalid friend, who often didn't recognize him. Yet his frequent visits showed the extent of his devotion. The feeble old man would sit with his nearly comatose friend and try to extract a flicker of recognition or reaction from him. Quite fittingly, when Sheekman died in January of 1978, his obituary, in addition to listing his survivors, also noted that he was Groucho's friend.

Groucho was about to celebrate his eighty-fourth birthday, and a party was planned. "Gloria is a gregarious, gay-spirited woman who loves parties and giving and doing," Dorris Johnson said. "Groucho called and invited her to the party. He'd been at our house to visit Nunnally and asked me if I wanted to come. I said, 'Grouch, I can't do it. I don't like to leave Nunnally alone up here.'" (Johnson was incapacitated by emphysema.) "That was partly it. Also, the crowd had changed at Groucho's. . . . I neither was much interested in what they did and could not imagine their having any interest in me or what I did or what I represented or who I was or who I was not. . . . Then Gloria called, very subdued, very hurt, a day or two before the party. She asked, 'Are you going to Groucho's birthday party?' I said no. She laughed and said, 'You didn't get invited either!'"

Mrs. Sheekman went on to say that she had indeed been invited by Groucho, but that he later took back the invitation. "Erin doesn't like what you did to Arthur," Groucho explained.

Mrs. Johnson said, "I was indignant. . . . From that time I never asked Erin to our home."

Mrs. Johnson was livid because she felt the action was cruel and grossly unfair. For in Gloria Sheekman, Groucho never had a better friend. "He had never had anyone do any more for him and demand *nothing* in return," Mrs. Johnson said. "She was a giver. She didn't need *anything* he had. And she looked out for him. During those few years from the time he fell on the streets in Beverly Hills, when he had a first mild stroke, Gloria was the one that went in, got the doctor, called in nursing care, let the children know. She had him to her home, she cooked for him, she entertained for him.

"During the last few years, most of the wives were very outspoken, very single-minded about Erin. Gloria and I were her longest defenders. We both said there was so much she had done that his children didn't do, that no one else could have restored some life and interest in him."

Mrs. Sheekman, typically, declined to be painted as a Florence Nightingale, and tactfully avoided making any statements that would imply Groucho's children neglected him. She would only say, "Groucho was a very dear friend, and Arthur was very, very loyal to him. My husband was very loving, very giving. Most people felt his humor and wit were as close to Groucho's as anyone's. But Arthur's was far gentler."

From that point on, although she remained cordial to Erin whenever they chanced to meet, Mrs. Johnson's mind was set. She carefully avoided making any waves about it. When Jack Benny died in December of 1974, Erin called Mrs. Johnson to invite her to accompany her and Groucho to the funeral. "I didn't want to go with them, because I wasn't feeling too kindly toward Erin. Groucho didn't want to go either, but he said it would be disrespectful not to. His absence would be conspicuous.

"I felt rather bitter toward Erin the last few years, because Groucho seemed so helpless in the face of all that whirled around his life. He had reached the age and diminished health that he needed *some* area of serenity. He needed calm, and his alliance was with a young girl who needed the excitement and stimulation of celebrities, of the big names of Hollywood. Oh my, what allure! You can't put down a longing like that when you only have one access to it . . . and the access was through Groucho."

Another relationship came to an end when Groucho's cook, Martha, left her job of almost fifteen years at the end of the year. The personality conflict between her and Erin had made the situation untenable. Mrs. Brooks quit, unaware that only three months before, Groucho in his revised will had bequeathed twenty-five thousand dollars to her . . . provided she was still working for him at the time of his death.

On yet another front, Melinda moved to northern California, where she and her husband planned to open a fishing tackle store.

Her half-brother, Arthur, in an interview with Hollywood columnist Marilyn Beck, said, "It reached a point—after she had married a part-time actor and they had a couple of kids—that she couldn't cut being around Dad anymore. She finally moved away and deliberately sought a simple lifestyle—I guess some would call it a 'Hippie existence'—that was. as far removed as she could get from the luxury in which she had been raised."

About the relationship between Groucho and his younger daughter, Dorris Johnson said, "I wouldn't try to say who was right or wrong. I think each one was too unyielding. I felt that Melinda should have been more understanding of her father, and the changes that came with extreme old age. If she had been a little more sympathetic and had reached toward him, I think it would have shown something in her character that maybe was lacking. She could preach and say what evil was, and be unaware that she was inflicting a certain pain by her own intolerance there. Groucho had diminished in his capacities, and it takes a lot of reaching out and understanding. In time, she will come to understand."

Melinda took with her a substantial cash gift from her father, equal amounts going that same year to his other children. Nevertheless, the principal beneficiary of his generosity that year was Erin.

Other changes were in the offing early in 1975. Groucho's stockbroker and business manager—who had represented him for years—were supplanted by others. He also retained a new attorney.

Hollywood columnist James Bacon wrote on January 7:

Groucho Marx is really serious about suing author Richard Anobile and the Darien House publishers over material appearing in "The Marx Brothers Scrapbook."

Groucho has retained legal eagles Ed Perlstein and Mickey Rudin to take the battle into court and determine if the questionable material represents a breach of the agreement between Groucho, the author and the publisher.

Rudin is the lawyer who got Frank Sinatra out of Australia, so you know he's tenacious. [Sinatra had recently appeared in Australia and made some comments affronting the national pride. Rudin had worked out a truce between his client and the country.]

Peter Shore is an elfin man of late middle age, and his witticisms are extensively quoted among the Hollywood set.

Erin thought a coffee table book of Shore's interior designs should be published. Shore asked me if I would be interested in writing the text for the book. Groucho Marx, he added, had already agreed to write the introduction.

A preliminary meeting on the Shore project was held at Erin's house. She said a publisher's advance of fifty thousand dollars for the book should be the minimum acceptable offer. I was doubtful, since picture books rarely command that large an advance. Besides, despite his status in Southern California, Shore was an unknown quantity to New York publishers.

Nevertheless, Shore and I continued preparing a book presentation. Erin invited me to Groucho's for lunch one Sunday to discuss his introduction to the book.

"Seated by the window, he looked frail and vulnerable," I wrote in *The Groucho Phile*. "Decades seemed to have passed since the last time I'd seen him. Here, despite the glory and the immortality that is Groucho Marx, was a far older man than even the world's intrusive press had led me to believe. Had Time committed that final indignity, sticking out its leg and tripping up that famous nimble wit?"

We went out on the terrace by the pool, where Erin was swimming, and sat down at the wrought iron table. Soon she and Steve Stoliar, who was working on the fan mail, joined us.

Groucho's was a tour de force performance for an audience of three, plus my tape recorder. His delivery was much slower, and Erin and I occasionally acted as his straight men, but his stream of consciousness was a delight:

"I first met Peter Shore through his brother Sandy . . . I met him in Bulgaria . . . he was herding goats. He didn't herd enough of them so he quit. He took a boat to Savannah, Georgia . . . met a colored girl there . . . wanted to marry her but she wouldn't have him because he was white. By the way, he's the greatest decorator of houses I've ever met. Most decorators talk with their hands on their hips."

"Does Peter Shore?" I asked.

"I don't know," Groucho responded. "You'll have to ask the goats . . . I once knew a man. His first name was Peter . . . because when he goes bathing you could see it. Peter's the best. I can tell by the bills I get . . . I was always crazy about his peter. The goats saw it too . . . that's what's known as sheep dip."

"What about Peter Shore's personality?" Erin asked.

"It's fiery," Groucho answered. "Whenever he comes in a room, the whole room lights up . . . especially if you have a match . . . the girls in Savannah Gee Aye are very pretty . . . they're Creole . . . I was in a whore house once . . . with the colored girl . . . she had a great bottom . . . she was sitting on it."

"What's your favorite color?" I asked, trying to get back to the point.

"Black," Groucho responded. "Like the girl from Savannah. She wasn't all black. She was true blue . . . and it was all white with me. And I think that gives you a true picture of Peter Shore and his brother Sandy."

Surely, he had more to say. "Why did you agree to do the introduction to the book?" I asked.

"Because I just had my piano tuned. I gave him carte blanche. He's an artist just like Kreisler or Heifetz. I've never heard Peter play. He plays with himself, you see."

How long did it take Peter Shore to work on the house?

"About five foot eight."

Is that any longer than usual?

"Mine? It's very short. I have trouble finding it."

Do you have names for your rooms?

"Son of a bitch is one of the names . . . that's my bedroom. I look at myself in the mirror . . . and I'm a son of a bitch! . . . You know when I die, I want an epitaph: 'Here lies Groucho Marx . . . and lies and lies and lies. He never kissed an ugly girl.' "

Is there any such thing as an ugly girl?

"You should see some of my relatives."

Groucho went on with other non sequiturs. "I'm having dinner with the head of NBC tonight. Actually, NBC has no head ... I have a sweet tooth ... I only have one. I love the table in the dining room. I only wish the food were better."

Throughout the colloquy a uniformed nurse had hovered in the background. When Groucho briefly excused himself, I asked Erin if he was ill. "No," she replied. "Nurses are here round-the-clock because of the strokes he's had. Sometimes I think they're not needed, since Groucho is fine now. But I wouldn't forgive myself if he had another stroke and there wasn't a nurse here to take care of him."

Groucho returned at this point, taking the tag word as his cue. "I've never had troubles keeping nurses," he said. "I'm charming. I've got what they want: the salary."

When a young woman attaches herself to an older man, stereotyped thinking about the relationship automatically sets in. I was pleased to be proven wrong, for I had nothing but respect for Erin's devotion.

In the brief time I had spent with Groucho, I thought I saw the reason why. Those who lash out, as he had done to such hilarious effect for so many years, often can't withstand the devastating critiques of others. But the Groucho of today was self-mocking, and funny about it, and that's an eminently attractive quality in people of any age.

He also was a paragon of indomitability, taking his daily constitutionals, still reading voraciously, looking in on sick friends, learning at age eighty-four to play the piano. This was an extraordinary old man. The sardonic laughter of the quiz show host had been replaced by an innocent twinkle. Whatever his past sins, an essential purity showed through. A great tragedy is that his children weren't around to perceive that. In his dotage, he had truly become a lovable man.

Soon after, Erin asked if I might be interested in collaborating with Groucho on a book about the quiz show. There was definite publisher interest.

I suggested that I take on the Groucho book immediately. Since it was to be basically a novelty book, it could be completed in three or four months. I was presented to Groucho as a *fait accompli*.

He had looked at me as just another guest, whose name he had trouble remembering, one of dozens who came by each week. When Erin said, "Hector is going to write the book on the quiz show with you," Groucho regarded me differently. It was not necessarily with new respect, but with an awareness of me as an individual.

A meeting with his lawyers was set. A previous writer who had been discussing the assignment had agreed to take the short end of a 90-10 split on the book, a price he was willing to pay to have his name associated with Groucho's. "We find that you're acceptable to us," one of the attorneys said. (Apparently, because of the Anobile book, a security check had been made.) After a more equitable financial agreement was reached, I was ready to begin work.

I was well aware that my work at Groucho's house was very much under the aegis of Erin, but it wasn't an impossible burden to live with. Although I perceived no great warmth in her, I also hadn't seen the angry fire of which she was capable. As I began to be included in more social gatherings, I found it unfair that several ladies I had asked to Groucho's house didn't want to go, primarily because they had absolutely no interest in meeting Erin.

Principally, one went to Groucho's home for entertainment and the talent was still top dollar: Sammy Davis, dancing on a coffee table; Bernadette Peters, singing a ballad to Groucho; Sally Kellerman, her songs all smoky allure; Shields and Yarnell, doing the pantomime routines that reminded the host of his brother Harpo; Carroll O'Connor, revealing a pleasant singing voice; Mae West, with Bill Marx accompanying her, vocally undulating "The Ballad of Diamond Lil"; Jack Lemmon, playing the piano; Fred MacMurray, the saxophone; Groucho himself, singing his repertoire of novelty songs.

There is, of course, an Old Guard Hollywood society—conservative, rigid, irremediably dull—that Erin could not aspire to, since her ambiguous relationship with Groucho placed her beyond the pale. Its members were contemporaries—if not confrères—of Groucho and his friends. Yet with such heady company coming through his front door several nights a week, Erin didn't have to aspire elsewhere. If some of his older friends had to be supplanted by the dazzling talents Erin was inviting to his house, for her sake, he would abide their company. It wasn't that great an ordeal, given their fawning attitudes.

My favorite times at Groucho's revolved around our work, which took place in his bedroom-study. Despite all that Erin had brought into his life, there was a core of loneliness to him. I supplied a partial distraction. To elicit a response to some difficult questions, I would occasionally phrase them in a different way. Invariably, the deepest reaches of his memory would deliver. Friends asked, "Is Groucho senile?" I would always answer, "He makes perfect sense to me." It just took a little more time.

Erin was often away during our daily lunches. Groucho and I would discuss any and all matters. It is indicative of his basic democratic nature that members of the household staff usually sat with him when he ate. Fortunately, his archivist, Steve Stoliar, would take in the exchanges, then rush to his desk after lunch to jot them down. Here are a few:

HECTOR: Isn't it strange that out of all the people on your show only Fenneman is still working in broadcasting?
GROUCHO: Yeah. I took care of them.

*

HECTOR: I've read that the reason Fred Astaire and Ginger Rogers worked so well as a team was that she gave him sex appeal and he gave her class.
GROUCHO: He gave her clap?

*

GROUCHO (to nurse): You're cute, but it's too late.
NURSE: Too late for what?
GROUCHO: For you.

*

460

ZEPPO: Robin, the weekend cook, said she'd marry me, but she's too tall.
ERIN: What part of her do you want?
ZEPPO: The part I can reach.
GUMMO: What do you want with her feet?

*

GROUCHO (eating a lamb chop): This tastes like rubber.
STEVE: It tastes good.
GROUCHO: This is the best tasting rubber I've ever eaten.

*

STEVE: (referring to Frankie, one of Groucho's two cats): It's a nice cat.
GROUCHO: Yes. It's the only pussy I'm getting.

*

GROUCHO: Wonderful mail today. Nothing but requests for money.
STEVE: You got Variety, didn't you?
GROUCHO: Yes, a variety of requests for money.

*

GROUCHO: A woman's husband died, so she had his body cremated and kept the ashes in a vase on her living room table. Every time people would come over they'd flick their cigarette ashes in the vase. Finally, one man said, "Say, your husband looks as if he's putting on a little weight."

*

ERIN (prior to a New York trip for the taking of depositions in the Anobile suit): What are you going to wear to court?
GROUCHO: A court suit.

461

ERIN: What about the evidence you're going to deliver?
GROUCHO: Well, it's a package about this big.
ERIN: No, what elements are in it?
GROUCHO: Elephants? I shot an elephant in my pajamas and how it got in my pajamas I'll never know.

*

ERIN: Did you know it's Steve's birthday this Tuesday?
GROUCHO: Is it? Well, we'll have to give him something, even if it's only his discharge.

*

NURSE: It's damp and dreary outside.
GROUCHO (singing): All the folks are damp and dreary.

*

As we worked, I never got the impression that he had any special regard for me until one morning when, as was my usual custom, I walked through his open bedroom door unannounced.

I startled him, and he reacted with the only display of anger I had ever experienced.

"If you ever do that again, I'm going to kick your ass out of this house!"

"Do what, Groucho?"

"Don't come into my room without knocking. I'm entitled to my privacy."

"I've been coming into your room like this for at least two months now," I replied, "and only now you're telling me you don't like it?"

He thought about that for a while. Then he sheepishly nodded. Nevertheless, the exchange was upsetting for I would never do anything that would cause him the least discomfort. I left him alone for the rest of the morning.

His attorney came for lunch. We were discussing the process of

462

film-making, and the attorney said the director was the most important contributor to the enterprise.

"It's the writer," Groucho insisted. He looked meaningfully at me. If this was an apology, none was needed, although his gesture was greatly appreciated.

A few days later, since we were going to be discussing areas that Steve Stoliar as a budding comedy writer would be interested in, I asked him if he wanted to sit in on our session. When Steve and I joined Groucho in his room, his employee was rather unceremoniously asked to leave. It was then that I realized he considered our exchanges privileged information.

After Steve left, I said to Groucho, "He's afraid of you, you know."

"I don't want him to be afraid of me," he said softly.

Perhaps my words were extreme, so I tempered them. "I mean he has a healthy respect for you." This he could accept.

Groucho and Lucille Ball were scheduled to appear as presenters of the best comedy-variety series at the 27th Annual Emmy Awards on May 19. Groucho had unwittingly created a minor scene the previous year when she was honored as Sunair Humanitarian of the Year. Other comedians who had gathered to do her honor were Milton Berle, George Burns, Jack Benny, and Bob Hope. During a picture-taking session at the event, Groucho said, "Lucy, you're known for your beautiful legs. Could you show us one of them?" She daintily lifted up the skirt of her chiffon gown and extended one leg. Suddenly, Groucho began taking off his coat and shirt. Hope and Berle interpreted this as an act of senility and escorted him away. "I don't know why they were so concerned," Groucho later said. "I was only going to show her my Groucho T-shirt." He was hurt that his colleagues should think he had lost control of his faculties.

Groucho's spot with Miss Ball was the last Emmy presentation of the evening. Groucho—wearing a beret with his formal outfit and the French *Commandeur* rosette around his neck—was escorted by two girls, one on either side.

He and Lucy received a standing ovation.

"Thank you, thank you, thank you," Groucho said.

463

"If it's all right with you, Groucho, I'll read the nominees and you can read the winner," Miss Ball said.

"It's *not* all right with me," Groucho replied. She poked him with her elbow. After she read the names of the nominees, Groucho asked, "Where is it? Where is the envelope?" The duck from "You Bet Your Life" came down, bearing the envelope, which Miss Ball removed. She opened it and read the winner's name: Carol Burnett.

Groucho was angered because he felt he had been shunted aside. Miss Ball released a statement claiming that shortly before the presentation, word had reached her backstage that one of her children had been seriously injured in an automobile accident. She said she was so overwrought she wasn't aware of what she was doing. Over the next week, Groucho received many letters from television viewers, highly critical of Miss Ball's behavior. At no time did Lucille Ball try to offer him a personal explanation for her actions.

Eventually, I thought, his anger had dissipated. Yet, when at dinner a couple of weeks later, a guest asked if he'd made any personal appearances lately, Groucho replied, "I did 'The Lucille Ball Show' the other night."

By summer, Groucho and I had become good friends. There was no great deliberateness on his part. His were minor signs, and yet they spoke volumes to me. He voluntarily inscribed a photograph to me, calling me "a good writer," his highest compliment. Then he gave me a nickname, "Ben Hector." We began trading books, and discussed them over lunch. I was impressed by his grasp of authors' writing styles. He could read three or four pages of a book and pass quick judgment on the writer's worth. He was invariably right. He began gently nagging me about the advantages of marriage. Groucho had been married for forty-one years of his life. Despite three divorces, he was convinced that marriage is a necessity for a man. He didn't let up. I in return said that a writer makes the worst kind of husband, that his shy and lonely megalomania makes him unfit for long-lasting relationships of any kind. On a larger scale, I told him, I knew of very few happily married couples, no matter what their profession.

"My son Arthur is happy," he pointed out. "He's a writer." The view was expressed with no anger or malice.

I had become a fixture in his house. Erin graciously said I was welcome to raid the refrigerator at any time for a snack, a liberty Groucho also extended to me, which was also extended to the others in the household. I was there for one and sometimes two meals a day. Taking afternoon coffee breaks, I sat in on the intrigues—"Upstairs, Downstairs" with a California setting—and the common object of the staff's displeasure was the part-time mistress of the house. I had arrived one day to find a member of the staff informing some fans at the door they couldn't see Groucho because "that terrible woman would kill us." It wasn't my place, but after the fans left, I told the offender that he owed "that terrible woman" a certain loyalty, since it was at her pleasure that all the members of the staff had been hired.

I also found the Actor's Method in Erin's madness. Her rages were sometimes calculated to move people into action. One time, she went through an angry tirade over the telephone, her screams carrying into the farthest reaches of the house. She slammed down the receiver and started to laugh. "Do you think that will get some action?" she asked.

No one was exempt from her abrupt changes in mood, not even Groucho himself. One day, the three of us were sitting by the pool. Groucho quietly said that he'd called his accountant and instructed him to send two hundred dollars to Kay, who needed some dental work. "I'm going to fire that son of a bitch!" Erin screamed. "How do you know she won't use it for alcohol? It's all been set up. She gets her money. She shouldn't bother you."

"I don't want you to fire him," he quietly replied. The tirade resumed. Groucho turned to me and said, "She has no compassion."

"No compassion?" Erin yelled. "Do you call it compassion to give that woman money so that she can go on a bender?"

Groucho got up and went to his room. After her anger had subsided, Erin apologized to me for the outburst, and went into the reasons why she had reacted as she did.

Groucho's remark seemed an apt one at the time, and it was not the type of comment that a senile, totally manipulated man would make.

He saw her faults and could even joke about them. The three of us were sitting at lunch one Saturday when Groucho turned to Erin and playfully asked, "Aren't you feeling well?" Erin said she felt fine. "Why do you ask?" Groucho replied, "You haven't fired anybody today."

If Erin was retribution for his maltreatment of women over the years, Groucho was unaware of it. Had he thought that, it was a price he was glad to pay. He would forfeit his friends and hand over a considerable part of his fortune to keep Erin by his side. I have no doubt that he would have married her if she only would have him. Had this happened, the impending headlines would never have occurred. Erin, however, professed to want children of her own. The only way to keep her by his side would be to adopt her.

One day Erin entered the house in a fury, because a psychiatrist had given it as his professional opinion that Groucho was not of a rational enough mind to make that important decision. Up to now, every major token of Groucho's generosity to Erin had been cleared through both his psychiatrist and his lawyer. A thoroughly confused Groucho did not know what to make of Erin's harangue. He had the noblest of intentions, and he didn't understand what all the yelling was about.

The time would come when I too would bear the brunt of her anger. Groucho and I had been working for several weeks, and although the publisher's advance money had been paid, I still didn't have a signed collaboration agreement from Groucho. My attorney attempted to expedite the matter. He called Erin, who hung up the phone in anger, and started to berate me. I picked up all my materials and prepared to move everything out of the house. As soon as I arrived home, Groucho's lawyer called and said the agreement was on its way. When I returned to the house the next day, carrying back all the materials I took with me, I accepted Erin's apology for her outburst. In so doing, it seems as if I had given her license to scream at will. The one apology paid for the future tirades in advance.

There is a very obvious question that should be asked in the face of the foregoing. Why did I sit by and do nothing when all the turmoil surrounded me? One reason was the nature of the relationship between Groucho and Erin. It was a perverse romance. When he told me his favorite author was W. Somerset Maugham, I immediately thought of *Of Human Bondage*. Groucho evidently was playing Philip Carey to Erin's Mildred. That was his need and, short of mayhem, who was I to thwart his desires? I didn't like seeing Groucho berated by a woman he would have properly dealt with twenty years previously. But I had to admit that Erin kept him motivated and stimulated. She got the adrenalin flowing, and Groucho could function. I was sure she had added years to his life.

If Erin used Groucho, she in turn was used. Hangers-on who came to dinner would make snide remarks about her out of her hearing. One actor was virtually a live-in guest, staying for months in Melinda's old room, getting up at noon and going off to start his day. That Christmas, he invited over fifty people to Groucho's for a party without asking the permission of either Groucho or Erin. When Groucho heard what was in the offing, he called the actor to his room.

"Do you know the meaning of chutzpah?" Groucho asked.

The actor was contrite, but he begged Groucho not to humiliate him by making him call the party off. Groucho relented. We were subjected that evening to a procession of underground movie makers, Sunset Strip hustlers, and drug freaks. After Groucho's death, the actor gave interviews telling of his intimate friendship with Groucho. He didn't add that he had to be virtually black-mailed into occasionally accompanying Groucho on his daily walk. The actor had all the time in the world to be photographed with the glorified legend, and little time to spend with the very lonely man.

I tried to tell Erin that these were not her friends. By helping her I felt I was helping Groucho. She would agree, but then continued to see the same people.

It was a significant milestone, as evidenced by the barrage of requests from major publications for exclusive interviews. Los Angeles Mayor Tom Bradley had proclaimed it "Groucho Marx Day." Special preparations were called for. The party was scheduled for Sunday afternoon, October 5, three days after his actual eighty-fifth birthday, and two hundred guests—among the most celebrated people in Hollywood—were invited.

It was a private party, nevertheless, and no photographers were included. As my birthday gift I hired photographer Frank Diernhammer to shoot pictures which I later presented to Groucho in a leather album.

Erin wanted this to be an extra special day, and she even recruited Peter Shore to advise on floral arrangements and table settings. The caterers suggested a birthday cake with the Groucho caricature from his A&M album painted on it in icing.

I arrived with Diernhammer before the party started, to find that there were several other photographers outside trying to get in. When I informed one of them that this was a private party, he asked why Diernhammer was being allowed to enter. I explained.

Inside, one of the staff informed me that a photographer from *Rolling Stone* had managed to make his way into the house. Erin was sitting in Groucho's bedroom, while a nurse was helping Groucho dress. As I walked in, Erin was laughing. Groucho, his hearing aid not turned up, had only partially heard that it was a *Rolling Stone* photographer who would have to be asked to leave. "I don't want any holy rollers at my party," he said. He refused to come out until the uninvited young man left.

Zeppo and Gummo came from Palm Springs, and the three surviving Marx Brothers were photographed together. None of Groucho's children was present. His grandson Andy, however, was there, as well as Andy's grandmother, Grace Kahn, and his mother, Irene Atkins. His colleagues from "You Bet Your Life" were also invited. Groucho and I had put the finishing touches on *The Secret Word Is Groucho* that very week, and they had recently shared their reminiscences with us. Other performers came to pay their respects to the master. They included Peter Sellers, Elliott Gould, Sally Kellerman, Milton Berle, Steve Allen, Red Buttons, Carroll O'Connor, Sally Struthers, Jack Lemmon, and Liza Minnelli. Later, Bob Hope arrived. "One of the best comedians of our time has just come in," Groucho said. "Why don't you come up and say a few words, Bob?"

"You don't have to say those words just because I'm here," Hope said.

"If you weren't here I wouldn't have said them," Groucho shot back.

Hope shook his head. "I've never been able to top you."

The party ushered in a new round of honors, activities, and public appearances for Groucho. I had met a studio executive named Stanley Musgrove during a previous book collaboration. He was also the head of the University of Southern California Friends of the Libraries, as well as one of Mae West's closest friends. Musgrove had brought Miss West to dinner at Groucho's recently. He thought his group should honor Groucho at a literary luncheon, and it was scheduled for a week after the birthday party.

George Fenneman agreed to moderate, and Jack Lemmon, Lynn Redgrave, and Roddy McDowall were set to read excerpts from Groucho's six books. I put the program together. Groucho advised me on the excerpts he thought should be read. We then worked out what his contributions would be.

A few weeks previously, Andy had said, "I understand USC is going to have a testimonial for you. When is it?"

"October 12," Stoliar replied.

"That's right around your birthday," Andy observed.

"I can wait," Groucho said. "They're coming fast now."

"What do you want for your birthday?" his grandson asked.

"Last year."

Groucho seemed listless when he arrived with Erin at the USC hall where the event was to be held. People who came up to him before the lunch which preceded the program found him distracted. Bob Dwan expressed his concern about Groucho's condition. Bob had worked with Groucho for years, and could sense when things weren't running smoothly.

Groucho mustered his forces during lunch, for when he rose from his table to take his place on the stage, he was almost his old self.

"Not only were there audience questions," Jack Lemmon recalled, "but there were prepared questions that we had to ask Groucho because we thought they would be edifying to the audience. My question was particularly long. I listed certain of his films. 'Now, Groucho,' I said, 'all or part of those films were not actually written as the credits were. They were aided and abetted by you as a writer and you have always been a prolific writer and yet, you did not take credit for the writing.' It must have taken me three minutes. I said, 'Why is it that you declined to take the writing credit of these most famous of your works?' Without a beat, he said, 'I'm nuts about your wife!' Well, it was a hell of an answer, and the place fell in and it's one of those I-guess-you-should-have-been-there things. The longer the question was, the funnier that idiot answer was because it was totally obtuse, as he often was. He seemed to make no sense very often and yet it's funny."

It was an extraordinarily happy, smoothly flowing program, the audience relishing all the comic lines, laughing even at those they had heard a dozen times before.

Afterwards, Groucho was again deflated and remote. I marvelled at the reserves of strength he must have called on to bring himself up for his performance. Groucho himself told his nephew Bill, who accompanied him when he sang, "I couldn't have done it without you."

"That was the first time in all my life that he ever said anything gracious to me," Bill said.

By this time, Erin and I had made an accommodation. She may have looked on me as an afternoon sitter for Groucho. My presence freed her to pursue other matters. They were, however, harder to come by than they had been when she first started working with Groucho.

The problem was rooted in Erin's personality itself. "I've become a monster!" she once exclaimed to me. "When I first started with Groucho, I was sweet and agreeable and everyone walked all over me. Now I'm a bitch, and they listen."

She had assumed an attitude that made it increasingly more difficult to deal with her as Groucho's personal manager and closest advisor. Erin approached negotiations on the premise that everyone was out to exploit Groucho. No matter how amicable and fair the negotiations, the other side was the enemy. Gradually, a reaction set in. Merchandisers and television and film producers decided that dealing with Erin for the rights to Groucho meant trouble, frustration, and exasperation.

After we completed *The Secret Word Is Groucho*, we worked together on an introduction to the revised paperback edition of

Beds, Groucho's first book. He posed for new pictures, entertaining famous people in his own bed. Lynn Redgrave, Elliott Gould, Valerie Perrine, and a Great Dane jumped into bed with him ... separately of course. He jumped into other people's beds, calling on Phyllis Diller and Burt Reynolds. Reynolds, during the taking of his picture with Groucho, struck a Not-tonight-I-have-a-headache pose. To Groucho it was *déjà vu.*

Putting together the paperback took about a month. Before it was completed, another offer was accepted for a picture book of Groucho's life, similar to Chaplin's *My Life in Pictures*, which had been recently published. In the meantime, Groucho was working on a Bob Hope television special, a takeoff on *Jaws*, in which forty comedians would be devoured. Called "Joys," it offered few of them.

Gathering more than seven hundred photographs and illustrations and placing them in a logical sequence was a much more difficult job than I expected. Drawing Groucho out was much easier. The pictures jogged his memory, and he would come forth with anecdotes that he had long forgotten and that consequently had not been published.

Looking at pictures of Groucho as a young man, I observed, "You were a good-looking fellow, Grouch."

"I look better now," he replied. "I don't wear a false mustache. I don't smoke." He apparently felt more comfortable within his own skin than he'd ever felt before.

While we were working on the project, the publisher's editor came to California to see how the book was progressing. She was witness to a household emergency and also got a look at Erin's temper.

The housekeeper, who'd recently emigrated from South America, developed a mysterious rash. Erin took her to a doctor. It was diagnosed as syphilis. Without ceremony, the housekeeper was sacked, Erin refusing to come into Groucho's house until the hapless woman was gone. Every other member of the household was sent to Groucho's doctor to get a Wassermann test. Erin feared the disease could be contracted by using the same utensils the housekeeper had handled.

"What would happen if *Groucho* came down with syphilis?" she asked me.

"James Bacon might run the item," I replied, referring to the Hollywood columnist. She wasn't amused. No amount of cajoling and appealing to her sense of fair play could change her mind about the disease or about the woman who was left to look for a job without a recommendation from her previous employer.

Groucho, of course, was never apprised of what happened. He had surrendered the responsibility of running the household to Erin as part of her supervision of his entire life.

The first public broadside against Erin, though effectively veiled, came early in 1976. Sidney Sheldon's third novel, *A Stranger in the Mirror*, was published. A mass market *roman à clef* in the Harold Robbins-Jacqueline Susann mold, the book—according to its jacket blurb—was the story of "Toby Temple, super star and super bastard, adored by his vast TV and movie public yet isolated from real, human contact by his own suspicion and distrust . . . and the story of Jill Castle, who came to Hollywood to be a star and discovered she had to buy her way with her body." The coming together of these two characters created a best-seller.

Jill Castle, a failed actress, attached herself to Toby Temple, making herself indispensable as dutiful wife and helpmate and just incidentally extracting revenge on the people who had exploited her in the past.

There were uncomfortable similarities to Groucho and Erin in the two characters. Toby Temple was the son of an ambitious mother and a charming schlemiel of a father, as was Groucho. There the resemblance ended, however, Temple having achieved his original fame as a nightclub comic. Since the character was genitally well-endowed, some readers thought the character was patterned after Milton Berle, since the latter comedian had made frequent mention of that fact in his autobiography. As for Jill Castle, not only did she estrange Temple from his oldest friends— as Erin had been accused of doing—she became celebrated for her selflessness in nursing Temple back to health after a crippling stroke. At book's end, after a second stroke leaves Temple with no hope for recovery, and having been reunited with her first lover, Jill

Castle pushes Temple, strapped in his wheelchair, into a swimming pool. He drowns. At the subsequent inquest, Temple's physician comes forward and attests to Jill's devotion. The death is ruled an accident.

There had been a real-life incident in the past when Groucho had almost drowned, and Erin had pulled him out of the pool. If Sheldon adapted the incident in his novel, it must have been revealing for Erin to discover how he had changed the situation to create a villainess.

By dedicating the novel to Groucho, Sheldon seemed to be challenging Erin to identify herself and Jill Castle as one. The mass reader market, unaware of the near-drowning incident, would be unable to make the same connection.

"What can I do?" she asked friends. "Sidney was so devoted to Groucho when no one else would have anything to do with him. After all, it's just a novel."

A few days after the book was published, Groucho was honored with the Sunair Humanitarian Award at a $100 per plate fund-raising dinner. Groucho and Erin bought two tables. Sidney and Jorja Sheldon were among the guests. Erin, seated at the second table, came over during the proceedings, and made chitchat with the Sheldons. Sheldon asked her if she had read the book. "I just haven't had time," she replied.

If Sheldon wrote the book with the intention of subtly telling Groucho he should see Erin in the same light as many saw her—a fact he couldn't admit because of possible legal repercussions—he was destined to be disappointed. Groucho never read the book.

One day, we were discussing his friends of the past. "Groucho," I said, "you've been friends with some of the great writers of our time. Now look at your friends." I mentioned Sheldon and the producer of highly commercial, artistically deplorable films.

Groucho thought for a moment. "To tell the truth, I'm not that crazy about the producer," he said. "But Sidney ... he's a good writer." He could not ignore Sheldon's past and continuing devotion.

Goldwyn, a biography Arthur had written, was published that spring. During an interview with Stanley Eichelbaum of the *San*

Francisco Examiner, Arthur talked about the *Minnie's Boys* misadventure, and told how Groucho felt Totie Fields was too Jewish to play Minnie Marx.

About Erin, Arthur said, "I'm out of the will, and as far as I know, so are my sisters, Melinda and Miriam. She brainwashed Groucho, and made him get rid of his long time business manager and even his maid, Martha, who'd been with him for thirty years. We all got along great until Erin came into the picture."

In a later interview with James Bacon, Arthur jokingly said Groucho was anti-Semitic because he didn't want Minnie portrayed as being too Jewish.

A friend showed Erin Arthur's comments in the San Francisco newspaper. Together with Arthur's quote in the Bacon column, it drove her into a frenzy. Bacon was invited to lunch. Arthur Whitelaw, who had produced the play, was also summoned.

Erin wanted the record set straight. Whitelaw, during lunch, told Bacon how happy Groucho was with Erin. He was not particularly kind to Arthur.

As Erin recited a litany of Arthur's past neglect, Groucho started to cry. "He's no good," he said between sobs.

"Please, Groucho, don't cry," Erin said. "You'll make me cry too."

Groucho regained his composure.

Soon after, Groucho had his attorney draft a letter, in which he told Arthur he was being taken out of his will and his legacy would go to the United Jewish Appeal instead. Groucho, of course, never changed his will, and had no intention of doing so. But by sending the letter, he further alienated his son, making it nearly impossible for a reconciliation to take place.

From that point on, Groucho would occasionally start crying for no discernible reason. If a woman's tears tear a man up, try listening to those of an old man, looking back over his life and yearning for what might have been. Erin soon invited a group of psychologists to dinner. I asked one of them how to handle Groucho's tears. "Wouldn't you cry too," he asked, "if your children didn't want anything to do with you?" My question was never answered.

In September, Groucho was due to appear in a tribute to television on the "Donny and Marie Show." His appearance was promoted, and he appeared in the show's finale, but Erin withdrew with him before Groucho's spot could be taped. Perhaps she felt Groucho wasn't receiving the veneration he deserved. Whatever the reason, Groucho would absolutely not appear, despite his contractual obligation.

Erin was gradually being consumed by a desperation I couldn't understand. Her financial arrangements with Groucho were beyond my ken. All of my collaboration agreements were made with Groucho himself and not with Groucho Marx Productions, of which Erin was a fifty percent partner. They had been hammered out with Groucho's attorneys, who were tough negotiators, but eminently fair.

When, at dinner one night, Erin showed me a letter Groucho's attorney had written her, resigning as Groucho's representative, the red alert went up. The law firm could no longer represent Groucho, the letter stated, because they were convinced that Groucho's best interests and Erin's were not the same. It stopped short of accusing her of exploiting Groucho for her personal gain, yet the implication was there. I still wonder why she would show me a letter that was so personally damaging.

When Groucho's and my mutual literary agent suggested I write the definitive, authorized biography, I hesitated. Much as I'd come to love Groucho, and as concerned as I was about his future, I didn't want to make a career of writing Marxiana. But my agent stressed the extraordinary opportunity I'd been handed by my association with Groucho, and so I agreed.

On Sunday, October 31, 1976, Groucho and Erin attended a banquet of the American String Teachers Association honoring Zubin Mehta. Lenny Atkins, Arthur's successor as Irene's husband, was banquet chairman. Before the three hundred in attendance, Groucho got up, and with Grace Kahn accompanying him on the piano, sang her composition, "Oh, How That Woman Could Cook." On that evening, at Los Angeles's Ambassador Hotel, Groucho unknowingly gave his final performance.

He had been scheduled to appear two weeks later in Washington, D.C., at a fund-raising tribute sponsored by the Ralph Nader organization. Several other celebrities had also promised to appear: Chevy Chase, Valerie Perrine, George Fenneman, and Shields and Yarnell.

Erin, for some time now, had been voicing ambivalence about the trip. The Sunday before our scheduled Tuesday departure, George and Peg Fenneman came to lunch at Groucho's to discuss his participation in the show. Erin surprised us all by saying she didn't think the trip was a good idea.

"I just can't get up and perform in front of people anymore," she told me after the Fennemans left. Did she truly believe the public was coming to see her? Or had she taken on Groucho's persona? It was a spooky afternoon.

She called Lauren Bacall in New York, who told Erin she thought Groucho should be honored at the Kennedy Center, and not at some downtown movie house. The Nader people had been forced to find another hall when they discovered the Center was already booked.

The next day, Tom Wilhite had scheduled a meeting with Chevy Chase to discuss the script I was blocking out for the event. Chase was hesitant about reading from a text, and preferred to wing it on his own. Nothing much was accomplished, and it was just as well. After we left the conference room at Rogers and Cowan, Tom and I went back to his office, where Tom informed me that Erin had called just before the meeting to say the trip was off. He hadn't mentioned it during the meeting with Chase because he thought I might be able to dissuade her from cancelling. The Nader people had already spent more than fifteen thousand dollars on publicity and travel arrangements to take us all to Washington. Erin had explained that a recent change in medication had caused Groucho to become incontinent, and she wouldn't risk embarrassing him in public. The trip was called off.

Groucho received some negative publicity as a result of the cancellation. The bulk of the criticism, however, was aimed at Erin. And it is true that despite her continuing reservations, she had let the planning for the event proceed.

I was going East anyway on a research trip, and the cancellation served only to delay my departure an extra day. On the evening before I left, actually the day we had all been due in Washington, I had dinner with Groucho. Erin was expected, but she never arrived. After dinner, as was his habit, Groucho excused himself "to take a leak and brush my fangs—fangs for the memory." A few minutes later, after he had changed into pajamas and was sitting in bed watching television, I went into his bedroom to say good-bye.

His look was beatific. "You're a wonderful man," he told me. "I love you."

I was enormously moved. "I love you too, Groucho," I replied. Trying to keep the exchange light, I went on, "The whole world loves you." He smiled and turned his attention to the television.

As I drove home, thinking how completely this little old man had gotten under my skin, I was aware how easy it had been for him to say the words to a relative stranger he'd known for a comparatively short time. And I wondered if his son Arthur had, in his entire fifty-six years, ever heard the same words.

CHAPTER FIFTEEN

The color of truth is grey.

André Gide

Seated in his Manhattan office on an achingly cold, late November day in 1976, Goddard Lieberson talked about his future duties as executor of Groucho's will, the provisions of which he was not fully aware. Lieberson was a man of renowned integrity and as fair an arbiter as either Groucho's children or Erin Fleming could hope to have. He was not in California to see the effect that his children's indifference was having on Groucho these days. Nor could he feel the fallout, three thousand miles away, of Erin's many tempests and rages.

Lieberson felt, as many of Groucho's friends did, that the end was near for Groucho. Indeed, Lieberson's own death the following May was untimely for it would sidetrack Groucho's carefully laid plans.

At the moment, however, Lieberson was talking about Groucho's children, whom he didn't know well, and Erin Fleming, whom he knew better.

"Whatever Groucho leaves Erin," he said, "I'm sure she deserves every penny."

The sentiment was to be repeated often over the next several months, as I interviewed Groucho's friends and business associates, even by those who bore no great fondness for Erin. Anyone who'd known Groucho knew what an impossible man he could be.

Erin, in gaining his confidence and his love, had to cut through more than eighty years of bitterly built-up defenses. She was not immune to the bite of Groucho's still waspish tongue, but fortunately she could give as well as receive. She refused to be intimidated by him. Erin also had to overcome Groucho's madonna-versus-whore attitude toward women. There's a lyric from *Funny Girl,* in which the Fanny Brice character sings she has twenty-six expressions, sweet as pie to tough as leather. Erin had mastered the two extremes, if few of the nuances between. Along with these accomplishments she was expected to be inordinately amusing and devoted to Groucho. No matter what others thought, in his eyes she delivered. It was not beneath her to empty the bedpan when Groucho was sent to bed by his doctor. And, to get him out of bed, when misery and despair threatened to keep him there, she had to irritate him, to challenge him, to build his will to resist the encroachments of old age. If he refused to eat his meals, she would anger him with her comments. "Why don't you eat your lunch?" she'd ask. "I work hard. I'm supporting you. Do *you* think you paid for all this? *I'm* Groucho Marx, and what I did for you I can do for anyone." How well he knew what she had done for him. The thought of losing her was unbearable. Invariably, he finished the meal. If Groucho was momentarily resentful, his attitude would soon change. Her stratagems had longer-lasting effects on others, for they created largely unspoken enmity. In addition, a certain loss of her own self-respect was inevitable. Who wants to be known as a real-life villain, particularly when others feel you are playing the role so well?

Undeniably, her chosen role placed an enormous strain on Erin. And when it was coupled with the withdrawal by the attorneys she had come to look on as her protection against Groucho's children, the tensions she felt were almost tangible.

Shortly after my arrival in New York, Erin also came East. The two of us were invited to Arthur Whitelaw's for dinner one night, and I picked her up at her suite at the Sherry Netherland. Having a drink while she finished dressing, Erin told me that she wasn't returning to California until Groucho made peace with his children. She stressed that it would be up to Groucho to make the necessary overtures.

Henry Golas, a nineteen-year-old student at the California Institute of the Arts, had been hired part-time to catalog Groucho's film collection and to screen movies every Friday in the projection room. Groucho and young Golas usually watched the movies together, Groucho offering parenthetical observations on how scenes had been shot. If others should join them, Groucho would take a keen interest in watching their reactions to the film being shown.

Now another responsibility was delegated to Henry. Erin told him to inform Groucho that she wasn't coming back if he didn't see Arthur.

"I didn't deliver the ultimatum to Groucho," Golas said. "I just asked if he'd like to see Arthur and Lois. 'Certainly,' he said. I only had Arthur's address. I asked Andy for the telephone number. He didn't have it. Groucho said to him, 'What kind of a son are you that you don't have your father's phone number?' He dictated a telegram to send to Arthur: 'Please call me. Want to see you. Love Father.' When I told Erin, she said it should have been signed Padre." (This was the nickname Arthur and Miriam had coined for him.)

When Arthur called, Henry arranged for him and his wife to come to dinner. Erin had suggested that Nat and Helen Perrin also be invited, but they declined the invitation. The meeting between father and son was cordial enough, if a touch awkward. Groucho gave Arthur an autographed copy of *The Groucho Phile*.

At one point Henry pulled the younger Marxes aside while two musician friends of Erin's played the piano and sang for Groucho.

"He's at the point in his life where he should have his family around him," he told them.

"There's a time when his family needed him," Lois said.

Arthur looked pained. "That's not important now," he told Henry. "He's in good health and he seems well taken care of."

Henry had been instructed to tell Arthur he was welcome to look at all of Groucho's books, to assure himself that his father's finances were in order.

"Now that she's taken everything," Lois said bitterly, "she wants to drop them on us."

Again Arthur softened his wife's comments, repeating, "That's not important. It won't be necessary to look at the books."

481

Henry assured the Marxes that the prime loyalties of the household staff were to Groucho.

"You're in love with the legend," Lois said.

"I think pretty realistically," the young man answered, "and it's pretty silly to hate a man for his past cruelties when that man doesn't exist anymore."

Before Arthur and Lois left, Henry asked them to call if they had any questions. An uneasy truce had been effected.

Getting Miriam to the house was much more difficult. She accepted two invitations, but didn't show up either time. When Erin returned from New York, she drove with Groucho and Henry to Miriam's house in Culver City, which she shared with a caretaker couple.

"I remember sitting in a dumpy little living room," Henry told me. "Groucho told Miriam he wanted to buy her another house."

Over the next few weeks, Henry acted as liaison between father and daughter. "When Miriam was together," Henry recalled, "she was charming and witty. But when she was off on the other side, she didn't make sense. She was full of fear and told obvious lies."

The woman caring for Miriam would occasionally call the house, asking to speak to Groucho, saying Miriam wanted to talk to her father. When Henry told her to put Miriam on the phone, the woman would become threatening. Groucho rarely spoke to his daughter. He couldn't and wouldn't cope with her problems, even when it was she and not her caretakers calling.

Then, a local hospital called the Marx household to say that Miriam had been admitted as a patient. Erin again sent Henry to see what had happened. Groucho was not informed. "It was obvious she'd been beaten," Henry recalled, "but she kept claiming she'd fallen down. As she gained confidence in me, she told me she'd been locked in her room for days, with only a chamber pot."

Actor Warren Berlinger, who also operates a financial planning service, had recently been hired to advise Groucho. He was soon recruited to perform more mundane duties, going to Culver City with Henry to pick up some clothes for Miriam.

When Miriam recovered from her injuries, she agreed to be transferred from Cedars-Sinai Hospital in Los Angeles to St. John's in Santa Monica, to again embark on an alcoholic rehabilitation program.

After I returned from New York early in 1977, Groucho and I resumed deliberations on the book. When I asked him to expound on his standing as a living legend, he said, "It's an empty phrase. It means nothing. I'm pleased, but I don't put up an American flag. My responsibility to the audience is to give as good a show as I can. I've been a star for fifty years. I think I can see why. I find myself funny. I never think I could have done it better. I always did it as well as I could at the time. I see a lot of comedians today on television that are good. But these are not funny times we're living in."

When I asked him what his greatest career satisfaction had been, Groucho quickly replied, "The kids. They're crazy about me. I'm crazy about them too."

He bristled when I suggested he was affected by a lifetime of insecurity. "I'm eighty-six years old," Groucho snapped. "If I'm not secure now, when in the hell am I going to be?"

Intimations of his mortality followed. "I don't think I want to live past ninety," he said one day over lunch. "That's long enough for anyone. But that's a long way off. I don't plan to die for quite a while. When I go, I'll probably die alone with Erin crying. The one I love is Erin. And she loves me. She changed my whole life in every way." Then he beamed. "Erin says that when I go I deserve a monument!"

Groucho was cooperating with me as well as he could, although his memory often failed him. I had fallen into the habit of bringing picture books for him to see, for I found that he would come up with reminiscences about people once he'd seen their pictures. One of the books was a pictorial history of the theater. Looking at Ethel Barrymore's picture one day, he quoted her famous curtain line in a voice an octave lower than his own, "That's all there is . . . there isn't any more."

We all laughed at his imitation. "I'm convinced Ethel Barrymore was a man," Groucho continued. "No woman could have a voice that low."

"Sammy Colt is going to be surprised," I said.

"Who's that?"

"He's a social man-about-town I know," I replied. "Ethel Barrymore's son."

Groucho's eyes widened. And when I ventured his opinion about

Ethel Barrymore to others a few days later, Groucho corrected me. "She can't be a man," he said. "She has a son."

That didn't deter him from continuing the Barrymore imitation, since it was always good for a laugh. Once, looking at his emptied dinner plate, he volunteered, "That's all there is . . . there isn't any more."

The same couldn't be said about Groucho's career. He was eighty-six his last birthday and still being sought for appearances. The most immediate was a syndicated television program, "Groucho's Special," which was being put together by director Stanley Dorffman. The plan was to film a series of parties at Groucho's house, with his famous guests performing in his living room. An accompanist came every afternoon to rehearse Groucho, who planned to sing the songs he'd made famous, as well as some special material.

Late in January, Henry Golas remarked that he found it increasingly difficult to function around Erin. He had recently come to me and suggested something should be done to give Groucho serenity. Although I too felt this would be preferable to the turmoil around him, this was my judgment and not Groucho's. His need for an Erin Fleming in his life was difficult to explain to an impressionable young student who adored the man as well as the legend. "He's being well taken care of," I told Henry. "Only his children can do something about it. If they don't care enough, I don't see what anybody else can do."

Melinda's monthly allowance had recently been cut off. Groucho's daughter called the house, and one of the nurses spoke to her. The nurse, appalled that she was being dragged into a domestic matter, promptly resigned.

"Melinda can have her allowance back," Erin told me. "All she has to do is pay some attention and respect to her father." Melinda did so soon after, arriving from northern California with a friend— who also happened to be an attorney—to see her father. Erin made herself scarce, and the only regular member of the household who was available was Henry.

Henry told me Melinda had come because she heard Groucho was being verbally and physically abused by Erin. Henry confided in Melinda, telling her of ugly scenes he'd witnessed. He then suggested that I also had damaging things to say about Erin. When he informed me what he'd done, I told him I would have nothing to say. My role was to write an impartial book about Groucho's life, not to be drawn into family disputes.

Because Melinda had sought to give Henry the impression that she received no money from Groucho, when in fact he had seen the cancelled checks, Henry now saw that he was involved in a situation that was over his head. Total honesty was called for, and he told Erin what he'd done. He chose to do so by telephone though, rather than in person.

The day he called, Groucho and I were conferring in his bedroom when Erin came charging in. "Henry just called and he said Melinda is asking questions," she told Groucho. "She says I abuse you. She's been to see you five times in seven years. Is *she* going to take care of you?"

Groucho exploded. "That little bitch! She'll never set foot in this house again."

Erin walked out of the room to continue her conversation with Henry. I looked at Groucho. He was shivering.

"Grouch," I offered, "she's your daughter." He began to cry. I ineffectually patted his arm. After a few minutes, he regained his composure.

"Let's go on," he said.

"Maybe we shouldn't," I said. "We can pick up again some other time."

He was insistent, however, that we should continue talking as if nothing had happened. I started to speak, but Groucho again started to cry.

"I can't," he said. "I'm too upset."

When I saw him the next day, I didn't mention Melinda. Although he seemed depressed, he bounced back within a few days, being chipper enough to accept an invitation to George Burns's eighty-first birthday party. His gift was a brass duck, and he arrived at the party with Erin and Adam Schapiro, the teen-age son of a photographer friend of Erin's. Adam often entertained at Groucho's parties, being introduced as The Great Amazo, the eminent magician.

People traditionally entertain at Hollywood parties, and Adam was brought along to show off some of his tricks. Groucho also planned to serenade his old friend with a song or two. The party, however, was more structured and less intimate than Groucho had anticipated. He became irritated when he found out he wasn't expected to entertain, when that was his main reason for coming.

Milton Berle received the brunt of Groucho's anger. "I don't think you're funny," he snapped at him.

Berle, trying to lighten Groucho's mood, said, "Everything I know I stole from you."

"Then," Groucho testily replied, "you weren't listening."

Erin spotted one of Groucho's recently resigned attorneys and created a scene. The host asked her to leave. Norman Krasna, one of dozens who saw the incident, came to Groucho's aid. Erin snarled to leave them alone. She then took Groucho down to the tented tennis courts where dinner was being served.

Groucho was upset about the incident when I saw him the following day. Erin was outraged, as if it was someone else and not she who'd created the scene.

I was surprised to find out, in the retelling of the preceding evening's events, that Norman Krasna was in California. For someone who'd been devoted to Groucho for so many years, it struck me as strange that he hadn't made any effort to see Groucho since his arrival from Switzerland. I checked with Groucho, who invited Krasna to Saturday lunch.

I picked Krasna up at his hotel. We'd never met, but I related to him immediately. He's a cheerful, outgoing, delightful man. Besides that, we had one precious thing in common, having collaborated with Groucho on his writings.

"What do you think of Erin?" he asked me on the drive over.

No one had ever put the question so bluntly. I had my opinions, but whenever Erin's name was brought up at dinner parties, I'd deliberately been noncommittal.

"I guess everyone has a friend whose wife you don't particularly like," I told him. "But you are polite to her because you don't want to lose the friend."

Norman then told me he'd felt thrust aside since Erin had come into Groucho's life. He talked about the Burns party and how humiliated he'd felt seeing Groucho caught up in such a display. The whole town was talking about Erin's behavior, he said.

Lunch was pleasant. As we prepared to leave, Norman asked Groucho if he'd like to join him and Arthur at Hillcrest one day for lunch, after which he and Arthur would play a round of golf. Groucho declined the invitation.

As I drove Norman back to his hotel, he offered his assistance on my book, saying he would talk to Arthur about conferring with me. This, he informed me a couple of days later, Arthur agreed to do. I called Arthur and we agreed to meet as soon as he had some free time. He was then at work on an unauthorized biography of Carroll O'Connor.

Work with Groucho continued, but it was becoming harder to draw him out, since he was distracted by more immediate concerns. The incident at the Burns party still rankled. Preparations for the television special were sapping his energies. What he most brooded about was what appeared to be the finality of his estrangement from Melinda. He still felt great ambivalence about Miriam, and his attitude toward Arthur did not seem to be a caring one. That's why I put the question to him.

"Do you love Arthur?" I asked.

"Of course, I love him," Groucho replied, surprised that I would have any doubt. "He's my son!"

When a person is party to events which later attract great notoriety, one's instinct is to build up one's part in the proceedings. This I do not want to do. Suffice it to say I was there.

No one had to tell me about my special standing with Groucho. He liked and trusted me, otherwise he would not have agreed to my writing an authorized biography of him without setting any conditions whatever. This last was especially significant to me, given his recent experience with the Richard Anobile book, as well as a recently concluded collaboration with yet another writer, Charlotte Chandler. She had conducted a *Playboy* interview with Groucho, and had worked off and on for two years gathering anecdotes and reminiscences. For some reason, Erin had banished Miss Chandler from Groucho's house shortly after his eighty-fifth birthday party.

"She was an impostor," Groucho told me about the departed writer, whom he never saw again.

Miss Chandler, over lunch, had told me that she did not have a signed contract for the book as yet, but there was a verbal agreement with Doubleday & Co. which would be formalized when the manuscript was finished.

Erin asked Julia Coopersmith, the literary agent for Groucho and myself, to confirm whether this was true. Since Julie was a former Doubleday editor, she seemed the logical person to ferret out the information. The report back from New York was that there was no signed contract in existence, and Julie was unable to determine if a verbal agreement with one of Doubleday's countless editors was in effect.

On the strength of this partial information, Erin severed the relationship with Miss Chandler. As I saw it, she had not misled anyone, and her months of work were being abruptly terminated.

Groucho looked on his sessions with Miss Chandler and his celebrity friends as being unproductive. He told me the book would never be published. In a separate conversation with me, Erin disagreed. "As soon as the old man dies," she said, "that book will be sold."

As was often the case, Erin was correct. The book, published by Doubleday in the spring of 1978, painted an intimate association between Groucho and Miss Chandler which no regular in the household could confirm.

Nevertheless, because of the shabby treatment Miss Chandler received, I kept my relationship with Erin friendly but formal. Although we were never close, no one was more aware that she had been instrumental in bringing Groucho and me together. Yet, Erin had never done me any harm. If she often chose not to hear what I thought were helpful words, it was not due to my lack of trying. I was well aware that in her eyes I was a bit of a drudge, since I had absolutely no interest in the people she found so endlessly fascinating. I didn't want to endure boring people just because they also happened to be stars. Groucho and I had worked quietly and well together, and we had no conflicts.

Things, however, were happening that were beyond anyone's control, and Erin was in no condition to cope with them. One evening Groucho had gone to bed after rehearsing for the television special. In the morning it was apparent he had suffered another small stroke. He was disoriented, bumping into walls, seating himself at the dining room table with the back of the chair to his right side, facing the wall instead of the table. It was later determined that his peripheral vision had been affected.

The house took on a morbid air. Everyone seemed to sense that this was the end ... again. It was now doubtful that Groucho would be able to perform in the special. Rehearsals by others nevertheless continued. On one afternoon, a very frail Groucho was helped into Erin's office, which was filled with hangers-on, myself included. He was seated at a desk and several papers were placed before him. Erin showed him where he was to sign. In the past, any agreements Groucho signed with me had been carefully drawn by his attorney. Today there was no attorney present, and Groucho was not told what he was signing. Once the signing was over, Groucho was helped back to his room. I felt great misgivings about what I'd just seen.

Amazingly, Groucho's condition improved, albeit slowly. Olivia de Havilland was in town to attend the American Film Institute tribute to Bette Davis, and I thought a visit from her would cheer Groucho up. I called her, and she was delighted to accept an invitation for afternoon tea.

The morning of her visit, Groucho fell. His nurse put him to bed. I arrived later and was told he was having difficulty walking.

"Are you going to get up for Olivia?" I asked him. He assured me he would, and that he wanted the accompanist to play while he sang for her. When Erin asked if he was going to get up, he also assured her he would. He said he was not in pain. Yet, when he got up to go to the bathroom, he couldn't put any weight on his right leg. It was decided to serve tea in the bedroom instead of the living room.

Miss de Havilland was warm and gracious as she reminisced about the happy times they'd spent together. When Groucho looked at her and said, "You're not getting any younger," she threw back her head and laughed. Erin, as usual, was polite and deferential when she met a celebrity for the first time. Talking about her work on Groucho's behalf, she volunteered, "Hector says the most irritating thing about me is that I'm always right."

Before Miss de Havilland left, Groucho torturously inscribed a book to her.

I didn't return to Groucho's house after I took Miss de Havilland back to the Beverly Hills Hotel. Erin had assured me that Groucho's doctor would be called to see him.

Both Groucho and Erin were unreachable the following day, a Friday. So I called Steve Stoliar, and we went to the house the following morning. No one was there. Groucho's bed was made.

Erin occasionally used a legal secretary, and I called her from the house to find out if she knew Groucho's whereabouts.

"Erin took him to Palm Springs for the weekend to see Zeppo," she said.

"She couldn't be that irresponsible," I told Stoliar after hanging up the phone. "I know how sick Groucho was."

A few minutes later the secretary called back. "I forgot to tell you," she said. "Erin said the house should be shut up for the weekend, and that Steve shouldn't work."

There were a dozen or so cartons stacked up in both Erin's and Steve's offices, containing legal papers which had been returned by yet another attorney.

Late Sunday night, Erin called. "Do you know where we are?" she asked.

"No," I replied.

"We're at Cedars-Sinai. Groucho's all right. He had to have a hip operation. Can you come over? He's asking for you."

When I arrived at Groucho's room, Erin was sitting there alone. She showed me a sketch drawn by the surgeon, showing that the hip joint had been replaced. Shortly afterward, we went into the Intensive Care room to see Groucho.

"Hector's here," Erin told him.

Groucho looked up. "Any questions?" he asked.

I was suffused with an enormous feeling of tenderness toward this helpless old man. Ours hadn't been a demonstrative relationship, yet I impulsively bent over and kissed him on the forehead.

"What do you think of our getting married, Julius?" Erin asked him. "Hector can be our best man."

"I don't want him to be our best man," Groucho replied.

"Why not?" I asked. "I'd want you to be *my* best man."

"You're too fat."

I swore I'd immediately go on a diet. Before the stroke, we'd talked about how his older writer friends coped with the basically sedentary nature of their work without putting on weight, an adjustment I hadn't been able to make. Groucho had no answer, for he was having weight problems himself. He had maintained the same weight of 140 pounds all his adult life. Over the last year, however, he had gained about ten pounds, largely due to his unbridled lust for chocolates. I had accompanied him to the rest room at a recent screening, and he was mortified that, after relieving himself, he couldn't button his pants. "I'm going to kill myself," he loudly complained as we returned to the darkened theater. "I'm ten pounds overweight." "Yeah, Grouch," I replied. "I hate to see you when you're 110."

A few moments after my arrival at Groucho's bedside, Elliott Gould and Warren Berlinger walked in. Erin prompted Groucho, and he serenaded us with a weak but tuneful rendition of "Father's Day," the song he'd composed with Harry Ruby.

His sedation took hold. Soon, a fitful Groucho was under its effect, squirming uncomfortably. He called out several times, "Give me a break, Jack! Give me a break." Later he chanted, "I'm going to my father's house." Were these his equivalents to Citizen Kane's Rosebud? I could envision Groucho auditioning for a vaudeville job, and pleading to that ubiquitous Jack how badly he needed the booking. I couldn't figure out the reference to a father. Although Frenchy had been pretty much the housekeeper of the Marx household, Minnie was the dominant parent whom one would expect Groucho would refer to. Perhaps he was speaking for his children, who had been too long away from Groucho.

When Erin and I returned to his hospital suite, I told her Arthur had to be informed of the situation.

"You know how Groucho feels about Arthur," she said. "He doesn't want him around."

"He has to be told," I insisted.

The public relations man from the hospital soon joined us, followed by the surgeon. She turned to them, explained the situation as she saw it, and they in turn agreed that Arthur could be told the following day.

Erin informed me the next morning that Martin Gang, the attorney who'd drawn up Groucho's will, had called the children to inform them. Tom Wilhite, Groucho's public relations man, was at the hospital when I arrived. We worked out the wording of a press release.

491

Erin insisted that the circumstances behind the operation be clearly spelled out. With that in mind, she'd written down a summary of the operation as the attending physician had described it:

Groucho complained of pain in his right leg. He was brought in under Dr. Morley Kert's care. A floating fracture of the right hip was revealed in the X rays, probably due to the pressure on his right leg from a mild stroke two years ago. This caused the bone to gradually float. Groucho made the decision himself that the operation be performed. The surgeon was Dr. Robert Rosenfeld, a specialist who has treated many prominent athletes and stunt men. He underwent the insertion of a Gilberti or Bateman prosthesis in the right hip. The anesthesiologist was Dr. James Schauble. It was a thirty-nine-minute operation. Groucho was wide awake immediately and was walking by Sunday at 5:30 P.M. He will be moved out of Intensive Care today and will be released by the weekend.

Wilhite completed the taking of notes. "And don't forget to say," Erin added, "that I've been at his bedside for three days and nights."

Erin next suggested that I should call Arthur to find out when he was coming to see his father. When I reached him by phone, Arthur claimed the lawyer hadn't called him. "Why did I have to be the last one to know?" he asked.

"I didn't know about it myself," I awkwardly answered. Arthur said he was on deadline with his current book, but that he would try to come by at three that afternoon. After I hung up the phone, I wondered why I had deliberately told Arthur I didn't know about the operation until that morning. Of course, I knew, but I didn't want to share the responsibility of keeping the news from Arthur, since I had been saying he should be informed all along.

Andy Marx came to see his grandfather before Arthur's arrival. We sat together in the lobby waiting for his father. When Arthur arrived, having come in through a back elevator, he'd already seen Groucho. He'd asked Arthur to get him the daily newspapers. While we waited for a hospital volunteer to get them for us, Arthur and I got acquainted. He was a much easier man to talk to than I'd anticipated. We went back to see Groucho after the papers arrived, and found Erin standing over his bed, cooing at him. Erin looked up and noticed Arthur. The two didn't speak.

We stayed for a few moments, then Andy and I walked Arthur to an elevator. When we returned to Groucho's room, Erin said his blood pressure had risen dangerously as a result of Arthur's visit.

"I didn't want to call Arthur," she said, looking accusingly at me. "But I was convinced otherwise." Andy didn't comment on this indirect indictment of his father.

Later that day, I received a phone call from Erin's temporary legal secretary. "She wants you to tell Sid Lockitch everything you and Arthur talked about," the secretary told me. (Lockitch was Groucho's new accountant, the third in as many months.) "What do you mean?" I asked. "I'm not going to get involved in any of this."

Lockitch called later to ferret out details of my conversation with Arthur. "I said, 'How are you?'" I told him. "And he said, 'It's a nice day.'"

The next time I talked to Erin I told her I was not going to be used in this way. "Well, you know Sid," she said. "Sometimes he gets too eager."

During the two and a half weeks Groucho was in the hospital, Erin and I settled into an informal routine. I would stay with him every morning, keeping him company and monitoring phone calls. Erin would come in the afternoon and stay until bedtime.

During this time, I had a conversation with Dr. Rosenfeld. He said Groucho was coming along well. He had a good appetite. The doctor was alarmed, however, about one thing. "He may be eighty-six, and that's old enough," the doctor said, "but he has the arteries of a man who's 105." The prognosis wasn't good, despite the success of the operation.

If irritability and a desire to get out of the hospital were good signs, then Groucho should have been home already. He'd always hated being confined to his bed. He didn't know the hospital nurses, and resented their probings and ministrations. His private nurses had moved over from the Trousdale house to care for him during the hospital stay, serving as a little familiarity away from home.

The familiarity was too little, as far as Groucho was concerned. On his good days, he would try to get one of his nurses to kiss him. She operated by the book, however, and couldn't be tempted. One morning, after an uncomfortable night, she was trying to pacify him.

"Groucho," she said, "if you were the nurse and I were the patient, what would you do to make me more comfortable?" With only a trace of his wicked leer, he said, "I'd kiss you." It still didn't work.

Since my mornings were devoted to Groucho, I attempted to go about my work in the afternoons. It was a decided conflict to be writing negative things about Groucho's earlier life when I was feeling concern about his present condition. There were documents and tapes that had to be examined. Most were located at Groucho's house, but some were in a recording studio Erin had set up in one of her houses. A sound engineer was at the studio, and I called him to get the tape of a "Monitor" radio program played for me. When Erin heard I'd been at the house, she called and said her insurance didn't cover my being there. When I continued my research at Groucho's house, I received a call from Warren Berlinger, who informed me that the insurance coverage at that house had expired. Until it was renewed, no one but the household staff would be allowed there.

Henry Golas was asked to leave, too. He decided to join me for a visit with Groucho. On the way to the hospital, he said, "Erin said to get you out of the house, but that I can go back as soon as I get rid of you."

"Why would she say that?" I asked.

"She said that you don't understand about her and Groucho. She thought you did, but now she feels she was mistaken."

Had she seen my function as part of a grand design, an apologia, a rationale and justification of her role? Groucho had set no conditions on my writing of his biography. Did Erin feel she and I had some tacit agreement? I was still totally trusted with Groucho—keeping him company, wheeling him down the hospital corridors for his daily constitutional, helping hospital technicians when they administered breathing exercises—and yet I was not allowed in his home.

I don't know why Erin should settle on me as the spy from the other camp. Although I'd given her a wide berth during her many furies, I had never been less than frank about my feelings to her. I had adopted a code of behavior about the situation. While I told her when I thought her actions were wrong, I had not bruited it around to outsiders as members of the household had.

She was making it nearly impossible for me to keep my objectivity. Something had to be done. I then remembered Norman Krasna's offer of help in case any difficulties arose. I called and told him about the situation. He invited me to join him and his wife for dinner. During our conversation, I told Norman and Erle Krasna about my apprehensions. The prime one dealt with Erin's inexplicable behavior. Before, I thought I could see the gears of her mind working. Now I couldn't. She was becoming increasingly more erratic and suspicious, not only of me, but of everyone around her. The motives of all were suspect.

Norman said he had talked to Arthur, and we were expected at his Bel-Air home after dinner. Never was a line so clearly drawn. Should I agree to repeat my misgivings to Arthur and his wife Lois, there was no doubt I would become part of the storm that was obviously gathering. I had to quickly decide whether it would be disloyal to Groucho to confide in Arthur. It couldn't be, not since Groucho had told me of his love for his son.

Yet, Norman had drafted me more than I had volunteered. "When someone from Erin's camp comes forward," he told Arthur, "and tells you of things that are happening in the household, you can't sit back any longer and ignore them." I had never considered myself part of Erin's so-called camp. In the emotions of the moment, it seemed superfluous to correct Norman's statement. During the discussions, I was largely silent while the two couples plotted strategy. Both Arthur and Lois told of a stream of fired employees and guests at Groucho's who had come to them with stories of Erin's abuse of Groucho. One of them was a noted entertainer. Arthur and Lois had been stockpiling their ammunition, and now, they decided, they would proceed to do something about the situation. I didn't ask what their action would be, nor did they volunteer the information.

As we drove back to the hotel where the Krasnas were staying, I asked, "Have I done the right thing?"

"You have to understand something," Norman said. "This isn't just a fight for Groucho. It's a fight for money." Of the latter point I never had any doubt.

495

Now that I had broken my objective silence, I decided I wouldn't volunteer information, but I would openly answer questions from any factions. Yet, Erin never asked.

I ran into Norman a few days later at the hospital. While Groucho was napping and we waited to see him, a nurse told us Erin had brought a psychiatrist to examine Groucho the previous day. "Groucho wasn't feeling well," she said. "He wasn't making much sense. He has his good days and his bad days, and yesterday happened to be a bad day. The psychiatrist refused to certify him as being of sound mind. Yet, he's fine today."

Groucho was released from the hospital on Tuesday, March 22. The local newspapers reported that his first guest at his home was Carroll O'Connor, who'd joined him for lunch. Arthur was caught up in a dispute with O'Connor about the unauthorized biography, and reports of Groucho's socializing with the television star could only antagonize his son. That same day, Arthur had quietly gone to Santa Monica Superior Court and had himself named as Groucho's conservator, along with the trust department of the Bank of America, which would handle the financial affairs.

The following day, I received a call from Erin. "Get over to Groucho's house right away!" she hurriedly said. When I tried to question her, she interrupted. "That's all I can say. Get over there right away!"

I surmised that Groucho had died and even in his death Erin was trying to keep the news from Arthur. The parking area in front of the house looked like a used car lot. When the housekeeper admitted me, I rushed in and encountered Warren Berlinger. "What happened?" I asked.

He explained that Arthur and Lois had arrived that morning with representatives from the bank, ready to take charge of Groucho's life. Attorneys and other factotums were called, and the house was overrun with strangers from both camps.

The faction representing Erin was gathered in the living room. Arthur's people had taken over the den. Groucho, oblivious to the commotion in the front of the house, was resting in his bedroom in the back.

When I walked into the den, Arthur rose from a sofa and came over to talk to me. He had already promised his cooperation in the writing of the biography, but now he set conditions. He wanted me to testify on his behalf. I had not seen any great protestations of affection for Groucho when I'd been at Arthur's house a few nights previously. Lois was particularly vituperative about her father-in-law.

"There has to be another way," I told Arthur. "Taking Erin away from Groucho could kill him. This can cause a lot of negative publicity, too." Arthur said the notoriety was unavoidable. I remembered a previous conversation with Groucho, when he had rather proudly told me, "There has never been any scandal attached to my name. I like pretty young girls, but that's no scandal." Now, through no fault of his own, it looked as if his reputation was about to be tarnished.

One of Arthur's attorneys then collared me. He said that Norman Krasna had talked to him about me, and that my help was needed to force a solution once and for all. This I was unwilling to do. I had already told what I knew, but as much as I felt some control over Erin's activities was needed, I wouldn't be a party to removing her from Groucho's life. She had been his only constant for six years, and it would have been totally callous to separate her from him.

Erin's attorneys had contacted the court, intending to present papers Groucho had signed three years previously naming her as his permanent conservator. Both sides were waiting to hear from the court, to find out what the next step should be. About the proceedings, Bert Granet would later say, "No matter how it starts, it always ends up like *The Little Foxes*."

Shortly thereafter, there was a mass exodus from the house, the judge agreeing to entertain Erin's new motion. Later that afternoon, the court set a hearing for two weeks later.

That evening, I called Arthur's house to see what could be done about keeping the situation out of the newspapers. Lois answered the telephone and, in talking about the strains of the day, started to cry. She complained that people should have come forward to support Arthur's claim. I was among those who were remiss, she implied, since it was apparent I was trying to protect the book I was working on. What I'd considered a matter of conscience was now being seen as opportunistic and expedient.

497

"It's a sorry situation," I said. "I feel sorry for Groucho and his children and for Erin too."

"If that's the way you feel," she bridled, "we have nothing to talk about. It's been a long day."

"Then let me talk to Arthur," I said.

"No," she firmly replied. "I won't let you." With that, the phone was hung up.

Erin called me the following day to tell me the matter was settled. Arthur's petition was withdrawn. She would remain as conservator with Arthur's designated bank, The Bank of America, named as fiscal conservator. The arrangement would be formalized at a routine court hearing on April 15. This seemed like the proper solution to me. Erin could stay with Groucho, with his children welcome to see him at any time, while the bank would concern itself with financial matters. A civil truce had been declared.

Throughout his stay in the hospital, according to Erin, Groucho was recuperating on schedule. She claimed he was walking up to fifty feet a day. He would put his arms around the shoulders of two orderlies and be virtually dragged down the hospital corridor, but he had in fact not walked at all. It was more apparent at home that he was not responding to treatment.

Groucho's household became even more melancholy with the death of Nunnally Johnson on March 25, three days after Groucho was released from the hospital.

Erin was determined that Groucho shouldn't be told of the death of one of his oldest friends. In a letter to Johnson, Groucho had written, "If you, Thurber, Ruby, Sheekman and a few others knock it off, I'll be about ready to say the hell with everything."

Now that time had come. Thurber and Ruby were dead, and Sheekman was lost to the rational world because of arteriosclerosis.

Erin and I culled an assortment of lines from Groucho's letters to Nunnally, and she sent a message to the Johnson family with a covering note:

Because of Groucho's physical condition just now, I dare not tell him of our tragic loss ... With your permission, and with all my love and deepest respect, I have extracted a few lines ... They go like this:

498

Dear Lonely,

I don't know what will be said about you when you shuffle off this mortal coil *(there's* a cheery way to start a letter) . . . I have said many legendary things which I am sure will ultimately echo down through the ages . . . Here it is the Ides of March. (Actually it's November 15th, but if it's good enough for Shakespeare, I'm not going to complain. Last things first.)

Nunnally, it won't be easy to get a replacement for you. Is there only one Lonely Johnson? I know the obvious answer— "THANK GOD"—nevertheless it is true. Oh, I've tried other writers but they're always on strike, and broke, and I wind up with the check. I've even tried producers, but they insist I go to their previews (the early ones, before they're trimmed by Abe Lastfogel).

You know the old line about "man is the only animal that doesn't relinquish its young." I might add—here sits one old male that doesn't relinquish his friends. I would hate like hell to have anything come between us, except perhaps, a beautiful dame who is crazy about sodomy . . .

I send love to you all and hope this is not the end of our affair.

Groucho

A memorial service was scheduled for the near future. I went by myself. Nunnally Johnson would have appreciated the overflow crowd, which was to hear Helen Hayes, Alistair Cooke, and George Seaton pay tribute to their departed friend. I went back to Groucho's. Erin was waiting to be taken to the reception at Chasen's. The blouse she was wearing was dangerously low cut, and not suitable—I felt—for the occasion. "When a girl wears a neckline like that," I told Erin, "I don't know where to look." She laughed. "Nunnally would have loved it."

Although they had been at the memorial services, Arthur and Lois did not go on to Chasen's. When we arrived, we ran into the Krasnas. While Erin got into a violent discussion with Norman about the court proceedings, Mrs. Krasna and I beat strategic withdrawals, she to the buffet table and I to the bar. Other than that outburst, Erin was properly respectful to the Johnson family, who nevertheless weren't as amused by her low neckline as Erin claimed Nunnally would be.

I drove Erin back to Groucho's after the reception. He was wheeled into her office shortly after we arrived. "I want you to get out," he told Erin.

"What did you say?" she asked.

"Get out!"

"Who's going to take care of you?" she inquired.

Groucho shrugged. "Just get out."

Erin wheeled him back to his room, attempting to mollify him. When she returned a few minutes later, she said she was exhausted. It was my cue to leave. I didn't know what to make of Groucho's remarks.

The weeks slowly passed with Groucho listless and apathetic. He seemed to be giving up the struggle.

When, on a Sunday, Lilly Hamlisch and her daughter, Terry Liebling, came to see him, they couldn't ignore the obvious. Groucho was pushed into the living room in his wheelchair. The three women stood around him. Groucho looked at Erin. "You're beautiful," he lovingly said. Erin smiled. Then she urged him to sing. But all Groucho could manage, he who had always sung with great verve and on pitch, was a tuneless croak. It brought tears to our eyes.

Groucho's condition remained unchanged. Since he had returned home to his household staff, I hadn't spent as much time with him as when he'd been in the hospital. On a Thursday afternoon in mid-April, I paid him one of my thrice-weekly visits. Groucho seemed glad enough to see me, but he didn't show any great enthusiasm, not even for the two pounds of chocolates I'd brought him. As I was leaving, I asked Erin's legal secretary, "Is all the craziness over?"

"I think so," she replied. "But there's something strange happening. Erin had some detectives in over the weekend. They found some syringes in the storm drain."

Now, when both factions should have been living up to the spirit of the agreement, one of them was about to be accused not only of bad faith, but also of having committed a criminal act. On Easter Sunday, Erin had hired two private detectives to determine if there were any listening devices hidden in Groucho's house. What they found instead were syringes in the storm drain in front of the house. They were not necessarily hidden there. Garbage cans were placed on a cement abutment above the storm drain, and the syringes could have fallen there during routine trash collections.

When court convened on Friday, April 15, private detective Norman Perle testified at what was to be a routine hearing that he had found the drugs and syringes in the storm drain. He claimed that when he told Erin about them, she disclaimed any knowledge of them and said they were placed there to frame her.

Santa Monica Superior Court Judge Edward Rafeedie ordered the hearing held over until the following Monday. On that day a detective from the Beverly Hills police department testified that a criminal investigation was underway. (Nothing was to come of it.) A second private detective, Fred Wolfson, testified that same day that Erin suggested the drugs and syringes "be buried in the yard." The two private detectives, according to Wolfson, first discussed the matter with an attorney, who advised them to go to the Beverly Hills police. Traces of short-acting barbiturates were found in the syringes, according to the findings of a toxicologist.

Testimony over the next few days was given by three of Groucho's former private nurses. One alleged that Erin had given Groucho tranquilizers against his physician's orders. All said they had seen Erin physically abuse Groucho.

When court reconvened on Wednesday, April 20, the two private detectives said they had confronted Erin in the courtyard of a Los Angeles condominium the previous night. Erin had gone there to seek out a nurse who had accompanied the detectives on their surveillance mission on Easter Sunday. The detectives said Erin had threatened to kill them.

The accusations of Groucho's three nurses were devastating. I had been friendly with them all. They were attractive, efficient young women. Of the three, one had voluntarily resigned and the two others had been fired. None of them hesitated to testify about Erin's behavior, yet I had never heard any of them say anything in the past about illegal prescriptions being administered to Groucho. It was a gossipy household, and other confidences had been revealed. Nor did they talk of Erin physically abusing Groucho. I had been agonizing about the proper thing to do, but if I'd been

501

armed with the damaging information the nurses claimed to possess, I wouldn't have hesitated to act. If, as they maintained, Erin's treatment of Groucho was life-threatening, why had none of them come forward before now?

The court didn't delve into the matter, nor did Erin's attorneys. They were concerned with larger matters. During the week of hearings, they were making gradual concessions in Erin's name. It was determined that a temporary conservator would be named until the legal matter was resolved.

Bert Granet had never found Arthur Marx to be an inherently warm man. He was thus puzzled when Groucho's son called and asked if he would agree to act as his father's conservator. Granet had the impression the assignment would last about three weeks and, although he had some reservations, he accepted the responsibility.

In the meantime, the Erin faction contacted Zeppo, who also agreed to act as conservator should the court choose him. Both sides filed their nominations. For some reason, Zeppo was totally unacceptable to his nephew. Soon, it seemed Granet would be acceptable to Erin. When J. Brin Schulman, Arthur's attorney, called him, Granet agreed to take the responsibility for three weeks. Schulman informed him the task might take longer. In that case, Granet offered Nat Perrin's name, since Groucho's old writer was a nonpracticing attorney.

Unknown to Groucho, his brother Gummo died on Thursday, April 21. Funeral arrangements were pending when, on the following day, Nat Perrin was named Groucho's temporary conservator. He told interviewers Erin would be permitted to visit Groucho, as would his children, and all other friends. He agreed to serve in the capacity until a permanent conservator, either Arthur or Erin, was named after the hearing, now set for May 13.

One of Nat Perrin's first orders of business was to arrange for Melinda to come and visit her father. During his conversations with her, Nat said, "As you grew up and got into your twenties, you used to run away. It struck me as very strange because I know how much your father loved you."

She replied, "I love him very, very much too. I always did. I still do, not for what he is, but just for himself. He didn't seem to understand that I didn't want to be in show business. I was being pushed into an area for which I had no talent. It was torture. I had to run away from that and from general life-styles that really did not appeal to me. I got off into a totally opposite kind of life, and I've never been happier. I still love my father as deeply as any child could love her father."

I was witness to the great affection she showed Groucho. Totally forgotten was her last visit and the circumstances surrounding it. Groucho couldn't get enough of Melinda, kissing his pretty daughter time and again. As she prepared to leave, he virtually begged, "Try and stay a little longer." Naturally, she did.

Groucho brightened for the next few days. When I observed how pleased he seemed with Melinda's visit, he said, "Yes, and she's coming back!"

Miraculously, after nearly thirty years of turmoil, Groucho's other daughter Miriam had started to turn herself around. Groucho's imminent demise seemed to destroy the goblins with which she'd been afflicted for too long. She had tried Alcoholics Anonymous before, but it hadn't worked for her. Now she was ready to forgive herself. Within weeks, she was the staunchest supporter of AA, throwing herself into the saving of human lives with the same fervor she'd used in supporting unpopular causes as a teen-ager. From a condition of total dependency on others, she had swiftly become a strong shoulder for others to lean on. At this writing, she is still self-reliant, very much among the living. She will be heard from yet.

Arthur continued his periodic visits, as he had before the headlines made his name almost as big a household word as his father's.

Nat Perrin was performing an impossible juggling act, mediating between Groucho's children, Erin, and friends who wanted to make Groucho's last days comfortable.

"I had seen Erin now and again," he said, "but purely socially. She was always nice to me and I have nothing against her. I know she hated my guts during the conservatorship. I had to cut down on her time to allow for others. I had to assume that if everything was great she would have still been the conservator. A lot of people said they wouldn't come if she was around. I tried to make it equal time."

Among the group of friends who called were Norman Panama

and Julius Epstein and their wives. Groucho began to ogle the ladies.

"You can have your pick of either one of them," Panama said.

"They both love me," Groucho replied.

"Everyone loves you, Groucho," Panama said.

"Yes," Groucho responded, "everyone except me."

Epstein changed the subject. "We're going to play poker this evening."

"I don't play cards," Groucho said.

"I remember years ago you used to play," Epstein recalled, "for very small stakes."

"And French-fried potatoes," Groucho cracked.

When George Fenneman came to visit, he was recruited by a nurse to help transfer Groucho from his wheelchair to his bed. Fenneman put his arms around the upper trunk of Groucho's body and Groucho in turn put his arms around Fenneman's neck. As he was swivelled into bed, Groucho said, "Fenneman, you always were a lousy dancer."

Steve Allen also called. Groucho had been napping when he arrived. He was pushed into the living room in his wheelchair. Because his peripheral vision was now totally gone, Groucho didn't see Allen at first.

"How do you do, Groucho," the visitor said, "I'm Chevy Chase."

Groucho didn't grasp the joke. His nurse had to tell him who Allen was. Before long, the two were at the piano. As he started to play, Allen talked about a show he'd seen. "This MC got a guy out of the audience," he started. "Did you get people out of the audience, Groucho?"

"Yes," he replied. "We got them out and kept them out."

"Then, there was a cannon act," Allen continued in Groucho's non sequitur style. "Groucho, were you ever shot out of a cannon?"

"No," he replied, "but I was shot into one."

"Anyway," Allen continued, "this guy had a novel approach."

"Yes," Groucho interrupted, "he didn't use a cannon."

The two men stayed at the piano, Allen playing and Groucho plunking a few notes. Every once in a while, Groucho would turn to his nurse and Steve Stoliar, and comment, "He's great."

"Oh, you like him?" the nurse asked.

"No," Groucho said, "he's lousy."

Allen, mortally hurt, stopped playing. "Are you going to play some more?" Groucho asked.

"Only if you keep up the other half of the duet," Allen answered. They whiled away a good portion of the afternoon. That evening at dinner, Groucho talked about "that great piano player that was here."

Allen had overstayed the allotted time for visitors, but in his case it had a beneficial effect on Groucho.

"Many times doctors specified there should be no more than half-hour visits from anybody," Perrin said. "You couldn't do that with Erin. I made it an hour with her, and she would stay two or three. Nobody ever asked her to leave, to my knowledge. She would have dinner with Groucho every night.

"At the beginning, I had no qualms at all about leaving Erin with Groucho," he told me. "When I got concerned was one day, when Groucho got a stomach upset and she, it seems, got ill at the same time. She was furious. She called and said Arthur and Lois had tried to poison her and Groucho. That was a pretty awful thing to say, and I suddenly realized how ugly this thing was. I began thinking anything was possible, and it was possible Erin would be in a position to later say, 'I told you so.' From that point, I ordered that nobody but the cook was to touch the food or go into the kitchen. I didn't cut anybody's visiting time down. Nobody but the nurses were to feed him. Incidentally, I found he took food better from the nurses than from anybody else.

"Other than that, it went along well . . . except that Erin was always after me. She said, 'You should be handling the business. You understand about that. I should be the conservator.' I said, 'Erin, I didn't stop you from being the conservator. The court did. If you want, go to the court and ask to remove me. I won't put up a fight.' After four weeks, my application to be removed as a conservator went right in. It took a few weeks to process. Erin was after me constantly. When she wants to be angry at you, there's nothing in the world you can say. She never heard me.

"The other side said that on the basis of the evidence that had been adduced in the courtroom, I should bar Erin completely. I said, 'I refuse to do that. You're asking me to judge the evidence. She has really not had her day in court, and I will not judge that evidence. That's the judge's job. He has not ordered me to bar her, and I refuse to bar her. If you want to bar her, you'd better petition the court to force me to bar her.' They said they would. They started a petition, then withdrew it. I would not bar her, and was willing to go to court to defend her right.

"One night, because Erin had run a slight fever, she was told she would have to get a clearance from a doctor before she could see Groucho. She came anyway. I never raised any real issues unless they were overpowering. I couldn't undo six or seven years of relationships simply because I could point at one thing that was the wrong thing to do."

On another night, Erin was trying to coax Groucho into eating his dinner.

"Come on, baby, can't you feed yourself?" she challenged. Then she started to laugh.

"What's so funny?" Groucho asked.

"You are," she said. "You're the funniest man in the world."

"Not anymore I'm not," he softly replied.

He now seemed ambivalent toward Erin. When she wasn't at the house, he often forgot her name. Then he took to describing Erin as "the woman who has my money."

Henry Golas had been hired to supervise the household during the week, and had dropped out of Calarts for one term. Steve Stoliar came in on weekends. One day, Groucho called Henry to his room. "I want to go down in the car and turn left," he said. "That's where my money is." He seemed to be wanting to get his affairs in order.

In the middle of May, the hearing to determine Groucho's permanent conservator was postponed until July 18. Judge Rafeedie ordered the postponement to allow Erin's new attorneys time to prepare her case. At that time, Erin would be permitted to make a defense against the past accusations.

A few days later, Nat Perrin—his energies sapped—made public his desire to be removed as temporary conservator. "The job has become quite a responsibility," he told United Press International. "I get calls all the time from the house—when I'm home, when I'm out to dinner and when I'm at parties. It's a continuous job and I can't even get out of town. It has become quite a responsibility." He gave notice that he wouldn't serve after the end of July. "There's so much bad feeling between the contesting parties that I have to work as traffic manager to see that they don't get in each other's way."

Yet another friend died soon after. Goddard Lieberson, who'd been named executor of the will, succumbed to cancer on May 29. Again, Groucho was not told of the death of another intimate. Nor was he aware that Norman Krasna had left for his home in Switzerland.

Upon his arrival there, Norman found an autographed copy of *The Groucho Phile* waiting for him. He wrote his invalided friend:

Dear Hackenbush:

I have just put down your book and I write you instantly before my emotional reaction to it is tempered by embarrassment.

Oh, I knew about your being a living legend and there's a William Auerbach-Levy original of the three of you in front of me when I eat breakfast in my boudoir every morning, and an original Thurber caricature in another room and a picture of my arms entwined around you in my study, but I had forgotten.

The seventeen years we have been physically separated are a partial explanation but I guess the treadmill of living and striving occupies us sometimes too much at the expense of certain obligations.

And I am obligated to you for a relationship which influenced my life. When you took me in during my early twenties, yours was the only family I had ever seen intimately. I was raised as a single child with no hint that a group existed like your own. I wouldn't say you were a surrogate father to me but certainly an older brother. You gave me Shufro, the ambiance of *Dear Ruth* and an endorsement by your companionship that undoubtedly boosted me many rungs up the Hollywood pecking order. I would imagine that contemporaries felt that anyone Groucho was interested in sufficiently to be seen that often in public with must be a damn sight brighter than was suspected.

This emotion concerning your life, and Harpo's, whose picture I can see at the moment, crept up on me slowly and unexpectedly, but by the time I finished the book I found myself quite close to tears.

I have asked Arthur to read this letter to you because I want to be certain it would be transmitted.

I am sorry that I missed many opportunities to repay some of the debt I owe you. I have excuses why I was neglectful but they are weak ones.

You have been one of the great influences in my life and I love you very much.

Norman

His friend had written Groucho a description of a happy home life that had only briefly existed, but one Groucho passionately wanted to believe in. He kept the letter close to him for days, asking his nurses to read it over and over, tears coming to his eyes each time.

The letter clearly required an answer. Groucho laboriously dictated a letter to be sent to his friend. It was the last Groucho letter ever sent:

Dear Norman,

I miss not seeing you. We had a lot of great times together, until you moved to Switzerland.

Come back. We need you.

Love,
Hackenbush

Groucho was back in the hospital within a matter of days. The new hip joint had become dislocated and additional surgery was called for. Hospital spokesmen perpetuated the great American myth that invests celebrities with superhuman qualities by saying the old Groucho wise-cracking spirit was still alive. Actually he was desperately ill, all his ailments of the past being compounded by his extremely low resistance. He was released after a week's stay. Less than twenty-four hours later, Groucho was rushed back to Cedars-Sinai Hospital because of an aspiration problem which made him susceptible to pneumonia. His condition worsened, for he contracted pneumonitis, normally a benign form of pneumonia, but dangerous for a man with Groucho's low resistance to infection.

Two days after his admission to the hospital, the *Los Angeles Times* printed excerpts of a 368-page deposition given by Groucho's one-time chef, John Ballow. In it he alleged that Erin had bullied and drugged Groucho, and he likened the atmosphere in the house to a battlefield. Coming on the heels of the nurses' testimony, Ballow's deposition further damaged Erin's reputation.

By this time, the legal fees over Groucho's conservatorship totaled nearly $50,000. Groucho and his estate would pay that amount and more, since a provision in California law provides that legal fees for both factions are to be absorbed by the estate in dispute. Erin's lawyers had submitted a bill for $16,000 to cover 175 hours of work representing both Groucho and Erin before she was removed as conservator. After that Erin had to absorb her own legal costs. Arthur's lawyers billed nearly twice as much for 330 hours of work, which Groucho was also required to pay.

If Groucho was unaware of the costs involved, Erin said later that he was aware of the court proceedings. If so, he was too ill to discuss them during the times I spent with him.

One day, I greeted him with, "Are you behaving?" His look was injured and accusatory. How could I be so flippant and insensitive? If only he were capable of withering me with a well-deserved sarcasm. I didn't attempt any more mock cheerfulness. On my next visit, an even weaker Groucho looked up at me. "This is no way to live," he said. And no way to die, either.

Yet, when he wasn't overly uncomfortable, a faint smile played on his lips, and his look was totally loving. "How are you?" he would ask, as if at that point the welfare of a reasonably healthy man was of any importance. Then he'd reach out to shake my hand, his grip surprisingly strong, as if he were holding on for dear life.

Nat Perrin noticed that Groucho still loved to kiss and touch women. "When Lois came to visit, he kissed her about fifty times. He would never have stopped if she hadn't gotten tired of bending over." If he had been unfair in his attitude toward her, he seemed to want to compensate for it as best he could.

509

In early July, Erin's 912-page deposition was filed in Santa Monica Superior Court. In it, she said she loved Groucho with all her heart, adding that he had often proposed marriage.

"I didn't accept because of my vanity," she stated. "It's my vanity in wanting to have my own children. He felt we could adopt children." Erin categorically denied she had abused Groucho.

The date of the court hearing, which had been reset for July 18, was rescheduled for August 31. Judge Rafeedie granted the request of Joseph Donahue, one of Erin's attorneys.

A compromise in the fight for conservatorship was hinted at less than a week later, when, on July 15, after a series of chamber conferences between Rafeedie and the attorneys involved, it was revealed that both sides had agreed to the appointment of Andy Marx, Groucho's twenty-seven-year-old grandson, as permanent conservator.

Andy would have been named permanent conservator on July 19, but Erin requested a few weeks more time to evaluate Andy's performance as temporary conservator before agreeing to his permanent appointment.

Yet, even this final impediment was soon removed. Erin and her attorneys had made continual concessions since the dispute began. Aside from her deposition, in which opposing attorneys questioned her rationality, she had never told her side of the story. After a twenty-minute court session in Groucho's hospital room, Andy was named permanent conservator. William Farr, in the *Los Angeles Times* of July 28, wrote, "Wednesday's event signaled a surrender by Erin Fleming, Groucho's constant companion the last seven years, in her efforts to be named his conservator."

CHAPTER SIXTEEN

I don't mind dying. I just don't want to be there when it happens.
Woody Allen

Driving over to Cedars-Sinai Hospital on that August morning, I don't know why it should be such a disconcerting surprise to hear a news flash on the radio: "Groucho Marx has taken a turn for the worse."

The hospital corridors would soon be staffed by guards to keep out the curious, but as of yet the area around Groucho's eighth-floor suite was quiet and unperturbed. One of his nurses was at the reception desk when I arrived. She informed me that Arthur, Lois, and Andy were with Groucho. I had said my farewell to Groucho the day before, as I'd said it each time I'd left him. There was no need to intrude myself in the scene. After years of semiestrangement, his son was with him and Miriam was on her way. Groucho's peace had been made with Melinda. He couldn't have been better prepared for the journey.

Andy came out of Groucho's room to talk with me. I offered the

511

usual consoling words and went home to wait for the inevitable news.

Death came on that Friday, August 19, 1977, at 7:25 P.M. Groucho's condition had been listed as "fair" until the previous day, when his periods of unconsciousness became more frequent.

Erin was at his bedside before his death, but had stepped outside for a few minutes when the end came. Newsmen reported seeing her crying in a hospital corridor. Miriam arrived too late to see her father one last time, but she had made her peace with him and now possessed an equanimity of which Groucho would have been proud.

An outpouring of tributes from colleagues was recorded in the world's press, placing Groucho and his brothers in the pantheon alongside W.C. Fields, Charlie Chaplin, and Laurel and Hardy. Friends called Groucho's house, to discover only the household staff was present. "I don't know who to console," Betty Comden told Steve Stoliar. "I guess we should console ourselves," Stoliar replied.

Further calls inquired about funeral arrangements. Nobody at Groucho's house knew what the family's plans were, nor were they ever informed.

On Sunday afternoon, Arthur and Lois held a memorial gathering at their home, inviting thirty friends who, as Arthur told the press, were persons excluded from close contact with Groucho during the period when Erin was his companion.

Melinda did not come down from northern California, although Miriam was present. Pointedly excluded from the gathering were Gummo's son Bob, Groucho's third wife Eden, and Zeppo, the last surviving Marx brother. In a bitter statement to the press, Zeppo said he had been barred from the gathering because he had backed Erin in the conservatorship hearing. He repeated his belief that Erin had extended Groucho's life by providing a stimulating influence for him.

I was invited that evening, not to Arthur's, but to dinner at Stanley Musgrove's ranch house in the San Fernando Valley. He is a man I normally don't socialize with, yet his invitation was extended with kindness. "I know how you must be feeling," he said. "Come out and join us. You need some cheering up. Mae's coming."

The most unlikely place to have Mae West as your dinner partner is in a suburban backyard. One living legend had died, and here I was sitting next to one of the few surviving ones. Miss West had recently finished making a film, *Sextette,* and I asked her if she'd enjoyed the experience.

"It was very easy," she said, her bravado reminding me of Groucho. It was that indomitability that had kept them both viable and vital for so long.

On Monday, the *New York Daily News* ran an article in which George Jessel and George Burns expressed their disappointment in not being invited to honor Groucho. Erin was quoted as saying she and "dozens" of show business personalities might organize a party in Groucho's honor, "with lots of laughter."

Late that morning Groucho's body was cremated while Arthur and Andy prayed at private services at Temple Beth El in Hollywood. No decision on deposition of the ashes had been made, according to a spokesman for Groman Mortuary.

That night, the star-filled reception was held at Erin's West Hollywood house. About thirty people were present, the only certifiable star there being Carroll O'Connor. George Segal had attended a memorial service which Erin had organized at Temple Emanuel in Beverly Hills, but none of the invited guests I talked to remembered seeing him at Erin's house later.

When Groucho's will was filed for probate, his three children were left the bulk of his estate, then estimated at $2.8 million to $6 million, but later revised to $1.8 million. Erin was left $150,000, plus control of Groucho's film and television rights. His collection of memorabilia was willed to the Smithsonian Institution. Groucho bequeathed a single dollar to any beneficiary who contested the will, with the remainder of that individual's bequest to go to the Jewish Federation Council of Greater Los Angeles.

That same week, attorney J. Brin Schulman was awarded a $60,000 fee and almost $18,000 in expenses by the Santa Monica Superior Court for representing Arthur in the conservatorship hearing. Schulman was later retained by Groucho's fiscal conservator, the trust department of the Bank of America, to bring suit against Erin. This was done in late October, in the name of the bank and not Groucho's children, who couldn't be accused of contesting the will with the filing of the action. Erin was charged with fraudulently taking $400,000 out of the estate. The suit, totaling $1,680,000 asked for punitive damages, double damages, and the return of real estate and personal gifts gained by using undue influence. The court authorized payment of up to $20,000 for Schulman to proceed with the litigation.

In February of 1978, attorneys for Erin Fleming filed a creditor's claim against the estate, alleging that she was owed a sum in excess of $74,000. The amount included nearly $70,000 in unpaid statements from the two legal firms that previously represented her in the conservatorship hearings. In addition, she requested distribution of her share, as Groucho's personal manager, of the royalties on the two books on which he and I collaborate as well as on this authorized biography. In addition, she requested her manager's share of the royalties from an album recorded during Groucho's Carnegie Hall concert in 1972.

Three months later, attorneys for the Bank of America's trust department filed their objection to the distribution of these moneys, as well as her $150,000 tax-free legacy, claiming that the Marx estate was pursuing monetary claims against Erin far in excess of the amount of her bequest. They also stated that the estate was not yet in a condition for a preliminary distribution to be made. The court nevertheless awarded Erin $25,000 to pursue the pending litigation—" a partial victory, as Erin described it to the press.

At this writing, attorneys for both factions are discussing the possibility of an out-of-court settlement in which Erin would renounce any claim to half-partnership in Groucho Marx Productions. Neither side is confident that the settlement will be made before the suit is placed on the court calendar two years or more from now. At that time, it will be decided whether Groucho's acts of generosity toward Erin—put in legal form by high-powered attorneys and certified as rational acts by distinguished psychiatrists—were indeed extracted, as the complaint against her charged, through "connivance, control, direction, wheedling, intimidation, extortion, tormenting, threats, inveiglement, deceit, duress, menace, manipulation. . . ."

EPILOGUE

As you drive through the main gates of Eden Memorial Park, located at the most declassé northern reaches of the San Fernando Valley, you see a sign to the right of the entrance: NO ARTIFICIAL FLOWERS ALLOWED ON GRAVESITES.

The asphalt-topped curving roads at the relentlessly middle-class Jewish cemetery don't open to the startling vistas—nor the pretentious kitsch—of Forest Lawn, where Chico, Harpo, and Gummo are buried. It's a no-frills cemetery, and nowhere is this more apparent than behind a black steel gate with a star of David fashioned out of wrought iron thereon. Tiny gnats are always present in the stark and functional columbarium beyond, where, at eye level, a six-inch square bronze plaque can be seen:

Groucho Marx

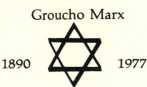

1890   1977

A dark bronze plastic flower container held a worn red felt rose when Henry Golas and I visited.

In death, Groucho's final suppressed desire has been thwarted. The monument he yearned for, but dared not believe he deserved, has not been constructed. Yet, such pomp and grandeur are hardly needed, for the body of his work is monument enough. In the joy he brought to the world and forfeited in himself, he was no ordinary mortal, despite the too human desire to be loved. Groucho Marx was not of an age, but for all time, and I want to believe that he would laugh at the eternal irony of his final resting place. It cost four hundred and thirty-seven dollars.

Acknowledgments

In writing about my favorite legend and the many eras in which he lived, I have been extremely fortunate in receiving the unstinting cooperation of many.

Chief among them is Paul G. Wesolowski of Drexel Hill, Pennsylvania, who over a four-year period has compiled undoubtedly the most comprehensive bibliography on the Marx Brothers, containing more than five thousand entries stretching back more than seventy years and culled from dozens of periodicals throughout the United States and Europe. In addition, he has served as chief researcher on this book, and for his resourcefulness and thoroughness he has my deepest thanks.

Special debts of gratitude are due to three others: To Mrs. Jerome Greene (the first Mrs. Chico Marx) and her daughter, Maxine Marx, who have broken a lifetime of public silence in order to share their insights on Groucho Marx and his brothers; and to Norman Krasna, whose encouragement sustained me more than he realizes.

I am also grateful to those who shared their memories of Groucho, happy as well as sad: Goodman Ace, Robert Allen, Woody Allen,

Mrs. Lenny Atkins (the first Mrs. Arthur Marx), Irving Brecher, Kitty Carlisle, Dick Cavett, Marc Connelly, George Cukor, Hattie (Darling) Weinstein, Olivia de Havilland, Robert Dwan, George Fenneman, Jerry Fielding, Fred Fox, Henry Golas, Bert and Charlotte Granet, E. Y. (Yip) Harburg, the late Victor Heerman, Margaret Irving James, Mrs. Nunnally Johnson (Dorris Bowden), Allan Jones, Mrs. Gus Kahn, Pauline Katz, Jack Lemmon, Ralph Levy, the late Goddard Lieberson, Roxie Johnson Lonergan, Andrew Marx, Robert Marx, Sam Marx, William Marx, Sunny Nadel, Maureen O'Sullivan, Nat Perrin, Mrs. Arthur Sheekman (Gloria Stuart), Peter Shore, Salwyn Shufro, Steve Stoliar, and Arthur Whitelaw.

I have also benefited from the generosity of two writers: Joe Adamson, of Malibu, California, the authority on teakwood and other Marx Brothers esoterica, and Edward Eliscu, of Newton, Connecticut, for sharing his thoughts on the late Harry Ruby.

My thanks also go to the researchers and interviewers who supplied additional information and perceptions: James Bell, Los Angeles and Chicago; Bob Cooper, San Francisco; Shaun Considine, New York; Henry Golas, Los Angeles; Mark Hopman, Chicago; Dana Snow, Los Angeles; Steve Stoliar, Los Angeles; John Tefteller, Los Angeles; and Steve Wolf, New York.

Finally, posthumous thanks go to the man who allowed me to share his sweet and bitter life: Groucho Marx.

H. A.

BIBLIOGRAPHY

Ace, Goodman. *The Book of Little Knowledge*. New York: Simon & Schuster, Inc., 1955.

Adamson, Joe. *Groucho, Harpo, Chico and Sometimes Zeppo*. New York: Simon and Schuster, Inc., 1973.

Agee, James. *Agee on Film*. New York: McDowell Obolensky, 1958.

Allen, Fred. *Much Ado About Me*. Boston: Little, Brown & Company, 1956.

Allen, Steve. *The Funny Men*. New York: Simon and Schuster, Inc., 1956.

Batterbury, Michael and Ariane. *On the Town in New York*. New York: Charles Scribner's Sons, 1973.

Bercovici, Konrad. *Around the World in New York*. New York: The Century Co., 1924.

Bernstein, Burton. *Thurber*. New York: Dodd, Mead & Company, 1975.

Birmingham, Stephen. *Our Crowd*. New York: Harper & Row, Publishers, Inc., 1967.

Black, Mary. *Old New York in Early Photographs 1853-1901.* New York: Dover Publications, Inc., 1973.

Blum, Daniel. *A Pictorial History of the American Theatre 1900-1956.* New York: Greensburg, 1956.

Brown, Henry Collins. *In the Golden Nineties.* Hastings-On-Hudson: Valentine's Manual, Inc., 1928.

Burns, George. *Living It Up. Or, They Still Love Me in Altoona.* New York: G. P. Putnam's Sons, 1976.

Cahn, William. *A Pictorial History of the Great Comedians.* New York: Grosset & Dunlap, Inc., 1970.

Campbell, Robert. *The Golden Years of Broadcasting.* New York: Charles Scribner's Sons, 1976.

Cavett, Dick and Porterfield, Christopher. *Cavett.* New York and London: Harcourt Brace Jovanovich, Inc., 1974.

Churchill, Allen. *The Great White Way.* New York: E. P. Dutton & Co., Inc., 1962.

Cooke, Alistair. *Six Men.* New York: Alfred A. Knopf, Inc., 1977.

Crichton, Kyle. *The Marx Brothers.* Garden City, N. Y.: Doubleday & Co., Inc., 1950.

Dedmon, Emmett. *Fabulous Chicago.* New York: Random House, Inc., 1953.

Durgnat, Raymond. *The Crazy Mirror.* London: Faber and Faber Limited, 1969.

Epstein, Morris. *A Pictorial History of Jewish Holidays and Customs.* New York: KTAV Publishing House, Inc., 1959.

Eyles, Allen. *The Marx Brothers, Their World of Comedy.* Cranbury, N. J.: A. S. Barnes & Co., Inc., 1969.

Farb, Peter. *Word Play.* New York: Alfred A. Knopf, Inc., 1974.

Fields, Ronald J., Commentary by. *W. C. Fields By Himself.* Englewood Cliffs, N.J.: Prentice-Hall, Inc., 1973.

Gilbert, Douglas. *American Vaudeville. Its Life and Times.* New York: Whittlesey House (McGraw-Hill Book Co., Inc.), 1940.

Golden, Harry. *The Greatest Jewish City in the World.* Garden City, N. Y.: Doubleday & Co., Inc., 1972.

Goodrich, David L. *Horatio Alger Is Alive and Well and Living in America.* New York: Cowles Book Co., 1971.

Gordon, Max with Lewis Funke. *Max Gordon Presents.* New York: Bernard Geis Associates, Inc., 1963.

520

Green, Abel and Laurie, Joe, Jr. *Show Biz from Vaude to Video.* Port Washington, N. Y.: Kennikat Press Corporation, 1951.

Halliwell, Leslie. *The Filmgoer's Book of Quotes.* New York: A Signet Book, New American Library, 1973.

Harriman, Margaret Case. *The Vicious Circle.* New York: Rinehart & Co., Inc., 1951.

Hecht, Ben. *A Child of the Century.* New York: Simon & Schuster, Inc., 1954.

Hodge, Marshall Bryant. *Your Fear of Love.* Garden City, N. Y.: Doubleday & Co., Inc., 1967.

Jessel, George with John Austin. *The World I Lived In.* Chicago: Henry Regnery Company, 1975.

Kanin, Garson. *Hollywood.* New York: The Viking Press, 1974.

Kauffmann, Stanley, editor. With Bruce Henstell. *American Film Criticism.* New York: Liveright, 1972.

Kaufman, Beatrice and Hennessey, Joseph, editors. *The Letters of Alexander Woollcott.* New York: The Viking Press, 1944.

Krueger, Miles, editor. *The Movie Musical from Vitaphone to 42nd Street.* New York: Dover Publications, Inc., 1975.

Lahr, John. *Notes on a Cowardly Lion.* New York: Alfred A. Knopf, Inc., 1969.

Lax, Eric. *On Being Funny. Woody Allen and Comedy.* New York: Charterhouse, 1975.

LeRoy, Mervyn, as told to Dick Kleiner. *Take One.* New York: Hawthorn Books, Inc., 1974.

McCabe, John. *Mr. Laurel and Mr. Hardy.* New York: A Signet Book, New American Library, 1961.

Marx, Arthur. *Not as a Crocodile.* New York: Harper & Bros., 1958.
———. *Son of Groucho.* New York: David McKay Co., Inc., 1972.

Marx, Harpo, with Rowland Barber. *Harpo Speaks!* New York: Freeway Press, 1974.

O'Connor, Richard. *Heywood Broun.* New York: G. P. Putnam's Sons, 1975.

Riis, Jacob A. *Children of the Poor.* New York: Charles Scribner's Sons, 1892.

Rosenberg, Bernard and Wilverstein, Harry. *The Real Tinsel.* New York: The MacMillan Company, 1970.

Roth, Lillian with Mike Connolly and Gerold Frank. *I'll Cry*

Tomorrow. New York: Frederick Fell, Inc., 1954.

Sennett, Mack as told to Cameron Shipp. *King of Comedy.* New York: Pinnacle Books, 1954.

Shulman, Irving. *Valentino.* New York: Trident Press, 1967.

Singer, Isaac Bashevis. *The Magician of Lublin.* New York: Farrar, Straus & Giroux, Inc., 1960. (Translated from the Yiddish by Elaine Gottlieb and Joseph Singer.)

Sobel, Bernard. *A Pictorial History of Vaudeville.* New York: Citadel Press, 1961.

Spears, Jack. *Hollywood: The Golden Era.* Cranbury, N.J.: A. S. Barnes & Co., Inc., 1971.

Stagg, Jerry. *The Brothers Shubert.* New York: Random House, Inc., 1968.

Still, Ed. Bayard. *Mirror for Gotham, New York as Seen by Contemporaries from Dutch Days to the Present.* New York: Universal Press, 1956.

Teichmann, Howard. *George S. Kaufman: An Intimate Portrait.* New York: Atheneum Publishers, 1972.

————. *Smart Aleck.* New York: William Morrow & Co., Inc., 1976.

Thomas, Bob. *Thalberg: Life and Legend.* Garden City, N. Y.: Doubleday & Co., Inc., 1969.

————.*Winchell.* Garden City, N. Y.: Doubleday & Co., Inc., 1971.

Thomas, Tony and Terry, Jim with Busby Berkeley. *The Busby Berkeley Book.* Greenwich, Conn.: New York Graphic Society, 1973.

Wagner, Walter. *To Gamble, Or Not to Gamble.* New York: World Publishing, 1972.

White, E. B. *Charlotte's Web.* New York: Harper & Row, Publishers, Inc., 1952.

Wilk, Max. *The Golden Age of Television.* New York: Delacorte Press, 1976.

————. *The Wit and Wisdom of Hollywood.* New York: Atheneum Publishers, 1971.

Woollcott, Alexander. *The Portable Woollcott.* New York: The Viking Press, 1946.

Zierold, Norman. *The Moguls.* New York: Coward-McCann, Inc., 1969.

Zimmerman, Paul D. and Goldblatt, Burt. *The Marx Brothers at the Movies.* New York: Berkley Windhover Books, 1975.

Zolotow, Maurice. *Billy Wilder in Hollywood.* New York: G. P. Putnam's Sons, 1977.

INDEX

537